(home) 201716.
(cabletel).

NORTHERN IRELAND PLANNING LAW

Northern Ireland Planning Law

J. A. Dowling

GILL & MACMILLAN

Gill & Macmillan Ltd
Goldenbridge
Dublin 8
with associated companies throughout the world
© J.A. Dowling 1995
0 7171 2340 5
Index compiled by Julitta Clancy
Print origination by
Carrigboy Typesetting Services, Co. Cork
Printed by ColourBooks Ltd, Dublin

All rights reserved.
No part of this publication may be reproduced, copied or transmitted in any form or by any means without written permission of the publishers or else under the terms of any licence permitting limited copying issued by the Irish Copyright Licensing Agency, The Writers' Centre, Parnell Square, Dublin 1.

A catalogue record is available for this book from the British Library.

Table of Contents

Foreword	vii
Acknowledgments	viii
Preface	ix
Table of Cases	xi
Table of Statutes	xxv
Table of Statutory Instruments	xxxix
Abbreviations	xlii

Part One: Introduction — 1

Chapter 1	Historical Introduction to Planning Law in Northern Ireland	3
Chapter 2	Administration of Planning Control	9

Part Two: Strategic Planning — 23

Chapter 3	Development Plans	25
Chapter 4	Development Schemes	32
Chapter 5	Simplified Planning Zone Schemes and Enterprize Zone Schemes	33
Chapter 6	Conservation Areas and Other Areas of Special Interest	39
Chapter 7	Acquisition of Land for Planning Purposes	44
Chapter 8	Planning Blight	50

Part Three: Development Control — 61

Chapter 9	The Meaning of Development	63
Chapter 10	Planning Permission	83
Chapter 11	Applications for Planning Permission	91
Chapter 12	Determining Applications for Planning Permission	107
Chapter 13	The Decision and its Consequences	124
Chapter 14	Termination of Lawful Development Rights	149

| Chapter 15 | Enforcement Powers | 159 |
| Chapter 16 | Planning by Agreement | 194 |

Part Four: Special Control 205

Chapter 17	Listed Buildings and Historic Monuments	207
Chapter 18	Tree Preservation	224
Chapter 19	Hazardous Substances	228
Chapter 20	Advertisements	233
Chapter 21	Caravans	237
Chapter 22	Environmental Protection	248

Part Five: Miscellaneous 253

| Chapter 23 | Roads | 255 |
| Chapter 24 | Purchase Notices | 257 |

Appendices 265

Appendix A Planning (Use Classes) Order (NI) 1989, Sch.	267
Appendix B Planning (General Development) Order (NI) 1993, Sch. 1	271
Appendix C Planning (Assessment of Environmental Effects) Regulations (NI) 1989, Schs 1 and 2	303

Index 307

Foreword

With the introduction of the Planning (Northern Ireland) Order 1972, planning law in Northern Ireland was set on a broadly comparable basis with relevant legislation in England, Scotland and Wales. Given this context and the fact that there is no shortage of textbooks on planning law, the question might well be asked 'Why another one?' The answer lies mainly in the unique nature of the Northern Ireland planning system within the United Kingdom. The essential components of this sytem, which combine to distinguish it from others, are that planning is administered by central Government on a regional basis, as opposed to being a local government function, and appeals are made to an independent body, the Planning Appeals Commission. Dr Dowling's book provides not only a concise analysis of the administrative framework of planning in Northern Ireland, but also a comprehensive explanation of the provisions of principal and subordinate legislation.

The courts, in their review of decisions made by relevant planning authorities and appeal bodies throughout the United Kingdom, play a pivotal role in interpreting what is a substantial and complex area of environmental law. Dr Dowling's book draws upon a wide range of relevant case law, and the inclusion of judicial decisions by the Northern Ireland courts is of particular value. His book will be of great benefit to students and practitioners whether their field of study or background be in law, planning or any other related discipline.

JOHN WARKE
Deputy Chief Commissioner
Planning Appeals Commission, Belfast
22 March 1995

Acknowledgments

I would like to record my thanks to a number of people without whose assistance completion of this work would have taken longer or would not have occurred at all. To begin with my gratitude goes to Mr T. W. Stewart, Director of the Planning Service of the Department of the Environment for Northern Ireland, who at an early date kindly indicated that his department would be willing to answer queries, and whose offer in this regard was taken up by me on a number of occasions. I would also like to thank the several members of staff of the Planning Service who responded to the queries I raised. Thanks are also due to Mr John Warke, Deputy Chief Commissioner in the Planning Appeals Commission, who kindly agreed to write the Foreword for the book. Finally amongst those with a professional interest in Planning Law, I must thank Mr T. C. Smyth SC for his helpful comments on the manuscript.

As ever, colleagues in the Faculty of Law at Queen's University Belfast deserve mention. I would like to thank Miss Norma Dawson, Dean of the Faculty, and Professors Brigid Hadfield and Herbert Wallace for their encouragement while the book was in preparation. Finally, my thanks to Ms Finola O'Sullivan and Messrs Gill & Macmillan for bringing the book to publication.

Crown copyright is reproduced with the permission of the Controller of HMSO.

Preface

Planning law is the body of law under which the State controls the right of landowners to do as they please with their land, in the interest of the public as a whole. The idea of the social control of land in favour of the public at large is a concept which evolved early in this century. In recent years the protection of the environment has become a major concern both in Parliament and the community in general. This concern manifests itself in planning law. Assessment of the impact of the development proposed by landowners is a requirement in the process of obtaining planning permission for certain types of development. Planning control should not however be seen as limited only to the protection of the environment. The day to day transfers of property from vendors to purchasers proceed against the background of planning control. The problems which conveyancers encounter today are at least as likely to be concerned with infringements of planning control as with defects of title in the traditional sense. Whether the purchaser can use the property as he wishes is as much, if not primarily, a question of planning control as the existence of any covenants in the title to the property. Whether he can safely buy his country residence is as likely to require investigation of whether the house is tied by a condition in the planning permission restricting occupation to an agricultural worker as whether the vendor has title to sell it.

In the twenty years or so since the introduction of modern planning law in Northern Ireland there has been no textbook in which the provisions of the relevant legislation and case law have been explained. Professor Wylie's *Irish Conveyancing Law*[1] contains a useful section on the subject, but is of course concerned with the transfer of land, albeit that knowledge of planning law is an important requirement in that process. David Trimble has written on the provisions for enforcement of planning control in Northern Ireland in John Alder's *Effective Enforcement of Planning Control*[2] to indicate the similarities and differences between the provisions of the legislation here and that in England and Wales which is the subject of the book. Where more detailed commentary is required, students and practitioners have had to make use of texts on planning law in England and Wales. Such a situation is not peculiar to planning law in Northern Ireland and, fortunately, is changing with the advent in recent years of a number of publications dealing specifically with various areas

1 Wylie, *Irish Conveyancing Law* Abingdon, Oxon.: Professional Books 1978.
2 Alder, John, *Effective Enforcement of Planning Control* Oxford: BSP Professional Books, 1989.

of Northern Ireland law. Nonetheless, in the case of planning law use of English textbooks is less straightforward than in other branches of law because of the differences in the administration of planning law and local government which exist in the two jurisdictions. In addition, the provisions of the Planning and Compensation Act 1991 have brought about changes in planning law in England and Wales which as yet have no counterpart here and mean that new editions of the standard works will have to be handled with care.

The object of this book is to provide a concise statement of the law relating to planning in Northern Ireland. The work focuses primarily on the provisions of the Planning (Northern Ireland) Order 1991 (hereafter 'the 1991 Order') and the principal decisions of the courts as to the interpretation of those provisions. Other statutory provisions relating to the control of land use or protection of amenity are mentioned where relevant.

The law is stated as at 1 January 1995.

Table of Cases

Adams & Wade Ltd v Minister of Housing and Local Government
(1965) 18 P & CR 60 .... 261, 263
Agricultural, Horticultural and Forestry Industrial Training Board v
Aylesbury Mushrooms Ltd [1972] 1 All ER 280 15
Alderson v Secretary of State for the Environment (1985) 49 P & CR 307 130
Allen v City of London Corporation [1981] JPL 685 116
Allen v Department of the Environment for Northern Ireland [1985] NI 195
.... 261, 263
Allnatt London Properties Ltd v Middlesex CC (1964) 15 P & CR 288 129
Amalgamated Investment and Property Co. Ltd v John Walker & Sons Ltd
[1976] 3 All ER 509 221
Anisminic Ltd v Foreign Compensation Commission [1969] 1 All ER 208 38
Arcam Demolition and Construction Co. Ltd v Worcestershire CC
[1964] 2 All ER 286 185
Arlington Securities Ltd v Secretary of State for the Environment
(1989) 57 P & CR 407 116
Ashbridge Investments Ltd v Minister of Housing and Local Government
[1965] 3 All ER 371 38
Ashford BC v Secretary of State for the Environment [1992] JPL 362 130
Associated Provincial Picture Houses Ltd v Wednesbury Corporation
[1947] 2 All ER 680 .... 128, 145, 242
Attorney-General v Logan [1891] 2 QB 100 160
Attorney-General v Pontypridd [1905] 2 Ch. 450 48
Attorney-General ex rel Bedford CC v Trustees of the Howard United
Reformed Church, Bedford [1975] 2 All ER 337 212
Attorney-General ex rel Co-Operative Retail Services Ltd v Taff-Ely BC
(1982) 42 P & CR 1 87
Attorney-General ex rel Egham UDC v Smith [1958] 2 All ER 557 ...... 160, 191
Attorney-General ex rel Hornchurch UDC v Bastow [1957] 1 All ER 497 ..... 160, 191
Attorney-General ex rel Scotland v Barratt Manchester Ltd
(1992) 63 P & CR 179 .... 197, 201
Attorney-General ex rel Suttcliff v Calderdale BC (1982) 46 P & CR 399 208
Attorney-General of the Gambia v N'Jie [1961] 2 All ER 504 37
Avon CC v Millard (1985) 50 P & CR 275 .... 199, 202
Ayles v Romse and Stockbridge RDC (1944) 108 JP 176 91

Babbage v North Norfolk DC (1990) 59 P & CR 248 241
Backer v Secretary of State for the Environment [1983] 2 All ER 1021 237
Backer v Secretary of State for the Environment (1982) 47 P & CR 149 ... 64, 169
Balco Transport Services Ltd v Secretary of State for the Environment
(1981) 45 P & CR 216 150
Balco Transport Services Ltd v Secretary of State for the Environment
[1985] 3 All ER 689 262

Table of Cases

Bangor Flagship Developments Ltd's application,
In re |1991| 5 NIJB 57 .... 94, 95, 111
Bangor Flagship Developments Ltd's application (No 2),
In re |1992| 8 BNIL 91 .... 101, 125, 152
Barber v Secretary of State for the Environment |1991| JPL 559 194
Barclays Bank plc's application, Re (1990) 60 P & CR 354 201
Barnet LBC v Eastern Electricity Board |1973| 2 All ER 319 226
Barnet LBC v Secretary of State for the Environment |1992| JPL 540 118
Barvis v Secretary of State for the Environment (1971) 22 P & CR 710 65
Bath Society v Secretary of State for the Environment
(1991) 62 P & CR 565 41
Bedwell Park Quarry Co. Ltd v Hertfordshire CC |1993| JPL 349 201
Belfast Corporation v O D Cars Ltd |1960| NI 60 4
Bell v Canterbury CC (1988) 56 P & CR 211 227
Bell, R & Co. (Estates) Ltd v Department of the Environment for
Northern Ireland |1982| NI 322 .... 82, 135
Bell & Colvill Ltd v Secretary of State for the Environment
|1980| JPL 823 115
Bendles Motors Ltd v Bristol Corporation |1963| 1 All ER 578 69
Bennett v Secretary of State for the Environment |1993| JPL 134 172
Bernard Wheatcroft Ltd v Secretary of State for the Environment
(1982) 43 P & CR 233 .... 97, 126
Betty's Cafes Ltd v Phillips Furnishing Stores Ltd |1956| 2 All ER 497 ... 56
Binns v Secretary of State for Transport (1985) 50 P & CR 468 55
Birmingham Corporation v Secretary of State for the Environment and
Habib-Ullah |1963| 3 All ER 668 74
Biss v Smallburgh RDC |1964| 2 All ER 543 .... 237, 238
Blair's application, In re |1985| NI 68 .... 101, 146
Bolton Corporation v Owen |1962| 1 All ER 101 52
Bovis Homes (Scotland) Ltd v Inverclyde DC 1982 SLT 473 138
Bowling v Leeds CBC (1974) 27 P & CR 531 52
Brayhead (Ascot) Ltd v Berkshire CC |1964| 1 All ER 149 132
Breckland DC v Secretary of State for the Environment (1993) 66 P & CR 34 97
British Railways Board v Secretary of State for the Environment
|1994| JPL 32 129
Bromley LBC v Secretary of State for the Environment
(1990) 59 P & CR 100 41
Bromsgrove DC v Secretary of State for the Environment
(1988) 56 P & CR 221 130
Brookdene Investments Ltd v Minister of Housing and Local Government
(1969) 21 P & CR 545 261
Brooks & Burton Ltd v Secretary of State for the Environment
|1978| 1 All ER 773 .... 69, 77
Brown v Secretary of State for the Environment (1980) 40 P & CR 285 117
Buckinghamshire CC v Callingham |1952| 1 All ER 1166 65
Buckley v Law Society |1983| 2 All ER 1039 148
Bullen v Dunning (1826) 5 B & C 851 224
Bullock v Secretary of State for the Environment (1980) 254 EG 1097 224
Burdle v Secretary of State for the Environment |1972| 3 All ER 240 ..... 71, 72

Table of Cases

Burn v North Yorkshire CC (1992) 63 P & CR 81 .... 55, 56
Bushell v Secretary of State for the Environment |1980| 2 All ER 608 140
Buxton v Minister of Housing and Local Government |1960| 3 All ER 408 37,159

Calcaria Construction Co. Ltd v Secretary of State for the
  Environment (1974) 27 P & CR 435 94
Calder Gravel Ltd v Kirklees MBC (1990) 60 P & CR 322 82
Cambridge CC v Secretary of State for the Environment |1991| 9 EG 119
  (HC); |1992| 21 EG 108 (CA) 66
Camden LBC v ADC Estates Ltd (1991) 61 P & CR 48 93
Camden LBC v McDonalds Restaurants Ltd (1992) 65 P & CR 423 152
Camden LBC v Secretary of State for the Environment
  (1993) 67 P & CR 59 82
Caravans & Automobiles Ltd v Southall BC |1963| 2 All ER 533 174
Cardiff Rating Authority v Guest Keen Baldwins Iron & Steel Co. Ltd
  |1949| 1 All ER 27 65
Carpet Decor (Guildford) Ltd v Secretary of State for the Environment
  (1982) 261 EG 56 .... 77, 158
Carter v Secretary of State for the Environment |1991| JPL 131 238
Carter v Secretary of State for the Environment |1994| 29 EG 124 237
Chambers v Department of the Environment for Northern Ireland
  |1985| NI 181 112
Charman v Dorset CC (1986) 52 P & CR 88 56
Chelmsford Corporation v Secretary of State for the Environment
  (1971) 22 P & CR 880 96
Chelmsford RDC v Powell |1963| 1 All ER 150 238
Chertsey UDC v Mixman's Properties Ltd |1964| 2 All ER 627 242
Cheshire CC v Woodward |1962| 1 All ER 577 ....64, 65
Chiltern DC v Hodgetts |1983| 1 All ER 1057 186
Chris Fashionware (West End) Ltd v Secretary of State for the
  Environment |1980| JPL 678 120
Christchurch BC v Secretary of State for the Environment |1993| EGCS 217 119
City of Bradford MC v Secretary of State for the
  Environment (1987) 53 P & CR 55 .... 129, 130, 195, 196
City of London Corporation v Secretary of State for the
  Environment(1971) 71 LGR 28 158
Clugston v Secretary of State for the Environment |1994| JPL 648 96
Clwyd CC v Secretary of State for the Environment |1982| JPL 696 90
Clyde & Co. v Secretary of State for the Environment
  |1977| 3 All ER 1123 .... 114, 118
Cole v Somerset CC |1956| 3 All ER 531 85
Coleen Properties Ltd v Minister of Housing and Local Government
  |1971| 1 All ER 1049 140
Coleshill and District Investment Co. Ltd v Minister of Housing and
  Local Government |1969| 2 All ER 525 .... 65, 67, 68
Collis Radio Ltd v Secretary of State for the Environment
  (1974) 29 P & CR 390 118
Cook's application, In re |1986| NI 242 .... 159, 191, 193
Co-Operative Retail Services Ltd v Taff-Ely BC (1979) 38 P & CR 156 87
Copeland v Secretary of State for the Environment (1976) 31 P & CR 403 88

Costain Homes Ltd v Secretary of State for the Environment
 (1989) 57 P & CR 416 82
Cotswold DC v Secretary of State for the Environment (1986) 51 P & CR 139.... 212
Council of Civil Service Unions v Minister for the Civil Service
 [1984] 3 All ER 935 .... 145, 146
Courtney-Southan v Crawley UDC [1967] 2 All ER 346 174
Covent Garden Community Association Ltd v Greater London Council
 [1981] JPL 183 147
Cox's application, Re (1986) 51 P & CR 335 201
Crodaun Homes Ltd v Kildare CC [1983] ILRM 1 108
Cynon Valley BC v Secretary of State for Wales (1987) 53 P & CR 68 ....151, 152

Davies v London Borough of Hammersmith and Fulham [1981] JPL 682 116
Davis v Miller [1956] 3 All ER 109 167
Davy v Spelthorne BC [1983] 3 All ER 278 .... 55, 148, 178
Deane v Bromley BC (1992) 63 P & CR 308 227
Debenhams plc v Westminster CC [1987] 1 All ER 51 .... 208, 209
Department of the Environment for Northern Ireland v Thompson
 [1992] 2 BNIL 126 177
Department of the Environment for Northern Ireland v Watson
 (Suede and Leather Cleaners) Ltd [1979] 6 NIJB 80, 81
Dibben v Secretary of State for the Environment [1991] JPL 260 118
Don & Don t/a Northern Markets v Department of the Environment for
 Northern Ireland [1981] 1 NIJB 165
Doncaster BC v Green [1991] EGCS 117 192
Doncaster BC v Secretary of State for the Environment
 (1992) 63 P & CR 437 169
Dooley v Galway CC [1992] 2 IR 136 108
Dudley Bowers Enterprises Ltd v Secretary of State for the Environment
 (1985) 52 P & CR 365 171
Dunlop v Woollahra MC [1981] 1 All ER 1202 112
Dunoon Developments Ltd v Secretary of State for the Environment
 (1992) 65 P & CR 101 158
Durham CC v Secretary of State for the Environment
 (1990) 60 P & CR 507 .... 125, 152
Dyer v Dorset CC [1988] 3 WLR 213 208

Ealing BC v Jones [1959] 1 All ER 286 37
Ealing BC v Ryan [1965] 1 All ER 137 74
East Barnet UDC v British Transport Commission [1961] 3 All ER 878 69
East Hampshire DC v Davies (1991) 61 P & CR 481 192
East Lindsey DC v Secretary of State for the Environment [1994] EGCS 119 82
Easter Ross Land Use Committee v Secretary of State for
 Scotland 1970 SC 182 15
Eastwood v Department of the Environment [1983] 4 BNIL 109 54
Edgewarebury Investments Ltd v Minister of Housing and Local
 Government [1963] 1 All ER 124 79
Edwards (PG) v Secretary of State for the Environment [1994] EGCS 60 117
Eldon Garages Ltd v Kingston-upon-Hull CBC [1974] 1 All ER 358 .... 169, 170
Electricity Supply Board v Gormley [1985] IR 129 108

Table of Cases

Ellis v Worcestershire CC (1961) 12 P & CR 178 125
Elmbridge BC v Secretary of State for the Environment [1994] JPL 242 140
Emma Hotels Ltd v Secretary of State for the Environment
    (1980) 41 P & CR 255 78
Emin v Secretary of State for the Environment (1989) 58 P & CR 416 76
English Speaking Union of the Commonwealth v Westminster CC
    (1973) 26 P & CR 575... 79
Entwhistle Pearson (Manchester) Ltd v Chorley BC (1993) 66 P & CR 277 ... 55, 56
Epping Forest DC v Scott (1985) 53 P & CR 79 177
Esdell Caravan Parks Ltd v Hemel Hempstead RDC
    [1965] 3 All ER 737.................................... 69, 241, 242
Essex CC v Essex Incorporated Church Union [1963] 1 All ER 326....... 55, 263
Etheridge v Secretary of State for the Environment (1984) 48 P & CR 35..... 90
Ewen Developments Ltd v Secretary of State for the Environment
    [1980] JPL 404 .... 168, 169

Fanning, Re [1979] NI 79 47
Fawcett Properties Ltd v Buckinghamshire CC [1960] 3 All ER 503 130
Ferris v Secretary of State for the Environment (1988) 57 P & CR 127 170
Fitzpatrick Development Ltd v Minister of Housing and Local
    Government (unreported) 116
Fletcher v Chelmsford BC (1992) 63 P & CR 312 227
Fletcher v Minister of Town Planning [1947] 2 All ER 496 15
Forkhurst v Secretary of State for the Environment (1982) 46 P & CR 8 78
Francis v Yiewsley & West Drayton RDC [1957] 3 All ER 529 170
Freeney v Bray UDC [1982] 2 ILRM 29.......................... 87, 110
Frescati Estates Ltd v Walker [1975] IR 177 91

Garbutt v Secretary of State for the Environment (1989) 57 P & CR 234 126
General Estates Co. Ltd v Minister of Housing and Local Government
    (1965) 194 EG 202 260
Genova Ltd's application, In re [1992] 10 NIJB 1 152
Gill v Secretary of State for the Environment [1985] JPL 710 158
Gillick v West Norfolk and Wisbech Area Health Authority
    [1985] 3 All ER 403 148
Gillingham BC v Medway (Chatham) Dock Co. Ltd (1992) 63 P & CR 205 126
Good v Epping Forest DC [1994] 2 All ER 156 .... 195, 196
Gouriet v Union of Post Office Workers [1977] 3 All ER 70 .... 159, 160, 192
Graham v Secretary of State for the Environment
    [1993] JPL 353 .... 82, 168, 169, 182
Grampian RC v City of Aberdeen DC (1984) 47 P & CR 633 131
Granada Theatres Ltd v Secretary of State for the Environment
    (1980) 257 EG 1154 118
Gransden & Co. Ltd v Secretary of State for the Environment
    (1987) 54 P & CR 86 115
Gravesham BC v Secretary of State for the Environment
    (1984) 47 P & CR 142 74
Great Portland Estates plc v Westminster CC [1984] 3 All ER 744 .... 114, 122
Greater London Council v Secretary of State for the Environment
    (1986) 52 P & CR 158 117

Gregory v Camden LBC [1966] 2 All ER 196 147
Griffiths v Secretary of State for the Environment [1983] 1 All ER 439 .... 86, 87
Groveside Homes Ltd v Elmbridge BC (1988) 55 P & CR 214 226
Guildford RDC v Penny [1959] 2 All ER 111 69

Hall & Co. Ltd v Shoreham-by-Sea UDC [1964] 1 All ER 1 .... 129, 130
Hambledon and Chiddingfold PC v Secretary of State for the
  Environment [1976] JPL 502 121
Hamilton v West Sussex CC [1958] 2 All ER 174 96
Hammersmith LBC v Secretary of State for the Environment
  (1975) 30 P & CR 19 182
Hammond v Horsham DC (1989) 59 P & CR 410 237–38
Hanily v Minister of Local Government and Planning [1952] 1 All ER 1293 91
Harris v Belfast Education and Library Board [1974] NIJB (Nov) 87
Harrogate BC v Secretary of State for the Environment
  (1986) 55 P & CR 224 .... 171, 182
Harrow CC v Secretary of State for the Environment (1990) 60 P & CR 525 ... 41
Hartley v Minister of Housing and Local Government [1969] 3 All ER 1658 ... 150
Harvey v Secretary of State for Wales (1990) 60 P & CR 152 168
Heron Corporation Ltd v Manchester CC [1978] 3 All ER 1240. ... 94, 95, 96, 98
Hertfordshire CC v Secretary of State for the Environment [1994] JPL 448 ... 168
Hewlett v Secretary of State for the Environment (1985) 273 EG 401 75
High Peak BC v Secretary of State for the Environment [1992] JPL 446 116
Hill v Department of the Environment [1976] NI 43 .... 52, 56
Hillingdon LBC v Secretary of State for the Environment [1990] EGCS 5 90
Hobday v Secretary of State for the Environment (1990) 61 P & CR 225 181
Hopcraft's application, Re (1993) 66 P & CR 475 .... 201, 202
Horner v Department of the Environment for Northern Ireland [1971] NIJB ... 103
Horsham DC v Secretary of State for the Environment [1992] JPL 334 115
Hoveringham Gravels Ltd v Chiltern DC (1977) 76 LGR 533 125
Hoveringham Gravels Ltd v Chiltern DC (1978) 35 P & CR 295 89
Hoveringham Gravels Ltd v Secretary of State for the Environment
  [1975] 2 All ER 931 122
Howard v Secretary of State for the Environment [1974] 1 All ER 644 179
Howes v Secretary of State for the Environment [1984] JPL 439 .... 168, 169
Hughes v Doncaster MBC [1991] 1 All ER 295 167
Hughes v Secretary of State for the Environment [1994] EGCS 86 75
Hughes, H T & Sons Ltd v Secretary of State for the Environment
  (1985) 54 P & CR 134 170–71

Iddenden v Secretary of State for the Environment [1972] 3 All ER 883 66
Impey v Secretary of State for the Environment (1984) 47 P & CR 157 64
Inver Resources Ltd v Limerick Corp. [1987] IR 159 91
Iveagh (Earl) v Minister of Housing and Local Government
  [1963] 3 All ER 817 210

J L Engineering Ltd v Secretary of State for the Environment [1994] JPL 453 ... 151
J L Engineering Ltd v Secretary of State for the Environment
  [1994] EGCS 110 151

James v Minister of Housing and Local Government
  [1965] 3 All ER 602 .... 69, 110, 111, 237
James v Secretary of State for Wales [1966] 3 All ER 964 .... 69, 110, 237
James v Secretary of State for the Environment [1991] JPL 550 209
Jeary v Chailey RDC (1973) 26 P & CR 280 165
Jennings Motors Ltd v Secretary of State for the Environment
  [1982] 1 All ER 471 .... 70, 72, 152
Johnston v Secretary of State for the Environment (1974) 28 P & CR 424 71
Johnston's application, Re [1984] 10 NIJB 20, 140, 144
Jones v Secretary of State for Wales (1991) 61 P & CR 238 129
Jones' & White & Co.'s application, Re (1989) 58 P & CR 512 ...... 197, 201, 202

Kane v Northern Ireland Housing Executive [1986] NI 145 22
Kane's application, In re [1984] 17 NIJB 98, 120
Kaur v Secretary of State for the Environment (1991) 61 P & CR 249 172
Keleghan v Corby (1977) 111 ILTR 144 108
Kent CC v Batchelor (1976) 33 P & CR 185 224
Kent CC v Kingsway Investments (Kent) Ltd [1970] 1 All ER 70 131
Kerrier DC v Secretary of State for the Environment
  (1980) 41 P & CR 284 .... 90, 170
Kingsley v Hammersmith & Fulham LBC (1991) 62 P & CR 589 236
Kingston-upon-Thames Royal BC v Secretary of State for the
  Environment [1974] 1 All ER 193 .... 128, 129
Kwik Save Discount Group Ltd v Secretary of State for Wales
  (1975) 37 P & CR 170 72
Kwik Save Discount Group Ltd v Secretary of State for Wales
  (1980) 42 P & CR 166 69

Lade and Lade v Brighton Corporation (1971) 22 P & CR 737 53
Lambeth LBC v Secretary of State for the Environment [1992] EGCS 17 209
Leighton and Newman Car Sales Ltd v Secretary of State for the
  Environment (1976) 32 P & CR 1 152
Lenlyn Ltd v Secretary of State for the Environment (1984) 50 P & CR 129 ... 179
Lever (Finance) Ltd v Westminster Corporation [1970] 3 All ER 496 .... 81, 82, 89
Lewis v Rook [1992] EGCS 21 209
Lilo Blum v Secretary of State for the Environment [1981] JPL 278 70
London Borough of Enfield v Secretary of State for the Environment
  [1973] JPL 155 113
London Borough of Hounslow v Secretary of State for the Environment
  [1981] JPL 510 171
London Borough of Southwark v Frow [1989] JPL 645 192
London City Corporation v Bovis Construction Ltd
  (1988) 86 LGR 660; [1992] 3 All ER 697 .... 191, 192, 193
London Corporation v Cusack-Smith [1955] 1 All ER 302 .... 174, 257
London Residuary Body v Lambeth LBC [1990] 2 All ER 309 119
Lord Advocate v Dumbarton DC [1990] 1 All ER 1 101
Louisville Investments Ltd v Basingstoke DC (1976) 32 P & CR 419 56
LTSS Print and Supply Services Ltd v Hackney LBC [1976] 1 All ER 659 166
Lucas, F & Sons Ltd v Dorking and Horsham RDC (1964) 17 P & CR 111 88

Table of Cases

McCann's application, In re [1992] 7 NIJB 60 .... 15, 16, 101, 249
McClurg & Spiller v Department of the Environment for
  Northern Ireland [1990] 2 NIJB 68 .... 87–8, 97
McGuigan's application, In re (unrep. 5 July 1990) 114
McInerney Properties Ltd v Department of the Environment for
  Northern Ireland [1984] 2 NIJB 112
McKay v Secretary of State for the Environment [1994] JPL 806 172
McKernan v McGeown [1983] 4 NIJB 112
Magill's application, In re [1986] 7 NIJB 37 .... 115, 144, 145, 146
Mahon v Sharma [1990] 2 NIJB 76 159
Maidstone BC v Mortimer [1980] 3 All ER 552 226
Main v Swansea CC (1985) 49 P & CR 26 105
Malvern Hills DC v Secretary of State for the Environment
  (1983) 46 P & CR 58 90
Mancini v Coventry CC (1982) 44 P & CR 114 53
Mancini v Coventry CC (1985) 49 P & CR 127 56
Mansi v Elstree UDC (1964) 16 P & CR 153 172
Marshall v Nottingham CC [1960] 1 All ER 859 69
Martins' application, Re (1988) 57 P & CR 119 .... 197, 201, 202
Mason v Secretary of State for the Environment [1984] JPL 332 127
Medina BC v Proberun Ltd (1991) 61 P & CR 77 .... 95, 127, 129
Merton LBC v Edmonds *The Times* 6 July 1993 236
Metallic Protectives Ltd v Secretary of State for the Environment
  [1976] JPL 166 171
Methuan-Campbell v Walters [1974] 1 All ER 606 208
Mid-Glamorgan CC v Bargoed Coal Co. Ltd [1992] JPL 832 175
Miller-Mead v Minister of Housing and Local Government
  [1963] 1 All ER 359 .... 88, 170, 171, 176
Minister of Agriculture Fisheries and Food v Jenkins [1963] 2 All ER 147 101
Minister of Housing and Local Government v Hartnell [1965] 1 All ER 490 241
Mirai Networks Ltd v Secretary of State for the Environment [1994] JPL 337 158
Mitchell v Secretary of State for the Environment [1992] JPL 553 168
Mitchell v Secretary of State for the Environment [1994] EGCS 111 114
Monaghan UDC v Alf-a-Bet Promotions Ltd [1983] ILRM 64 108
Moran v Secretary of State for the Environment [1988] JPL 24 79
Morelli v Department of the Environment for Northern Ireland
  [1976] NI 189 108
Munnich v Godstone UDC [1966] 1 All ER 930 174
Murfitt v Secretary of State for the Environment [1980] JPL 598 .... 168, 172
Murphy v Secretary of State for the Environment [1994] JPL 156 140
Murphy, J & Sons Ltd v Secretary of State for the Environment
  [1973] 2 All ER 26 120

Nash v Secretary of State for the Environment (1985) 52 P & CR 261 184
Nelsovil Ltd v Minister of Housing and Local Government
  [1962] 1 All ER 423 180
New Forest DC v Secretary of State for the Environment [1984] JPL 178 122
Newbury DC v Secretary of State for the Environment
  [1980] 1 All ER 731 .... 127, 128, 151, 195, 242
Newbury DC v Secretary of State for the Environment (1990) 61 P & CR 258 182

Newbury DC v Secretary of State for the Environment
   (1993) 67 P & CR 68 168–169
Newbury DC v Secretary of State for the Environment [1995] JPL 329 168
Newham LBC v Secretary of State for the Environment (1987) 53 P & CR 88 115
Niarchos v Secretary of State for the Environment (1978) 35 P & CR 259 115
Nicholls v Secretary of State for the Environment [1981] JPL 890 151
Norfolk CC v Secretary of State for the Environment [1973] 3 All ER 673 ... 82, 87
North Down BC's application, In re [1986] NI 304 .... 13, 139, 140, 144, 147
North Warwickshire BC v Secretary of State for the Environment
   (1985) 50 P & CR 47 77
North Wiltshire DC v Secretary of State for the Environment [1992] EGCS 65 118
Northavon DC v Secretary of State for the Environment [1990] JPL 579 150
Northumberland CC v Secretary of State for the Environment
   (1990) 59 P & CR 468... 121
NUPE & COHSE's application, In re [1988] NI 255 .... 15, 16

O'Neill v Clare CC [1983] 3 ILRM 141 112
O'Reilly v Mackman [1982] 3 All ER 1124 .... 147, 148
O'Reilly's application, Re (1993) 66 P & CR 485 201
Oakimber Ltd v Elmbridge BC [1992] JPL 48 .... 90, 96
Orchard Caravans Ltd v Department of the Environment for
   Northern Ireland [1980] 11 NIJB 93

Parkes v Secretary of State for the Environment [1979] 1 All ER 211 ..... 63, 64
Peacock Homes Ltd v Secretary of State for the Environment
   (1984) 48 P & CR 20 168
Pedgrift Ltd v Oxfordshire CC (1992) 63 P & CR 246 129
Pehrsson v Secretary of State for the Environment (1990) 61 P & CR 266 ... 140
Pennine Raceway Ltd v Kirklees MC [1982] 3 All ER 628 154
Perkins v Secretary of State for the Environment [1981] JPL 755 168
Perkins v West Wiltshire DC (1975) 31 P & CR 427 53
Perrins v Perrins [1951] 1 All ER 1075 177
Peters v Yiewsley & West Drayton UDC [1963] 1 All ER 64 243
Petticoat Lane Rentals Ltd v Secretary of State for the Environment
   [1971] 2 All ER 743 .... 151, 152
Pilkington v Secretary of State for the Environment
   [1974] 1 All ER 283 .... 89, 98, 124, 152
Pine Valley Developments Ltd v Minister of the Environment
   [1987] 7 ILRM 747 112
Pioneer Aggregates (UK) Ltd v Secretary of State for the Environment
   [1984] 2 All ER 358 .... 125, 133, 150, 151, 152, 203
Plymouth CC v Secretary of State for the Environment
   [1972] 3 All ER 225 263
Pope v Secretary of State for the Environment [1991] EGCS 112 72
Porritt v Secretary of State for the Environment [1988] JPL 414 175
Port Louis Corporation v Attorney-General of Mauritius [1965] AC 1111 14
Postill v East Riding CC [1956] 2 All ER 685 170
Poulton's Application, Re (1992) 65 P & CR 319 201
Poundstretcher Ltd v Secretary of State for the Environment [1989] JPL 90 118

Prestige Homes (Southern) Ltd v Secretary of State for the
 Environment [1992] EGCS 66; [1992] JPL 842 152
Prosser v Minister of Housing and Local Government (1968) 67 LGR 109 ...152
Prosser v Sharp (1985) 274 EG 1249 76
Purbeck DC v Secretary of State for the Environment (1982) 263 EG 261 ...260, 262
Pye, J A (Oxford) Estates Ltd v West Oxfordshire DC
 (1984) 47 P & CR 125 ....115, 116
Pyx Granite Co. Ltd v Minister of Housing and Local Government
 [1959] 1 All ER 625 ....128, 131

Quartley's application, Re (1989) 58 P & CR 518 ....199, 202

R v Alath Construction Ltd (1990) 60 P & CR 533 225
R v Amber Valley DC, ex p Jackson [1984] 3 All ER 501 111
R v Birmingham CC ex p Ferrero Ltd [1993] 1 All ER 530 144
R v Bradford-on-Avon UDC, ex p Boulton [1964] 2 All ER 492 ....96, 103, 104, 105
R v Bromley LBC, ex p Sievers (1981) 41 P & CR 294 93
R v Canterbury CC, ex p Halford [1992] EGCS 23 39
R v Canterbury CC ex p Springimage Ltd [1994] JPL 427 147
R v Chichester Justices, ex p Chichester DC (1990) 60 P & CR 342........176
R v City of London Corporation, ex p Allan (1980) 79 LGR 223 30
R v Collett [1994] 2 All ER 372 185
R v Crown Court at Reading, ex p Hutchinson [1988] 1 All ER 333 148
R v Elmbridge BC, ex p Health Care Corporation Ltd [1992] JPL 39 ......90, 96
R v Elmbridge BC, ex p Wendy Fair Markets Ltd [1994] EGCS 159 190
R v Exeter CC ex p Terry [1990] 1 All ER 413 ....122, 129
R v Gillingham BC, ex p Parham Ltd (1980) 58 P & CR 73..............195, 196
R v Great Yarmouth BC, ex p Botton Brothers Arcades Ltd
 (1988) 56 P & CR 99 ....111, 147
R v Greenwich LBC, ex p Patel (1985) 57 P & CR 282 ....175, 185
R v Hammersmith & Fulham LBC, ex p Greater London Council
 (1985) 51 P & CR 120 ....94, 147
R v Hammersmith & Fulham LBC, ex p People Before Profit Ltd
 [1981] JPL 869 139
R v Harfield [1993] JPL 914 172
R v Hillingdon BC, ex p Royco Homes Ltd [1974] 2 All ER 643 .....128, 132, 144
R v Jenner [1983] 2 All ER 40 190
R v Kent Justices, ex p Crittenden [1963] 2 All ER 245 ....240, 243
R v Lambeth LBC, ex p Sharp (1985) 50 P & CR 284 108
R v Leominster CC, ex p Antique Country Buildings Ltd
 (1988) 56 P & CR 240 220
R v Minister of Housing and Local Government,
 ex p Chichester RDC [1960] 2 All ER 407 260
R v Monmouth DC, ex p Jones (1985) 53 P & CR 108 ....97, 111, 147
R v Newbury DC ex p Stevens and Partridge (1992) 65 P & CR 438 94
R v North Hertfordshire DC, ex p Sullivan [1981] JPL 752 147
R v Pettigrove and Roberts (1991) 62 P & CR 355 188
R v Plymouth CC ex p Plymouth and South Devon Co-Operative
 Society Ltd (1993) 67 P & CR 78 ....114, 115, 196

Table of Cases

R v Rochester upon Medway CC, ex p Hobday
(1989) 58 P & CR 424 .... 166, 176, 178
R v Runnymede BC, ex p Sarvan Singh Seehra (1986) 53 P & CR 281 188
R v Ruttle, ex p Marshall (1988) 57 P & CR 299 185
R v Secretary of State for the Environment, ex p Davies (1990) 61 P & CR 481 ... 179
R v Secretary of State for the Environment, ex p J B I
Financial Consultants (1988) 58 P & CR 84 179
R v Secretary of State for the Environment, ex p Kent
(1989) 57 P & CR 431 105
R v Secretary of State for the Environment, ex p Leicester CC
(1988) 55 P & CR 364 45
R v Secretary of State for the Environment, ex p Ostler [1976] 3 All ER 90 38
R v Secretary of State for the Environment ex p Percy Bilton Industrial
Properties Ltd (1975) 31 P & CR 154 94
R v Secretary of State for the Environment, ex p Rose Theatre
Trust Co. [1990] 1 All ER 754 147
R v Secretary of State for the Environment ex p Slough BC [1994] EGCS 67. 88
R v Secretary of State for Social Services, ex p Association of
Metropolitan Authorities [1986] 1 All ER 164 15
R v Secretary of State for Transport, ex p de Rothschild
[1989] 1 All ER 933 38
R v Sevenoaks DC, ex p Terry [1985] 3 All ER 226 111
R v Smith (1984) 48 P & CR 392 177
R v St Edmundsbury DC, ex p Investors in Industry Commercial
Properties Ltd [1985] 3 All ER 284 .... 111, 128
R v South Northamptonshire DC, ex p Crest Homes plc
(1994) 68 P & CR 187 194
R v Swale BC, ex p Royal Society for the Protection of Birds [1991] JPL 39. ... 64
R v Swansea CC ex p Elitestone Ltd [1993] 46 EG 181 65
R v Tower Hamlets LBC, ex p Ahern (London) Ltd
(1990) 59 P & CR 133 .... 170, 177, 182
R v Tunbridge Wells BC, ex p Blue Boys Development Ltd
(1990) 59 P & CR 315 .... 79, 136
R v Wealdon BC, ex p Charles Church South East Ltd (1990) 59 P & CR 150 195
R v Wells Street Stipendiary Magistrate, ex p Westminster CC
[1986] 3 All ER 4 .... 212, 217
R v West Oxfordshire DC, ex p Pearce Homes Ltd [1986] JPL 523 .... 86, 87
R v Westminster CC, ex p Monahan [1989] 2 All ER 74 .... 114, 121, 196
R v Wychavon DC, ex p Saunders [1991] EGCS 122; (1992) 64 P & CR 120 ... 184
R v Yeovil Corporation, ex p Trustees of Elim Pentecostal Church
(1971) 23 P & CR 39 .... 86, 87
R (Antrim CC) v Minister of Housing and Local Government [1960] NI 1 5
R (Thallon) v Department of the Environment for Northern Ireland
[1982] NI 26 .... 108, 111, 118, 119, 125, 144, 145
Ransom & Luck v Surbiton BC [1949] 1 All ER 185 203
Rawlins v Secretary of State for the Environment [1989] JPL 439 70
Regent Lion Properties Ltd v Westminster CC [1990] 4 EG 131 152
Reigate & Banstead DC v Brown [1992] EGCS 26 192
Rhyl UDC v Rhyl Amusements Ltd [1959] 1 WLR 465 48
Richmond upon Thames LBC v Secretary of State for the Environment
[1984] JPL 24 116

Robbins v Secretary of State for the Environment [1989] 1 All ER 878 218
Rochdale MBC v Simmonds (1980) 40 P & CR 432 170
Rolf v North Shropshire DC (1988) 55 P & CR 242 218
Rollo v Minister of Town Planning [1948] 1 All ER 13 ....15, 16
Roy v Kensington and Chelsea FPC [1992] 1 AC 624 148
Royal Borough of Kensington v Secretary of State for the Environment
  [1981] JPL 50 70
Runnymede BC v Ball [1986] 1 All ER 629 192
Runnymede BC v Smith (1986) 53 P & CR 132 189
Ryeford Homes Ltd v Sevenoaks DC [1990] JPL 36 ....112, 113

Safeway Properties Ltd v Secretary of State for the Environment
  [1991] EGCS 68 194
Save Britain's Heritage v Secretary of State for the Environment
  [1991] 2 All ER 10 ....132, 141
Scarborough BC v Adams [1983] JPL 673 175
Scott v Secretary of State for the Environment [1983] JPL 108 170
Secretary of State for the Environment v Cambridge CC [1922] EGCS 16 ... 140
Seddon Properties Ltd v Secretary of State for the Environment
  (1978) 42 P & CR 26 ....31, 141
Sevenoaks UDC v Twynam [1929] 2 KB 440 37
Sharkey v Secretary of State for the Environment (1992) 63 P & CR 332...... 45
Shephard & Love v Secretary of State for the Environment [1992] JPL 827 168
Sidebotham, Re (1880) 14 ChD 458 37
Simpson v Edinburgh Corporation 1960 SC 313 113
Slough Estates Ltd v Slough BC (No 2) [1969] 2 All ER 988............. 86, 87
Smart & Courtney Dale Ltd v Dover RDC (1972) 23 P & CR 408 258
Smith v East Elloe RDC [1956] 1 All ER 355........................... 38
Smith v Secretary of State for the Environment [1994] JPL 640 150
Somak Travel Ltd v Secretary of State for the Environment [1987] JPL 630 168
South Bucks DC v Secretary of State for the Environment [1989] JPL 351 85
South Lakeland DC v Secretary of State for the Environment
  [1992] 1 All ER 573 41
South Oxfordshire DC v Secretary of State for the Environment
  [1981] 1 All ER 954 ....90, 118
South Ribble BC v Secretary of State for the Environment
  (1991) 61 P & CR 87 172
South Somerset DC v Secretary of State for the Environment
  [1993] 26 EG 121 115
Southend-on-Sea Corporation v Hodgson (Wickford) Ltd
  [1961] 2 All ER 46 82
Sovmots Investments Ltd v Secretary of State for the Environment
  [1976] 3 All ER 178 121
Spackman v Secretary of State for the Environment [1977] 1 All ER 457 ....90, 118
Square Meals Frozen Foods Ltd v Dunstable BC [1974] 1 All ER 441 177
Stafford v Roadstone Ltd [1980] 1 ILRM 1 159
Stafford BC v Elkenford Ltd [1977] 2 All ER 519 192
Staffordshire Moorlands DC v Cartwright [1992] JPL 138 90
State, The (Alf-a-Bet Promotions Ltd) v Bundoran UDC (1978) 112 ILTR 9 ... 91
State, The (Murphy) v Dublin CC [1970] IR 253........................ 87

Table of Cases

State, The (Pine Valley Developments Ltd) v Dublin CC [1984] IR 407 96
State, The (Tern Houses (Brennanstown) Ltd) v An Bord Pleanala
 [1985] IR 725 96
Steeples v Derbyshire CC [1984] 3 All ER 468 111
Steinberg v Secretary of State for the Environment
 (1989) 58 P & CR 453 .... 40, 41
Stevens v London Borough of Bromley [1972] 1 All ER 112 174–75
Stoke-on-Trent CC v B & Q plc [1991] 4 All ER 224 192
Stoke-on-Trent CC v B & Q (Retail) Ltd [1984] 2 All ER 332 .... 160, 192
Strable v Dartford BC [1984] JPL 329 112
Stratford on Avon DC v Secretary of State for the Environment
 [1994] JPL 740 .... 27, 111
Stringer v Minister of Housing and Local Government
 [1971] 1 All ER 65 .... 114, 116, 120
Stubbings v Beaconsfield Justices (1987) 54 P & CR 327 247
Swale BC v Secretary of State for the Environment [1994] JPL 236 99
Swinbank v Secretary of State for the Environment
 (1988) 55 P & CR 371 172

Tameside MBC v Secretary of State for the Environment [1984] JPL 180 122
Tesco Stores Ltd v Secretary of State for the Environment
 (1994) 68 P & CR 219 .... 115, 196
Thayer v Secretary of State for the Environment [1991] EGCS 78 90
Thomas David (Porthcawl) Ltd v Penybont RDC [1972] 3 All ER 1092 ... 68, 168
Thompson's application, In re [1985] NI 170 .... 79, 80, 81, 82
Thrasyvoulou v Secretary of State for the Environment
 [1988] 2 All ER 781 .... 98, 183
Tidman v Reading BC [1994] EGCS 180 113
Tidswell v Secretary of State for the Environment [1977] JPL 104 ...... 165, 166
Times Investment Ltd v Secretary of State for the Environment
 (1991) 61 P & CR 98 .... 133, 146
Top Deck Holdings Ltd v Secretary of State for the Environment
 [1991] JPL 961... 140
Towner & Goddard's application, Re (1989) 58 P & CR 316 201
Trentham, G Percy Ltd v Gloucestershire CC [1966] 1 All ER 701........ 70
Trio Thames Ltd v Secretary of State for the Environment [1984] JPL 183 73
Trustees of the Castell-y-Mynach Estate v Secretary of State for Wales
 [1985] JPL 40... 150
Trusthouse Forte Ltd v Secretary of State for the Environment
 (1987) 53 P & CR 293 117

Unex Dumpton Ltd v Secretary of State for the Environment
 (1991) 61 P & CR 103 .... 40, 41
Union of the Benefices of Whippingham and East Cowes,
 Re [1945] 2 All ER 22 15
Uttlesford DC v Secretary of State for the Environment [1992] JPL 171 72

Valentina of London Ltd v Secretary of State for the Environment
 [1992] EGCS 77 171
Van Dyck v Secretary of State for the Environment [1992] JPL 356 169

Wain v Secretary of State for the Environment (1982) 44 P & CR 289 261
Wakelin v Secretary of State for the Environment (1983) 46 P & CR 214 72
Wallace & Co.'s application, Re (1992) 66 P & CR 124 201
Wallington v Secretary of State for the Environment (1991) 62 P & CR 150 . . . 76
Watson-Smyth v Secretary of State for the Environment
  [1992] JPL 451 (1992) 64 P & CR 156 208–09
Watts v Secretary of State for the Environment (1991) 62 P & CR 366 208
Waverley BC v Hilden [1988] 1 All ER 807 . . . . 192, 193
Wealdon DC v Taylor [1992] JPL 1036 152
Wealson DC v Secretary of State for the Environment [1983] JPL 234 182
Webber v Minister of Housing and Local Government
  [1967] 3 All ER 981 73
Wells v Minister of Housing and Local Government
  [1967] 2 All ER 1041 . . . . 79, 80, 81, 82
Wessex Regional Health Authority v Salisbury DC [1984] JPL 344 97
West Bowers Farm Products v Essex CC (1985) 50 P & CR 368 64
West Oxfordshire DC v Secretary of State for the Environment
  (1988) 56 P & CR 434 . . . . 153, 170
Western Fish Products Ltd v Penwith DC [1981] 2 All ER 204 . . . . 81, 82
Westminster Bank Ltd v Minister of Housing and Local Government
  [1970] 1 All ER 734 122
Westminster CC v British Waterways Board [1984] 3 All ER 737 119
Westminster CC v Secretary of State for the Environment
  (1990) 59 P & CR 496 233
Wheatfield Inns (Belfast) Ltd v Croft Inns Ltd [1978] NI 83 150
White v Secretary of State for the Environment (1989) 58 P & CR 281 150
Whitley & Sons Ltd v Secretary of State for Wales [1992] JPL 856 . . . . 90, 170
Wilson v Secretary of State for the Environment [1974] 1 All ER 428 . . . . 38, 108
Wilson v West Sussex CC [1963] 1 All ER 751 87
Windsor Royal BC v Brandrose Investments Ltd [1983] 1 All ER 818 . . . . 195, 198
Windsor and Maidenhead Royal Borough v Secretary of State for the
  Environment (1988) 56 P & CR 427 . . . . 211, 212
Winton v Secretary of State for the Environment (1983) 46 P & CR 205 72
Witherspoon v Secretary of State for the Environment [1992] JPL 547 118
Wood v Secretary of State for the Environment [1973] 2 All ER 404 71
Worthing BC v Secretary of State for the Environment [1991] EGCS 113 74
Worthing BC v Secretary of State for the Environment
  (1992) 63 P & CR 446 169
Wychavon DC v Secretary of State for the Environment [1992] JPL 753 175
Wycombe DC v Michael Shanly Group Ltd [1994] 2 EG 112 236
Wycombe DC v Secretary of State for the Environment
  (1989) 57 P & CR 177 115
Wyndham v Way (1812) 4 Taunt 318 224
Wyre Forest DC v Secretary of State for the Environment
  (1984) 58 P & CR 291 116
Wyre Forest DC v Secretary of State for the Envrionment
  (1990) 60 P & CR 195 238

Young v Secretary of State for the Environment
  (1983) 47 P & CR 165 (CA); [1983] 2 All ER 1105 (HL) 150, 151
Young v Secretary of State for the Environment (1990) 60 P & CR 560 184

Table of Statutes

Access to the Countryside (NI) Order 1983 .... 12, 16
   Article
      16(1) 12
      29 12
      40 12
      50 12
Aerodromes Act (NI) 1971
   Section 19(1) 295
Agriculture Act (NI) 1949 280
Agriculture (Environmental Areas) (NI) Order 1987 43
Amenity Lands Act (NI) 1965 6

Business Tenancies Act (NI) 1964
   56

Caravan Sites Act 1968 238
Caravan Sites and Control of Development Act 1960
   Section 29(1) 238
Caravans Act (NI) 1963
   .... 16, 237–38
   Section
      1(1) 238
      1(2) 238
      1(3) 244
      1(4) 237
      2 245
      3(1) 238
      3(2) 238
      3(3) 238
      3(4) 239
      3(5) 239
      3(6) 239
      4(1) 239
      4(2) 239
      5 240–42
      5(1) 239–40, 240
      5(1)(a) 242, 243, 244
      5(2) 240
      5(3) 240, 240, 242
      5(4) 240, 242
      5(5) 240
      5(6) 242
      5(7) 240, 243
      5(8) 244
      6 239
      7(1) 243
      7(2) 243
      7(3) 243
      7(4) 243
      7(5) 243
      8(1) 243
      8(2) 243, 244
      8(3) 244
      8(4) 244
      8(6) 243
      8(7) 243
      8(9) 243
      9(1) 244
      9(2) 244
      9(4) 244
      10(1) 244
      10(1)(c) 247
      10(2) 244
      10(3) 244
      10(4) 244
      11(1) 243
      12 244
      21 246–47
      21(1) 246
      21(2)(a) 246
      21(2)(b) 246
      21(3) 246
      21(6) 246
      22(1) 246
      22(2) 244
      23(1) 246
      23(5) 246
      25(1) 237
   Schedule 245, 247

Chronically Sick and Disabled Persons (NI) Act 1978 125
Conveyancing and Law of Property Act 1881
   Section 19 59

Electric Lighting (Clauses) Act 1899
   48
Electricity (NI) Order 1992 103
Enterprize Zones (NI) Order 1981
   .... 27, 35, 47, 84
   Article
     3(1) 35
     3(2) 36
     3(3) 36
     4(1) and (2) 36
     5(2) 36
     6 36–37
     6(1) 36, 37, 38
     6(2)(b) 38
     6(4) 37, 38
     7 36
     7(1) 35
     8(1) 35
     11 36

Gas (NI) Order 1977
   Article 14(1) 289
General Rate Act 1967
   Schedule 1
     para. 2(c) 208
Government of Ireland Act 1920
   Section 5 4

Historic Monuments Act (NI) 1971
   .... 11, 207, 212, 218, 222
   Section
     1 223
     1(1) 11
     6 223
     7 223
     9 223
     9(1) 11
     10(1) 223
     11(1) 223
     11(4) 223
     14 223
     27 222
   Schedule 2 223

Housing (NI) Order 1981 ..... 11, 51
   Article
     3(1) 22
     47 .... 11–12, 22
     48 27
     48(1) 12
     49 27
Housing Executive Act (NI) 1971
   22
Housing, Town Planning etc. Act 1909
   3
   Section 76(2) 3
Housing, Town Planning etc. Act 1919
   3
   Section 51 3

Income and Corporation Taxes Act 1988
   Section 776 48
Interpretation Act (NI) 1954
   Section 38 25

Judicature (NI) Act 1978
   Section
     18 .... 31, 193
     18(1) 144, 148
     18(2) 147

Laganside Development (NI) Order 1989 12
   Article
     3(1) 12, 21
     4(1) 12, 21
     10(1) 21
     10(2) 22
     10(3) 22
     11(1) 12
   Schedule 1
     para. 2(1) 21, 22
     para. 4(2) 22
Land Acquisition and Compensation (NI) Order 1973 51
   Article 24(1) 52
Land Development Values (Compensation) Act (NI) 1965 .. 6, 141–48, 261
   Section
     1 142
     2(1)(a) 142
     2(1)(b) 142

5	142
8	142
9	142
10(1)	142
10(2)	142
13(1)	142
14	133, 134, 135, 137, 142, 143
14(1)	133
14(1)(a)	142
14(2)	135
15	143
15(1)(a) and (b)	137
15(2)	137
15(3)	134
15(4)	134
15(5)	134
16	143
16(1) and (3)	137
17(1)	134
18	134
19	134
20(2)	142, 155
20(4)(a)	143
22(1)	143
22(5)	143
24	143–44
24(1)	143
24(10) and (11)	143
24(12)	143
24(3)(a)	143
24(3)(b)	143
24(6)	144
26	235, 264
26(1)	155
26(2)	155
26(3)	155
26(3)(b)	155
26(4) and (5)	155
26(6)	155
29	133, 134–35, 137, 142, 143
29(1)	134, 134
29(2)	135
29(2A)	137
29(3)	135
29(3A)	134
29(9)	143
30	135
43(1)	133, 134, 141, 155, 215
Schedule 1	134, 141, 261

Schedule 2	141
Schedule 3	142

Land Improvement Act (Ireland) 1765 ... 224

Land Improvement Act (Ireland) 1775 ... 224

Land Improvement Act (Ireland) 1783 ... 224

Land Registration Act (NI) 1970 ... 199, 200

Section
41	174, 178
88	203
Schedule 7	174, 178
Schedule 11	210, 219, 226
para. 39	203, 204

Local Government Act (NI) 1934
Section 22(2)(b) ... 47

Local Government Act (NI) 1972 ... 7, 12
Section 1(1)	13
Schedule 6	45, 47
para. 2(a)	45
para. 2(b) and (c)	45
para. 3(1)	46
para. 3(2)	46
para. 4	46
para. 5(1)(a)	46
para. 5(1)(b)	47
para. 5(1)(c)	46
para. 5(1)(d)	46
para. 5(2)	46
para. 6(1)	46
para. 6(3)	46
para. 11(1)	47
para. 12(1) and (2)	47
para. 14(1)	48
para. 14(2)	48
para. 15(1)	48
para. 18	48
para. 18(2)	264

Local Government (Boundaries) Act (NI) 1971 ... 13

Local Government (Miscellaneous Provisions) (NI) Order 1985 ... 237, 246

Article
8(1)	246
8(3)	247

9 247	4(1) 20
10 247	4(2) 20
11 . . . . 237, 246, 247	4(3) 20

Local Government (Postponement of Elections and Reorganisation) (NI) Order 1972
Article 4(1) 7–8

Nature Conservation and Amenity Lands (NI) Order 1985
. . . . . . 11, 16, 20, 39, 199, 202–4
Article
2(2) 202
3(1) 11
8 202–3
8(1) 202
8(2) 203
8(3) 203, 204
9(1) 204
9(2)(a) 204
9(2)(b) 204
9(3) 204
12 . . . . 11, 33
12(3) 20
14 . . . . 11, 33
14(1) 43
16 11
17(1) 204
17(2) 204
17(3) 204
17(4) 204
17(5) 204
17(6) 204
18 33
19(3) 20
21(3) 20
24 . . . . 11, 33
24(1) 43
24(2)(b) 43
24(9) 204
25(1) 43
25(7) 43
34(1) 203
Schedule 4 203

Nature Conservation and Amenity Lands (Amendment) (NI) Order 1989 39
Article
3(1) 20

10(1) 43
Schedule
para. 1 20
para. 2 20
para. 5 21
para. 6(1) 21

New Towns Act (NI) 1965 . . . . . . 6, 11
Section
1 27
1(1) 11
4(1) 11

Northern Ireland Act 1962
Section 14 4

Open Spaces Act 1906 16

Planning (NI) Order 1972
. . . 5, 6, 7, 9, 12–13, 25, 159, 166
Article
3(1) 9
4(1) 25
4(2) 25
30 81
64(1)(a) and (b) 215
64(2) 215
65(1) 216
65A(2) 157
65A(3) 158
65A(4) 158
65A(5) 158
65A(6) 158
65A(7) 158
66(1) 227
66(2)(a) 227
66(2)(b) 227
66(3) 227
66A(1) 230
66A(2) 230
66B 255
67(2) 190
67(3) 191
67(4) 191
67(5) 162, 191
67(6) 191
68 . . . . 135, 137
69A(1) 134

69A(2)	135
82(1)	21
88(1)	16
97(1)	155
97(2)	155
109	166
124	190

Schedule 5
   para. 2(1) 166

Planning (Amendment) (NI) Order 1978 8
   Article 3 155

Planning (Amendment) (NI) Order 1982 .... 8, 50
   Article
17(3)	51
17(5)	52
17(6)	58
18(b)	137
18(c)	134

Planning (NI) Order 1991
.... 7–8, 9, 13, 159–61
   Article
2(1)	208
2(2)	64–65, 67, 76, 77, 100, 174, 233, 257
3(1)	9, 25, 114, 160
3(2)	9
4(1)	25
4(2)	26
4(3)	30, 98
4–10	9
5	30
5(2)	13, 28
5(3)	116
5(3)(a)	28
5(3)(b)	28
5(3)(c)	28
5(4)	28, 51
5(5)	28
5(6)	29
6	30
6(2)	13, 30
6(3)	51
6(4)	30
6(5)	31
7	17, 29
8(1)	29
8(2)	30
9(1)	27
9(2)	27
10	26
10(5)	18
11	77
11(1)	63, 69
11(2)	63, 75
11(2)(b)	76
11(2)(c)	76
11(2)(d)	77
11(2)(e)	77
11(3)	67, 74
11(3)(a)	74
11(3)(b)	75
11(3)(c)	75
11(4)	84
12	63, 83, 197
13	13, 80, 125
13(1)	9, 84
13(2)	13
13(2)(b)	83, 84
14(2)	35, 83
14(3)	83
14(4)	34
14(5)	33
14(6)	34
14–18	27
15(1)	84
15(1)(a)	83
15(1)(b)	84
16(1)	34
18(1)	33
19	36
19(1)	84
19(3)	84
19(4)	84
19(5)	84
19(7)	84
19(8)	84
19(9)	84
20	83
20(1)	13, 80, 91
21	108–9, 181
21 to 28	139
21(1)	109
21(1)(a)	108, 110
21(1)(b)	110, 181
21(2)	108
21(3)	110, 181

22	96
22(1)	91, 103
22(1)(a)	103, 104
22(1)(b)	104
22(1)(c)	92, 104, 110
22(1)(d)	104, 110
22(2)(a)	103
22(2)(b)	103
22(3)	104
22(4)	104
22(5)	104
22(6)	104
22(7)	103
23	161, 162–64, 171
23(1)	161, 162, 163
23(2)	163
23(3)	163
23(4)	163
23(5)	164
23(6)	164
23(7)	164
23(8)	164
23(9)	163
23(10)	163
23(11)	163
23(12)	162
24	17, 164
24(1)	164
24(2)	164
24(3)	164
24(4)	164
24(5)	164
24(6)(a)	164
24(6)(b)	164
24(7)	164
25	30, 83, 160, 240
25(1)	80, 113–14, 116, 124, 127
25(2)	110, 181
25(3)(a)	110
26(1)	125
27	240
27(1)	127
27(1)(a)	127
27(1)(b)	67, 86, 127, 149
27(2)	86, 149
28(1)	99, 136
28(3)	136
28(3)(a)	99
28(3)(b)	99
28(4)	99
29	67, 89
29(1)	98, 119, 136
29(1)(a) and (b)	99
29(3)	99
30	219
30(1)	89, 124, 132
30(2)	89
31	10, 17, 18, 100, 101, 133, 251
31(1)	101
31(2)	18, 101
31(3)	101
31(4)	101
31(5)	101
31(6)	100
32	80, 134, 137, 239, 251, 262
32(1)	17, 112, 125, 133, 136, 138
32(2)	133
32(3)	136, 139
32(5)	139
32(6)	139
33	80, 111, 112, 138, 251
34	86, 87, 89, 90, 99, 134, 135, 153, 261
34(1)	89
34(2)	89
34(3)	89
35	86, 87, 89, 90, 99, 134, 135, 153, 261
35(1)	86, 89
35(2)	90
35(2)(a)	90, 93
35(2)(b)(ii)	96
35(4)	90
36	90
36(1)	90, 163
36(4)(a)	89
36(4)(b)	90, 93
37	153, 216
37(1)	153
37(2)	153
37(3)	154
37(4)	153
37(5)	154
37(6)	154
38	30, 235, 258
38(1)	154
38(2)	18, 154

Table of Statutes

38(3)	154	44(2)	217, 220
38(3)(a)	154	44(2)(b)	211
38(3)(b)	154	44(3)	217, 220
38(4)	154	44(4)	211
38(5)	154	44(5)	217, 220
39	30, 67, 156–58, 258–59, 260	44(7)	217
39(1)	156	44(8)	212
39(2)	156	44(8)(a)	212, 213
39(3)(a)	156	45(1)	214
39(3)(b)	156	45(2)	214
39(4)	18, 156	45(3)	215
39(5)	156	45(4)	215
39(6)	156	45(5)	215
40	79, 153, 194–202, 202, 203	46	261
40(1)	194, 195, 200	46(1)	216
40(2)(a)	199	47	30
40(2)(b)	197	47(1)	216
40(2)(c)	197	47(2)	18, 216
40(3)	200	47(3)	216
40(3)(b) and (c)	199, 200	48(1)	213
40(4)	200	48(2)	213
40(5)	200	48(3)	213
40(6)	200	49	217
40(7)	200	50(1)	14, 33, 39
40(8)(a)	198	50(2)	39
40(8)(b)	198	50(3)	14, 40
41	80–82, 98, 136	50(4)	39
41(1)(a)	79	50(5)	40, 41
41(1)(b)	79	50(6)	33
41(2)	17, 80, 81	51	42, 67
41(3)	80	51(1)	42
42	42, 207	51(2)	42
42(1)	13, 207	51(3)	42
42(1)(b)	207	51(4)	42
42(2)	207	52(1)	40
42(2)(a)	210	52(2)	40
42(2)(b)	210	52(3)	40
42(3)	13, 210	53(1)	14, 228
42(4)	210	53(3)(a)(i)	228
42(5)	210	53(3)(a)(ii)	228, 230
42(6)	210	53–63	14
42(7)	208, 209, 212	54(1)	228
42–49	21	54(2)	228
43	222	54(4)	228
43(1)	13, 222	54(4)(b)	14
43(2)	222	54(4)(b) and (c)	228
43(3)	222	55(1)	228, 229
44	67, 259	55(2)	229
44(1)	207, 211, 217, 220	55(3)	229

55(4)	229
55(5)	229
56(1)	18, 228
56(2)	18
57(1)	17, 229
57(3)	229
58(1)	228
59(1)	230
59(2)	230
59(3)	230
59(4)	230
59(5)	18, 230
59(6)	230
60(1)	229
60(2)	229, 230
60(4)	229
60(8)	229
61(1)	230
61(2)(a)	230
61(2)(b)	230
61(3)	231
61(5)	231
61(6)	231
61(7)	231
62	230
62(1)	231
62(2)(a)	231
62(2)(b)	231
62(3)	231
64(a)	224
64(b)	224
65(1)	225
65(1)(a)	225, 226
65(1)(b)	224, 225
65(2)	18, 225
65(2)(c)	18
65(3)	225, 226
66(1)	226
67	233
67(1)	18
67(3)	236
67(4)	18
67(5)	84
68	30, 163, 171
68(1)	161, 162, 165, 167, 174
68(2)	165
68(3)	169
68(3)(a)	166
68(4)	167
68(5)	173, 174, 175, 180, 187, 220, 226
68(5)(b)	163
68(6)	166, 169
68(7)(b)	173
68(8)	173
68(9)	67, 171
68(10)(a)	173
68(11)	173
68(12)	184, 220, 226
68(13)	173
68(14)	175, 220, 226
68(15)	175, 220, 226
68(16)	184
69	100, 163, 262
69(1)	17, 173, 178, 179
69(3)	178, 183–84
69(3)(a)	100
69(3)(g)	175
69(3)(h)	173, 187
69(4)	177, 179
69(4) to (8)	221
69(5)	181, 182
69(6)	181
69(7)	181
69(8)	183
69(9)	164, 176, 177–78
69(10)	178
69–71	232
70	221, 227
70(1)	181, 183, 221
70(2)	170, 182
70(3)	175, 181, 182
71(1)(a)	182
71(1)(b)	183
71(2)	182, 183
71(2)(a)	182
71(2)(b)	182
71(3)	180, 183
71(3)(a)	182
71(3)(b)	182, 183
71(3)(c)	182
72	184, 220, 226
72(1)	185
72(2)	185
72(3)(a)	185
72(3)(b)	185
72(4)	186
72(5)	67, 174, 178

72(5)(a)	186	80(5–10)	219
72(5)(b)	186	80(8)	219
72(6)	184	81(1)	231
73(1)	161, 188, 189	81(2)	231
73(1)(a)	188	81(3)(a)	231
73(1)(9b)	188	81(3)(b)	232
73(2)(a)	189	81(4)	232
73(2)(b)	189	81(5)(b)	232
73(3)	188	81(7)	232
73(4)	189	81(8)	232
73(5)	189	81(9)	232
73(6)	189	81(10)	17
73(7)	189, 190	81(11)	232
73(8)	190	81(12)(a)	232
73(9)	188	82(1)	226–27
74	193, 220, 226	82(2)	226
74(1)	185	82(3)	226
74(2)	184, 185	82(4)	227
74(3)	185	82(5)	227
74(4)	185	82(6)	227
74(5)	185	83	67
74(6)	185	83(1)	157
74(7)	185	83(2)	157
74(8)	185	83(3)	157
75	67	83(4)	157
75(1)	176	83(5)	157
75(2)	176	83(6)	157
75(3)	176	83(7)	157
76	67	83(8)	157
76(1)	184	83(9)	157
76(2)	171, 184	84(1)	236
76(3)	184	84(2)	233, 236
76(5)	186	84(3)	236
77(1)	219, 220	85	14, 32
77(3)	220	86	27, 44, 51
77(4)	219	86(1)	32
77(6)	220	86(3)	32
78	262	86(4)	32
78(1)	17, 221	86(5)	32
78(2)	220	87	10, 45, 255, 264
78(3)	221	87(1)	14, 44
78(4)	221	87(1)(a) and (b)	32
78(6)	221	87(2)	45
78(7)	221	87(3)	45
79(1)	220	87(5)	14
79(2)	220	87(6)	45
80(1)	219	87(7)	44
80(3)	219	87–93	218
80(4)	219	89	48, 255

90	48	102(1)	255
90(1)	48	103(1)	256
90(2)	48	103(2)	256
91	44	103(3)	256
91(1)	49	103(4)	256
91(2)	49	103(5)	256
91(3)	49	105(1)	21
92	48	105(2)	21
93	46	106	207
94	133, 137, 257–62	106(1)	211
94(1)	133, 156, 257, 263	106(4)	211
94(1)(a)	133, 257	107	217
94(1)(b)	155, 258	108	222
94(1)(i)	258, 260	108(2)	222
94(2)	215, 263	108(3)	222
94(2)(1)	260	109	211, 218–19
94(2)(a)	259	109(1)	218
94(2)(b)	216, 259	109(2)	218
94(2)(i)	259	109(3)	218
94(3)	158, 259, 260, 263	109(4)	215, 218, 262
94(4)(a)	262	110(1)	16
94(5)	261	110(2)	17
94(6)	261	110(3)	17
94(7)	215, 262	110(4)	17
94(8)	259	111	139
95(1)	263	111(1)	17
95(2)(a)	262	111(1)(a)	19
95(2)(b)	262	111(1)(b)	18, 19
96	263	111(1)(c)	19
97(1)	263	111(2)	17, 20
97(2)	263	111(2)(a)	19
97(3)	263	111(2)(b)	18, 19
98(1)	263	111(2)(c)	19
98(2)	264	111(3)	19
98(3)	264	111(4)	19, 93
98(5)	264	111(5)	19
98(6)	264	111(6)	20
98(7)	264	112	67
98(8)(a)	264	112(2)	67
98(8)(b)	264	112(2)(a)	67, 75
99	264	112(2)(b)	67
100	51, 255	113(1)(c)	208
100(1)	255	113(4)	219
100(2)	255	114	102
100(7)	255	114(1)	102
101(1)(a)	255	114(2)	102
101(1)(b)	255	114(3) to (5)	102
101(2)	255	115(1)	227
102	51, 255	115(2)	227

115(3)	227
115(4)	227
116	30
116(1)	17, 186
116(2)	186, 187
116(3)	187
116(4)	187
116(5)	187
116(6)	187
116(7)	186
117(2)	102
118	50
118(1)	101, 102, 186, 187
119	9
120	10
121	161
121(1)(a)	161
122(1)(a)	161
122(1)(b)	161
122(2)	161
123(1)	9
124	163, 199
124(1)(a) and (b)	109
124(2)	109
124(3)	109
125	10, 191
125(1)	162
125(2)	162
125(3)	162
125(4)	162
126	9
127	105
128	185, 186, 226
131	210, 219, 226
133	134, 230, 244, 255
Schedule 1	213
para. 1	213
para. 2(a)	213
para. 3	213
para. 4(1)	214
para. 4(2)	214
para. 5	215
para. 5(3)	215
para. 6	216
para. 7	214, 262
para. 8	214
Schedule 2	45
para. 4(a)	45
para. 4(b) and (c)	45
para. 7(a)	46
para. 7(b)	47
para. 7(c)	46
para. 7(d)	46
Schedule 3	
para. 2	21
para. 4(1)	21
para. 4(2)	21
para. 4(4)	21
para. 5	21
para. 6	21
Schedule 5	51, 134, 230, 238, 240, 244, 255

Planning (Interim Development) Act (NI) 1944
.... 3, 4, 5, 6, 16, 25, 134, 166

Section	
1(1)	5
2(2)	5
2(6)	6, 16
2(10)	5
4	5
4(1)(a)	5–6
4(1)(b)	6
6	6
9(1)	133, 141

Planning Acts Amendment Act (NI) 1944 5

Planning and Building Regulations (Amendment) (NI) Order 1990
.... 8, 34, 50

Article	
21	157
29(1)	50
30(3)	166

Planning and Compensation Act 1991

Section	
10	167
13	67

Planning and Housing Act (NI) 1931
.... 3–4, 5, 6, 25

Section	
1	4
1(2)	3
2(1)	3
4	4
5	4

5(2) 4
7 4
8 4
9(1) 4
9(2)(b) 4, 6
10(2) 4
16 3
Planning and Land Compensation Act (NI) 1971 ....6, 50
Planning Blight (Compensation) (NI) Order 1981 ....32, 50
Article
  1(2) 52, 53, 58
  3(1) 51, 54
  4(1)(a) 52
  4(1)(b)(i) 52
  4(1)(b)(ii) 52
  4(2)(a) and (b) 52
  4(4)(a) and (b) 52
  4(5) 52
  5(1) 53
  5(1)(a) 52
  5(1)(b) 53
  5(1)(c) 53
  6(2) 54, 55, 58, 60
  6(2)(c) 56, 57, 59
  6(2)(h) 59
  6(4) 55
  7(1) 55
  7(3) 55
  7(4) 56
  7(5) 55
  7(6) 57
  7(7) 57
  8(1) 57
  8(2) 57
  8(3) 57
  8(4) 58
  8(5) 58
  8(6) 57
  8(10) 57
  9 ....54, 58
  9(1) 58
  10(1) 54, 58
  10(6) 57
  11(1) 57
  11(2) 58
  11(3) 59
  11(4) 59
  12(1) 59
  12(1)(a) 59
  12(1)(b) 59
  12(3) 59
  12(4) 59
  12(5) 59
  13(1) 60
  13(2) 60
  13(3) 60
  14(1) 59
  14(1)(e) 60
  14(2) 60
  14(3) 54
  14(3)(a) 60
  14(3)(b) 60
  15 60
  15A(1) 50
  17(4) 51
Pollution Control and Local Government (NI) Order 1978 16
Private Streets (NI) Order 1980
  Article 3(1) 275
Property (NI) Order 1978
  ....136, 197, 201, 203
Article
  3(1)(a)(i) 201
  3(1)(b) 136
  5(1) 201
  5(5)(c) and (d) 201
  5(6)(b) 202
Public Health (Ir) Act 1878 16

Rates (NI) Order 1977
  Articles 42(1A) to (1E) 35
Rates (Amendment) (NI) Order 1983
  Article 5 35
Registration (Land and Deeds) (NI) Order 1992
  Article 21 178
Registration of Clubs Act (NI) 1967
 81
Registration of Deeds Act (NI) 1970
 200
Section
  1 199
  39 199
  Schedule 6, para. 12 199

Rent (NI) Order 1978
  Article 3(1) 74
Roads (NI) Order 1980 100
  Article
    30 302
    44(1) 302
    Schedule 2 302
Roads (NI) Order 1993 51
  Article
    14 ....27, 100
    15 ....27, 100
Rhyl Improvement Act 1892 48

Social Security and Housing Benefits Act 1982
    Section 28 15

Telecommunications Act 1984 .. 299
  Section
    4(1) 299
    7 299
    Schedule 2 299
Town and Country Planning Act 1947
    .... 172, 257

Town and Country Planning Act 1971
   262
  Section
    23(9) 151
    52 195
    52(3) 198
    243 178
    280 161
Town and Country Planning Act 1990
   83
  Section
    19(2) 167
    55(1)(A) 67
    57(2) 83
    57(3) 83
    57(4) 83, 151
    106(2)(a) 195
    171(B)(1) 169
    174 178
    196A 161
    226 44
    284 31
    287 ....31, 37
    287(1)(a) and (b) 31
    289 184

Table of Statutory Instruments

Caravan Sites (Licence Applications) Order (NI) 1963 239

Department of Housing, Local Government and Planning (Dissolution) (NI) Order 1976
Article 3 239
Departments (Transfer of Functions) (NI) Order 1976 222

Laganside Development Designation Order (NI) 1989 12
Land Development Values (Ascertainment and Certificates) Regulations (NI) 1965 142
Land Development Values (Compensation) Regulations (NI) 1965 .... 142, 155
Regulation
   6(1), (3), (4) 143

Ministries (Transfer of Functions) (Nos 1 and 2) Orders 1944 3
Ministries of Northern Ireland (Transfer of Functions and Adaptation of Enactments) Orders (NI) 1964 and 1972 239
Ministries of Northern Ireland Order 1964 3

Planning (1991 Order) (Commencement No 1) Order (NI) 1992 8
Planning (1991 Order) (Commencement No 2) Order (NI) 1993 8
Planning (Assessment of Environmental Effects) Regulations (NI) 1989 ....35, 100, 248
Regulation
   2(2) 248
   3(1) 248, 249
   3(1)(a) 248
   4 249
   4(1) 249
   4(2) 249
   4(3) 249
   4(4) 249
   4(6) 249
   4(7) 249
   4(8) 249
   5 249
   5(1) 250
   5(2) 250
   5(3) 250
   5(4) 250
   5(5) 250
   6 249
   6(2) 249
   7 249
   8(1) 250
   8(2) 249, 251
   9 251
   10(1)(a) 251
   10(1)(b) 251
   10(2) 251
   11(c) 251
   12 251
   13(1) 251
   14(1) 251
   14(2) 251
   15 251
   16 251
   17 248
   Schedule 1 .... 248, 249–50, 303–6
   Schedule 2 ....248, 249–50
   Schedule 3
     para. 2 250
     para. 3 250
     para. 4 250
Planning (Assessment of Environmental Effects) (Amendment) Regulations (NI) 1994 ....248, 249

Planning (Conservation Areas) (Demolition) Regulations (NI) 1988
Regulation 7 42
Schedule 2 42
Planning (Control of Advertisements) Regulations (NI) 1992 .... 84, 233
Regulation
3 236
3(1) 235
3(2) 235
3(3) 235
3(4) 234
4(2)(ii) 233
5 236
5(1) 235
6 236
6(1) 236
6(2) 236
6(3) 236
6(4) 236
7(1) 234
7(3) 234
8 ....14, 234
9(1)(b) 234
9(2)(c) 234
10(1) 235
10(2) 235
11(1) 234
12(1) 235
12(2) 235
13(1) 234
14(3) 235
Schedule 1 235
Schedule 2 233
Schedule 4 .... 234, 235, 235
Planning (Development Plans) Regulations (NI) 1991 26
Regulation
3 28
5(1) 27
5(2) 27
5(3) 27
6 26
8 ....26, 34
9 34
9(a) 26
11 34
11(1) 29
12(1) 29

12(2) 29
13 30
14 29
14(a) 30
14(b) 30
Planning (Development Plans) (Amendment) Regulations 1994
........................28
Planning (Fees) Regulations (NI) 1992 213
Regulation
3(1) 105
3(2) 106
3(3) 106
4(1) and (2) 106
6–9 106
10 106
10(2) 106
11(1) 105
13 106
18 106
18(1) 106
Schedule 1 106
Planning (Fees) (Amendment) Regulations (NI) 1993 105
Planning (Fees) (Amendment) Regulations (NI) 1994 105
Planning (General Development) Order (NI) 1993 .... 85, 91
Article
2 .... 86, 92, 93, 109
3 .... 247, 271
3(1) 85
3(2) 85
4 .... 85, 158
4(1) 85
4(2) 85
4(3) 85
5 271
5(1) 85
5(4) 85
7(1) 92
7(2) 92
7(3) 99, 100
7(4) 92, 103
8(1) 85
8(2) 92
9 96
11 110

1(2) 138
11(3)(c) 106
13 .... 132, 137, 138
15(a) 109
15(b) 109
17 .... 191, 262
Schedule 1 .... 247, 271–302
Schedule 3 101
Planning (Hazardous Substances) Regulations (NI) 1993 228
Regulation
    5–7 228
    7 228
    10 228
    11 228
    17(3) 232
Planning (Listed Buildings) Regulations (NI) 1973 213
Planning (Listed Buildings) Regulations (NI) 1992 213
Regulation
    2 213
    3(a) 213
    3(b) 214
    4(1) 214
    4(2) 214
    6 213
    8 .... 215, 216
Planning (Simplified Planning Zones) Regulations (NI) 1990 34
Regulation
    5 34
Planning (Simplified Planning Zones) (Excluded Development) Order (NI) 1994 .... 35, 83
Planning (Special Enforcement Notices) Regulations (NI) 1990
.... 186
Planning (Tree Preservation Order) Regulations (NI) 1973 225
Regulation
    3(1) 225
    3(2) 225
    4(1) 225
    5(1) 226
    5(2) 226
Planning (Use Classes) Order (NI) 1989 77–78
Article
    3(1) 77
    3(3) 78
    3(5) 77
    Schedule 267–70
Planning (Use Classes) (Amendment) Order (NI) 1993 77
Planning (Use Classes) (Amendment No 2) Order (NI) 1993
.... 77, 78, 267, 268
Planning Applications (Exemption from Publication) Order (NI) 1991
.... 109
Planning Blight Regulations (NI) 1989 .... 53, 54
Plant and Machinery (Valuation for Rating) Order 1927 65

Rules of the Supreme Court (NI) 1980
    Order 53 .... 31, 144
    rule 4 147

EC LEGISLATION

European Community Directives
    85/337/EEC 248

OTHER JURISDICTIONS

Local Government (Planning and Development) Act 1976 [Republic of Ireland]
Section
    27 159

Abbreviations

'The 1972 Order' the Planning (Northern Ireland) Order 1972

'The 1991 Order' the Planning (Northern Ireland) Order 1991

'The GDO' or
'The General Development Order' the Planning (General Development) Order (Northern Ireland) 1993

'The UCO' or
'The Use Classes Order' the Planning (Use Classes) Order (Northern Ireland) 1989

'The 1965 Act' the Land Development Values (Compensation) Act (Northern Ireland) 1965

PART ONE

Introduction

CHAPTER ONE

Historical Introduction to Planning Law in Northern Ireland

As has been the case in many other branches of law, legislation to control the development of land in Northern Ireland came into existence some years later than in England and Wales and, when it did, the Northern Ireland legislation followed its English counterpart to a greater or a lesser degree.[1] In England and Wales the first Planning Act had been the Housing, Town Planning etc. Act 1909 which introduced the 'planning scheme'. This became the central feature of the Northern Ireland legislation introduced in 1931.[2] The 1909 Act was followed by another bearing the same title a decade later, which brought the concept of interim development control to this country towards the end of the Second World War.[3] Neither the 1909 Act nor the 1919 Act extended to Ireland,[4] and it was not until 1931 that the Government here introduced an 'Act to provide for the making of schemes for the development or redevelopment of land ... '.[5] When it did arrive, the measure was well received by Parliament, the main criticism being that it was ten years too late.[6]

The 1931 Act vested responsibility for planning in the then local authorities,[7] which were empowered to prepare or adopt 'planning schemes' for land within their district (s. 2(1)). The Act also enabled the then Ministry of Home Affairs[8] to authorise planning schemes, where the Ministry considered it expedient, with the object of preserving and protecting areas of special architectural or historic interest (s. 1(2)). 'Planning schemes' were defined as schemes laying down a plan of development or redevelopment for land 'with the general object of securing proper sanitary conditions,

---

1 For an historical introduction to the legislation in England and Wales see Telling and Duxbury, *Planning Law and Procedure*, 9th ed. London: Butterworths 1993, ch. 1 and Heap, *An Outline of Planning Law*, 10th ed. London: Sweet and Maxwell 1991, ch. 1.
2 Planning and Housing Act (NI) 1931.
3 Planning (Interim Development) Act (NI) 1944.
4 1909 Act, s. 76(2); 1919 Act, s. 51.
5 Planning and Housing Act (NI) 1931.
6 See HC Debs (NI) Vol. 13 col. 1000, 22 April 1931.
7 The then borough or urban district councils; the county councils; or in the case of land belonging to the Belfast Harbour Commissioners, the Commissioners: s. 16.
8 The functions of the Ministry were later transferred to the Ministry of Health and Local Government (later renamed the Ministry of Development) by the Ministries (Transfer of Functions) (Nos 1 and 2) Orders 1944, SR & O 1944 Nos 43 & 61. For the renaming of the Ministry see Ministries of Northern Ireland Order 1964, SR & O (NI) 1964 No 205.

amenity and convenience in connection with the laying out and use of the land ... or in connection with the redevelopment of the land if already developed' (s. 1). The matters to be included in such schemes were specified in s. 5 of the Act, and included, for example, provisions as to the number of buildings, their height and use (s. 5(2)), streets, open spaces, and the control of advertisements.[9] In order to promote the objectives of the legislation, the Act gave the authority responsible for the planning scheme powers to purchase land included in the scheme either by agreement or compulsorily (s. 8). The Act also enabled the authority to remove any buildings or work which contravened the scheme, and to execute any work which it was the duty of any person to execute under the scheme (s. 7).

The second feature of the Act, which was to be amended some years later, was the provision for regulation of development during the interim period between the date on which a resolution to prepare or adopt a planning scheme had been passed by the local authority and the date on which such scheme came into effect (s. 4). The Ministry was empowered to make an order allowing such development to take place subject to the conditions contained in the order, or as might be required by the local authority, and such conditions could be enforced as if they were provisions of a planning scheme already in operation. This form of regulation of interim development became the subject of the other main legislative provision controlling planning in Northern Ireland until the substantial reorganisation effected in 1972, the Planning (Interim Development) Act (NI) 1944, discussed below.

The other innovation of the 1931 Act was to entitle anyone whose land was injuriously affected by the coming into operation of a planning scheme to obtain compensation from the local authority responsible for the scheme (s. 9(1)).[10] Claims could not be made however in respect of development carried out after the date on which the resolution to make the scheme was passed, unless the development was permitted under the interim development control provisions (s. 9(2)(b)). This ensured that unpermitted development was discouraged.

---

9   Second schedule, paras 1, 3 & 5. The schedule contains twenty paragraphs listing various matters covering a wide range of planning matters.
10 The compensation provisions in the Act gave rise to an issue of constitutional importance: s. 10(2) provided that property should not be deemed to be injuriously affected by reason of any provisions of a planning scheme prescribing certain matters regarding buildings. In *Belfast Corp.* v O D Cars Ltd [1960] NI 60 it was argued that this provision offended the provisions of s. 5 of the Government of Ireland Act 1920, which provided that the Government of Northern Ireland had no power to make any law so as to take away property without compensation, and that any such purported law was void. The House of Lords held that the restrictions contained in the Acts of 1931 and 1944 did not amount to a 'taking' of property and consequently the provisions of s. 10(2) of the 1931 Act were not void. The legislature took the opportunity however to dispose of any argument founded on s. 5 of the 1920 Act by abolishing the restriction on the legislative power of the Northern Ireland Government: see Northern Ireland Act 1962, s. 14; Wylie, *Irish Conveyancing Law*, Abingdon Oxon.: Professional Books 1978, para. 7.081.

In 1944 the Government introduced two measures. The Planning Acts Amendment Act (NI) 1944 effected some changes to the powers of the local authorities. The other Act, the Planning (Interim Development) Act (NI) 1944, despite its title and the assurances of Government Ministers,[11] became the principal means of development control in Northern Ireland until the changes effected by the Planning (NI) Order 1972. The Act did two things: first, it provided that all land which was not already the subject of a planning scheme prepared pursuant to the 1931 Act should be subject to a resolution to prepare such a scheme, which resolution was deemed to have been passed by the relevant local authority (s. 1(1)). This was necessary because since the 1931 Act came into operation only three authorities had taken any steps to formulate planning schemes.[12] Second, due to the lack of progress in the preparation of planning schemes, the Act provided for interim development control, i.e. control of development during the period between the passing (or deemed passing) of a resolution to prepare a planning scheme and the coming into operation of the scheme, replacing the provisions contained in the 1931 Act.[13] These provisions and other provisions of the Act concerning the Planning Board established in 1942 gave rise to some opposition.[14] What the Act did was to provide that the Ministry should make an order with respect to the development of land during the period between the date of the resolution to prepare a planning scheme and the date on which the scheme would come into operation (s. 1(1)).[15] Such an order could permit development or empower local authorities to permit development (s. 2 (2)). Development which was carried out without permission was not made unlawful,[16] but the local authority might exercise the powers conferred by s. 4 of the Act to remove unpermitted buildings or prohibit unauthorised uses of land (s. 4(1)(a)

---

11 See HC Debs (NI) Vol. 26 cols 1810 (the Prime Minister) and 1813 (the Minister of Public Security), 20 October 1943.
12 See the comments of the Minister of Home Affairs on the second reading of the Bill, HC Debs (NI) Vol. 26 col. 1788, 20 October 1943.
13 Planning (Interim Development) Act (NI) 1944, s. 2(10). 'The object is that while planning authorities are drawing up the plans they will not be set at naught by ill-conceived planning and development which may nullify in a large measure the efforts made to develop and build in a reasonable way, and not according to the fancy of each person . . .' HC Debs (NI) Vol. 26 col. 1791, 20 October 1943 (the Minister of Home Affairs).
14 Lord Glentoran describing the measure as 'one of the most dangerous Bills that has ever been brought before this House . . . If we pass this Bill . . . the whole business of this country in this connection will be run by a group of civil servants and specialists, and specialists are the most dangerous people in the world': HC Debs (NI) Vol. 26 cols. 1806–7. Less dramatically other members were concerned about the effect of the provisions of the Bill on farmers wishing to make improvements, especially when such improvements had been delayed due to shortage of materials required for the war. See ibid. cols 1798 and 1801.
15 See Planning (General Interim Development) Order (NI) 1944, SR & O 1944 No 58.
16 R (*Antrim* CC) v *Minister of Housing and Local Government* [1960] NI 1, 7 *per* Lord MacDermott LCJ.

and (b)) and, as we have seen, there would be no right to compensation under the 1931 Act.[17] Where local authorities were empowered to determine applications for interim development, the Act provided a right of appeal to the Ministry with the proviso that the appellant could require the appeal to be determined by an independent person appointed by the Ministry (s. 2(6)). Finally, the Act allowed for compensation in certain cases where the application for development was refused (s. 6). In the circumstances the comments of the Minister of Home Affairs on the Act seem a little harsh.[18]

The Acts of 1931 and 1944 remained the primary legislative provisions controlling development until 1972. Changes were made in the interim, notably by the Land Development Values (Compensation) Act (NI) 1965 and the Planning and Land Compensation Act (NI) 1971, but it was not until the Planning (NI) Order 1972 that a substantial reform of planning law and administration was effected.[19] That such reorganisation was needed had been pointed out as long ago as 1963. Commenting on the operation of the 1931 and 1944 Acts, Sir Robert Matthew reported:

> The idea of the 'statutory planning scheme', under the 1931 Planning and Housing Act, failed. Making of schemes was not obligatory, and none were, in fact, confirmed. Up to the War, it could be said with truth that development in every field was unplanned. The Planning (Interim Development) Act of 1944 'deemed' that a Resolution to prepare a Planning Scheme had been passed for every area in the country. Since then, a permanent 'interim' planning situation has been allowed to develop, pending the emergence of a 'Planning Scheme'. No planning schemes have been completed, and it would appear that the existing legislation is a dead letter.[20]

Although dead, the legislation was not laid to rest for another decade. In the meantime a review of local government had taken place and the recommendations of the review body were published in 1970.[21] Insofar as

---

17 Planning and Housing Act (NI) 1931, s. 9(2)(b).
18 'Be assured that it is no reflection on our very accomplished Parliamentary draughtsman when I describe the language of this Bill as highly technical almost to the point of repulsiveness': HC Debs (NI) Vol. 26 col. 1788, 20 October 1943.
19 Proposals for 'radical changes' in planning administration had been made in 1964 (White Paper on the reorganisation of planning, Cmd. 465; see HC Debs (NI) Vol. 61 cols 832–924, 16 June 1965), following which a Memorandum of Proposals was issued in 1966 setting out an outline of proposed legislation on administration and development control. What was envisaged was the establishment of a Central Development Office responsible for review of the regional plan and preparation of area plans under the guidance of steering committees composed of local authority representatives, and which would also determine applications for planning permission. See *Report of the Ministry of Development* for the period 1 April 1966 to 31 March 1967, Cmd. 516, pp 15–16. Note however, also, the New Towns Act (NI) 1965 and Amenity Lands Act (NI) 1965.
20 *Belfast Regional Survey and Plan* 1963 Cmd. 451 (Matthew Report).
21 *Report of the Review Body on Local Government in Northern Ireland* 1970 Cmd. 546 (Macrory Report).

planning administration was concerned the review body took the view that planning services hitherto provided by local authorities should be treated as a regional service, the responsibility for which should be vested in the Ministry of Development,[22] but that the new district councils should handle local planning applications.[23] The centralisation of planning administration had been one of the main recommendations of the Matthew Report, which had noted that 'the multiplicity of small authorities,[24] however suitable for purely local affairs, is an impossible impediment to the kind of broad co-ordinated planning and development, so urgently required for the future and prosperity of the Province.'[25]

In 1972 the Government at Stormont proceeded with the reorganisation of local government.[26] At the same time it announced its intention to implement the recommendation for centralisation of the responsibility for planning throughout the province. In February the Ministry of Development published a White paper called *Town and Country Planning—Proposals for Legislation* which foreshadowed new legislation to provide for (*inter alia*) a single planning authority, a Planning Appeals Commission, a statutory development plan system and a new definition of development.[27] However, before legislation could be brought forward, the Northern Ireland Parliament was prorogued and responsibility for government was taken over by the Parliament at Westminster.[28]

The proposals of the Northern Ireland Government on planning were taken up by the Government at Westminster and enacted in the Planning (NI) Order 1972,[29] and are now consolidated in the Planning (NI) Order

---

22 Macrory Report paras 74, 82 and 83.
23 Ibid., para. 122.
24 37 in all: Matthew Report para. 180; *Report of the Ministry of Development* for the period 1 April 1972 to 31 December 1973 (1975) p.25.
25 Matthew Report para. 182. The reasons given for the need for centralisation were (1) consistency in the treatment of development proposals throughout the province; (2) the degree to which Government itself participated in development; (3) the need to link planning decisions more closely with Government policy in relation to other administrative services in which Government was involved; (4) the need to guide development for the protection of natural amenities and assets transcending local administrative areas; (5) the control of population and employment throughout the province; (6) Government responsibility for compensation; and (7) the ability to recruit and deploy economically the available planning staff. See para. 196.
26 Local Government Act (NI) 1972.
27 See *Report of the Ministry of Development* for the period 1 April 1971 to 31 March 1972, Cmd. 572.
28 Northern Ireland (Temporary Provisions) Act 1972.
29 Moving the approval of the 1972 Order Mr Paul Channon explained that the proposals followed closely in all essential particulars the White Paper issued by the Northern Ireland Government in February. See HC Debs (5th series) Vol. 843 col. 588, 19 October 1972. The 1972 Order was made on 1 November 1972 but did not become effective (with certain exceptions) until 1 October 1973, which coincided with the date on which the reorganisation effected by the Local Government Act (NI) 1972 took place. See SR & O 1973 No 241 and Local Government (Postponement of Elections

1991.[30] Unfortunately, parts of the 1972 Order and later amendments[31] remain in force. These deal principally with compensation payable in certain circumstances by the planning authority.

---

and Reorganisation) (NI) Order 1972, Art. 4(1); *Report of the Ministry of Development* for the period 1 April 1972 to 31 December 1973, p.25.
30   Made 21 May 1991, coming into effect (with the exceptions of Arts 28, 53–63 and 81) three months after that date (Art. 1(2)). Arts 53–63 and 81 to come into effect on such day(s) as may be appointed by the Head of the Department of the Environment (Art. 1 (3)). Art. 28 came into force on 1 July 1992: see Planning (1991 Order) (Commencement No 1) Order (NI) 1992. Arts 53–63 and 81 in effect from 1 August 1993: see Planning (1991 Order) (Commencement No 2) Order (NI) 1993.
31   Planning (Amendment) (NI) Order 1978; Planning (Amendment) (NI) Order 1982; Planning and Building Regulations (Amendment) (NI) Order 1990.

CHAPTER TWO

The Administration of Planning Control

We saw in the previous chapter how the administration of planning control in Northern Ireland originated as a matter for local authorities and ended up as a matter for central government. It is proposed in this chapter to consider the division of responsibilities between central and local government which now obtain under the 1991 Order, and to consider also other authorities which have a role to play in the administration of planning control.

1 The Department of the Environment

Under the 1972 Order responsibility for planning control was vested in the Ministry of Development (Art. 3(1)). Not long after the Order came into effect the functions of the Ministry were transferred to the Department of the Environment which is now responsible under the 1991 Order for planning control.

(1) Duties of the Department

Art. 3(1) of the 1991 Order imposes a general duty on the Department to 'formulate and co-ordinate policy for securing the orderly and consistent development of land and the planning of that development.' To enable the Department to carry out its duty, the Order confers various powers on the Department. These are considered below. Apart, however, from this general duty, there are various specific duties created by the Order. Thus the Department is required to provide by Order for the granting of planning permission (Art. 13(1)). Apart from this, it is the Department which is responsible for preparing development plans and keeping them under review (Arts 4–10), and for the administration and enforcement of the development control provisions of the Order.

(2) Powers of the Department

As mentioned above, the 1991 Order gives the Department various powers to enable it to carry out its duties. Thus, for example, the Department may undertake surveys or studies (Art. 3(2)), hold local enquiries (Art. 123(1)), and appoint advisory bodies or committees to assist it (Art. 126). In addition, it may make grants for research (Art. 119) and in connection with education in respect of development proposals (Art. 120). Further, it has power under Art. 125 to require information from occupiers of land as to ownership of the land and the use to which the land is put, to enable the Department to serve or issue any notices or documents which are authorised by the Order. Finally, the power conferred on the Department to acquire land where it is required in connection with a development scheme or for 'proper planning' should be noted (Art. 87).

(3) *Organisation of the Department*

The Planning Service of the Department consists of planning Headquarters and six Divisional Planning Offices, together with two sub-offices, dealing with the administration of planning control in particular areas of the Province.

The functions carried out by Planning Headquarters are (a) the preparation of primary and secondary legislation; (b) the issue of policy guidance notes; (c) the issue of Divisional Office circulars and manuals to lay down policy and procedures to ensure that the processing of Area Plans and development control applications is carried out in a consistent manner; (d) production of regional policies; (e) monitoring development plan and control issues; (f) handling planning applications for the extraction of minerals, waste disposal and other developments involving major environmental issues, and the determination of applications to which Art. 31 of the 1991 Order applies and (g) offering assistance in dealing with particular problems which may arise in the processing of Area Plans and planning applications.[1]

The Divisional Planning Offices are concerned with the following matters: (a) preparation of Area Plans, including consultation, public enquiries and the consideration of any reports made by the Planning Appeals Commission; (b) handling the majority of planning applications and appeals;[2] (c) all pre-application enquiries and (d) the functions of the Department regarding e.g. applications for listed building consent and grants in conservation areas.[3] As well as being constituted by Planning Headquarters and the Divisional Offices, there is a body known as the Planning Directorate, which consists of the Director, the Assistant Director and the Assistant Secretary of the Planning Service. The function of the Directorate is to control, and manage, the Planning Service by the

---

1 Information supplied by the Department.
2 Major applications to which Art. 31 of the 1991 Order applies are dealt with partly by Planning Headquarters and partly by the relevant Divisional Office: the designation of the application as one to which Art. 31 is to apply is made by Planning Headquarters, and the determination of such applications is made by Headquarters, but the relevant Divisional Office is responsible for handling the application through any public enquiry held pursuant to Art. 31.
3 Information supplied by the Department.

allocation of resources to the Divisional Offices. In addition, however, the Department operates a referral system, under which applications for planning permission can be referred to the Directorate for consideration where the relevant district council disagrees with the proposed decision of the Divisional Office on the application.[4]

(4) Other powers and duties in relation to planning

Apart from its duties and powers created under the 1991 Order, the Department, as its name implies, is responsible under various other enactments for the protection of the environment, or planning in its widest sense. It is not possible here to examine all the powers and duties of the Department, but it is appropriate to mention the following:

(a) The Nature Conservation and Amenity Lands (NI) Order 1985

Under Art. 3(1) of this Order it is provided that the functions of the Department include formulating and implementing policies for nature conservation and the conservation and enhancement of the natural beauty and amenity of the countryside. The Order empowers the Department to designate areas of land as National Parks (Art. 12); Areas of Outstanding Natural Beauty (Art. 14); Nature Reserves (Art. 16); or Areas of Special Scientific Interest (Art. 24). The provisions of the Order are considered later.[5]

(b) The New Towns Act (NI) 1965

This empowers the Department to designate areas of land as sites for new towns (s. 1(1)), and where an order designating land has been made, to acquire land in the area (s. 4(1)).

(c) The Historic Monuments Act (NI) 1971

Ss 1(1) and 9(1) of the Historic Monuments Act (NI) 1971 give the Department powers respectively to acquire or to make protection orders in respect of historic monuments.[6] The provisions of the Act are considered later.[7]

(d) The Housing (NI) Order 1981

Where the Northern Ireland Housing Executive declares land to be redevelopment area under Art. 47 of the Housing (NI) Order 1981, it is required to prepare and submit to the Department a redevelopment scheme indicating the manner in which it is intended that the area should be laid out and

---

4 Information supplied by the Department.
5 Chapter 5.
6 For the definition of 'historic monument' see s. 27.
7 See Chapter 17.

the land used, and to apply to the Department for an order vesting the land in the Executive (Art. 48(1)). If objections to the redevelopment scheme are made, the Department is required to hold a local enquiry to consider the objections. If there are no objections, or after considering the objections, the Department may approve the scheme (with or without amendment) or may refuse to approve the scheme.

(e) The Access to the Countryside (NI) Order 1983

The Department has various powers under the Access to the Countryside (NI) Order 1983, notably under Art. 40, which enables the Department to acquire land which gives, or forms part of, access to open country, where the Department is of opinion that it is requisite that the public should have access to that open country for open-air recreation.[8]

(f) The Laganside Development (NI) Order 1989

Finally, the Laganside Development (NI) Order 1989 established the Laganside Corporation (Art. 4(1)) to secure the regeneration of the area of land designated for the purpose of the Order (Art. 3(1)).[9] In this regard the Department is the body responsible for designating the area in question, and under Art. 11(1) the Department has power to give directions of a general or specific nature to the Corporation as to how the Corporation is to discharge its functions.

2 *The local council*

The Macrory Report on local government[10] had recommended that the existing structure of district and county councils should be replaced by not more than twenty six district or borough councils[11] and that the functions of the new councils should be of four kinds: executive, representative, consultative and ceremonial.[12] It will be recalled from the previous chapter that the Review Body recommended that planning functions hitherto exercised by the local authorities should become a regional service under the control of central government, although the Review Body envisaged that the new district councils would handle local planning applications.[13] Taken together, the Local Government Act (NI) 1972 and the Planning (NI)

---

8 See also Art. 16(1) (power to make public path extinguishment orders); Art. 29 (confirmation by Department required for access orders); and Art. 50 (financial assistance of Department for exercise of powers of district councils under the Order).
9 For the designated area see Laganside Development Designation Order (NI) 1989, SR 1989 No 138.
10 *Report of the Review Body on Local Government in Northern Ireland* 1970 Cmd. 546.
11 Macrory Report, para. 115.
12 Ibid., para. 119.
13 Ibid., paras 74, 82, 83 and 122.

Order 1972 brought about the recommendations made by the Review Body, with the exception of the role of the councils to determine planning applications. S. 1(1) of the 1972 Act established a district council for every local government district established under the Local Government (Boundaries) Act (NI) 1971, and provided that such council should have the functions conferred on it by any statutory provision. The 1972 Order limited the functions of the councils in relation to planning to consultative functions only, and this remains the position under the 1991 Order.

(1) Cases where consultation is required

The cases where the district council is entitled to be consulted under the 1991 Order are as follows:

(a) In relation to development plans

Where the Department proposes to make, alter, repeal or replace a development plan for an area, it is obliged to consult the district council for the area to which the plan relates, both when it intends to adopt the procedure laid down in Art. 5 of the Order (Art. 5(2)) and when it intends to adopt the alternative procedure provided in Art. 6 (Art. 6(2)).

(b) In relation to applications for planning permission

Art. 13 of the 1991 Order requires the Department to make a development order to provide for the granting of planning permission. Such an order may either itself grant planning permission, or provide for the grant of permission by the Department on an application made to it (Art. 13(2)). Art. 20(1) of the Order requires that the development order shall require the Department before granting or refusing planning permission to consult with the district council for the area in which the land is situated. There is no onus, however, on the Department, to consult the council where an appeal has been made to the Planning Appeals Commission against refusal of permission.[14]

(c) In relation to listed buildings

Under Art. 42(1) of the 1991 Order the Department is required to keep a list of buildings of special architectural or historic interest. Before compiling or amending the list, the Department is obliged to consult the appropriate district council (Art. 42(3)). The Department must also consult the district council before it issues any certificate pursuant to Art. 43(1) that it does not intend to list a building.

---

14 In re North Down BC's application [1986] NI 304.

(d) In relation to conservation areas

The Department is empowered under Art. 50(1) of the 1991 Order to designate areas of special architectural or historic interest where it is desirable that the character or appearance of the areas should be preserved or enhanced. Art. 50(3) requires the Department to consult with the appropriate district council before making, varying or cancelling any designation made under Art. 50.

(e) In relation to hazardous substances

The 1991 Order provides a special form of control applicable where hazardous substances are located on land (Arts 53–63). Art. 53(1) provides that the presence of a hazardous substance on land requires the consent of the Department. It also requires the Department to make various regulations regarding applications for such consent, and such regulations may require the Department to consult the district council for the area in which the land is situated (Art. 54(4)(b)).

(f) In relation to development schemes

Where the Department considers it expedient that an area be developed, redeveloped or improved, it may prepare a scheme defining the area of the scheme and the manner in which it is intended the area should be laid out and the land used (Art. 85). Before doing so the Department is obliged to consult the district council for the area in question.

(g) In relation to land acquired for planning purposes

Before the Department can acquire land pursuant to the power conferred by Art. 87(1) of the Order, it must consult the district council in whose area the land is situated (Art. 87(5)).

(h) In relation to advertisements

Finally, under Reg. 8 of the Planning (Control of Advertisements) Regulations (NI) 1992, where an application is made to the Department for express consent to display an advertisement, the Department is under a duty to consult the relevant district council.

(2) **Meaning of 'consult'**

While the 1991 Order specifies a number of cases in which the Department is required to consult the local council, it does not specify what is meant by consultation, nor does it provide any procedure for consultation.[15] It would seem, however, that consultation involves the following:

---

15 It has been said that the nature and object of consultation must be related to the circumstances which call for it: *Port Louis Corp.* v *Attorney-General of Mauritius* [1965] AC

(i) The Department must supply the council with sufficient information to enable the council to tender advice on the matter in question.[16]

(ii) A sufficient opportunity must be given to the council to tender advice,[17] or, to put it another way, a full and sufficient opportunity must be given for members of the council to ask questions and to submit their opinions in any reasonable way.[18]

(iii) The purpose of consultation is to allow the council to put forward considered information or advice about aspects of the form or substance of the proposals in question, or their implications for the council, as to which the Department might not be fully informed or advised and as to which the council might have relevant information or advice to offer.[19]

(iv) Sufficient time must be available for the Department to consider the advice offered by the council, and in this context sufficient does not mean ample, but enough to enable the relevant purpose to be fulfilled.[20]

(v) The Department must consider any advice offered by the council.[21]

It seems also that in deciding whether consultation has taken place, regard must be paid to the *substance* of the events and it is not conclusive either way whether the parties said in terms that a consultation for the purposes of the legislation was taking place, or was to take place, or was intended, or whether nothing relating to this was said at all.[22] Further, the test appears to be an objective one.[23]

The essence of consultation was explained by Donaldson J in *Agriculture, Horticultural and Forestry Industry Training Board v Aylesbury Mushrooms Ltd*:[24]

1111, 1124 *per* Lord Morris, and that the requirement of consultation is never to be treated perfunctorily or as a mere formality. See also *Easter Ross Land Use Committee v Secretary of State for Scotland* 1970 SC 182.

16 *Rollo v Minister of Town Planning* [1948] 1 All ER 13; *R v Secretary of State for Social Services, ex p Association of Metropolitan Authorities* [1986] 1 All ER 164; *In re NUPE & COHSE's application* [1988] NI 255; *In re McCann's application* (HC) Carswell J, 10 July 1992 unrep.

17 *Rollo v Minister of Town Planning*; *R v Secretary of State for Social Services, ex p Association of Metropolitan Authorities*; *In re McCann's application*.

18 *Re Union of the Benefices of Whippingham and East Cowes* [1945] 2 All ER 22.

19 *R v Secretary of State for Social Services, ex p Association of Metropolitan Authorities* [1986] 1 All ER 164, 167 *per* Webster J, discussing the duty of the Secretary of State to consult local authorities before making regulations under s. 28 of the Social Security and Housing Benefits Act 1982.

20 Ibid.

21 Ibid; *In re McCann's application*.

22 *Fletcher v Minister of Town Planning* [1947] 2 All ER 496, 500 *per* Morris J.

23 *In re NUPE & COHSE's application* [1988] NI 255, 266 *per* Carswell J.

24 [1972] 1 All ER 280, 284.

The essence of consultation is the communication of a genuine invitation, extended with a receptive mind, to give advice (see *per* Bucknill LJ approving a dictum of Morris J in *Rollo* v *Minister of Town and Country Planning*). If the invitation is once received, it matters not that it is not accepted and no advice is proferred. Were it otherwise organisations with a right to be consulted could, in effect, veto the making of any order by simply failing to respond to the invitation. But without communication and the consequent opportunity of responding, there can be no consultation.

Again, in the words of Carswell J:

The duty of a person who has an obligation to consult another is to give the consultee sufficient information and time to consider the matter, then to give genuine consideration to his advice: see *Re* NUPE *and* COHSE's *Application* [1988] NI 255, 264–6. If the consultee fails to give any advice, or if the advice is incorrect or flawed in the manner suggested in this case by the applicant, I do not think that the consultation or any subsequent decision made is invalid.[25]

(3) Duties and powers under other enactments

It should be noted that, apart from the consultative provisions of the 1991 Order, the district councils do exercise powers, which may loosely be described as planning powers, in the sense of powers relating to environmental protection, under various other legislative provisions. The consideration of these duties and powers is outside the scope of this work.[26]

3 The Planning Appeals Commission

Before 1972, where an applicant for permission to carry out interim development under the 1944 Act was refused permission, a right of appeal lay to the Ministry, or if the appellant so wished, the appeal could be determined by an independent person appointed by the Ministry.[27] When responsibility for planning control was transferred from the local authorities to the Department of the Environment under the Planning (NI) Order 1972, it became necessary to establish an appellate tribunal to determine appeals from refusals of permission by the Department. Art. 88(1) of the 1972 Order accordingly established the Planning Appeals Commission, which continues to exist by virtue of Art. 110(1) of the 1991 Order.

---

25 In re *McCann's application*.
26 See e.g. Access to the Countryside (NI) Order 1983; Public Health (Ir) Act 1878; Pollution Control and Local Government (NI) Order 1978; Nature Conservation and Amenity Lands (NI) Order 1985; Open Spaces Act 1906. For the powers and duties however of district councils in respect of the control of caravans, see Caravans Act (NI) 1963 and Chapter 21.
27 Planning (Interim Development) Act (NI) 1944, s. 2(6).

(1) Constitution of the Commission

The Commission consists of a chief commissioner and such number of other commissioners as the Department may, with the consent of the Department of Finance and Personnel, determine (Art. 110(2)).[28] A commissioner is entitled to such remuneration, allowances and benefits as the Department may determine with the approval of the Department of Finance and Personnel (Art. 110(4)). It is provided that a commissioner is precluded from engaging in a gainful profession, occupation or business if to do so would be incompatible with his functions under the Order (Art. 110(3)).

(2) Duties of the Commission

The duties of the Commission under the 1991 Order[29] fall into three categories:

(a) Appellate functions

The first function of the Commission, as the name of the Commission suggests, is to hear appeals under various Articles of the 1991 Order against decisions taken by the Department. Thus, the Commission is required to hear appeals against notices requiring the submission of the application for planning permission (Art. 24); the refusal of an application for planning permission, consent required by a condition in a planning permission, or approval under a development order (Art. 32(1)); the determination whether planning permission is required (Art. 41(2)); refusal on an application for hazardous substances consent (Art. 57(1)); and enforcement notices, listed buildings enforcement notices and special enforcement notices (Arts 69(1), 78(1) and 116(6)). Further, Art. 81(10) provides that the Department is required to make regulations to provide for appeals to the Commission against hazardous substances contravention notices.

(b) Public enquiries

Apart from its appellate functions, the Commission may be required under several provisions of the Order to hold public enquiries in certain circumstances. First, under Art. 7 of the Order, the Department can cause an enquiry to be held by the Commission to consider objections to a development plan or to the alteration, repeal or replacement of a development plan. The second situation in which an enquiry by the Commission can be directed concerns the procedure in respect of major planning applications under Art. 31.[30] Briefly, where the Department considers that

---

28 At present the Commission consists of one full-time chief commissioner, five full-time professional commissioners, and six part-time members.
29 Note that the Order envisages that duties may be assigned to the Commission under other enactments: see Arts 111(1) and (2).
30 See Chapter 11.

the development for which permission is sought would involve a substantial departure from the local development plan, or would affect a substantial section of the community, it may direct that the provisions of Art. 31 shall apply to the application, and for the purpose of considering representations made in respect of the application, it may cause a public local enquiry to be held by the Commission (Art. 31(2)). A similar procedure and power to cause an enquiry to be held by the Commission exists in relation to applications for hazardous substances consent under Arts 56(1) and (2). Finally, Art. 67(1) requires the Department to make regulations regarding the display of advertisements. In one instance such regulations are to provide for (*inter alia*) the holding by the Commission of such enquiries or other hearings as may be prescribed (Art. 67(4)).

(c) *Hearings*

Under certain provisions of the 1991 Order the Department may be required to afford individuals a hearing by the Commission before the Department takes certain action. Thus, under Art. 38(2), before making an order revoking or modifying planning permission, the Department is required to serve notice of its intention to make such an order, and if the recipient so requests, the Department is required to afford him an opportunity of a hearing before the Commission. Again, under Art. 39(4), the recipient of a notice of intention to make a discontinuance order is given a similar power. Similar provisions exist under Art. 47(2) in the case where the Department intends to revoke listed buildings consent, and under Art. 59(5) in the case of revocation of hazardous substances consent. Under the provisions of the 1991 Order relating to the protection of trees, the Department is empowered to make regulations regarding tree preservation orders (Art. 65(2)), and such regulations may provide for affording an individual the opportunity of a hearing before the Commission (Art. 65(2)(c)). Finally, the provisions of Art. 67(4) concerning advertisement regulations have already been noted.

(3) Assistance in carrying out duties

Where the Commission is bound to carry out functions specified in the Order it may be assisted by persons appointed by the Department who may be remunerated by the Department (Art. 10(5)). The qualifications of such persons or the nature of the assistance which they can be appointed to give are not specified. Apart from this, the Chief Commissioner is empowered, under Art. 111(1)(b) in the case of appeals to be determined by the Commission[31] and under Art. 111(2)(b) in the case of enquiries or

---

31 Except where the appeal is to be decided solely by reference to written representations: Art. 111(1)(b).

hearings, to appoint an assessor to sit with the Commissioner hearing the appeal or holding the enquiry to advise him on any matter arising. Before making any such appointment the Chief Commissioner must consult both the Commission and the Department (Arts 111(1)(b) and 111(2)(b)). Where the assessor is appointed he may be remunerated by the Commission (Art. 111(3).

(4) Procedure for proceedings before the Commission

(a) Regulations

Art. 111(5) of the 1991 Order empowers the Department after consultation with the Commission to make rules for regulating the procedure for proceedings before the Commission. Subject to the provisions of the Order and any rules which may be made pursuant to the power in Art. 111(5), the procedure for proceedings before the Commission is such as is determined by the Commission itself (Art. 111(5)). To date no rules governing procedure have been made.

(b) Procedure at appeals

Where the Commission is required to hear an appeal under any of the provisions of the Order, the appeal is heard by a member of the Commission appointed by the Chief Commissioner (Art. 111(1)(a)). The appointed member reports back to the Commission with a recommendation as to whether the appeal should succeed or fail. The Commission then considers the report of the appointed member, and gives the decision on the appeal.[32] While it is usual that the Commission follows the recommendation of the appointed member, this is by no means always the case.

On an appeal the Commission has power to confirm, reverse or vary the decision of the Department which is the subject of the appeal and the decision of the Commission has the like effect as a decision of the Department.[33]

(c) Procedure at enquiries

As with appeals where the Commission is required to hold an enquiry under the Order, the enquiry is held by a member of the Commission appointed for that purpose by the Chief Commissioner (Art. 111(2)(a)), who then reports to the Commission. Once again, it is the Commission as a whole which makes a report on the matter dealt with at the enquiry (Art. 111(2)(c)).

---

32 Note that it is the decision of *the Commission* rather than that of the appointed member which determines the appeal: Art. 111(1)(c).
33 Except as to appeals: Art. 111(4).

(d) Procedure at hearings

The procedure in connection with cases where someone is given an opportunity to be heard by the Commission is the same as that for the cases where an enquiry is held by the Commission (Art. 111(2)). Following the hearing the Commission makes a report to the Department which the Department is obliged to consider (Art. 111(6)).

(5) Judicial review

The proceedings of the Commission are open to judicial review by the courts.[34]

4 Other relevant bodies

The Department, the district councils and the Planning Appeals Commission are the principal bodies entrusted with the administration of planning control in Northern Ireland. Apart from these, however, there exist other bodies which have various functions, principally of an advisory nature in connection with certain aspects of planning control.

(1) The Council for Nature Conservation and the Countryside

Art. 3(1) of the Nature Conservation and Amenity Lands (Amendment) (NI) Order 1989 established the Council for Nature Conservation and the Countryside, which replaced the Committee for Nature Conservation and the Ulster Countryside Committee which had been set up under the Nature Conservation and Amenity Lands (NI) Order 1985. The functions of the old committees were transferred to the Council by Arts 4(1) and (2) of the 1989 Order. These are advisory functions connected with the exercise of the powers and duties of the Department under the 1985 Order.[35] The new Council also has an advisory role in connection with payment of grants under Art. 29(1)(a) of the 1985 Order, and in connection with promotional and educational activities in relation to conservation (1989 Order, Art. 4(3)).

The Council consists of a chairman and deputy chairman appointed by the Head of the Department together with a maximum of eighteen other members appointed by the Head of the Department (1989 Order, sch., para. 1). Each member of the Council holds office for a maximum of three years but is eligible for reappointment (1989 Order, sch., para. 2).

---

34 Re Johnston's application [1984] 10 NIJB.
35 E.g. in connection with the establishment and management of national parks (1985 Order, Art. 12(3)) and in the making of byelaws for protection of nature reserves (Art. 19(3)) and marine nature reserves (Art. 21(3)).

Procedure of the Council is regulated by the Council itself (1989 Order, sch., para. 5), which may constitute a committee for advising in the discharge of its functions (1989 Order, ibid., para. 6(1)).

(2) The Historic Buildings Council

As will be seen later,[36] the Department exercises a special form of control over buildings of special architectural or historic interest (1991 Order Arts 42–49). To assist with these functions the Historic Buildings Council was established by Art. 82(1) of the 1972 Order, and continues to exist by operation of Art. 105(1) of the 1991 Order.

The Council consists of a chairman appointed by the Head of the Department and as many other members so appointed as the Head of the Department determines (1991 Order, sch. 3, para. 2). A member of the Council holds office for a maximum of three years, but is eligible for reappointment (1991 Order, sch. 3, para. 2). The Council is required to appoint such committees as may be determined by the Department, which may, by regulations or direction, make provision with respect to the appointment, constitution or functions of such committees (1991 Order, sch. 3, paras 4(1) and (4)). A committee appointed by the Council may include persons who are not members of the Council (1991 Order, sch. 3, para. 4(2)). Procedure of the Council and its committees is regulated by the Council subject to approval of the Department (1991 Order, sch. 3, para. 5), to which the Council is required to make periodic reports on its activities (1991 Order, sch. 3, para. 6).

The functions of the Council are set out in Art. 105(2) of the 1991 Order. These are: (a) to keep under review and, from time to time, report to the Department on the general state of preservation of listed buildings; (b) to advise the Department on such matters relating to the preservation of buildings of special architectural or historic interest as the Department may refer to it and (c) such other functions as are conferred on it by any statutory provision.

(3) The Laganside Corporation

Under Art. 4(1) of the Laganside Development (NI) Order 1989 the Laganside Development Corporation was established to secure the regeneration of the area designated by the Department under Art. 3(1) of the Order (Art. 10(1)).[37] The Corporation is a body corporate[38] consisting of not less than seven or more than ten members appointed by the Head of

---

36 Chapter 17.
37 For the designated area see Laganside Development Designation Order (NI) 1989 SR 1989 No 138.
38 Laganside (NI) Order 1989, sch. 1, para. 2(1).

the Department.[39] Members of the Corporation hold office for a fixed term not exceeding five years.[40]

The general object of the Corporation, viz. the regeneration of Laganside, is to be achieved in particular by (a) bringing land and buildings into effective use; (b) encouraging investment; (c) by creating an attractive environment and (d) by ensuring appropriate facilities are available to encourage people to live and work in the area (Art. 10(2)). To this end the Corporation is empowered to do various things including to acquire and dispose of land, carry out building and other operations and 'anything necessary or expedient for the purposes of the object or for purposes incidental to those purposes' (Art. 10(3)). Thus, in contrast to the Council for Nature Conservation and the Countryside and the Historic Buildings Council, the Corporation is not an advisory body; rather, it is given responsibility for development of the area designated by the Department for the purposes of the Laganside Order, subject to the overall control of the Department and the requirement of planning permission for such development.

(4) The Northern Ireland Housing Executive

The Northern Ireland Housing Executive is the body responsible for public housing in Northern Ireland.[41] The power of the Executive to make redevelopment schemes under Art. 47 of the Housing Order 1981 has already been noted.[42]

(5) The European Community

The United Kingdom is part of the European Community and as such is required to implement Directives issued by the Council of Ministers of the Community. One of the concerns of the Council is the protection of the environment. In 1989 a directive issued by the Council led to the formulation of regulations requiring environmental assessment studies to be prepared for certain types of development and submitted to the planning authority which would take the study into account when determining the application for planning permission for the proposed development.[43] Other Directives are presently the subject of new regulations in preparation. It is likely that the Community's role in planning matters will increase in years to come.

---

39 Ibid., para. 2(1).
40 Ibid., para. 4(2).
41 The Executive was established under the Housing Executive Act (NI) 1971, and continues to exist by virtue of Art. 3(1) of the Housing (NI) Order 1981.
42 For the content of such schemes see *Kane v Northern Ireland Housing Executive* [1986] NI 145.
43 See Chapter 23.

PART TWO

Strategic Planning

CHAPTER THREE

Development Plans

We have seen how the Planning and Housing Act (NI) 1931 and the Planning (Interim Development) Act (NI) 1944 provided for a system of planning control based on 'planning schemes' which were intended to be made by local authorities, and how the system had, in the words of the Matthew Report, become a dead letter. Planning schemes were too cumbersome to be workable and none were in fact made.[1] Following the Matthew Plan in 1963[2] a series of (non-statutory) Area Plans were prepared either by the Ministry or by private consultants and by 1972 most of Northern Ireland was covered by such plans.[3] These plans became the way forward for planning policy. Art. 4(1) of the 1972 Order provided that the Ministry might prepare a development plan for any area, which would consist of a map and written statement formulating proposals for the development and other use of the land in the area to which the plan related (1972 Order, Art. 4(2)). The system of development plans established by the 1972 Order remains the basis for planning policy under the 1991 Order.

(1) *Power to make development plans*

Art. 4(1) of the 1991 Order restates the power conferred by the 1972 Order, providing that the Department may at any time make a development plan for any area or alter, repeal or replace a development plan which has already been adopted by the Department for any area.[4] Thus, the legislation *empowers* the Department to make plans, but does not *require* it to.[5] Nonetheless, the duty of the Department to formulate policy for securing the orderly and consistent development of land and the planning of that development should be borne in mind (1991 Order, Art. 3(1)). Rather than the possibility of the Department failing to prepare a plan for any area, Regulations made under the 1972 Order clearly contemplate that more than one plan for an area may exist, as they provide that in the case of contradictions between development plans for the same part of any area the provisions which are more recently adopted by the

---

1 See White Paper *Town and Country Planning—Proposals for Legislation* (February 1972) published by the Ministry of Development, para. 3.
2 *Belfast Regional Survey and Plan* 1963 Cmd. 451.
3 *Town and Country Planning—Proposals for Legislation* para. 3.
4 For adoption of plans see below.
5 See Interpretation Act (NI) 1954, s. 38.

Department shall prevail (Planning (Development Plans) Regulations (NI) 1991).

(2) Form and content of development plans

The Order provides that a development plan shall consist of a map and written statement formulating, in such detail as the Department thinks appropriate, proposals for the development and use of land in the area to which the plan relates; and such diagrams, illustrations and descriptive matter as the Department thinks appropriate to explain or illustrate the proposals in the plan (1991 Order, Art. 4(2)). In addition to these requirements, the form and content of development plans is regulated by regulations which the Department is empowered to make under Art. 10 of the Order.

Thus the contents of a development plan comprise three elements: a map; a written statement; and explanatory matter.

(a) *The map*

Reg. 8 of the Development Plans Regulations made under the 1972 Order provides that the map comprised in a development plan should be based on the Ordnance Survey Map, to such scale as the Department might think appropriate.

(b) *The written statement*

In addition to the proposals for development of the area to which the development plan relates, Reg. 9(a) of the Development Plans Regulations requires that the written statement should contain proposals relating to such of the following matters as the Department thinks appropriate: population; employment; housing; industry and commerce; transportation; shopping; education; health and personal social services; other social and community services; recreation and leisure; conservation, townscape and landscape; utility services; and any other relevant matters including minerals. The written statement is also required to contain such indications as the Department thinks appropriate of the following: the character, pattern and function of the existing development and other use of land in the area and the prompt needs and opportunities for change; any changes already projected, or likely to occur, which might materially affect matters dealt with in the plan, and the likely effect of those changes; the criteria to be applied as respects the control of development in the area; the extent and nature of the relationships between the proposals formulated in the plan; any other relevant matters.

Of the three elements of a development plan, the written statement is the most important, as Reg. 6 of the Development Plans Regulations provides that in the event of any contradiction between the written statement and any other document forming part of the plan, the written statement prevails.[6]

(c) *The explanatory matter*

Neither the 1991 Order nor the Regulations specify what the explanatory matter required to be included in a development plan must contain. The Order refers simply to 'such diagrams, illustrations and descriptive matter as the Department thinks appropriate'.

(d) *Incorporation of orders and schemes*

Where a development plan relates to land to which one of the orders or schemes mentioned in Art. 9(2) of the 1991 Order applies, the development plan operates as if the provisions of the relevant order or scheme were included in it (1991 Order, Art. 9(1)). The orders and schemes to which Art. 9 applies are: (a) an order under s. 1 of the New Towns Act (NI) 1965;[7] (b) an order under Art. 14 or 15 of the Roads (NI) Order 1993;[8] (c) a redevelopment scheme approved under Art. 49 of the Housing (NI) Order 1981;[9] (d) an enterprize zone scheme;[10] (c) a simplified planning zone scheme[11] and (f) a development scheme under Art. 86 of the 1991 Order.

(3) Types of development plan

Although the 1991 Order refers only to development plans, the Regulations made under the 1972 Order distinguish three types of development plan. First, *Area Plans*, i.e. development plans based on consideration of matters affecting the development and other use of land for the whole or a substantial part of the area of one or more district councils;[12] second, *Local Plans*, i.e. development plans based on consideration of matters affecting the development or other use of land for part of the area of one or more district councils;[13] and third, *Subject Plans* i.e. development plans based on consideration of a particular description of development or other use of land to which they relate.[14]

---

6 On the role of the written statement see *Stratford on Avon DC v Secretary of State for the Environment* [1994] JPL 740, 749.
7 Orders designating land as the site of a proposed new town.
8 Power to designate roads as trunk roads (Art. 14) and special roads (Art. 15).
9 Schemes prepared by the Northern Ireland Housing Executive under Art. 48 of the Order indicating the manner in which land included in a proposed redevelopment area should be laid out.
10 See Enterprize Zones (NI) Order 1981 and Chapter 4.
11 See 1991 Order, Arts 14–18 and Chapter 4.
12 Development Plans Regulations, Reg. 5(1).
13 Ibid., Reg. 5(2).
14 Ibid., Reg. 5(3).

(4) Procedure for making development plans

Development plans do not come into existence overnight or by surprise. Their importance requires that their preparation and contents be carefully considered. Accordingly, the 1991 Order provides a detailed procedure to be observed before a development plan can come into being. Such a procedure is designed to ensure that the proposals of the Department are given publicity from the earliest moment and that those who have views on them are given an adequate opportunity to make their views known.

The procedure laid down by the Order for the creation of a development plan involves four stages:

Stage 1

The Department *proposes* to make a development plan. This stage may be classified into four chronological steps:

First, the Department is required to consult with the district council for the area to which the plan or proposed plan relates (1991 Order, Art. 5(2)).

Second, the Department is required to secure publicity for its proposals. This requirement has two aspects. The Department is required to ensure adequate publicity for its proposals in the area to which the plan relates (Art. 5(3)(a)) and that anyone who might be expected to make representations to the Department about the Department's proposals is made aware that he or she is entitled to do so (Art. 5(3)(b)). Thus, the Department is obliged to ensure adequate publicity both *in the area and among relevant persons*. The Order does not give any guidance as to who such persons might be.

Third, Art. 5(3)(c) requires that an adequate opportunity is given to anyone who may be expected to make representations regarding the proposals to do so.

Finally, the Department is required to consider any representations made to it within the prescribed period. The Development Plans Regulations prescribe fourteen weeks, beginning on the date specified by the Department when publicising its proposals.[15]

Stage 2

This begins after the Department has considered any representations made following publication of its proposals. Art. 5(4) of the Order provides that the Department shall 'then' i.e. after considering representations, prepare the plan, and make copies of the plan available for inspection at such places as it considers appropriate. Each copy of the plan available for inspection is to be accompanied by a statement of the prescribed period within which objections may be made to the Department (Art. 5(5)).

---

15 Reg. 3 (as substituted by Planning (Development Plans) (Amendment) Regulations (NI) 1994).

As with stage 1, stage 2 of the procedure may be broken down into sub-stages. The preparation of the plan discussed in the preceding paragraph is the first. The second is publicity for the plan. Art. 5(6) requires the Department 'then' i.e. after preparation of the plan and making copies of it available for inspection, to take such steps as may be prescribed for the purpose of advertising (a) the fact that the plan is available for inspection; (b) the places and times at which and the period during which, the plan may be inspected; and (c) the prescribed period within which objections may be made to the Department.

Again, like stage 1, stage 2 requires that following preparation of the plan, time is allocated within which objections to the plan may be made to the Department. During this period the Department is empowered to require a public local enquiry to be held by the Planning Appeals Commission to consider such objections (Art. 7). Under the Development Plans Regulations where the Department requires an enquiry it is obliged to give notice by advertisement at least four weeks before the date of the enquiry, and to serve notice on any person who has made and not withdrawn an objection to the plan.[16]

Finally, at the end of the period for objecting to the plan, the Department is required to consider the objections and, if a public local enquiry was held, the report of the Planning Appeals Commission made following the enquiry (Art. 8(1)). Under the Development Plans Regulations, the Department is required to prepare a statement of the decisions that it has reached in the light of the report and any recommendations contained in it, and the reasons for those decisions (Reg. 12(1)). The Department is also required to make copies of the report of the Commission available for inspection (Reg. 12(2)).

Stage 3

This is really the culmination of stage 2. After considering the objections to the plan and the report of the Planning Appeals Commission if applicable, the Department may by order adopt or reject the plan (Art. 8(1)). Notice of adoption or rejection must be advertised.[17]

Under the Development Plans Regulations, where the Department proposes to modify a plan it is required, if it considers it expedient to do so having regard to the nature and importance of the proposed modifications, (a) to prepare a list of the proposed modifications, giving reasons for proposing them; (b) to advertise where copies of the list of the proposed modifications have been deposited for inspection, the time within which any objections may be lodged, and that such objections must be in writing; (c) to serve notice on persons who objected to the plan and such other persons as the Department thinks fit; (d) to consider

---

16 Development Plans Regulations, Reg. 11(1).
17 Ibid., Reg. 14.

any objections to the proposed modifications; (e) to decide whether or not to cause a further public local enquiry to be held to consider objections; and (f) if an enquiry is held, to afford objectors an opportunity of being heard at the enquiry (Reg. 13).

Where a development plan has not been adopted (either because it has been rejected or because no order adopting it has yet been made) then the provisions of the 1991 Order which require or authorise regard to be had to the development plan[18] have effect as if any reference to the development plan were omitted (Art. 4(3)). Thus, references in such provisions are to be construed as references to adopted plans only. It would seem however that an unadopted plan is a 'material consideration' which must be taken into account under the relevant provisions.[19]

Stage 4

This is when the date on which the plan, following adoption, becomes operative. Art. 8(2) provides that a plan becomes operative on the date appointed for the purpose in the order by which the plan was adopted by the Department. As noted earlier, following adoption the Department is obliged to publish notice in the *Belfast Gazette* and locally and to serve notice on anyone who has requested to be notified,[20] and to make copies of the plan available for inspection (Reg. 14(b)).

(5) Alterations, repeal and replacement of development plans

Where a development plan has been made, the Department may wish to alter, repeal or replace it at a later date. The procedure for doing so is the same as for making the plan in the first place.[21] Where, however, it appears to the Department that the issues involved in the alteration, repeal or replacement are not of sufficient importance to warrant the procedure set out in Art. 5 (stages 1 and 2) the Department may instead adopt the short procedure provided in Art. 6.

As with the full procedure in Art. 5, under Art. 6(2) the Department is required to consult the district council for the area affected by the plans. The Department prepares the relevant documents and makes copies available for inspection. These must be accompanied by a statement of the timescale within which representations or objections may be made (Art. 6(4)). The Department then advertises that the documents are available for inspection, and where and when they may be inspected, and

---

18 E.g. Arts 25 (applications for planning permission); 38 (revocation of planning permission); 39 (discontinuance orders); 47 (revocation of listed building consent); 68 (enforcement notices); 116 (special enforcement notices).
19 R v *City of London Corp., ex p Allan* (1980) 79 LGR 223.
20 Development Plans Regulations, Reg. 14(a).
21 See Arts 5, 7 & 8.

invites representations or objections. As with the full procedure, the Department is required to consider any objections made within the prescribed time (Art. 6(5)).

(6) *Challenging validity of plans*

Unlike the situation in England and Wales[22] there are no provisions in the 1991 Order for challenging the validity of development plans. This does not mean, however, that, once made, a development plan is immune from enquiry by the courts. The preparation of a development plan is an administrative act by a public body and as such is open to scrutiny by judicial review under Order 53 of the Rules of the Supreme Court (NI) 1980.[23] What the court will want to see is whether the Department in the preparation of the plan has acted *ultra vires*. Under the statutory procedure for challenging plans contained in the legislation in England and Wales, challenge may be made on two grounds: first, that the plan is not within the powers conferred by the Act in respect of plans; and second, that any requirements of the Act or regulations as to approval or adoption of the plan have not been complied with (Town and Country Planning Act, s. 287(1)(a) and (b)). It has been suggested that the grounds on which the courts can intervene on an application for judicial review are essentially the same as on an application under the statutory provisions in the English legislation.[24]

---

22 Town and Country Planning Act 1990, ss 284 and 287.
23 See also Judicature (NI) Act 1978, s. 18.
24 Purdue, Young and Rowan-Robinson, *Planning Law and Procedure*, London: Butterworths 1989, p. 595. On the provisions of s. 287, see *Seddon Properties Ltd v Secretary of State for the Environment* (1978) 42 P & CR 26.

CHAPTER FOUR

Development Schemes

Development *schemes*, which the Department is empowered to prepare under Art. 85 of the 1991 Order, are distinct from development plans. Art. 85 provides that where the Department considers it expedient that any land should be developed, re-developed or improved as a whole, it may prepare a scheme indicating in general terms the manner in which it is intended that the area should be laid out and the land in the area used.

(1) *Procedure for making schemes*

As with development plans and the other schemes considered in this Part, the Department is required to consult the district council for the area where the land affected by the scheme is located before the scheme is prepared by the Department (1991 Order, Art. 85). After doing so, the scheme is prepared by the Department and publicised. Art. 86(1) requires that notice be published twice in at least one local newspaper describing the area to which the scheme relates and stating that the scheme is being prepared; specifying the place where copies of the scheme may be inspected; and the time during which objections to the scheme may be sent to the Department.[1] If objections are made and not withdrawn, the Department is required to cause a public local enquiry to be held by the Planning Appeals Commission, unless the Department considers the objections to be of a frivolous or vexatious nature (Art. 86(3)).[2] Thereafter the Department is required to consider the objections and the report of the Planning Appeals Commission and to decide whether or not to adopt the scheme. It may do so with or without amendments (Art. 86(3)). Once adopted, the scheme may be amended (Arts 86(4) and (5)).

(2) *Effect of schemes*

Where a development scheme has been adopted, the Department is empowered to acquire land which is required in connection with the scheme or which it is expedient to hold in connection with land so acquired (Arts 87(1)(a) and (b)). This power is considered later.[3] The land is also blighted for the purposes of the Planning Blight (Compensation) (NI) Order 1981.[4]

---

1 A minimum of twenty eight days for objections must be allowed, beginning on the date of the second appearance of the notice in the newspaper: Art. 86(1).
2 Note the *requirement* to cause an enquiry to be held by the Planning Appeals Commission under Art. 86(3), in contrast to the *power* to do so where objections to development plans are made: Art. 7.   3 Chapter 7.   4 Chapter 8.

CHAPTER FIVE

Simplified Planning Zone Schemes and Enterprize Zone Schemes

Development plans are the means by which the Department makes known its policy for development of the area to which the plans relate. In addition to development plans, however, there are two further means by which the Department can communicate its policy for development of certain areas and can influence the development which takes place in those areas. This chapter is concerned with the powers of the Department to make simplified planning zone schemes and enterprize zone schemes, the effect of each of which is to grant planning permission for the type of development specified in the scheme. Thus, by the use of such schemes, the Department not only declares the type of development which it would like to see in the areas to which the schemes relate, it also provides that such development is automatically permitted, so avoiding both doubt and expense for the would-be developer.

1 Simplified planning zone schemes

(1) Power to make schemes

Art. 14(5) of the 1991 Order empowers the Department to make a simplified planning zone scheme in respect of any area. The nature of such a scheme and its effect are considered below. For the moment, however, it should be noted that despite the breadth of Art. 14(5), certain types of land may *not* be included in a simplified planning zone scheme (Art. 18(1)). These types of land are (1) land in a conservation area;[1] (2) land in an area designated as a national park under Art. 12 of the Nature Conservation and Amenity Lands (NI) Order 1985; (3) land in an area designated as an area of outstanding natural beauty under Art. 14 of the 1985 Order; (4) land in an area declared to be of special scientific interest under Art. 24 of the 1985 Order; (5) land declared to be a national nature reserve under Art. 18 of the 1985 Order; (6) land identified in the development plan for the area as a green belt;[2] and (7) land of any other description which may be prescribed.

---

1   I.e. land designated by the Department under Art. 50(1) of the 1991 Order being land the character or appearance of which it is desirable to preserve or enhance: Art. 50(6). For conservation areas see Chapter 6.
2   Chapter 6.

(2) Form and content of schemes

A simplified planning zone scheme consists of a map and written statement and such diagrams, illustrations and descriptive matter as the Department thinks appropriate for explaining or illustrating the provisions of the scheme (1991 Order, Art. 14(4)). The similarities to the form of development plans should be noted. This similarity extends also, as we will see, to the procedure by which schemes come into being.[3] Apart from the requirements of a map, written statement and descriptive matter, the Order requires that a simplified planning zone scheme shall specify (a) the development or classes of development permitted by the scheme; (b) the land in relation to which permission is granted by the scheme; (c) any conditions, limitations or exceptions subject to which permission is granted;[4] and (d) such other matters as may be prescribed. Under Regulations provided for by the previous legislation[5] schemes are required to be given a title which indicates the area to which they relate.[6]

(3) Procedure for making schemes

The procedure for making and altering schemes is essentially the same as that for making and altering development plans (Art. 14(6)). The procedure provided in the Order is amplified by the Regulations, which provide *inter alia* that the period for making representations about proposals for schemes is six weeks from the date specified by the Department when publicising its proposals (Reg. 3), and that there is a similar period of six weeks for making objections to a proposed scheme, beginning on the date when copies of the proposed scheme are made available for inspection (Reg. 4). The Regulations contain provisions as to the holding of public local enquiries (Regs 8 and 9) and modifications the Department intends to make to the proposed scheme, similar to those contained in the Development Plans Regulations. Finally, the Regulations require that notice of adoption of a simplified planning zone scheme be advertised in the *Belfast Gazette* and locally (Reg. 11).

(4) Duration of schemes

Unlike development plans, simplified planning zone schemes take effect on the date of their adoption (Art. 16(1)). Schemes cease to have effect at the end of ten years beginning on that date (ibid.).

---

3 See below.
4 Chapter 11.
5 Planning (Simplified Planning Zones) Regulations (NI) 1990, made pursuant to the provisions of the 1972 Order as substituted by the Planning and Building Regulations (Amendment) (NI) Order 1990.
6 Simplified Planning Zones Regulations, Reg. 5.

(5) Effect of schemes

The adoption of a simplified planning zone scheme grants, in relation to the area covered by the scheme, planning permission for the development specified in the scheme (Art. 14(2)),[7] except in cases to which the Planning (Assessment of Environmental Effects) Regulations (NI) 1989 apply.[8]

(6) Challenging validity of schemes

As with development plans, there is no statutory procedure for challenging the validity of simplified planning zone schemes. Again, however, the remedy of judicial review is available.

2 Enterprize zone schemes

Simplified planning zone schemes are one way in which, in addition to preparation of a development plan, the Department can make local policy. The other way such policy can be made is in the form of an enterprize zone scheme under the provisions of the Enterprize Zones (NI) Order 1981. These schemes resemble simplified planning zone schemes in that their effect is to grant planning permission for the development specified in the scheme.[9] However, unlike simplified planning zone schemes, enterprize zone schemes have effects in relation to the rating of certain hereditaments included in the land to which the schemes relate.[10]

(1) Power to make schemes

The Department is empowered by Art. 3(1) of the Enterprize Zones (NI) Order 1981 to prepare, with a view to designation of an area as an enterprize zone, an enterprize zone scheme. Where a scheme is made and adopted, the Department may then designate the area to which the scheme relates as an enterprize zone (Art. 7(1)). After designating an area to be an enterprize zone, publicity of such designation is required under Art. 8(1) of the 1981 Order.

(2) Procedure for making schemes

The procedure for making an enterprize zone scheme bears some similarities to the procedure for making development plans. As with development

---

7 For a full discussion of the consequences so far as planning permission is concerned, see Chapter 9.
8 See Planning (Simplified Planning Zones) (Excluded Development) Order (NI) 1994.
9 See below.
10 See Rates (NI) Order 1977, Arts 42(1A) to (1E), as contained in Art. 5 of the Rates (Amendment) (NI) Order 1983.

plans, the Department is required to consult the district council for the area to which the scheme relates before preparing the scheme (1981 Order, Art. 3(2)). The scheme is then prepared and the Department is required to take steps to ensure that (a) adequate publicity is given to the provisions of the scheme; (b) that any order made designating an enterprize zone will have the effect of granting planning permission; (c) that persons who may be expected to want to make representations to the Department on the ground that the development specified in the scheme should not be granted planning permission are aware that they are entitled to make such representations; and (d) that such persons are given an adequate opportunity to make representations (Art. 3(3)). Following the period for representations, and after considering any representations made, the Department may adopt the scheme, with or without modifications (Arts 4(1) and (2)). After a scheme has been adopted by the Department the Department is required to publish a notice stating that the scheme has been adopted and that copies of it may be inspected (Art. 5(2)).

(3) *Effect of schemes*

As noted above, enterprize zone schemes have effects insofar as the rating of hereditaments included in the enterprize zone is concerned and as regards planning permission. The matter of rating is outside the scope of this book. Insofar as planning permission is concerned however, Art. 19 of the 1991 Order provides that an order designating an enterprize zone shall, without more, have the effect of granting planning permission for the development specified in the scheme.[11] The provisions of the 1991 Order as to planning permission are considered in Chapter 9.

(4) *Challenging validity of schemes*

In contrast to development plans and simplified planning zone schemes, a procedure exists under the Enterprize Zones Order for challenging the validity of enterprize zone schemes (Art. 6).[12] Under Art. 6(1) a person aggrieved by a scheme may within one month from first publication of adoption of the scheme apply to the High Court for an order that the Department shall not make an order designating the enterprize zone to which the scheme relates. The grounds on which the scheme may be challenged under Art. 6 are that the scheme is not within the powers

---

[11] Note that in contrast to the provisions concerning simplified planning zone schemes, it is not the adoption of the scheme which has the effect of granting permission, but the order designating the enterprize zone under Art. 7 of the Enterprize Zones Order which has this effect.
[12] A similar procedure exists for challenging the validity of modifications to schemes under Art. 11.

conferred by the Order or that a requirement of the Order has not been complied with (Art. 6(1)). The procedure for challenge laid down in Art. 6(1) is the only means of challenging the validity of the scheme (Art. 6(4)).

(a) Persons aggrieved

In order to obtain the relief available under Art. 6, the applicant must be a 'person aggrieved'. This expression has been popular with the legislature,[13] despite criticism by the judiciary.[14] The frequent use of the expression, however, may not be of much help in ascertaining the meaning of the words for the purpose of the Enterprize Zones Order.[15] Nonetheless there are some *dicta* in the authorities which seem to be of general application. In *Re Sidebotham*[16] James LJ said that the expression referred to someone who had suffered a legal grievance, against whom a decision had been pronounced which has wrongfully deprived him of something, or wrongfully refused him something, or wrongfully affected his title to something.[17] In *Attorney-General of the Gambia* v N'Jie[18] Lord Denning said that this definition was not, however, to be regarded as conclusive.[19] The words 'person aggrieved' are of wide import and should not be subjected to a restrictive interpretation. Outside the expression are mere busy-bodies who are interfering in things which do not concern them, but persons who have a genuine grievance because an order has been made which prejudicially affects their interests are within the expression.[20] It has been suggested of similar provisions now contained in s. 287 of the Town and Country Planning Act 1990 relating to challenges to development plans, that persons aggrieved include objectors, persons selected to appear at the public examination of the plan, persons who appeared at a local enquiry, bodies which have to be consulted in the making of a plan and any person whose property is affected by a plan.[21] There seems to be no reason to distinguish enterprize zone schemes and the provisions of the 1981 Order from the plans and procedure in the 1990 Act for this purpose.

---

13 See e.g. entries in *Stroud's Judicial Dictionary*, 5th ed., London: Sweet and Maxwell 1986.
14 *Ealing BC* v *Jones* [1959] 1 All ER 286, 287 *per* Lord Parker CJ, repeated by Salmon J in *Buxton* v *Minister of Housing and Local Government* [1960] 3 All ER 408, 411.
15 See *Sevenoaks UDC* v *Twynam* [1929] 2 KB 440, 443 *per* Lord Hewart CJ: 'The problem with which we are concerned is not, what is the meaning of the expression "aggrieved" in any one of a dozen other statutes, but what is its meaning in this part of this statute?'
16 (1880) 14 ChD 458.
17 Ibid., 465.
18 [1961] 2 All ER 504.
19 Ibid., 511.
20 Ibid.
21 Purdue, Young and Rowan-Robinson, *Planning Law and Procedure*, London: Butterworths 1989, p.575.

(b) The grounds of challenge and Article 6(4)

As we have seen, the grounds on which challenge may be made under Art. 6(1) are that the scheme is not within the powers conferred by the Enterprize Zones Order, or that any requirement of the Order has not been complied with. We have seen also that Art. 6(4) provides that except as provided by Art. 6, the validity of an enterprize zone scheme cannot be questioned in any legal proceedings whatever. The question arises whether the two grounds specified in Art. 6(1) are the *only* grounds on which challenge can be mounted, and are they the same as *ultra vires*? In particular, does the legislation prevent a person aggrieved from challenging the validity of a scheme on the ground that the scheme was made *mala fide*, or would a challenge on this ground be a challenge on the ground that the scheme was outside the powers of the Department conferred by the Order?[22] It would seem that if the Department in adopting the scheme has acted on no evidence; or has come to a conclusion which on the evidence it could not reasonably have come to; or has interpreted the legislation incorrectly; or has taken into consideration matters it ought not to have; or has failed to taken into account matters which it ought to have; or has otherwise gone wrong in law, the courts can intervene under Art. 6(1).[23]

(c) Substantial prejudice

On an application under Art. 6(1) on the ground of failure to comply with the requirements of the Order, the court must be satisfied that the interests of the applicant would be substantially prejudiced before it can grant the relief available (Art. 6(2)(b)). In *Wilson* v *Secretary of State for the Environment*[24] Browne J held that a person suffers substantial prejudice not only if he is deprived, by the failure to comply with the legislative provisions, of the opportunity of making representations or objections and of the chance of a public enquiry being held, but also if his interests require that representations or objections should be made by someone and those who would make such representations or objections are deprived of an opportunity of so doing.[25]

---

22 For differing views on similar provisions in the Acquisition of Land (Authorisation Procedure) Act 1946 see *Smith* v *East Elloe RDC* [1956] 1 All ER 855 HL. Also Purdue, *et al, op. cit.*, p. 568. In connection with *Smith* v *East Elloe RDC* and Art. 6(4) of the 1981 Order reference should be made also to *Anisminic Ltd* v *Foreign Compensation Commission* [1969] 1 All ER 208 and *R* v *Secretary of State for the Environment, ex p Ostler* [1976] 3 All ER 90. For the relationship between judicial review and the statutory grounds of challenge see *R* v *Secretary of State for Transport, ex p de Rothschild* [1989] 1 All ER 933, and discussion by Davies, [1989] All ER Rev, p.1.
23 See *Ashbridge Investments Ltd* v *Minister of Housing and Local Government* [1965] 3 All ER 371, 374 *per* Lord Denning MR.
24 [1974] 1 All ER 428.
25 Ibid., 439.

CHAPTER SIX

Conservation Areas and Other Areas of Special Interest

We have seen in the previous chapters how the Department is able to plan the development of areas of land by the preparation of development plans and the designation of enterprize zones and simplified planning zones. In this chapter we consider further means of planning the development of certain areas under the 1991 Order and under the Nature Conservation and Amenity Lands (NI) Order 1985.[1] The provisions of these enactments enable the Department to designate areas of Northern Ireland to be areas where special controls apply. The factor common to the various designated areas considered in this chapter is that the areas in question are of special interest either because of their natural characteristics, or because of the architectural or historic merit of their buildings. A full consideration of the powers and duties of the Department under the Nature Conservation and Amenity Lands Order is outside the scope of this book, but some comment is appropriate as the various possible designations, *viz.* National Parks, Areas of Outstanding Natural Beauty and Areas of Special Scientific Interest, are based on the desirability of conserving these areas. This, it is thought, would be undoubtedly a 'material consideration' to be taken into account for planning purposes.

1 Conservation areas

(1) Power to designate conservation areas

Art. 50(1) of the 1991 Order empowers the Department to designate areas as conservation areas (see also Art. 50(6)). Such areas are areas of special architectural or historic interest, the character or appearance of which it is desirable to preserve or enhance (Art. 50(1)).[2] It is provided also that the Department may vary or cancel a designation of a conservation area (Art. 50(2)). When designation of a conservation order is made, varied or cancelled, the Department is required to publicise this in a newspaper circulating in the locality (Art. 50(4)).

---

1 As amended by the Nature Conservation and Amenity Lands (Amendment) (NI) Order 1989.
2 See R v *Canterbury* CC, *ex p Halford* [1992] EGCS 23.

(2) Consultation requirements

Before making, varying, or cancelling a designation of a conservation area the Department is required to consult both the Historic Buildings Council and the appropriate district council (Art. 50(3)).[3]

(3) Effect of designation as conservation area

The consequences of designating an area as a conservation area are threefold:

(a) Financial assistance

Art. 52(1) of the 1991 Order empowers the Department to make grants or loans for the purpose of defraying in whole or in part any expenditure in connection with, or with a view to the promotion of, the preservation or enhancement of a conservation area. Such grants or loans may be made subject to such conditions as the Department thinks fit (Art. 52(2)). Where a loan rather than a grant is made, it may contain provisions as to repayment, payment of interest, or otherwise, as the Department (after approval by the Department of Finance and Personnel) determines (Art. 52(3)).

(b) Effect on exercise of other powers

Art. 50(5) of the 1991 Order requires that 'special attention' be paid to the desirability of preserving or enhancing the character or appearance of the conservation area in the exercise of any powers under the 1991 Order as regards any buildings or land in the conservation area. Thus, for example, the duty under Art. 50(5) will apply in relation to applications for planning permission to carry out development in the conservation area. What then is the nature and extent of the duty created by Art. 50(5)? It is suggested that the following principles emerge from the authorities:

(1) It is the character and appearance of the conservation area as a whole, and not the individual components of it, that are to be considered under Art. 50(5).[4] Thus, a proposal to replace one building in the area with another might have no material effect on the conservation area.[5]
(2) In the exercise of its powers under the 1991 Order, the Department (and presumably the Planning Appeals Commission on appeals) is not required specifically to refer to the statutory duty under Art. 50(5) in giving its decision. It must be clear however that the duty imposed by the Article was carried out.[6]

---

3   For the meaning of 'consult' see Chapter 2.
4   *Unex Dumpton Ltd v Secretary of State for the Environment* (1991) 61 P & CR 103, 109.
5   Ibid.
6   *Steinberg v Secretary of State for the Environment* (1989) 58 P & CR 453.

(3) The Article does not require that proposals for development in a conservation area should themselves preserve or enhance, or serve to preserve or enhance, the character or appearance of the conservation area. All that the Article requires is that special attention be paid to the desirability of preservation or enhancement. Other important factors may exist which render the development acceptable, notwithstanding the conservation considerations. Such factors can be weighed by the Department provided it pays special attention to the conservation objectives.[7]

(4) It is unclear whether the duty created by Art. 50(5) calls on the Department to do more than merely consider whether the development proposals would cause harm to the conservation area. In *Steinberg v Secretary of State for the Environment*[8] it was said that merely to say that the proposals would cause no harm does not fulfil the obligation to consider the preservation and enhancement of the conservation area.[9] The avoidance of harm is essentially negative, whereas the statutory duty imposed by Art. 50(5) is essentially positive.[10] If this is correct, it seems that the Department would not discharge its duty by simply asking 'Does the proposal preserve the character of the area?' and granting permission if the answer is yes.[11] Certainly the duty would not be fulfilled if the Department were to consider the development proposed to be 'not as bad as we thought'.[12] The view that preservation denotes something positive was however doubted in *South Lakeland DC v Secretary of State for the Environment*.[13] There it was said that where it is found that the area will not be harmed by the proposals, this amounts to a finding that it will be preserved, as 'preserve' does not have the narrow meaning of referring to development intended to make a positive contribution to preservation and excluding development of a neutral character.

What the Department must do to discharge the duty created by Art. 50(5) with regard to the question of harm is to consider whether the degree of harm should lead to a refusal of permission.[14]

---

7 *Harrow CC v Secretary of State for the Environment* (1990) 60 P & CR 525, 529; also *Bath Society v Secretary of State for the Environment* (1991) 62 P & CR 565.
8 (1989) 58 P & CR 453.
9 *Steinberg v Secretary of State for the Environment* (1989) 58 P & CR 453, 457.
10 Ibid.
11 Ibid., though the issue was left open.
12 *Bromley LBC v Secretary of State for the Environment* (1990) 59 P & CR 100, 116 per McCowan J.
13 [1992] 1 All ER 573.
14 *Unex Dumpton Ltd v Secretary of State for the Environment* (1991) 61 P & CR 100, 110. See also *Bath Society v Secretary of State for the Environment* (1991) 62 P & CR 565.

(c) Control of demolition

The third consequence of an area being designated a conservation area concerns the demolition of buildings in the area. Demolition of such buildings[15] is not to be carried out without the consent of the Department (Art. 51(2)).[16] Before determining an application for consent the Department is required to give at least fourteen days notice to the district council for the area in which the conservation area is situated and to consult with the council.[17] The Department, however, can direct that the requirement of consent shall not apply to the kind of building described in the direction (Art. 51(3)). Any such direction made by the Department must be prescribed as provided in Art. 51(4). Apart from the provisions of Art. 51, various provisions of the 1991 Order relating to listed buildings[18] apply also to buildings in conservation areas.[19]

2 Green Belts and Countryside Policy Areas

Apart from the statutory power under the 1991 Order to designate conservation areas, the Department has adopted a policy for development in the countryside which distinguishes between ordinary land and land in a Green Belt (formerly known as an Area of Special Control), or Countryside Policy Area.[20]

3 National Parks

Art. 12(1) of the Nature Conservation and Amenity Lands (NI) Order 1985 provides that the Department may designate an area as a National Park where it considers it desirable that measures be taken for the purpose of: (a) conserving or enhancing the natural beauty or amenities of the area; (b) conserving wildlife, historic objects or natural phenomena in the area; (c) promoting the enjoyment by the public of the area; and (d) providing or maintaining public access to the area.

---

15 Excluding listed buildings (buildings of special architectural or historic interest listed under Art. 42 of the 1991 Order: see Chapter 16), churches, historic monuments and buildings excluded by a direction of the Department under Art. 51(3): see Art. 51(1).
16 For the requirements for obtaining consent, see Planning (Conservation Areas) (Demolition) Regulations (NI) 1988, Reg. 3.
17 Ibid., Reg. 4.
18 See Chapter 16.
19 See Art. 51(5), and Planning (Conservation Areas) (Demolition) Regulations (NI) 1988, Reg. 7 and sch. 2.
20 See A *Planning Strategy for Rural Northern Ireland* (1992).

4 Areas of Outstanding Natural Beauty

Apart from the power to designate land as a National Park, the Department has power to designate land as an Area of Outstanding Natural Beauty.[21] As with National Parks, where land is designated as an Area of Outstanding Natural Beauty, the Department may formulate proposals for conserving or enhancing the natural beauty or amenities of the area; for conserving wildlife, historic objects or natural phenomena; for promoting enjoyment of the area by the public; and for providing or maintaining public access to the area.[22]

5 Areas of Special Scientific Interest

Where the Department is satisified that an area is of special scientific interest and accordingly needs to be specially protected, the Department is required[23] to declare the area an Area of Special Scientific Interest (1985 Order, Art. 24(1)). One of the effects of designation of an Area of Special Scientific Interest is that landowners are prevented from carrying out any operations or activities in the Area which are specified in the declaration of the Area as an Area of Special Scientific Interest (see Arts 25(1) and 24(2)(b)). Failure to observe the provisions of Art. 25 is an offence (Art. 25(b)) although it is a 'reasonable excuse' to carry out an operation for which planning permission has been granted (Art. 25(7)).

6 Environmentally Sensitive Areas

Finally, the Department of Agriculture has power under Art. 3 of the Agriculture (Environmental Areas) (NI) Order 1987 to designate an area an environmentally sensitive area where it appears to the Department desirable to conserve and enhance the natural beauty of the area; to conserve flora and fauna or physiographical features of the area; or to protect buildings or other objects of archaeological, architectural or historic interest in the area. The power is exercisable where adoption of particular agricultural methods is likely to facilitate conservation enhancement or protection.

---

21 Nature Conservation and Amenity Lands (NI) Order 1985, Art. 14(1).
22 Ibid., Art. 14(5).
23 Nature Conservation and Amenity Lands (Amendment) (NI) Order 1989, Arts 10(1), substituting 'shall' for the original 'may' in Art. 24(1) of the 1985 Order.

CHAPTER SEVEN

Acquisition of Land for Planning Purposes

The final means of 'strategic planning' to be considered here is the power of the Department to acquire land for planning purposes. Here the Department becomes an active participant in the development process, through the acquisition and disposal of the land, or development by the Department itself,[1] and is not merely involved through the formulation of policies and the exercise of its discretion to grant or refuse planning permission.

(1) Power to acquire or appropriate land

Art. 87(1) of the 1991 Order gives the Department power to acquire land either by agreement or compulsorily, in four cases. In addition, the Department has power to appropriate land already vested in it for other purposes, for the purposes set out in Art. 87(1).[2] The Department may acquire or appropriate land where it is satisfied (a) that the land is required in connection with a development scheme;[3] (b) that it is expedient in the public interest that the land should be held with land acquired in connection with a development scheme; (c) that the land is required for development or redevelopment or both, as a whole for the purpose of providing for the relocation of population or industry or the replacement of open space in the course of the redevelopment or improvement of another area as a whole; or (d) that it is expedient to acquire the land for a purpose which it is necessary to achieve in the interests of the proper planning[4] of an area in which the land is situated (Arts 87(1)(a) to (d)).

It will be seen that the power to acquire land under paras (a) and (c) exists where the land is 'required' for the purposes mentioned, in contrast to the test applicable under paras (b) and (d), namely that it is expedient to acquire the land for the purposes mentioned in those paragraphs.[5]

---

1 See 1991 Order, Art. 91.
2 1991 Order, Art. 87(7). See *Sutton LBC v Bolton* [1993] EGCS 14.
3 See Art. 86 and Chapter 4.
4 An expression which is not defined in the Order.
5 The meaning of 'required' has recently been considered under the provisions now contained in s. 226 of the Town and Country Planning Act 1990, which provide local planning authorities in England and Wales with similar, but not identical, powers. Unfortunately, the decisions are of limited assistance in view of the differences in the

(2) Procedure

Before it acquires any land under the power contained in Art. 87, the Department is required to consult the district council in whose land the area is situated. Having done so, the procedure for acquisition will depend on whether the acquisition is to take place by agreement or compulsorily. Before considering these alternative procedures, it should be noted that where the land is being acquired in connection with a development scheme, the acquisition may proceed concurrently with proceedings under Art. 86 for adoption of the development scheme, but any vesting order vesting the land in the Department must not be made until the order adopting the development scheme has been made (Art. 87(6)).

(a) Acquisitions by agreement

Where the acquisition is to take place by agreement, then the usual procedure for the transfer of land from one individual to another will be followed. Thus, there will usually be a contract for the sale of the land prepared by the landowner's solicitor, followed by an assurance of the land at a later date prepared by the Department's solicitor.

(b) Acquisitions by vesting order

Where, however, the Department wishes to acquire the land otherwise than by agreement, it may make an order vesting the land in itself (Art. 87(2)), and the provisions as to the making of vesting orders set out in sch. 6 of the Local Government Act (NI) 1972 apply, subject to the modifications contained in the 1991 Order (Art. 87(3)).[6] Under this procedure notice of the intended vesting order must be published by the Department on at least two occasions in the locality in which the land is situate.[7] The notice must be served on every person appearing to the Department to have an estate in the land, and must be served also on such government departments and public bodies as the Department thinks fit.[8] Publication affords an opportunity to make representations about the proposed vesting order. If representations are made the Department is required to cause a public local enquiry to be held by the Planning Appeals Commission or by 'any other person' unless the representations (1) are withdrawn; (2) relate solely to the amount of compensation; or (3) are in the opinion of the

---

statutory provisions. In *Sharkey v Secretary of State for the Environment* (1992) 63 P & CR 332, 340 McCowan LJ said that the acquiring authority does not have to show that the compulsory purchase is indispensable to the carrying out of the activity or the achieving of the purpose. 'Required' said his Lordship means 'necessary in the circumstances of the case.' See also *R v Secretary of State for the Environment ex p Leicester* CC (1988) 55 P & CR 364.
6   For the modifications of the 1972 Act, see sch. 2 of the 1991 Order.
7   Local Government Act (NI) 1972, sch. 6, para. 2(a); 1991 Order, sch. 2, para. 4(a).
8   1972 Act, sch. 6, paras 2(b) and (c); 1991 Order, sch. 2, paras 4(b) and (c).

Department solely of a frivolous or vexatious nature;[9] and to consider the report of the person who held the public enquiry.[10] After considering representations and, if applicable, the report, the Department may make or refuse to make the vesting order.[11]

A vesting order must contain such provisions as the Department thinks necessary or expedient for carrying it into effect.[12] Notice of the making of the vesting order must be published naming a place where a copy of the order may be inspected and a like notice must be served on persons who objected to the making of the order and who appeared at the local enquiry in support of those objections.[13] The vesting order becomes operative at the end of one month from the date on which notice of the making of the order is published.[14] Once this happens the Department is required to serve a copy of the order or a notice stating that the order has become operative on every person appearing to it to have an estate in the land.[15] The notice must also name a place where a copy of the vesting order may be inspected.[16] Finally, notice of the vesting order must be served on such government departments and public bodies as the Department thinks fit.[17]

Once the vesting order becomes operative, its effect is to vest in the Department on that date without any need of conveyance or transfer, an estate in fee simple or such other estate as is specified in the order, freed and discharged from all claims or estates save those specified in the order.[18] In the case of registered land however the date of vesting is different. The Department is required to endorse on the vesting order lodged in the Land Registry the date on which the vesting order would, under the provisions just considered, become operative. The date on which the order actually becomes operative is that date or the date on which the order is lodged for registration, whichever is the later.[19] Insofar as the former owners are concerned, after the vesting order becomes operative their interests are in the compensation fund only.

Where a vesting order has been made, any person aggrieved by the order may apply to the High Court to challenge the validity of the order, on the grounds that the vesting order was not within the powers conferred

---

9   1972 Act, sch. 6, para. 3(1); 1991 Order, sch. 2, para. 4.
10 1972 Act, sch. 6, para. 3(2).
11 Ibid., sch. 6, para. 3(1). Any objection to the proposed vesting order which, in the Department's opinion, amounts in substance to an objection to the provisions of the development plan may be disregarded by the Department: 1991 Order, Art. 93.
12 1972 Act, sch. 6, para. 4; 1991 Order, sch. 2, para. 6.
13 1972 Act, sch. 6, para. 5(1)(a); 1991 Order, sch. 2, para. 7(a).
14 1972 Act, sch. 6, para. 5(1)(c).
15 Ibid., para. 5(1)(d); 1991 Order, sch. 2, para. 7(c).
16 Ibid.
17 1972 Act, sch. 6, para. 5(2); 1991 Order, sch. 2, para. 7(d).
18 1972 Act, sch. 6, para. 6(1).
19 Ibid., para. 6(3).

by the 1991 Order on the Department, or that the procedure laid down has not been complied with.[20] Such an application must be made within one month from publication of the notice of the making of the vesting order.[21] On an application to challenge, the court may (1) suspend the operation of the vesting order either generally or insofar as it affects any property of the applicant, until the final determination of the proceedings; (2) quash the order either generally or insofar as it affects any property of the applicant, where the court is satisfied that the vesting order was not within the powers of the Department, or where the interests of the applicant have been substantially prejudiced by the failure to observe the procedure laid down; or (c) dismiss the application.[22] Apart from challenge on such grounds a vesting order cannot be questioned in any legal proceedings whatsoever (sch. 6, para. 5(1)(b)).[23] In *In re Fanning*[24] it was argued that the provisions of s. 22(2)(b) of the Local Government Act (NI) 1934 (corresponding to those now contained in sch. 6 of the 1972 Act) required the applicant actually to obtain an order suspending the operation of the vesting order within the prescribed time to enable the court thereafter to quash the order. Murray J rejected the argument holding that all that is required is that an application to quash the order be made within the prescribed time. The question whether an interim order suspending the operation of the vesting order could be made after the date on which the order became operative was left open, although Murray J thought that the matter might be of little practical significance as the court could, in appropriate cases, preserve the status quo by granting an interim or interlocutory injunction against entry on the land by the Department, pending determination of the application to quash the vesting order.[25]

As mentioned above, the interests of the former owners become interests only in the compensation fund. Where a former owner and the Department cannot agree on the amount of compensation to be paid by the Department, the question is to be referred to and determined by the Lands Tribunal.[26] The Department is required to make out maps and schedules of the lands affected by the vesting order and the names of the former owners and supply such information to the Lands Tribunal.[27]

---

20 1972 Act, sch. 6, para. 5(1)(b); 1991 Order, sch. 2, para. 7(b).
21 1972 Act, sch. 6, para. 5(1)(b).
22 For discussion of the expressions 'person aggrieved', 'substantial prejudice' and the grounds of challenge, see Chapter 5 in connection with similar provisions in the Enterprize Zones (NI) Order 1981.
23 See again Chapter 5.
24 [1979] NI 79.
25 Ibid., 84.
26 1972 Act, sch. 6, para. 11(1). For the establishment and constitution of the Lands Tribunal see Lands Tribunal and Compensation Act (NI) 1964.
27 1972 Act, sch. 6, paras 12(1) and (2). For the powers of the Lands Tribunal see ibid., para. 13.

On payment of the compensation by the Department, where the amount has been settled between the parties or by the Lands Tribunal, the Department is required to obtain a receipt which releases the compensation fund from all claims of the former owner.[28] Finally, the Department is required to pay interest on the compensation money from the date of vesting until the money is actually paid,[29] as well as the costs of the former owner in furnishing any evidence of title required by the Department.[30]

(3) *Dealing with the land acquired*

Where land has been acquired or appropriated by the Department for planning purposes, the Department has three options for dealing with it. The first two involve disposal of the land[31] but the third involves the Department being actively involved in its development.

The first option is for the Department to appropriate the land for any other purpose for which it is authorised to acquire land (1991 Order, Art. 89)). In other words the Department is empowered to appropriate land *to* and *from* planning purposes.

The second option involves actual disposal of the land. Under Art. 90(1) of the 1991 Order the Department may dispose of the land to such persons as it thinks expedient for best use of the land[32] or to secure building or other work which it considers is needed for the proper planning of the area where the land is situated. In disposing of land pursuant to Art. 90(1) the Department is required to ensure, as far as practicable, that people who were living or working on the land before it was acquired and who wish to be accommodated again on the land are given an opportunity of so doing (Art. 90(2)).

The expression 'dispose of' is not defined in the 1991 Order. In other enactments the expression has been held to mean out-and-out transfer, as opposed to letting,[33] but letting seems to be included in the term for the purposes of the 1991 Order, as Art. 92 refers to tenancies created by the Department under Art. 90 and provides for the recovery of premises so let.

---

28 Ibid., para. 14(1). For situations where the Department is unable to obtain a receipt, see ibid., para. 17(1).
29 Ibid., para. 18.
30 Ibid., para. 14(2). Where the compensation does not exceed £100, a statutory declaration as to occupation will suffice: ibid., para. 15(1).
31 Used here loosely to denote the fact that the land ceases to be held by the Department for planning purposes. This may be by appropriation to other functions of the Department, or by actual disposal to someone else: see below.
32 Or other land, or buildings or works already in existence or to be constructed, whether by the Department or anyone else: Art. 90(1).
33 See e.g. *Attorney-General* v *Pontypridd* [1905] 2 Ch. 450 (Electric Lighting (Clauses) Act 1899); *Rhyl UDC* v *Rhyl Amusements Ltd* [1959] 1 WLR 465 (Rhyl Improvement Act 1892). See the definition for tax purposes in the Income and Corporation Taxes Act 1988, s. 776.

The third option is to develop the land. Thus, the Department may erect, construct or carry out any building or work (Art. 91(1)) and may repair, maintain and insure any buildings or works on the land and generally deal with the land in a proper course of management (Art. 91(3)). The Department is also empowered to enter agreements for the development of the land (Art. 91(2)).[34]

---

34 On such agreements see Grant, *Urban Planning Law*, London: Sweet and Maxwell 1982, pp 522–528.

CHAPTER EIGHT

Planning Blight

We have seen in previous chapters that the Department may prepare development plans for areas of land and how it may formulate policy for areas in other ways, e.g. by the preparation of development schemes. The inclusion of land in a plan or scheme prepared by the Department or its public bodies, such as the Housing Executive, may have beneficial or adverse consequences for the owners of the land included in the plan or scheme, causing the land to increase or decrease in value. 'Planning blight' is the expression loosely used to describe any effect of plans or schemes which is detrimental to the landowner. We will see that for the purposes of the legislation to be considered in this chapter the term is given a more precise meaning, but, for the moment, it will suffice to describe the adverse effect which proposals of public bodies may have on land. Since 1971 Parliament has recognised a responsibility to compensate landowners whose land has depreciated in value because of such proposals.[1] The relevant provisions are now contained in the Planning Blight (Compensation) (NI) Order 1981.[2] The scheme of the Order is to enable landowners whose land is affected by the proposals of public bodies identified in the Order to serve a blight notice, the effect of which is to require the body in question to acquire the landowner's estate in the land from the landowner.

Blight notices are thus a means of 'inverse compulsory purchase' where the compulsion comes not from the acquiring authority, but from the landowner. The provisions of the 1981 Order apply to Crown land,[3] enabling claimants who satisfy the conditions discussed below to require the purchase of their interest in such land.[4]

(1) *Entitlement to serve blight notice*

To be able to serve a blight notice and activate the provisions of the 1981 Order, four conditions must be fulfilled:

---

1 The Planning and Land Compensation Act (NI) 1971 introduced compensation for planning blight to Northern Ireland.
2 As amended by the Planning (Amendment) (NI) Order 1982 and the Planning and Building Regulations (Amendment) (NI) Order 1990. For an explanation of the 1981 Order before the amendments see Trimble, 'Planning Blight' (1982) 33 NILQ 60.
3 As defined in the 1991 Order, Art. 118.
4 1981 Order, Art. 15A(1) (inserted by Planning and Building Regulations (Amendment) (NI) Order 1990, Art. 29(1)).

(a) The land must be blighted land

Land is affected by planning blight for the purpose of the 1981 Order only if it falls within any of the cases set out in Art. 3(1) of the Order. This provision lists twelve instances common to which is the prospect of land being acquired by compulsory purchase in the future.[5] The cases described in Art. 3(1) may be summarised as follows:

(a) land authorised by any Local or Public Act to be compulsorily acquired;

(b) land shown on a map approved by the Housing Executive, or described in a resolution of the Executive, as land which may be acquired for the purpose of redevelopment under the Housing (NI) Order 1981;

(c) land in an area declared by the Housing Executive as a proposed redevelopment area;

(d) land on which the Department proposes to construct, improve or alter[6] a road and has notified the relevant district council accordingly;

(e) land on which the Department proposes to construct, improve or alter[7] a road and on which the Department has exercised its power under the 1991 Order to prevent or restrict development of that land;[8]

(f) land on or adjacent to the line of a road proposed to be constructed, improved or altered under certain provisions of the Roads (NI) Order 1993, being land in relation to which a power of compulsory acquisition exists under that Order or the Land Acquisition and Compensation (NI) Order 1973;

(g) land indicated in a development plan[9] adopted under the 1991 Order as land which may be required for the purposes of a government department, district council or authority possessing compulsory purchase powers;

(h) land indicated in a plan (not being a development plan) as land which may be required for the purposes of the bodies in para. (g) above, being land in respect of which the Department has given written notice to the district council of its intention to exercise its development control powers under the 1991 Order by reference to such a plan;

(i) land in respect of which the Department has exercised its development control powers to safeguard it for development for the purposes of any function mentioned in para. (h);

(j) land indicated in an adopted development scheme[10] as land which may be required for the purpose of any function of a government

---

5 See Trimble, *op. cit.*, 62.
6 See Planning (Amendment) (NI) Order 1982, Art. 17(3).
7 See ibid., Art. 17(4).   8 See 1991 Order, Arts 100 and 102.
9 Including a plan, alteration to a plan or replacement plan of which copies have been made available for inspection under Art. 5(4) or 6(3) of the 1991 Order, and modifications proposed to be made in any such plan, alteration or replacement plan of which notice has been given: see 1991 Order, sch. 5.
10 See 1991 Order, Art. 86 and Chapter 4. The reference here to development schemes includes schemes copies of which have been made available for inspection, and proposals for amending such schemes: 1991 Order, sch. 5.

department, district council or authority possessing compulsory purchase powers;
(k) land shown on a map published by the Department as land proposed to be acquired by it for the purpose of Art. 24(1) of the Land Acquisition and Compensation (NI) Order 1973; and
(l) land in a housing action area, being land which the Housing Executive has said it intends to acquire.

To be served with a blight notice the land must fall fairly and squarely within one of the descriptions outlined above.[11]

(b) The claimant must have a qualifying interest

The second requirement which must be fulfilled for the landowner to serve a blight notice is that he should have an interest qualifying for protection under the Order (Art. 5(1)(a)). He will do so if he is a resident owner-occupier (Art. 4(1)(a)), i.e. someone who occupies, in right of an owner's interest, the whole, or a substantial part of, the hereditament[12] as a private dwelling, and has so occupied it for six months ending with service of the blight notice or, where the land is unoccupied at the service of the notice, ending not more than one year before service of the notice (Art. 4(2)(a) and (b)). Where the landowner wishing to serve a blight notice is not a resident owner-occupier, he will have a qualifying interest if he is an owner-occupier of an agricultural unit[13] or part of a unit (Art. 4(1)(b)(i)). Here 'owner-occupier' means a person who has occupied the whole of the unit for six months ending with service of the blight notice, or ending not more than twelve months before service of the blight notice, and in either case, has been entitled to an owner's interest in the unit.[14] Finally, a landowner will have a qualifying interest if he is an owner-occupier of a hereditament the annual value of which does not exceed £2,250 or such other amount as may be specified by the Department (Art. 4(1)(b)(ii)). For this purpose 'owner-occupier' means a person who has occupied, in right of an owner's interest, the hereditament for six months ending with the service of the blight notice, or where the hereditament is unoccupied when the notice is served, ending not more than twelve months before the date of service (Art. 4(4)(a) and (b)).

---

11 See *Bolton Corp.* v *Owen* [1962] 1 All ER 101. For the argument that the legislation should be given a less restrictive interpretation, see Trimble, *op. cit.*, 63, citing *Bowling* v *Leeds* CBC (1974) 27 P & CR 531. This view seems to accord with that of McGonigal LJ in *Hill* v *Department of the Environment* [1976] NI 43, who said that any ambiguity in construction of the legislation should be resolved in favour of the landowner: [1976] NI 43, 46.
12 I.e. the aggregate of the land forming a single entry in the valuation list: Art. 1(2).
13 I.e. land occupied as a unit for agricultural purposes, including a farmhouse: Art. 1(2).
14 'Owner's interest' means a freehold interest (legal or equitable) or a legal tenancy of which there are at least three years still to run at the date of service of the blight notice: Art. 4(5), as amended by Planning (Amendment) (NI) Order 1982, Art. 17(5).

(c) The claimant has made reasonable endeavours to sell his interest

The landowner must not only have an interest qualifying for protection but must have made reasonable endeavours to sell that interest (Art. 5(1)(b)). The question of course is what amounts to reasonable endeavours. In *Perkins v West Wiltshire DC*[15] the landowner consulted an estate agent who told him the property would be impossible to sell because no purchaser would take it on finding out about the adverse proposals. Nothing else was done by the landowner to try to sell the land. The landowner served a blight notice, but the court held he had not made 'reasonable endeavours' to sell: all he had done was to take professional advice. In *Lade v Brighton Corp*.[16] the landowner considered putting a 'for sale' sign outside the premises, but thought that this would be bad for business. She decided to put a notice in the window and let it be known to those frequenting the premises that the premises were for sale. The court held that in the circumstances potential purchasers were more likely to be drawn from visiting dealers than from advertising in the press and that the owner had fulfilled the requirement of having made 'reasonable endeavours' to sell. Finally, in *Mancini v Coventry CC*[17] the claimant had made two attempts to sell his premises to the council. He then advertised the premises for sale in the local press and put the property in the hands of an estate agent. The council argued that this was insufficient because of the nature of the business carried on in the premises. The court rejected this argument as the claimant was selling the premises, not the business.

(d) Premises saleable only at substantial undervalue

The final condition an owner has to satisfy to be able to serve a blight notice is that having made reasonable endeavours to sell his interest he has been unable to do so except at a price substantially lower than that which it might reasonably have been expected to sell for if the land were not blighted (Art. 5(1)(c)).

(2) Procedure

(a) Blight notices

Where a landowner is able to satisfy the four requirements considered above he may serve a blight notice requiring the authority to purchase his interest in the blighted land (Art. 5(1)). Such a notice must be in the prescribed form[18] and must be served on the appropriate authority.[19] In

---

15 (1975) 31 P & CR 427.
16 (1971) 22 P & CR 737.
17 (1982) 44 P & CR 114.
18 See Planning Blight Regulations (NI) 1989.
19 For the meaning of 'appropriate authority' see Art. 1(2).

Eastwood v *Department of the Environment*[20] it was argued that an owner is entitled to serve one blight notice only, so that the Lands Tribunal would have no jurisdiction to deal with a second notice served after the first had been withdrawn by agreement between the owner and the appropriate authority. This argument was rejected by the Lands Tribunal, as the terms upon which the first notice had been withdrawn expressly preserved the rights of the owner in any future proceedings.[21]

(b) Counternotices

If the authority on which the blight notice is served wishes to object to the blight notice, it is required within two months of service of the blight notice to serve a counternotice objecting to the blight notice.[22] Objections to the blight notice can be made on any of the following grounds (Art. 6(2)):

(a) that no part of the land is blighted land;
(b) that the appropriate authority does not propose to acquire any part of the land;
(c) that the authority proposes to acquire part only of the land;
(d) that on the date of service of the blight notice the owner did not have an interest in the property;
(e) that for reasons specified in the counternotice the interest was not a qualifying interest;
(f) that the claimant has not fulfilled the conditions that he has made reasonable efforts to sell and that the land can be sold only at a substantial undervalue;
(g) that in certain cases[23] the appropriate authority does not intend to acquire the property during the next fifteen years.

Further grounds of objection exist where the blight notice has been served by a mortgagee[24] and where the notice has been served by a personal representative.[25]

Finally, where the blight notice has been served by virtue of Art. 9[26] the counter-notice may contain an objection on the ground that the claim made in the notice has not been made out (Art. 10(1)).[27]

---

20 [1983] 4 BNIL 109.
21 For withdrawal of blight notices see below.
22 For the form of the counternotice see Planning Blight Regulations (NI) 1989.
23 Cases (b), (d), (e), (g), (h), (i), (j) and (l) specified in Art. 3(1).
24 See Art. 6(2)(h) and below.
25 See Art. 14(3) and below.
26 Which enables the owner to acquire the authority to purchase the whole of his agricultural land, even though part only is blighted if the unaffected area cannot be farmed without the blighted land.
27 See below.

The counternotice is required to specify on which of the above grounds the authority objects to a blight notice (Art. 6(4)). Where the ground of objection is not within any of the paragraphs in Art. 6(2) there is no power to include the objection in a counternotice.[28] The correct procedure seems to be an action for a declaration that the blight notice is invalid.[29]

(c) *Reference of objections to Lands Tribunal*

Where the authority has served a counternotice objecting to the blight notice, the owner may within two months of service of the counternotice refer the objection to the Lands Tribunal (Art. 7(1)), which may uphold or reject the objection. Where the Tribunal does not uphold the objection it is required to declare that the blight notice is valid (Art. 7(5)).

(i) Objections not raised in counternotice

It is not open to the acquiring authority to raise an objection to the blight notice at the hearing before the Lands Tribunal which the authority did not include in its counternotice.[30] Nor can the Lands Tribunal deal with any objection to the blight notice other than those specified in Art. 6(2).[31]

(ii) Onus of proof

Depending on which objections are being considered by the Lands Tribunal, the onus of proof may lie on the owner or the authority. Where the objections raised are those contained in Arts 6(2)(b)(c) or (g), the onus is on the authority to show that the objections are well founded, failing which the objections will not be upheld by the Tribunal (Art. 7(3)). Where, however, the objections before the Tribunal are any other objections, the onus is on the owner of the land to show that the objection has not been made out, failing which the Tribunal is required to uphold the objection (Art. 7(2)).

(iii) Relevant date

The question arises as to the date which the Lands Tribunal has to consider in determining whether the authority's objection to the blight notice has been made out. There seem to be three possibilities: (1) the

---

28 Binns v *Secretary of State for Transport* (1985) 50 P & CR 468.
29 See Purdue, Young & Rowan Robinson, *Planning Law and Procedure*, London: Butterworths 1989, p. 458. Compare the situation in relation to challenging the validity of enforcement notices and the decision in Davy v *Spelthorne BC* [1983] 3 All ER 278 HL. On this see Chapter 15. Purdue *et al* suggest that *Essex* CC v *Essex Incorporated Church Union* [1963] 1 All ER 326 HL may, however, mean that no challenge to a blight notice can be made other than by counter-notice, and on the grounds provided in the statute: *op. cit.*, p. 459.
30 *Essex* CC v *Essex Incorporated Church Union* [1963] 1 All ER 326 HL; *Burn* v *North Yorkshire* CC (1992) 63 P & CR 81; *Entwhistle Pearson (Manchester) Ltd* v *Chorley BC* (1993) 66 P & CR 277.
31 Binns v *Secretary of State for Transport* (1985) 50 P & CR 468.

date of the blight notice; (2) the date of the counter-notice; or (3) the date of the hearing before the Lands Tribunal. It would seem that the correct date is the date of the counternotice[32] though in *Mancini v Coventry CC*[33] Purchas LJ expressly left open the question whether in appropriate circumstances the material date could be the date of the hearing before the Lands Tribunal.[34] Further, in *Charman v Dorset CC*[35] the Lands Tribunal in England held that in judging the validity of the objections in the counternotice, and in particular the precise nature of the authority's declared intention, the Tribunal cannot shut its eyes to subsequent events as an indication of the weight to be attached to that declared intention.[36] A recent example of the operation of the rule is *Burn v North Yorkshire CC*[37] where a landowner served a blight notice on the ground that the land was blighted by proposals for a relief road. A counternotice was served in July 1990 objecting to the blight notice, but following a consultant's report after the counternotice had been served, the authority abandoned its proposals in December 1990. The Lands Tribunal held the relevant date to be the date of the counternotice, at which time the proposal had been abandoned.[38]

(iv) Objection under Article 6(2)(c).

It will be recalled that Art. 6(2)(c) provides that the authority may object to the blight notice on the ground that the authority proposes to acquire part only of the property. Art. 7(4) provides that the Tribunal shall not uphold an objection on this ground if the part of the property which the authority proposes to acquire is, or includes part of, a house, building or factory and the Tribunal is satisfied that the part cannot be acquired without causing material detriment to the building. If, in other words, material detriment would be caused by the acquisition of part, the authority cannot object to the blight notice on that ground. In *Hill v Department of the Environment*[39] a blight notice was served in respect of a house. The Department objected under what is now Art. 6(2)(c) on the ground that it intended to acquire part only of the property *viz.* part of the garden, and

---

32 *Louisville Investments Ltd v Basingstoke DC* (1976) 32 P & CR 419; *Mancini v Coventry CC* (1985) 49 P & CR 127; *Charman v Dorset CC* (1986) 52 P & CR 88; *Burn v North Yorkshire CC* [1991] EGCS 91.
33 (1985) 49 P & CR 127.
34 Ibid., 141.
35 (1986) 52 P & CR 88.
36 Compare the situation under the Business Tenancies Act (NI) 1964 where it is the date of the hearing rather than the date of the landlord's notice of objection to a new tenancy that is the relevant date for the purposes of determining whether the landlord's intention has been made out: see *Betty's Cafes Ltd v Phillips Furnishing Stores Ltd* [1956] 2 All ER 497.
37 [1991] EGCS 91.
38 See also *Entwhistle Pearson (Manchester) Ltd v Chorley BC* (1993) 66 P & CR 277.
39 [1976] NI 43.

this would not cause material detriment to the house. Evidence was given that when the road scheme which caused the blight was completed, the property would recover its full value. The Court of Appeal held the blight notice to be valid. Gibson LJ said that the test to be applied by the Lands Tribunal was whether the Tribunal was satisfied that the part of the garden could not be acquired without causing material detriment to the house. It would be unrealistic to consider the matter as though the acquisition were *in vacuo* and ask whether the loss of a small portion of the garden would cause a permanent loss in value of the house. The detriment to which the Lands Tribunal had to direct attention was detriment caused by the acquisition of part for the road scheme, which meant not only the permanent detriment caused by the loss of part, but also the detriment which might be reflected in market value caused by the operations.[40]

In considering whether part of a house, building or factory can be taken without material detriment to the building, the Lands Tribunal has to take into account not only the effect of the severance but also the use to be made of the part to be acquired and, where the part is proposed to be acquired for works or purposes extending to other land, the effect of the whole of the works and the use to be made of the other land (Art. 7(7)).

Finally, if the objection to the blight notice is upheld solely on the ground in Art. 6(2)(c) the Lands Tribunal is required to declare that the blight notice is valid as to the part to be acquired by the authority (Art. 7(6)).[41] Where this is the case, or where the owner without referring the case to the Lands Tribunal gives notice to the authority that he accepts the proposal to acquire part only, the acquisition proceeds only as to the part which the authority intends to acquire (Art. 8(6)).[42]

(d) *Effect of valid blight notice*

Where the acquiring authority does not object to the blight notice, or where any objection is withdrawn or not upheld by the Lands Tribunal, the acquisition by the authority proceeds. A contract is deemed to come into existence under which the Department will acquire the owner's interest in the land (Art. 8(1)), the purchase price being the amount which the authority would have paid for that interest had it acquired it under the relevant statutory provision (Art. 8(2)). Any dispute as to the amount of compensation to be paid by the authority will be determined by the Lands Tribunal (Art. 8(3)). The date on which the contract is deemed to come into existence is the date two months after service of the blight notice, or, in cases where the Lands Tribunal refuses to uphold an objection to the blight notice, the date of the Tribunal's determination (Art. 8(10)). The date for completion of the contract (subject to the parties

---

40 Ibid., 47.
41 For notices served pursuant to Art. 9 this does not apply: Art. 10(6). See below.
42 For notices served pursuant to Art. 9 this does not apply: Art. 11(1). See below.

agreeing otherwise) is three months from the date on which they agree on the amount of compensation to be paid, or the date on which the Lands Tribunal determines the amount (Art. 8(4)). If the authority fails to pay on the date for completion, it becomes liable to pay interest (Art. 8(5)).

(e) Withdrawal of blight notice

A blight notice may be withdrawn at any time before the amount to be paid for the interest of the claimant has been agreed between the parties or determined by the Lands Tribunal, or at any time before the end of six weeks, beginning at the date on which the amount is agreed or determined.[43] Where a blight notice is withdrawn, the contract deemed to be made with the acquiring authority is deemed not to have been made.[44]

(3) Special Cases

Special provision is made in the Planning Blight Order for certain situations.

(a) Article 9 blight notices

Where the land affected by blight is an agricultural unit (as defined by Art. 1(2)) and the blighted land is part only of that unit, the owner may include in his blight notice a claim that the area which is not blighted is not reasonably capable of being farmed as a separate unit, and require the authority accordingly to purchase his interest in *the whole of* the unit (Art. 9(1)). Where a notice containing such a claim and requirement is served, then in addition to the grounds of objection contained in Art. 6(2) which may be included in the authority's counternotice, the authority may object to the blight notice on the ground that the claim made in the blight notice (i.e. that the area unaffected by blight is incapable of being farmed alone) is not justified (Art. 10(1)). Where the authority intends to object to the blight notice on ground (c) in Art. 6(2) (i.e. that the authority proposes to acquire part only of the blighted land), the counternotice *must* contain an objection that the claim in the blight notice is not justified (Art. 10 (2)).

Where a blight notice has been served pursuant to Art. 9(1) requiring the authority to purchase not only the blighted land but the unaffected area as well and two conditions are met, then a contract is deemed to come into existence for the purchase of the blighted land only. The two conditions are (1) that the authority objects that the claim in the blight notice is not justified, and (2) that *either* the owner withdraws his claim for the unaffected area *or* the Lands Tribunal declares the notice valid as to the blighted land only (Art. 11 (2)).

---

43 Art. 8(3A) (as inserted by Planning (Amendment) (NI) Order 1982, Art. 17(6)).
44 Ibid.

If the authority objects *both* on the ground that the claim is not justified *and* under Art. 6(2)(c), a contract is again deemed to come into existence for the blighted land only if one of two conditions is met. These conditions are (1) that the owner accepts the authority's proposal to acquire the blighted land only, or (2) that the Lands Tribunal declares the notice valid as to the blighted land only (Art. 11 (3)).[45]

(b) Mortgaged land

Art. 12(1) provides that a blight notice may be served by a mortgagee, but certain special provisions apply. First, as with ordinary owners, the mortgagee must have made reasonable endeavours to sell the land, and be able to do so only at substantial undervalue (see Art. 12(1)(b)). This necessarily presupposes that the mortgagee has a power to sell, and that the power has become exercisable (see Art. 12(1)(a)).[46] Secondly, Art. 12(3) requires that the interest which the mortgagee has tried to sell is one which could be the subject of a blight notice by the owner of the land, or which could have been the subject of a blight notice by the owner on a date not more than six months before that of the mortgagee's blight notice. Finally, a blight notice cannot be served by a mortgagee where there is already a notice by the owner which is outstanding, and vice versa (Art. 12(4)).[47]

In the case of a blight notice served by a mortgagee, the authority can include in a counternotice objections that (1) on the date of service of the blight notice the mortgagee did not have an interest as mortgagee in any part of the land to which the notice relates; (2) the mortgagee did not have power to sell the land on the date of service of the blight notice; and (3) that the relevant conditions set out in Art. 12(3)[48] were not satisfied on the date of service of the blight notice (Art. 6(2)(h)).

(c) Personal representatives

Personal representatives of a person who was at his death the owner of a qualifying interest in blighted land may serve a blight notice where they have made reasonable endeavours to sell that interest and are able to do so only at a substantial undervalue (Art. 14(1)). The additional requirement in the case of personal representatives is that one or more

---

45 For the compensation to be paid for the area unaffected by blight, see Art. 11(4).
46 A mortgagee has a statutory power of sale where the mortgage has been created *by deed*: Conveyancing and Law of Property Act 1881, s. 19. For cases of mortgages not created by deed see Wylie, *Irish Land Law*, 2nd ed. Abingdon, Oxon: Professional Books 1986, para. 13.024. For where the statutory power becomes exercisable see 1881 Act, s. 20.
47 In this regard a notice is outstanding until it is withdrawn, or an objection in a counternotice has been upheld, or the period within which an objection may be referred to the Lands Tribunal has elapsed: Art. 12(5).
48 *Viz.* that the interest in the blighted land which the mortgagee claims to sell was not one which could have been the subject of a blight notice by the owner.

individuals are (to the exclusion of any body corporate) beneficially entitled to the interest of the deceased owner (Art. 14(1)(e)). A blight notice served by personal representatives, however, may not relate to part only of the land owned by the deceased (Art. 14(2)).

As with mortgagees, special provisions apply in the case of objections to blight notices served by personal representatives. The authority may object on grounds (a),(b),(c) and (g) of Art. 6(2), and on the following additional grounds: (1) that the persons serving the blight notice are not the personal representatives of the deceased owner (Art. 14(3)(a)); (2) that on the date of the deceased's death the deceased was not entitled to an interest in the blighted land (Art. 14(3)(a)); (3) that the interest of the deceased was not an interest qualifying for protection (Art. 14(3)(b)); or (4) that the personal representatives have not made reasonable endeavours to sell the land, that the condition that they can do so only at a substantial undervalue has not been satisfied, or that the requirement that one or more individuals are beneficially entitled to the deceased's interest has not been fulfilled (Art. 14(3)(c)).

(d) Partnerships

The provisions of the Order apply to blighted land occupied by a partnership for the purposes of the partnership (Art. 13(1)) as opposed to occupied by the individual partners (Art. 13(2)), and accordingly a blight notice may be served by the partnership. If the constitution of the partnership changes after service of the blight notice, the rights and obligations are preserved as far as the new partnership is concerned (Art. 13(3)).

(e) Death of owner after service of blight notice

Where an owner dies after having served a blight notice the provisions of the Order apply as if any reference to the owner were a reference to his personal representatives (Art. 15).

PART THREE

Development Control

CHAPTER NINE

The Meaning of 'Development'

The preceding chapter has dealt with the provisions of the 1991 Order concerning forward planning, i.e. the means by which the Department can plan the future use of land. In this chapter we consider the sections of the Order dealing with development control: how, in other words, the Department can permit or prevent the day to day development of land by individuals. The relationship between the two regimes, forward planning and development control, is considered in Chapter 12. In this chapter we consider what is meant by 'development'.

1 The meaning of 'development' and the requirement of planning permission

Art. 12 of the 1991 Order provides that, subject to the provisions of the Order, planning permission is required for the carrying out of any development of land.[1] The concept of development is therefore the central feature of the legislation and is defined in Art. 11(1) as:

> the carrying out of building, engineering, mining or other operations in, on, over or under land, or the making of any material change in the use of any buildings or other land.

The Article goes on to provide (Art. 11(2)) that certain operations are not to be taken as involving development of land, and these are considered later. For the moment we will concentrate on the definition of development contained in Art. 11(1).

The Article divides development into two classes: operational development (building, engineering, mining or other operations in, on, over or under land) and development by a material change in the use of any buildings or other land. The distinction between the two classes was discussed in *Parkes v Secretary of State for the Environment*[2] where Lord Denning said that 'operations' comprises activities which result in some physical alteration of the land, which has some degree of permanence to the land itself, whereas 'use' comprises activities which are done in, alongside or on the land but do not interfere with the actual physical characteristics of the land.[3] It should not be supposed from this that any given activity

---

1 For planning permission see Chapter 10.   2 [1979] 1 All ER 211.

must fall neatly into one or other of the classes of development: some activities may constitute a change of use or an operation according to what is the object of the activity.[4] Thus, deposit of waste on land to dispose of the material may constitute a change of use of the land, while if done to alter the character of the land it may amount to operational development.[5] Again, the same activity may constitute both an operation and a change of use.[6] An interesting example of the relation between the two classes of development is *Backer* v *Secretary of State for the Environment*.[7] There, a commercial building had been converted to use as a dwelling house by a date prior to July 1976, but the house had not been occupied as such until a date later than July 1976. The conversion had not been approved by the planning authority which served enforcement proceedings complaining of an unlawful change of use. The question arose as to whether the change of use took place before or after July 1976 and this in turn raised the issue as to whether the works of conversion which had taken place before then could amount to a change in use, or whether no change in use took place until the house was actually occupied as such. Unfortunately, the case does not answer the question, as the court was able to dispose of the matter by remitting the case to the Secretary of State for reconsideration on the basis that he had failed to consider a relevant authority, *Impey* v *Secretary of State for the Environment*[8] and the question therefore remains open.

(1) Operational development

Operational development consists of 'building, engineering, mining or other operations in, on, over or under land'. The word 'operations' is not defined but, as we have seen, has been interpreted as signifying activities which result in some physical alteration of the land which has some degree of permanence to the land itself.[9]

(a) Building operations

Art. 2(2) of the Order provides that 'building operations' *includes* rebuilding operations, structural alterations of or addition to buildings and other operations normally undertaken by a person carrying on business as a builder. The Article also provides that the word 'building' *includes* any

---

3 Ibid., 213. Art. 2(2) of the 1991 Order provides that 'use' in relation to land does not include the use of land for the carrying out of any building or other operations thereon. For mining operations, Art. 112(2) provides that 'use' does not include the use of land for the carrying out of mining operations, subject to the provisions of the subsection, discussed below. There is no exclusion in relation to engineering operations.
4 *West Bowers Farm Products* v *Essex* CC (1985) 50 P & CR 368, 377 *per* Sir John Donaldson MR. See also R v *Swale* BC *and anor, ex p* RSPB [1991] JPL 39.
5 Ibid.   6 Ibid.
7 (1982) 47 P & CR 149.   8 (1984) 47 P & CR 157n.
9 *Parkes* v *Secretary of State for the Environment* [1979] 1 All ER 211, 213 *per* Lord Denning MR. See also *Cheshire* CC v *Woodward* [1962] 1 All ER 517.

structure or erection, and any part of a building, but not any plant or machinery comprised in a building. Art. 2(2) does not provide an exhaustive list of what amounts to building operations, or what structures amount to buildings, but merely provides a list of what is *included* in those terms. In other words, while the Article may be helpful, it is not exclusive and the question may arise as to whether operations amount to building operations which cannot be answered by reference to Art. 2(2). The courts have had to consider what principles apply in answering this question.

The leading case is Barvis v Secretary of State for the Environment[10] in which Bridge J said that the test to determine whether what has taken place amounts to a building operation within the meaning of the section is whether what has been done has resulted in the erection of a building as defined in the legislation. If so, the court would want a great deal of persuading that the erection of it had not amounted to a building or other operation.[11]

Thus, the test is whether what has taken place has resulted in the erection of a building. This poses its own problems. In Cheshire CC v Woodward[12] Lord Parker CJ sought to answer the question whether what had resulted was a building by taking the test from land law of whether the resultant construction was a fixture or a fitting. If a fixture, then the structure was a building, and the activity which resulted in the building was a building operation. However, this adoption of the fixtures/fittings test was not followed by Bridge J in Barvis, who said that the court should not, in attempting to answer one question, ask itself a different one.[13] That said, in the same case the court derived assistance from Cardiff Rating Authority v Guest Keen Baldwins Iron & Steel Co. Ltd[14] which concerned the interpretation of the expression 'building or structure or in the nature of a building or structure' in the Plant and Machinery (Valuation for Rating) Order 1927. In that case Jenkins J had considered that the size of the structure, its degree of permanence and its physical attachment to the land were relevant factors in determining whether the structure was within the expression used in the Rating Order.[15] These tests, however, are no more than persuasive and the question is one of fact and degree in each case.[16]

Before leaving building operations, something must be said about demolition. For some time there was doubt whether demolition amounted to an operation which required planning permission. *Coleshill & District Investment Co. Ltd v Minister of Housing and Local Government*[17] suggested that demolition without any rebuilding, or without being part of any larger

10 (1971) 22 P & CR 710. See also R v Swansea CC ex p Elitestone Ltd [1993] 46 EG 181.
11 Ibid, 714.   12 [1962] 1 All ER 517.
13 (1971) 22 P & CR 710, 714.   14 [1949] 1 All ER 27.
15 Ibid., 36.
16 Thus, for example, a model village was considered as development in Buckinghamshire CC v Callingham [1952] 1 All ER 1166, and the fact that a crane was mobile did not prevent it from being a building in Barvis v Secretary of State for the Environment (1971) 22 P & CR 710.
17 [1969] 2 All ER 525.

operation, did not amount to development,[18] and in *Iddenden v Secretary of State for the Environment*[19] Lord Denning MR held that demolition of old buildings followed by erection of new ones in their place constituted two operations, planning permission being required only for the latter. The view that demolition does not constitute development received a setback in *Cambridge CC v Secretary of State for the Environment*[20] in which the court distinguished *Iddenden* and held that demolition *does* constitute development as it is an operation normally carried on by a builder and this is so whether or not the site is redeveloped following the demolition. The setback was shortlived as the Court of Appeal reversed the decision of the High Court on the ground that there had been nothing to justify the judge making a finding that the operations were operations normally carried on by a builder. Glidewell LJ said that the authorities established the following propositions:[21]

(1) Works of demolition of a building may, but do not necessarily or inevitably, constitute development.
(2) Such works constitute development if, but only if, they are properly to be regarded as either (a) building operations, (b) engineering operations, or (c) other operations on land.
(3) Demolition works may be building operations if they are a part of structural alterations of buildings. In such a case the demolition will inevitably be partial only, since if it were total there would be no building left to be altered.
(4) Demolition works of a particular type or scale may be operations normally undertaken by a person carrying on business as a builder.
(5) Demolition works or particular structures may be engineering operations.
(6) Whether demolition works are within any of these categories is a question of fact.
(7) The definition of development does not comprehend every operation on land.
(8) 'Other operations' are operations which, while not of one genus comprising also building operations and engineering operations, nevertheless must at least be of a constructive character, leading to an identifiable or positive result, or be similar to building operations or engineering operations.

---

18 Lord Wilberforce expressing the view that the planning legislation should be approached with a disposition not to bring within its ambit, unless specific words so required, operations which do not produce results of a positive, constructive, identifiable kind. Nothing in the legislation, the policy of development control, the charge on development, common sense or common expectation required, said his Lordship, that demolition should be subject to control, ibid., 538.
19 [1972] 3 All ER 883.   20 [1991] 9 EG 119.
21 [1992] 21 EG 108.

(9) Whether particular works of demolition constitute development must be decided in relation to those works and not to other projected works to which the demolition is a preliminary step.[22]

Finally, where the building to be demolished is a listed building, the consent of the Department is required (1991 Order Art. 44),[23] as is the case where the building is in a conservation area (Art. 51).[24]

(b) Engineering operations

Art. 2(2) of the 1991 Order provides that 'engineering operations' includes the formation or laying out of means of access to roads.[25] Apart from this the term is not defined in the Order. In *Coleshill and District Investment Co. Ltd v Minister of Housing and Local Government*[26] the court refused to overturn a ministerial decision that demolition of earth embankments constituted an engineering operation.

(c) Mining operations

Unlike the equivalent legislation in England and Wales, the 1991 Order does define 'mining operations', and does so in a comprehensive rather than an inclusive way. Art. 2(2) provides that 'mining operations' means the winning and working of minerals in, on, or under land whether by surface or underground working. 'Minerals' is also defined as including all minerals and substances in or under land of a kind ordinarily worked for removal by underground or surface working, but the word does not include turf cut for purposes other than sale (Art. 2(2)).

Insofar as mining operations are concerned, special provision is made by Art. 112 of the 1991 Order. The word 'use' does not include the use of land by the carrying out of mining operations (Art. 112(2)), save in the various provisions mentioned in Art. 112(2)(b), in which cases references to the use of land or the purpose for which land may be used include the carrying out of mining operations, and references to the continuance or discontinuance of a use include the continuance or discontinuance of mining operations.[27] The Order also provides that the deposit of waste in the course of mining operations involves a material change in the use of land (see Arts 11(3) and 112(2)(a)).

---

22 The matter has been settled in England and Wales where 'building operations' now expressly includes demolition: see s. 55(1)(A) of the Town and Country Planning Act 1990, introduced by s. 13 of the Planning and Compensation Act 1991.
23 For listed buidings generally see Chapter 17.
24 See generally Chapter 6.
25 For the meaning of 'means of access' see also Art. 2(2).
26 [1969] 2 All ER 525.
27 The provisions in question are Arts 27(1)(b) (planning conditions requiring discontinuance of use); 29 (application for planning permission for use already in existence); 39 and 83 (discontinuance orders); 68(9), 72(5), 75 and 76 (enforcement).

Finally, mining operations are unlike other operations in certain respects, notably the application of the 'four year rule' in connection with enforcement proceedings.[28] In *Thomas David (Porthcawl) Ltd v Penybont RDC*[29] Lord Denning MR said that mining operations are *sui generis* and that 'every shovelful is a mining operation'.[30] Accordingly, unlike the ordinary case of unlawful operational development, an enforcement notice can only require restoration of the site to the state it was in four years before the notice.[31]

(d) Other operations

The fourth category of operational development is 'other operations'. The meaning of this expression is in some doubt. In *Coleshill and District Investment Co. Ltd v Minister of Housing and Local Government*[32] Lord Morris[33] and Lord Pearson[34] pointed out that had development been intended to cover all operations there would have been no need to mention building, engineering and mining operations, so that 'other operations' must in some way be limited by reference to these terms. The argument however that 'other operations' must be construed *ejusdem generis* with building, engineering and mining, was rejected, on the gound that it is not possible to ascertain any common genus from these terms.[35] Lord Morris suggested that 'other operations' must denote operations which could be spoken of in the context of, or in association with, or as being in the nature of, or as having relation to, building operations or engineering operations or mining operations,[36] while Lord Pearson thought it was to be inferred that Parliament intended to deal primarily with building, engineering and mining operations, but intended secondarily to bring in some other operations similar to those specified operations or some of them.[37] Alternatively, it was possible that there were three genera and that 'other operations' must be similar to building operations, or to engineering operations, or to mining operations.[38] It has been suggested that the operations falling within the expression 'other operations' should be such as might alter the physical characteristics of land sufficiently substantially to be beyond the *de minimis* principle and in such a manner as to be within the general contemplation of planning legislation.[39]

---

28   See generally Chapter 15.
29   [1972] 3 All ER 1092.
30   Ibid., 1096.
31   Ibid. See generally Chapter 15.
32   [1969] 2 All ER 525.
33   Ibid., 529.
34   Ibid., 543.
35   Ibid., 532, *per* Lord Guest; 537 *per* Lord Wilberforce; 543 *per* Lord Pearson. The suggestion that building, engineering and mining operations have a common genus of positive actions was rejected.
36   Ibid., 529.
37   Ibid., 543.
38   Ibid.
39   Grant, *Urban Planning Law*, 2nd ed., London: Sweet and Maxwell 1982, p. 158. Professor Grant also makes the point that the breadth of exemption afforded by the GDO to various minor works renders the scope of 'other operations' largely theoretical.

(2) Material change in use

Art. 11(1) of the 1991 Order provides that development takes place in the making of any material change in the use of any buildings or other land. 'Material change in use' is not defined in the Act and the question is one of fact and degree in each case.[40] Insignificant changes of use may be ignored on an application of the maxim *de minimis non curat lex*.[41] The concept of a material change in the use of land has a number of aspects which must be considered to determine whether a material change has taken place amounting to 'development' within the meaning of the Order. Before looking at these, however, it should be noted that the concept of a material change in use presupposes an existing use which can be identified and a change in that use which is 'material'. The concepts which are to be examined here, such as the planning unit, have been developed by the courts in an attempt to answer whether a material change in use has taken place.

(a) Intensification

Assuming that there is a recognisable use carried on and that the level of such use is intensified, will such intensification be 'a material change in use' so as to constitute 'development' within the meaning of the Order? In other words, although the activity has not changed, can a change in the level of that activity amount to a material change in use?

In *Guildford* RDC v *Penny*[42] Lord Evershed MR rejected the submission by counsel that intensification of use could never be a relevant planning consideration, and in *Brooks and Burton Ltd* v *Secretary of State for the Environment*[43] Lawton LJ said 'we have no doubt that intensification of use can be a material change of use. Whether it is or not depends on the degree of intensification'.[44] In *Guildford* RDC v *Penny* Lord Evershed said that the increased intensity of use might involve a substantial increase in the burden of services which the local authority has to supply and this might in some cases at least be material in considering whether there had been a material change in use.[45] However, it should be remembered that what is

---

40 *Marshall* v *Nottingham City Corp.* [1960] 1 All ER 659, 666 *per* Glyn-Jones J, accepted as correct by Lord Parker CJ in *East Barnet UDC* v *British Transport Commission and anor* [1961] 3 All ER 878, 885. The court will not interfere with a finding that a change of use has been material unless the finding is such as could not properly have been reached: *East Barnet UDC* v *British Transport Commission and anor* at 885; *Bendles Motors Ltd* v *Bristol Corp.* [1963] 1 All ER 578, 580 *per* Lord Parker CJ.
41 See e.g. *Kwik Save Discount Group Ltd* v *Secretary of State for Wales* (1980) 42 P & CR 166.
42 [1959] 2 All ER 111.
43 [1978] 1 All ER 773.
44 Ibid., 774. See also *James* v *Minister of Housing and Local Government* [1965] 3 All ER 602 (reversed in part *sub nom. James* v *Secretary of State for Wales* [1966] 3 All ER 964) and *Esdell Caravan Parks Ltd* v *Hemel Hampstead RDC* [1965] 3 All ER 737.
45 [1959] 2 All ER 111, 114.

being done is to compare a former and a latter state of affairs to see whether there has been a material change in use. In this regard it has been said that the doctrine of intensification is 'somewhat artificial and semantic, and applies most usefully where there is no convenient description to distinguish a former and latter state of affairs except only in terms of their scale.'[46] And in *Royal Borough of Kensington* v *Secretary of State for the Environment*[47] Donaldson LJ criticised the doctrine saying that if the planners were incapable of formulating the use before intensification and the use after intensification, then there was no material change in use.

(b) The planning unit

One problem in ascertaining whether there has been a material change in use of buildings or land is defining what land is being referred to i.e. identifying the planning unit. For example, a block may contain ten residential flats. If one of the flats is used as a shop, has there been a material change in use? This may depend on the choice of planning unit: is the unit to be looked at the block itself, which remains ninety per cent residential, or the individual flat, which has changed its use? The doctrine of the planning unit in other words seeks to answer the question of whether there has been a material change in use by considering the amount of land involved; a change of use which relates to only a small part of the owner's land may not be material in relation to the land as a whole.[48] The question is whether the smaller area is a distinct 'planning unit'. As we will see, however, the concept of the planning unit is not merely geographical; it can connote also the planning history of the land.[49]

As a starting point in this discussion of the concept of the planning unit there is the statement in *G Percy Trentham Ltd* v *Gloucestershire CC*[50] that the planning unit is 'the whole of the area which was used for a particular purpose, including any part of the area whose use was incidental to and ancillary to the achievement of that purpose.'[51] In that case the vendor of a 75 acre farm sold the farmhouse and various farm buildings to a firm of contractors who used some of the buildings for storage of materials. Enforcement proceedings were brought in which the contractors argued that the buildings had previously been used by the farmer for storage and that accordingly planning permission was not required. The court held however that the planning unit to be considered was the whole of

---

46 Lilo Blum v *Secretary of State for the Environment* [1981] JPL 278.
47 [1981] JPL 50.
48 See *Rawlins* v *Secretary of State for the Environment* [1989] JPL 439 where the court pointed out the danger that selection of too small a unit as the planning unit might preclude the contention that the use of the small unit was ancillary to the use of a larger unit of which it forms part and that no material change has taken place in relation to the larger unit (at 441). For the decision on appeal see (1990) 60 P & CR 413.
49 *Jennings Motors Ltd* v *Secretary of State for the Environment* [1982] 1 All ER 471.
50 [1966] 1 All ER 701.   51 Ibid., 704 *per* Diplock LJ.

the unit acquired by the contractors i.e. the farmhouse and buildings, and that this unit had been used for agricultural purposes even though some of the buildings had an ancillary use for storage. As the unit was now being used for storage purposes a material change in the use of the unit had taken place. The relevant area to be considered as the planning unit was considered again in Burdle v Secretary of State for the Environment[52] where Bridge J suggested the criteria for determining the relevant planning unit were as follows:

(1) Whenever it is possible to recognise a single main purpose of the occupier's use of his land to which secondary activities are incidental or ancillary, the whole unit of occupation should be considered.
(2) It may equally be apt to consider the entire unit of occupation even though the occupier carries on a variety of activities and it is not possible to say that one is incidental or ancillary to another.
(3) However, it may frequently occur that within a single unit of occupation two or more physically separate and distinct areas are occupied for substantially different and unrelated purposes. In such a case each area used for a different main purpose (together with its incidental and ancillary activities) ought to be considered as a separate planning unit.[53]

In the same case his Lordship said 'it may be a useful working rule to assume that the unit of occupation is the appropriate planning unit, unless and until some smaller unit can be recognised as the site of activities which amount in substance to separate use both physically and functionally.'[54] In the case of a dwelling house, however, it has been said that it can rarely if ever be right to regard one room in it as a separate planning unit.[55] In the case of a block of flats in single ownership but let to different tenants the planning unit will usually be each individual flat.[56]

Two aspects of the doctrine of the planning unit call for particular mention. First, what is the effect of a division of the planning unit into separate occupation or separate ownership? Does this inevitably mean the creation of two new planning units in place of the one which existed beforehand and does the division involve a material change in the use of that unit? Second, does the construction of a new building inevitably result in the creation of a new planning unit?

In relation to the first of these matters, it has been said that the transfer of part of an existing planning unit to a separate owner or occupier does not result in the creation of a new planning unit for that part, as the boundaries of a planning unit are not primarily matters of title but of

---

52 [1972] 3 All ER 240.   53 Ibid., 244.
54 Ibid.
55 Wood v Secretary of State for the Environment [1973] 2 All ER 404, 408 per Lord Widgery CJ.
56 Johnston v Secretary of State for the Environment (1974) 28 P & CR 424.

activity.[57] This view has been criticised and it has been suggested that the separation of part of a planning unit can create a new planning unit so long as there is a change in occupation and not just a change in title.[58] Where a new planning unit is created, does this amount to a material change in the use of the previous unit? The view that it does is based on *Wakelin v Secretary of State for the Environment*[59] where Lord Denning MR said that if a garage block or stable attached to a large house was turned into separate accommodation and conveyed to a separate family that would amount to a material change in the use of the whole unit.[60] The view that Lord Denning had decided that division of the planning unit automatically results in a material change in use was rejected in *Winton v Secretary of State for the Environment*[61] by Woolf J who thought it would be surprising that division of the planning unit would amount to development if there were no planning consequences: whether division of the planning unit has the effect of amounting to a material change in use, said his Lordship, is a question of fact and degree.[62] *Wakelin* was recently considered in *Pope v Secretary of State for the Environment*.[63] There, a large house had been purchased in 1981. Following renovations to a boiler house the owner moved into the boiler house for a period until renovations to the main house were carried out. Once these were completed the owner moved into the main house and let the boiler house to tenants. The planning authority issued enforcement proceedings alleging an unauthorised change of use. The court held following *Burdle v Secretary of State for the Environment*[64] that the whole of the unit was the planning unit, whose use was as one dwelling, so that there was no change in use when the family moved from one building in the planning unit to another. When, however, the boiler house was rented to tenants as a separate dwelling a change occurred.[65]

The second question, whether the construction of a new building inevitably results in the creation of a new planning unit was considered in *Jennings Motors Ltd v Secretary of State for the Environment*.[66] The Court of Appeal rejected the view that a new planning unit is automatically created when a new building is constructed, this being a question of fact and degree in each case.[67] Lord Denning MR preferred to regard the matter not as one of the coming into being of a new planning unit, but as the opening of a new chapter in the planning history, which takes place when

---

57 *Kwik Save Discount Group Ltd v Secretary of State for Wales* (1975) 37 P & CR 170, 184 *per* Lord Widgery CJ. For the decision on appeal see (1980) 42 P & CR 166.
58 Purdue *et al*, *Planning Law and Procedure* London: Butterworths 1989, p. 100.
59 (1983) 46 P & CR 214.
60 Ibid., 217. Browne LJ agreed that a material change had occurred in the case itself, but left open the question whether the creation of a new planning unit would *always* amount to a material change in use: at 220.
61 (1983) 46 P & CR 205. 62 Ibid., 211.
63 [1991] EGCS 112. 64 [1972] 3 All ER 240.
65 See also *Uttlesford DC v Secretary of State for the Environment* [1992] JPL 171.
66 [1982] 1 All ER 471. 67 See ibid., 476 *per* Lord Denning MR; 478 *per* Oliver LJ.

there is so radical a change in the nature of the buildings on the site or the uses to which they are put that it can be looked on as a fresh start altogether in the character of the site.[68] Oliver LJ thought the difference in the two expressions, a new planning unit and a change in the planning history, was largely semantic, preferring to retain the former which was hallowed by long usage.[69]

(c) Primary and ancillary uses

Planning control is concerned with the *primary* use of land, and not with uses which are considered ancillary to the primary use. For example, a department store may have offices or a factory may have offices and laboratories and other uses which are ancillary to the primary use as a factory.[70] A primary use carries with it the right to carry on ancillary uses which may vary in duration and intensity while not amounting to development. Put simply, if the primary use of the land is unchanged, there has been no material change in use. If, however, the primary use of the land disappears, the uses ancillary to that primary use disappear also *ex hypothesi*. While the level of the ancillary use may fluctuate and new ancillary uses come and go, the intensification of the ancillary use as discussed above may be development. So, if one room in a dwelling house which is used as a consulting room were to become used substantially more frequently this might be held to amount to development. The use could be said no longer to be merely ancillary.

(d) Seasonal use

Where land is used for one purpose for a period of the year and then for another purpose during another period of the year, is there a material change in the use of the land each time the use is changed? For example, land may be used in the summer months as a caravan site while lying vacant over the winter. Again, a shopkeeper in a seaside town may put stalls on the forecourt of the shop to sell goods during the summer, while leaving it empty over the winter. In such cases the land has two uses, so that the change from one use to the other does not constitute development.[71] In the words of Diplock LJ: 'Provided that each activity is recurrent and accounts for a substantial part of the total amount of activity taking place on the land during the appropriate period to be taken for determining what use is made of the land, the natural answer to the question, "what use is made of the land?" is, in my view, "it is used for the two activities".'[72]

---

68 Ibid., 476.   69 Ibid., 480.
70 See *Trio Thames Ltd v Secretary of State for the Environment* [1984] JPL 183 per Forbes J.
71 *Webber v Minister of Housing and Local Government* [1967] 3 All ER 981.
72 Ibid., 985.

2 Acts which are expressly 'development'

Art. 11(3) lists a number of acts which expressly involve a material change in the use of land.

(1) Subdivision of dwelling house

First, the use as two or more separate dwelling houses of any building previously used as a single dwelling house involves a material change in the use of the building and each part which is so used (Art. 11(3)(a)). 'Dwelling house' is not defined in the Order.[73] Whether a house is a separate dwelling has been frequently considered for the purposes of Rent Acts,[74] but in *Ealing BC v Ryan*[75] Ashworth J left the question open as to whether the principles of the cases on the Rent Acts could be relevant for purposes of the Planning Acts. An earlier dictum of Lord Parker CJ in *Birmingham Corp. v Secretary of State for the Environment and Habib Ullah*[76] suggested that they were not. In *Ealing BC v Ryan* it had been suggested that the issue whether a building was being used as separate dwelling houses could be crystallised in the form of a question as to whether the people living in it were living separately or living together: in the former case the dwellings must be separate. Ashworth J rejected this submission, saying that a house may well be occupied by two or more persons to all intents and purposes living separately, without the house being thereby used as separate dwellings.[77] Multiple occupation itself is therefore not enough: before the subsection can apply there must be separate dwelling houses. His Lordship went on to suggest that factors which might be relevant in determining whether separate dwelling houses exist are the existence or absence of any form of physical reconstruction, and the extent to which the alleged separate dwellings can be regarded as separate in the sense of being self-contained and independent of other parts of the same property.[78] Each case depends on its own facts.[79]

(2) Deposit of waste on land

The second case which is expressly declared by Art. 11(3) to involve a material change in use is the deposit of refuse or waste material on land. This involves a material change in the use of the land, notwithstanding that the land is comprised in a site already used for that purpose, if either

---

73 See however *Gravesham BC v Secretary of State for the Environment* (1984) 47 P & CR 142 for the meaning of the term under the GDO. McCullough J considered that whether a building is a dwelling house is a question of fact in each case (at 146). A distinctive characteristic of a dwelling house in his Lordship's view is its ability to afford those who use it the facilities required for day to day private domestic existence.
74 See now Rent (NI) Order 1978, Art. 3(1).   75 [1965] 1 All ER 137.
76 [1963] 3 All ER 668, 674.   77 [1965] 1 All ER 137, 140.
78 Ibid.
79 Ibid. For a recent example see *Worthing BC v Secretary of State for the Environment* [1991] EGCS 113.

The Meaning of 'Development' 75

the superficial area of the deposit is thereby extended, or the height of the deposit is thereby extended and exceeds the level of the land adjoining the site (Art. 11(3)(b)).[80]

(3) Advertisements

The final activity expressly involving a material change in use relates to the display of advertisements. A use for the display of advertisements of any external part of a building which is not normally used for that purpose is treated as involving a material change in the use of that part of the building (Art. 11(3)(c)).[81]

3 Acts which are expressly not 'development'

Art. 11(2) provides a number of uses which are not 'development' for the purposes of the Order:

(1) Maintenance of interior

The carrying out of works of maintenance, improvement or other alteration of any building, being works which affect only the interior of the building or which do not materially affect the external appearance of the building is not development. In *Hewlett v Secretary of State for the Environment*[82] it was argued that the jacking up of the roof to allow repairs to the walls followed by repairs to the roof itself was maintenance or improvement of the original building rather than, as the Secretary of State contended, the construction of a new building. The court held, however, that whether there had resulted a new building was a question of fact and degree in each case. It would be possible, though very rarely the case, for rebuilding by stages to be held otherwise than a new building. Sir John Donaldson MR considered it 'very difficult to think how you can rebuild by stages in such a way as to produce what is in effect a new building and still be able to maintain that it was merely the old building in an improved form unless, as was pointed out in argument, there is a very substantial separation between the stages—a century or so was suggested.'[83]

(2) Maintenance of services

There is no development where a district council or statutory undertakers[84] carry out any works for the purpose of inspecting, repairing or renewing

---

80 Note that the subsection applies in relation to the deposit of refuse or waste materials during the course of mining operations: Art. 112(2)(a).
81 For the display of advertisements see Chapter 23.
82 (1985) 273 EG 401.
83 See now also *Hughes v Secretary of State for the Environment* [1994] EGCS 86.
84 For definition see Art. 2(2).

any mains, pipes, cables or other apparatus, including the breaking open of any street on other land for that purpose (Art. 11(2)(b)).

(3) Incidental uses

The use of any buildings or other land within the curtilage of a dwelling house[85] for any purpose incidental to the enjoyment of the dwelling house as such is not development. In *Prosser* v *Sharp*[86] there was a wooden hut in which the owner had installed water and gas, and which he used for preparation of food and recreational purposes, but not for sleeping as the family slept in a caravan stationed alongside. Enforcement proceedings for removal of the caravan were brought and one of the owner's defences was that the caravan was ancillary to a dwelling house under the equivalent provision in the English legislation. The court held however that no reasonable magistrates' court could have held the hut to be a dwelling house, and so the use of the caravan was not ancillary to a dwelling house. In *Emin* v *Secretary of State for the Environment*[87] it was said that in order for a use to be incidental to enjoyment of a dwelling house, the use had to be subordinate to enjoyment of the dwelling itself. The nature and scale of the proposed activities had to be considered; the physical scale of the buildings could be relevant in that it might provide some indicia as to the nature and scale of the activities. This was developed in *Wallington* v *Secretary of State for the Environment*[88] where the court refused to interfere with the decision of an inspector who had held that keeping forty four dogs at a house was not use incidental to the use of a dwelling house as such. Farquharson LJ said that in answering whether the use comes within Art. 11(2)(c) the following matters are relevant: (1) the situation of the dwelling house. Different considerations may apply depending on whether the house is in the country or in the centre of town. (2) The size of the dwelling house in the context of the use which is said to be incidental to its enjoyment. (3) The nature and scale of the activity which is said to be incidental to the enjoyment of the dwelling house as such. The more dominant the activity the less likely it is to be described as incidental. (4) The disposition and character of the owner. While the occupier's view of whether the activity is incidental or not is not conclusive it is something to which regard should be had.[89]

(4) Use for agriculture and forestry

The use of any land for the purposes of agriculture[90] or forestry and the use for any of those purposes of any building occupied together with

---

85 For the meaning of 'curtilage' see Chapter 17.
87 (1989) 58 P & CR 416.
89 Ibid., 161.
86 (1985) 274 EG 1249.
88 (1991) 62 P & CR 150.
90 For definition see Art. 2(2).

land so used does not constitute development (Art. 11(2)(d)). In *North Warwickshire BC v Secretary of State for the Environment*[91] a number of buildings on a farm were used for fox farming. Enforcement proceedings were brought in which the owner relied on the defence that the activities were not development. One point arose as to whether use of a *building* for agriculture *without use of land* came within the equivalent of Art. 11(2)(d). The court held that use of a building for agriculture was 'use of any land' as 'land' included buildings.[92] There was no requirement that in the case of buildings separate land should also be occupied.

(5) The Use Classes Order

Art. 11(2)(e) of the 1991 Order provides that in the case of buildings or land which are used for a purpose of any class specified in an order made by the Department for the purposes of Art. 11, the use of the buildings or other land or, subject to the provisions of the order, of any part thereof for any other purpose of the same class is not development. The present order is the Planning (Use Classes) Order (NI) 1989[93] (UCO) made under the equivalent provisions in the 1972 Order.

The scheme of the UCO is to list various uses of land in classes thus e.g. Class 1 contains seven use descriptions. The Order provides that the change of use from one of those uses to another is not development, so long as the former and latter uses are in the same class. So the change of use from a post office to a travel agency is not development because both uses are within the same class in the Order. But change of use from a post office to an office is development, as the uses are in different classes in the Order (Classes 1 and 3 respectively). Thus, the Order provides an easy way to ascertain whether a change of use amounts to development: if the former and latter uses are in the same class, there is no development (UCO, Art. 3(1)). This is so even if the change would otherwise be material.[94] Technically, the converse is not true: merely because the former and latter uses are in different classes does not automatically mean that the change amounts to development, though this must be a relevant and persuasive consideration.[95]

Two points must be made about the UCO. First, the Order is not comprehensive: certain uses are expressly stated to be outside the Order. Similarly Art. 3(5) expressly excludes from any class use (1) as an amusement arcade or centre or funfair; (2) as a betting office; (3) for the

---

91 (1985) 50 P & CR 47.
92 See definition in Art. 2(2).
93 Now amended by the Planning (Use Classes) (Amendment) (NI) Order 1993 and Planning (Use Classes)(Amendment No 2) (NI) Order 1993.
94 See *Carpet Decor (Guildford) Ltd v Secretary of State for the Environment* (1982) 261 EG 56; *Brooks and Burton Ltd v Secretary of State for the Environment* [1978] 1 All ER 733.
95 Purdue *et al, op. cit.*, p. 126.

purposes of a funeral undertaker; (4) as a hotel; (5) for the sale of fuel for motor vehicles; (6) for the sale or display for sale of motor vehicles; (7) for a taxi business or business for the hire of motor vehicles; (8) for the sale of food or drink for consumption on the premises or of hot food for consumption off the premises; (9) as a scrapyard, or as a yard for the storage or distribution of minerals or the breaking of motor vehicles; (10) for or in connection with public worship or religious instruction; and (11) for any work required to be registered under s.9 of the Alkali etc. Works Regulations Act 1906.[96] Where, therefore, the use of the land (either the former or the latter use) is one of the above, the UCO is of no assistance in determining whether development has taken place. Again, apart from these specified exclusions, a particular use of land may not be within the Order at all. The variety of uses to which land may be put is such that the particular use may not be listed in any of the classes in the Order. Again, the consequence is that the Order will be of no assistance in determining whether a change to or from that use is material.

The second point concerns uses falling within more than one class in the Order. Art. 3(3) of the Order provides that any use which is ordinarily incidental to a use which is specified in one of the classes in the Order does not cease to be incidental merely because it is specified in the Order in its own right as a separate use.[97]

The approach to the Order was explained in *Forkhurst v Secretary of State for the Environment*[98] There, Hodgson J suggested the following steps to ascertain whether the Order applies:

(1) arrive at an accurate description of the actual use of the property;
(2) decide whether that use fits into one of the classes;
(3) decide whether the description includes activities which fall into more than one class;
(4) decide whether, if the activities do fall into more than one class, one is incidental to the other.

In the same case his Lordship said that an activity either comes within a use specified in the UCO or it does not: there is no scope for measurement in terms of fact and degree. This view, however, has been criticised and the correct position said to be that the question of whether an activity comes within a class in the Order *is* a question of fact and degree, which should not be upset by the courts unless it is totally unreasonable.[99]

---

96 See Planning (Use Classes) (Amendment No. 2) Order (NI) 1993.
97 See *Emma Hotels Ltd v Secretary of State for the Environment* (1980) 41 P & CR 255.
98 (1982) 46 P & CR 89.
99 Purdue *et al, op. cit.,* p. 129.

4 Determination whether acts amount to development or not

It will be clear from the above that the question of whether the operations intended, or the change of use contemplated, amount to development may be difficult to answer. The consequences of arriving at the wrong decision may be serious. If, for example, a landowner decides that his change of use is not a material change of use and the Department takes a different view, the owner may be faced with enforcement proceedings resulting in loss. Fortunately, Art. 41 of the 1991 Order provides a solution. The Article provides that anyone proposing to carry out operations on land or to make any change in the use of land may apply to the Department to have it determined whether the carrying out of the operations or the making of the change in use would constitute or involve development of the land (Art. 41(1)(a)), and if so, whether an application for planning permission is needed, having regard to the provisions of the General Development Order (GDO) and any enterprize zone scheme or simplified planning zone scheme (Art. 41(1)(b)).[100]

In making a determination under Art. 41 the Department does not have jurisdiction to determine whether a planning permission already granted has been validly granted,[101] and in the case of an application to determine whether a proposed change of use is development or requires planning permission the existence of any planning permission is irrelevant, as what the Department is required to do is compare the proposed use with the *actual* use, not the use permitted by planning permission.[102] Where the application relates to operational development, the Department is not obliged to consider a change of use, even though it can perceive that a change is imminent, unless the Department is asked to do so or it becomes necessary to consider the bringing of enforcement proceedings.[103]

Where the Department determines that the proposed operations or change of use does not amount to development or that planning permission is not required, it seems that such determination is equivalent to the granting of planning permission[104] though the determination will not have the effect of annulling any conditions in a previous planning permission or covenants in a previous agreement under Art. 40 of the 1991 Order.[105]

Where such a determination is made, the fact that the applicant later makes an application for planning permission does not automatically

---

100 Note that the question is not whether *in all the circumstances* planning permission is needed, but whether permission is needed *having regard to the provisions of the development order etc.*; see Moran v Secretary of State for the Environment [1988] JPL 24, 28 per McCullough J.
101 Edgewarebury Investments Ltd v Minister of Housing and Local Government [1963] 1 All ER 124.
102 Moran v Secretary of State for the Environment [1988] JPL 24.
103 In re Thompson's application [1985] NI 170, 175 per Carswell J.
104 See Wells v Minister of Housing and Local Government [1967] 2 All ER 1041; English Speaking Union of the Commonwealth v Westminster CC (1973) 26 P & CR 575; R v Tunbridge Wells BC, ex p Blue Boys Development Ltd (1990) 59 P & CR 315.
105 R v Tunbridge Wells BC, ex p Blue Boys Development Ltd (1990) 59 P & CR 315.

mean that he has abandoned his right to rely on the determination.[106] An appeal against a determination under Art. 41 lies to the Planning Appeals Commission (Art. 32 as applied by Art. 41(2)) but judicial review of the Department's decision is also possible in appropriate circumstances.[107]

As far as applications for determinations under Art. 41 are concerned, the Order provides that various provisions of the Order regarding applications for planning permission apply to applications under Art. 41(2).[108] It is also provided that the Department may treat an application for planning permission as an application under Art. 41 where it appears to the Department that the activities for which permission is sought do not amount to development or that an application for planning permission is not required (Art. 41(3)).

The form and content of applications under Art. 41 are specified in the GDO. The application must be in writing and contain a description of the operations or change of use proposed and be accompanied by plans or drawings sufficient to identify the land and the nature of the operations. Where the application relates to a change of use, a full description of the proposed use must be given and also the present use of the land, or if the land is unused, its last use (GDO, Art. 10(1)).

The question arises as to the effect of an informal application and a determination made pursuant to it. This has usually arisen and been dealt with along with a similar problem, namely whether the planning authority is bound by statements made in response to requests for information from would-be developers. The courts have dealt with the questions in one of two ways.

(1) *Waiver of procedural requirements*

The courts have on occasion held that a request made to the planning authority for information whether proposed activities require planning permission is an application under Art. 41, and the response of the authority pursuant to the request a determination under Art. 41, despite the fact that the request does not comply with the formalities for an application under the Article. In *Wells v Minister of Housing and Local Government*[109] Lord Denning MR took the law to be that a defect in procedure could be cured and an irregularity could be waived, so as to render valid that which would otherwise be invalid.[110] Thus, the fact that the owners in that case had made no application at all under the equivalent provision to Art. 41[111] did not prevent the determination by the planning authority

---

106 *Department of the Environment for Northern Ireland v Watson (Suede and Leather Cleaners) Ltd* [1979] 6 NIJB.
107 *In re Thompson's application* [1985] NI 170.
108 The provisions applied are Arts 13, 20(1), 25(1), 32 and 33.
109 [1967] 2 All ER 1041.   110 Ibid., 1044.
111 They had made an application for planning permission. See now Art. 41(3).

that permission was not required from being a determination under the relevant provision. The authority had waived any formal application.[112] In *Western Fish Products Ltd v Penwith DC*,[113] however, an attempt was made to limit the decision in *Wells* to cases where an application for planning permission had been made, in the absence of which correspondence between the would-be developer and the planning authority could not constitute an application and determination under Art. 41.[114] *Wells* and *Western Fish* were considered by Carswell J in *In re Thompson's application*.[115] For the purposes of an application for a certificate of registration under the Registration of Clubs Act (NI) 1967 someone speaking on behalf of a sports club telephoned the Department requesting that a letter be sent stating that 'an unlicensed club does not require a change of use application under the Planning Order to become a licensed club.' In response the Department replied that 'there is no material change in use from an unlicensed club to a licensed club and planning approval is therefore not required.' A local resident sought judicial review of the ruling on the ground that the Department had been in error. In granting the relief sought the court held that the Department had waived the procedural requirement that an application under Art. 30 of the 1972 Order had to be in writing.[116] *Western Fish* was distinguished on the ground that the court there did not have to consider a clear and unequivocal request for a determination, made by telephone and not in writing, and a considered response prepared by the Divisional Planning Officer and sent out in writing.[117] Carswell J considered that what the Court of Appeal had decided in *Western Fish* was that it would not regard an informal meeting as constituting a sufficient application for a determination and with that he agreed.[118]

(2) Estoppel

As an alternative to holding the planning authority bound by statements made by it on the ground that such statements constitute determinations under Art. 41, the authority waiving any procedural requirements, some of the authorities have attempted to apply the doctrine of estoppel

---

112 [1967] 2 All ER 1041, 1045.
113 [1981] 2 All ER 204.
114 This involved criticism of the judgment of Sachs LJ in *Lever (Finance) Ltd v Westminster Corp*. [1970] 3 All ER 496.
115 [1985] NI 170.
116 This requirement no longer exists under Art. 41 of the 1991 Order, but an application must comply with the requirements of the GDO: Art. 20(1) as applied by Art. 41(2). The reasoning of Carswell J is equally applicable to the situation under Art. 41.
117 [1985] NI 170, 177.
118 Ibid. See also *Department of the Environment for Northern Ireland v Watson (Suede and Leather Cleaners) Ltd* [1979] 6 NIJB where again a letter from the Department was held to be a determination despite the absence of an application for planning permission.

against the authority. The authority is estopped in other words, where it informs the developer that what he intends to do is not development, from later denying the validity of that statement and taking enforcement action where the development has been carried out. The applicability of the doctrine of estoppel against the planning authority has been in doubt for some years. After an initial denial that the doctrine could apply against the planning authority on the basis that the doctrine cannot be raised to hinder the exercise of a statutory discretion of a public authority,[119] the view was put forward that a planning officer acting within the scope of his ostensible authority could bind the authority by any representation he made in the same way as he could bind a private concern.[120] However, in *Western Fish Products Ltd v Penwith DC*[121] Megaw LJ restated the view that an estoppel cannot be raised to prevent the exercise of a statutory discretion or to prevent or excuse the performance of a statutory duty,[122] a principle to which there were only two exceptions. The first is where the planning authority delegates to its officers powers to determine specific questions, such as applications under Art. 41. In such cases any decision by an officer cannot be revoked.[123] The second exception is where the authority waives a procedural requirement relating to any application made to it for the exercise of its statutory powers. In such cases the authority may be estopped from relying on lack of formality.[124] The court went on to say that before any estoppel could arise against the planning authority there had to be some evidence justifying the person who is dealing with the authority thinking that what the officer said would bind the authority[125] and that holding an office would not suffice.[126] The statement of the law in *Western Fish* was accepted as correct by Gibson LJ in *R Bell & Co. (Estates) Ltd v Department of the Environment for Northern Ireland*[127] though in the same case Jones LJ said that the line between the principles in *Lever (Finance)* and *Western Fish* is very fine. As already noted, *Western Fish* was distinguished by Carswell J in *In re Thompson's application*.[128]

---

119 *Southend-on-sea Corp. v Hodgson (Wickford) Ltd* [1961] 2 All ER 46.
120 *Lever (Finance) Ltd v Westminster Corp.* [1970] 3 All ER 496, 500 *per* Lord Denning MR, following his own decision in *Wells v Minister of Housing and Local Government* [1967] 2 All ER 1041. See also *Norfolk CC v Secretary of State for the Environment* [1973] 3 All ER 673; *Costain Homes Ltd v Secretary of State for the Environment* (1989) 57 P & CR 416; and *Calder Gravel Ltd v Kirklees* MBC (1990) 60 P & CR 322.
121 [1981] 2 All ER 204. For a recent discussion see *East Lindsey DC v Secretary of State for the Environment* [1994] EGCS 119.
122 Ibid., 219.   123 Ibid., 219.
124 Ibid., 221.   125 Ibid., 220.
126 Ibid.   127 [1982] NI 322.
128 For recent instances of the application of the principles involved see *Graham v Secretary of State for the Environment* [1993] JPL 353 and *Camden LBC v Secretary of State for the Environment* (1993) 67 P & CR 59 (CA upholding decision of inspector that a planning officer's letter, saying that variations to a planning application were minor and did not require separate permission, was binding on the planning authority).

CHAPTER TEN

Planning Permission

As has been noted already, planning permission is required for the carrying out of any development of land (1991 Order, Art. 12).[1]

(1) **How permission is obtained**

There are several ways under the 1991 Order by which planning permission may be granted:

(a) On an application to the Department

The best known means of obtaining planning permission is following an application for that purpose to the Department (see Arts 13(2)(b), 20 and 25). Such applications are considered in the next chapter.

(b) On the adoption of a simplified planning zone

Art. 14(2) of the 1991 Order provides that the adoption of a simplified planning zone scheme[2] has effect (save in cases to which the Planning (Assessment of Environmental Effects) Regulations (NI) 1989 apply)[3] to grant in relation to the zone, or any part of it specified in the scheme, planning permission for development specified in the scheme or for development of any class so specified. Planning permission under a simplified planning zone scheme may be unconditional or subject to such conditions, limitations or exceptions as may be specified in the scheme (Art. 14(3)). Such conditions or limitations may include conditions or limitations in respect of all development permitted by the scheme or in respect of particular descriptions of development so permitted (Art. 15(1)(a)), and conditions or limitations requiring the consent, agreement or approval of the Department in relation to particular descriptions of

---

1 The opening words of the Article are 'Subject to this Order . . .' There appear, however, to be no provisions in the Order allowing activities which constitute development to be carried out without planning permission. This contrasts with the situation in England and Wales under the Town and Country Planning Act 1990, where certain changes in use may be carried out without planning permission, notably the resumption of the normal use of land following a limited planning permission (1990 Act, s. 57(2)); following development permitted by a development order subject to limitations (s. 57(3)); or following an enforcement notice (s. 57(4)).
2 See generally Chapter 5.
3 See Planning (Simplified Planning Zones) (Excluded Development) Order (NI) 1994.

development (Art. 15(1)(b)). Different conditions or limitations may be specified for different cases or different classes of case (Art. 15(1)).

(c) On the designation of an enterprize zone

An order designating an enterprize zone[4] under the Enterprize Zones (NI) Order 1981 grants planning permission on the effective date for development specified in the scheme or for development of any class so specified (1991 Order, Art. 19(1)). The adoption of a modified scheme under Art. 4 of the 1981 Order modifies on the effective date the granting of planning permission for development specified in the modified scheme or for development of any class so specified (1991 Order, Art. 19). Such planning permission may be subject to conditions or limitations or may be unconditional (Art. 19(3)). The Department has power to direct that such permission shall not apply to a specified development, a specified class of development, or a specified class of development in a specified area within the enterprize zone (Art. 19(4)). If the scheme or modified scheme specifies matters in relation to any development it permits which will require approval by the Department, the permission has effect accordingly (Art. 19(5)).

If the area ceases to be an enterprize zone, planning permission ceases to have effect save where the development authorised by it has begun (Art. 19(9)) and, where development has begun, modifications to a scheme do not affect the permission (Art. 19(8)). Finally, the provisions as to planning permission being granted by an order designating an enterprize zone do not preclude the grant of permission by a development order or on an application to the Department (Art. 19(7)).

(d) By the advertisements regulations

Where the display of advertisements in accordance with regulations made under the Order[5] involves development (see also Art. 11(4)), planning permission for that development is deemed to be granted by Art. 67(5) of the 1991 Order and no application for permission is needed.

(e) By a development order

Art. 13(1) of the 1991 Order requires the Department to make an order to provide for the granting of planning permission. Such an order is called a development order. A development order may either provide for the granting of planning permission by the Department on an application made to it (Art. 13(2)(b)), or the development order may itself grant planning permission for the types of development specified in the order (Art. 13(1)(a)). It is this latter aspect which will be considered here.[6] The present

---

4 See generally Chapter 5.
5 See Planning (Control of Advertisements) Regulations (NI) 1992, and Chapter 20.
6 The provisions of the relevant development order as to the grant of planning permission by the Department on an application are considered in the next chapter.

development order is the Planning (General Development) Order (NI) 1993, (GDO). The effect of the GDO is to grant planning permission for the various types of development specified in the Order, without the need for an application to the Department (GDO, Art. 3(1)). The types of development for which permission exists by reason of the GDO are set out in Appendix B.

The permission granted by the GDO is subject to any conditions or limitations also specified (GDO, Art. 3(2)). The GDO does not operate to permit development contrary to a condition in any planning permission granted otherwise than by the GDO (Art. 3(2)).[7]

The operation of the GDO is subject however to the provisions of Art. 4, which provides that if the Department is satisfied, after consultation with the appropriate district council, that it is expedient that development of any of the classes specified in the GDO[8] should not be carried out in a particular area, or should not be carried out without specific planning permission being granted on an application to the Department, it may direct that the permission granted by the GDO shall not apply to all or any development in a particular area specified in the direction or to any particular development specified in the direction (GDO, Art. 4(1)).[9] Such a direction comes into force when notice of it has been served on the occupier of the land affected (GDO, Art. 5(1)).[10] Where in the case of a direction in respect of development in a particular area the Department considers individual service is impracticable, notice of the direction must be published in a local newspaper and, in such a case the direction comes into force on the date the notice is published (GDO, Art. 5(4)).

(2) Outline planning permission and approval of reserved matters

Where planning permission is sought for the erection of a building, it is possible for permission to be applied for and granted by the Department in two stages, outline planning permission and approval of reserved matters (GDO, Art. 8(1)). 'Outline planning permission' means planning permission for the erection of a building which is granted subject to a

---

[7] Thus, for example, if planning permission had been granted for a house with a condition that no garage should be constructed except with the consent of the Department, the owner would have to seek such consent despite the garage being permitted by the GDO.

[8] Except Part 16: GDO, Art. 4(1).

[9] No direction has effect in relation to the carrying out of any development specified in the GDO in case of emergency, or (unless expressly stated) to the carrying out of certain developments under private Acts or Orders or by telecommunications code system operators or by statutory undertakers: GDO, Art. 4(2) & (3). Nor can a direction make unlawful development which has already been carried out: *Cole v Somerset CC* [1956] 3 All ER 531. But see also *South Bucks DC v Secretary of State for the Environment* [1989] JPL 351.

[10] Notice must also be served on the owner: ibid.

condition (in addition to any other conditions which may be imposed) requiring subsequent approval to be obtained from the Department with respect to one or more reserved matters (GDO, Art. 2).[11] 'Reserved matters' are matters in respect of which details have not been given in the application for outline permission, and which concern the siting, design or external appearance of the building or the means of access to the building, or the landscaping of the site in respect of which the application was made (GDO, Art. 2). The scheme of outline planning permission and approval of reserved matters is therefore essentially one of approval in principle followed by approval of the details of the proposed development. The reasons why permission may be sought in this way and the requirements for applications for outline permission and approval of reserved matters are considered in the next chapter.

(3) Planning permission granted for a limited period

We will see later[12] that planning permission may be granted subject to conditions. Art. 27(1)(b) of the 1991 Order empowers the Department to grant permission subject to a condition requiring the removal of any buildings or works authorised by the permission or the discontinuance of any use authorised by the permission at the end of a specified period, and the carrying out of works required for the reinstatement of land at the end of that period. Such a permission is known as planning permission granted for a limited period (Art. 27(2)).

(4) When permission is granted

The date on which planning permission is granted is of significance as it provides the starting point for the period within which the development authorised by the permission must begin (see 1991 Order, Arts 34 and 35). There are two possible dates when permission may be said to be granted: the date on which the Department decides to grant permission, or the date on which it notifies that decision.[13] It seems that the latter is the correct date, and it is the notification which constitutes the grant of permission.[14] To take the earlier date would work an injustice against the

---

11 See also the definition in the 1991 Order, Art. 35(1) for the purposes of Arts 34 and 35 of that Order.
12 Chapter 13.
13 Contrast the provisions of Arts 34 and 35 with those of Art. 32, providing that an appeal must be made within six months from *notification* of the Department's decision.
14 R v Yeovil Corp., ex p Trustees of Elim Pentecostal Church (1971) 23 P & CR 39; Slough Estates Ltd v Slough BC (No 2) [1969] 2 All ER 988, 991 per Lord Denning MR (on appeal see [1970] 2 All ER 216); R v West Oxfordshire DC, ex p Pearce Homes Ltd [1986] JPL 523. See, however, also *Griffiths v Secretary of State for the Environment* [1983] 1 All ER 439. Notification cannot grant planning permission where the notification is made in error, and what should have been sent to the applicant is a notice of refusal of permission:

applicant, as time would be running against him for the purposes of Arts 34 and 35 when he did not know what the decision of the Department was.[15] The date of notification, however, may be interpreted as the date on which the decision notice is issued by the Department, or the date on which it is received by the applicant. It has been held in the Republic that the date on which the notice is given is the date on which it is *received* by the applicant, rather than the date on which it is sent by the planning authority, on the basis that the applicant should not be prejudiced if, for example, the decision notice goes astray in the post, this being a matter for which the planning authority should be regarded as responsible if it chooses this means of communicating the decision to the applicant.[16] Similar considerations however did not prevent the court in *Griffiths v Secretary of State for the Environment*[17] from holding that the date when action was taken by the Secretary of State on an appeal against refusal of permission was the date on which the decision letter was signed, rather than the date on which it was received by the appellant.

Until notification of the decision the Department can change its mind about the application.[18]

(5) Construction of planning permission

(a) Extrinsic evidence

In construing a will or a contract the court is required to put itself in the shoes of the testator or the parties by admitting in evidence all relevant facts known at the time by the testator or by both parties.[19] This rule allowing for the admission of extrinsic evidence does not in general apply to the construction of a planning permission, as planning permission may affect third parties e.g. purchasers of the land from the original applicant, who ought not to be subject to the risk of the apparent meaning of the permission being altered by the introduction of such evidence.[20] If, however, the permission incorporates any other document e.g. the application for permission or plans or drawings by reference, it is permissible to look at that document to construe the permission.[21] In *McClurg and Spiller v*

Norfolk CC v Secretary of State for the Environment [1973] 3 All ER 673. See also AG ex rel Co-Operative Retail Services Ltd v Taff-Ely BC (1982) 42 P & CR 1.
15 Co-Operative Retail Services Ltd v Taff-Ely BC (1979) 38 P & CR 156, 172 per Sir Douglas Frank QC, (on appeal see (1980) 39 P & CR 223 and (1982) 42 P & CR 1).
16 Freeney v Bray UDC [1982] 2 ILRM 29, not following The State (Murphy) v Dublin CC [1970] IR 253.
17 [1983] 1 All ER 439.
18 R v Yeovil Corp., ex p Trustees of Elim Pentecostal Church (1971) 23 P & CR 39; R v West Oxfordshire DC, ex p Pearce Homes Ltd [1986] JPL 523.
19 Slough Estates Ltd v Slough BC (No 2) [1970] 2 All ER 216, 218 per Lord Reid.
20 Ibid.
21 McClurg and Spiller v Department of the Environment for Northern Ireland [1990] 2 NIJB 68, following Wilson v West Sussex CC [1963] 1 All ER 751. Also Harris v Belfast Education and Library Board [1974] NIJB (Nov); see also Slough Estates Ltd v Slough BC (no. 2) [1970] 2

Department of the Environment for Northern Ireland[22] an application was made for planning permission for twenty apartments. The applicants were advised that the application was unacceptable but that further consideration would be given to a revised proposal omitting two of the apartments. Accordingly the applicants submitted revised drawings and a covering letter reducing the proposed development to eighteen apartments. The application was stored in the Department's computer, but the amendment was not. The application as amended was considered and planning permission was subsequently granted, in which the description of the proposal was 'Proposed development of twenty no apartments.' The applicants applied to the court for a declaration that they had planning permission for twenty apartments. Campbell J pointed out that while the applicants would have been aware of the letter amending the proposal a purchaser could only have become aware of it had he examined the planning register, and there was no evidence to show that he would have found the amendment in the register.[23] Accordingly the applicants were entitled to the declaration sought.[24]

(b) Single or multiple permission

Where planning permission is granted for any development, is it to be construed as meaning that what is permitted is *the whole* of the development authorised by the permission, or that *every stage* of that development is permitted? The question arises where the developer does not complete the development in the way authorised by the permission. For example, in *Copeland BC v Secretary of State for the Environment*[25] planning permission had been granted for construction of a house with a specified type of roof tile. The house was built with a different type of tile. The court held that the whole development was unauthorised. However in *Lucas (F) & Sons Ltd v Dorking and Horley RDC*[26] the court held that planning permission which had been granted for twenty eight houses was not to be regarded as permission to develop the land as a whole but as permission

---

All ER 216, 222 *per* Lord Pearson. It has been suggested that as the planning application is a public document open to inspection it is proper to look at the application for guidance even if it is not expressly incorporated, at least if there are doubts as to the meaning and validity of the permission: Purdue *et al*, *Planning Law and Procedure*, London: Butterworths (1989), p. 271. Contrast the earlier dictum of Lord Denning MR that the application cannot be looked at in *Miller-Mead v Minister of Housing and Local Government* [1963] 1 All ER 359, 463. See also Graham, 'The interpretation of planning permissions and a matter of principle' [1991] JPL 104.

22 [1990] 2 NIJB 68.
23 Indeed the evidence pointed the other way: a property certificate issued by the Department recording the planning history referred to the proposed development of twenty apartments and the grant of permission.
24 See also *R v Secretary of State for the Environment ex p Slough BC* [1994] EGCS 67.
25 (1976) 31 P & CR 403.
26 (1964) 17 P & CR 111.

for any of the development authorised in it. *Lucas* has however been described as 'rather exceptional'.[27]

(c) *Construction of buildings*

Where the planning permission is for the erection of a building, then, in the absence of any purpose specified in the permission, the permission is to be construed as including permission to use the building for the purpose for which it is designed (1991 Order, Art. 30(2)).

(6) **Extent of planning permission**

A planning permission not only covers the work specified in the approved plans, but it extends also to authorise any immaterial variation therein.[28] What is material is a matter for the Department.[29]

(7) **Duration of planning permission**

Except as provided in the permission to the contrary, planning permission enures for the benefit of the land and of all persons for the time being having an estate therein (1991 Order, Art. 30(1)). The development authorised by the permission must be commenced within the time specified in Arts 34 or 35.[30] Art. 34 provides that every planning permission[31] is granted subject to the condition that the development to which it relates must be begun within five years of the date on which permission is granted,[32] or such other period, whether longer or shorter, as the Department considers appropriate (Art. 34(1)).[33] In the case of outline planning permission[34] the development must be begun by the expiration of five years from the date of the grant of the outline permission or the expiration of two years from the final approval of reserved matters, whichever is

---

27 See *Pilkington* v *Secretary of State for the Environment* [1974] 1 All ER 283, 288 *per* Lord Widgery CJ; *Hoveringham Gravels Ltd* v *Chiltern DC* (1978) 35 P & CR 295, 302.
28 *Lever (Finance) Ltd* v *Westminster Corp.* [1970] 3 All ER 496, 500 *per* Lord Denning MR.
29 Ibid.
30 Development commenced and carried out after the relevant date is treated as not authorised by the permission: Art. 36(4)(a).
31 Other than outline planning permission (see Art. 35 and below); planning permission granted by a development order; planning permission granted for a limited period; planning permission granted under Art. 29 (development which has already taken place); planning permission granted by an enterprize zone scheme; or planning permission granted by a simplifed planning zone scheme: Art. 34(3).
32 See above.
33 If the permission contains no express condition, it is implied that the development be commenced within five years: Art. 34(2).
34 I.e. planning permission granted in accordance with the provisions of a development order, conditional on the subsequent approval by the Department of the particulars of the proposed development (reserved matters): Art. 35(1).

the later (Art. 35(2)).[35] Development is 'begun' for the purposes of Arts 34 and 35 on the earliest date on which any of the operations comprised in the development which are specified in Art. 36 begins to be carried out. The specified operations are (1) where the development consists of or includes the erection of a building, any work of construction in the course of the erection of the building; (2) where the development consists of or includes alterations to a building, any work involved in those alterations; (3) where the development consists of or includes a change of use of any building or other land, that change of use; and (4) where the development consists of or includes mining operations, any of those operations (Art. 36(1)). In applying Art. 36, the degree and extent of the work carried out is not relevant: the question is, whether the work is referrable to the planning permission[36] and genuinely done for the purpose of carrying the development out?[37] It seems, however, that work carried out without planning permission or commencing in breach of conditions in a planning permission is not development to which the permission relates and so will not count for the purposes of Arts 34 and 35.[38]

---

35 Approval of reserved matters must be sought within three years of the grant of outline permission: Art. 35(2)(a). An application for approval of reserved matters made after the specified date is treated as not having been made in accordance with the outline permission: Art. 36(4)(b). Reserved matters are finally approved for the purposes of Art. 35(2) when an application for approval is granted, or where there is an appeal, on the date the appeal is determined: Art. 36(2). The Department has power to substitute for the periods specified in Art. 35(2) such other periods as it considers appropriate: Art. 35(4).
36 *Thayer v Secretary of State for the Environment* [1991] EGCS 78. See also *Spackman v Secretary of State for the Environment* [1977] 1 All ER 257 and *South Oxfordshire DC v Secretary of State for the Environment* [1981] 1 All ER 954.
37 *Malvern Hills DC v Secretary of State for the Environment* (1983) 46 P & CR 58. See also *Hillingdon LBC v Secretary of State for the Environment* [1990] EGCS 5 and *Spackman v Secretary of State for the Environment* [1977] 1 All ER 257.
38 See *Etheridge v Secretary of State for the Environment* (1984) 48 P & CR 35, followed in *Oakimber Ltd v Elmbridge BC* [1992] JPL 48 and *R v Elmbridge BC, ex p Health Care Corp. Ltd* [1992] JPL 39. See also *Staffordshire Moorlands DC v Cartwright* [1992] JPL 138 and *Whitley & Sons Ltd v Secretary of State for Wales* [1992] JPL 856. There are however authorities to the contrary: see *Kerrier DC v Secretary of State for the Environment* (1980) 41 P & CR 284; *Clwyd CC v Secretary of State for Wales* [1982] JPL 696. See Martin, 'Keeping your permission alive' [1991] 45 EG 169.

CHAPTER ELEVEN

Applications for Planning Permission

In this chapter we consider the various provisions of the legisation, primary and secondary, relevant to applications to the Department for planning permission. Before doing so, however, it will be convenient to deal with a matter not covered by the legislation, viz. who may make an application for planning permission? The answer appears to be not everyone.[1] Nevertheless, ownership of the land for which permission is sought is not a prerequisite, neither is consent of the owner.[2] It has been said that anybody who genuinely hopes to acquire an interest in the land can apply for permission, thus covering e.g. potential purchasers of the land.[3] While the consent of the owner is not required for someone hoping to acquire an interest in the land to apply for permission, as we will see, the applicant in such a case is obliged to notify the owner of the application.[4]

1 Applications for planning permission

(1) Form and content of applications

Art. 20(1) of the 1991 Order provides that an application for planning permission shall be made in the manner specified in a development order, and shall include such particulars and be verified by such evidence as may be required by a development order or by any directions given by the Department under a development order. The present regulations are contained in the Planning (General Development) Order (NI) 1993 (GDO). The requirements for applications differ according to whether the application is for full permission, outline permission or for approval of reserved matters.

(a) Applications for full permission

Applications for full permission, i.e. applications for planning permission other than applications for outline planning permission or applications

---

1 Hanily v Minister of Local Government and Planning [1952] 1 All ER 1293, 1296 per Parker J, relying on Ayles v Romse and Stockbridge RDC (1944) 108 JP 176.
2 Ibid.
3 Ibid. See also Frescati Estates Ltd v Walker [1975] IR 177 and 184 (application made by someone with no estate in the land or prospect of acquiring one held invalid); The State (Alf-a-Bet Promotions Ltd) v Bundoran UDC (1978) 112 ILTR 9 and Inver Resources Ltd v Limerick Corp. [1987] IR 159.
4 See 1991 Order, Art. 22(1) providing that an applicant must lodge with his application one of the four certificates mentioned in the subsection. The certificate mentioned in

for approval of reserved matters, are required to be made on a form issued by the Department; to include the particulars specified in the form; to be accompanied by a plan which identifies the land to which the application relates and any other plans and drawings and information necessary to describe the development which is the subject of the application, together with six additional copies of the form plan and drawings submitted, except where the Department indicates a lesser number is required (GDO, Art. 7(1)). The Department may, by a direction in writing to the applicant, require such further information as it may specify in the direction to enable it to determine the application (GDO, Art. 7(4)).

(b) Applications for outline permission

Where the proposed development consists of the erection of a building, the applicant may, instead of applying for full permission, apply for outline planning permission. As we saw in the preceding chapter, 'outline planning permission' means planning permission for the erection of a building which is granted subject to a condition (in addition to any other conditions which may be imposed) requiring that full subsequent approval be obtained from the Department with respect to one or more reserved matters (GDO, Art. 2).[5] Although the developer will have to make two applications instead of one, the advantage for him is that his initial expenditure will be less as he need not submit detailed plans of the building with the application for outline permission. An application for outline permission is a way to keep down expenditure, particularly where the developer is not sure whether his proposals are likely to be permitted. It also offers flexibility where the applicant does not wish to develop the land himself, but to sell it as a building site, the building to be designed by the purchaser.

In the case of an application for outline planning permission details need not be given of any proposed reserved matters (GDO, Art. 7(2)). If the Department is of the opinion that the application for the proposed development ought not to be considered separately from reserved matters, it may require the applicant to give such further information as it may specify to enable it to deal with the application (GDO, Art. 8(2)).

(c) Applications for approval of reserved matters

Where an application for outline planning permission is successful, the developer will have to submit an application for approval of reserved matters before he can carry out the development. 'Reserved matters' are matters in respect of which details have not been given in the application

---

Art. 22(1)(c) states that notice of the application has been served on the owner of the land. See discussion below.

5 For the meaning of 'reserved matters' see below.

for outline permission and which concern the siting, design or external appearance of the building to which the outline permission relates, or the means of access to the building, or the landscaping of the site in respect of which the application for outline permission was made (GDO, Art. 2).

As we have seen, an application for approval of reserved matters must be made within three years of the date of the grant of outline planning permission (1991 Order, Art. 35(2)(a)).[6] All that is required to satisfy the terms of the Article is that an application is *made* within the prescribed period, not that the application should be successful within that period.[7] An application is 'made' on the date it is *received* by the Department rather than when it is sent by the applicant, if different.[8] In the words of Nourse LJ, 'The application is not made by A unless and until it impinges on B in some effective way. Whether you prefer to say that that requirement is satisfied by the application being received by or coming into the hands of B or, if that is something different, by its being communicated to him or coming to his knowledge may not matter very much.'[9] In R v *Bromley* LBC, *ex p Sievers*[10] outline planning permission had been granted on 24 January 1974. An application for approval of reserved matters was made on 24 January 1977, the preceding day being a Sunday. The court held that the application was valid.

If the application is made after the specified period, it is treated as not made in accordance with the terms of the outline permission (1991 Order, Art. 36(4)(b)). In *Orchard Caravans Ltd v Department of the Environment for Northern Ireland*[11] it was argued that where an appeal is pending in respect of conditions imposed in the outline permission the three year period is in suspension, and will resume running only when the appeal is determined. Murray J did not accept this. Where the applicant does appeal against the outline permission he can choose either to lodge an application for approval of reserved matters without prejudice to the appeal, or he can pursue his appeal keeping one eye on the calendar. Either way he must make an application for approval of reserved matters within the three year period.[12]

---

6 The Department, however, has power to substitute such other period, longer or shorter, as it considers appropriate: Art. 35(4). See generally Chapter 10.
7 *Orchard Caravans Ltd v Department of the Environment for Northern Ireland* [1980] 11 NIJB *per* Murray J.
8 *Camden* LBC v ADC *Estates Ltd* (1991) 61 P & CR 48, rejecting the argument that an application was made when the application was posted.
9 Ibid., 55.
10 (1981) 41 P & CR 294.
11 [1980] 11 NIJB.
12 *Quaere* whether the three year period begins anew following the determination of an appeal against the outline permission, the decision of the Planning Appeals Commission having the like effect as a decision of the Department (1991 Order, Art. 111(4)): *Orchard Caravans Ltd v Department of the Environment for Northern Ireland* [1980] 11 NIJB.

In the case of large developments, e.g. housing estates, it seems that it is not necessary for approval of reserved matters for every part of the development site to be sought at the same time.[13] Approval of reserved matters may be given on different occasions and subject to conditions.[14]

Because the scheme of outline planning permission and approval of reserved matters is one of principle and detail, it is not possible for the developer in his application for approval of reserved matters to deviate materially from the development approved in the outline permission.[15] In *Heron Corp. Ltd v Manchester CC*[16] Lord Denning MR said that an application for approval of reserved matters must be within the ambit of the outline permission and must be in accordance with the conditions annexed to the outline permission.[17] If the developer wishes to depart in any significant way from the outline permission or the conditions annexed to it he must apply for a new planning permission.[18] Whether the application for approval of reserved matters should be regarded as falling within the ambit of the outline planning permission is a matter for the Department, and it is not for the court to substitute its view or to determine whether on the merits of the case it considers that the application should not be so regarded.[19] The court may, however, set aside the decision of the Department if it has erred in law in the course of consideration of the question, e.g. if it has applied the wrong test of the validity of the application for approval of reserved matters or if the decision of the Department is so impossible to sustain that it cannot be said that the Department was entitled to come to the conclusion it did.[20]

It seems that in answering whether an application is within the ambit of the outline permission there may be cases where it is appropriate to look to matters apart from the outline permission itself.[21] Moreover, a distinction is drawn between cases where the developer seeks approval for *less* than was permitted in the outline permission and cases where the developer wants to carry out *more* than was authorised in the outline permission. In R v *Hammersmith and Fulham LBC, ex p Greater London Council*[22] outline planning permission had been granted for development including a bus garage, library, offices, carparking and transport interchange. The

---

13 See R v *Secretary of State for the Environment ex p Percy Bilton Industrial Properties Ltd* (1975) 31 P & CR 154.
14 R v *Newbury DC ex p Stevens and Partridge* (1992) 65 P & CR 438.
15 See e.g. *Calcaria Construction Co. Ltd v Secretary of State for the Environment* (1974) 27 P & CR 435.
16 [1978] 3 All ER 1240.
17 Ibid., 1244.
18 Ibid.
19 In re *Bangor Flagship Developments Ltd's application* [1991] 5 NIJB 57, per Carswell J.
20 Ibid.
21 R v *Hammersmith and Fulham LBC, ex p Greater London Council* (1985) 51 P & CR 120, 131 per Glidewell LJ.
22 (1985) 51 P & CR 120.

developer later applied for approval of reserved matters, but his plans did not include either the bus garage or the library. The planning authority considered that the application for approval of reserved matters was valid, but the Greater London Council as highway authority sought judicial review of the authority's decision, arguing that the application was outside the ambit of the outline permission. In refusing the relief sought Glidewell LJ considered that if the application for approval of reserved matters showed additional uses it would often be easy to say that it was not within the ambit of the outline permission. Where the application omitted one or more uses, however, the position was more difficult. There might be cases where a use in the outline permission was so significant that a departure from it in the application for approval of reserved matters might take the application outside the ambit of the outline permission, but that was not the case here.[23]

The principles in *Heron Corp.* and *Hammersmith and Fulham* LBC were recently considered in *In re Bangor Flagship Developments Ltd's application*.[24] Outline planning permission had been granted on a site of 11 hectares for a shopping centre, food court and leisure facilities, subject to conditions restricting the area of floorspace. An application for approval of reserved matters was submitted for part of the site comprising 7.8 hectares for a shopping centre and carparking. The proposal also showed construction of an access road outside the site for which approval was sought, but within the original 11 hectare site for which outline permission had been granted. Following the approval of the application an application was made for judicial review on the grounds that the application for approval of reserved matters was not within the ambit of the outline permission; that it was not within the conditions imposed on the grant of outline permission; and that the access road was outside the site for which approval of reserved matters had been sought. Carswell J held that the Department had been entitled to find that the application was within the ambit of the outline permission and that it was open to the Department to disregard the purported restriction in the application for approval of reserved matters to a portion of the 11 hectare site for which outline permission had been granted.

Just as the developer in his application for approval of reserved matters cannot go beyond the ambit of the outline planning permission, neither can the Department in dealing with the application for approval of reserved matters seek to restrict development which has been authorised by the outline permission. In *Medina* BC v *Proberun Ltd*[25] a developer had outline planning permission for development subject to approval of reserved matters, one of which was the means of access to the development site.

23　Ibid., 130–131.
24　[1991] 5 NIJB 57.
25　(1991) 61 P & CR 77.

An application for approval of the access was submitted, but the planning authority was not satisfied with the access proposed and failed to make a determination on the application. The developer appealed, arguing that while the access proposed might not be what the authority would like, it was the best available, and access in principle had been approved in the outline permission. The court accepted that as the access was the best available it fulfilled the requirements. If the planning authority thought it was unsatisfactory the proper procedure was to revoke the outline permission.[26]

The principle that the Department cannot restrict development permitted by the outline permission also means that the Department cannot impose a condition on the approval of reserved matters unless the right to do so was reserved in the outline permission.[27]

The form and content of an application for approval of reserved matters is governed by Art. 9 of the GDO. This provides that the application is to be made on a form issued by the Department and to give sufficient information to enable the Department to identify the outline planning permission in respect of which it is made, and to include such particulars and be accompanied by such plans and drawings as are necessary to deal with the matters reserved in the outline permission and to be accompanied by six additional copies of the form, plans and drawings except where the Department indicates that a lesser number is required. There is no need, however, for the application to be accompanied by one of the certificates required under Art. 22 of the 1991 Order[28] as an application for approval of reserved matters is not an application for planning permission within the meaning of that provision.[29]

In seeking approval of reserved matters the developer is not limited to one application: different matters may be approved in different applications[30] and where, for example, the outline permission relates to a large site, the developer may seek approval of various parts of the site or different phases of the development without being committed to the details of a later stage or phase.[31] Even where a particular matter has been the subject of an application for approval, the developer may submit another application in respect of the same matter.[32]

---

26 See also *Chelmsford Corp.* v *Secretary of State for the Environment* (1971) 22 P & CR 880; *Hamilton* v *West Sussex CC* [1958] 2 All ER 174; *Clugston* v *Secretary of State for the Environment* [1994] JPL 648; *The State (Pine Valley Developments Ltd)* v *Dublin CC* [1984] IR 407.
27 *R* v *Elmbridge BC, ex p Health Care Corp. Ltd* [1992] JPL 39; *Oakimber Ltd* v *Elmbridge BC* [1992] JPL 48. See also *Chelmsford Corp.* v *Secretary of State for the Environment* (1971) 22 P & CR 880. The contrary has been held in the Republic: *The State (Tern Houses (Brennanstown) Ltd* v *An Bord Pleanala* [1985] IR 725.
28 See below.
29 *R* v *Bradford-on-Avon UDC and ors, ex p Boulton* [1964] 2 All ER 492.
30 See 1991 Order, Art. 35(2)(b)(ii).
31 *Heron Corp. Ltd* v *Manchester CC* [1978] 3 All ER 1240, 1244 *per* Lord Denning MR.
32 Ibid.

Finally, an application for approval of reserved matters should be contrasted with an application for approval or consent which may be required under a condition imposed by the Department on the grant of planning permission. Unlike an application for approval of reserved matters, the latter is not an application in respect of which a fee is payable. Again, an application for approval or consent required under a condition may have to be made where the condition is contained in the grant of full permission, whereas an application for approval of reserved matters is required only after the grant of outline planning permission.

(2) Amendment of application

It seems that an application for planning permission may be amended[33] so as to obviate the need for a new application, at least where the amendment does not result in the application being substantially different from the original proposal. As will be seen, with few exceptions an application for planning permission must be publicised, thus affording interested parties an opportunity to make representations about the proposals contained in the application. To allow an amendment of the application which would result in the application being substantially different from that which has been publicised would therefore do an injustice to interested parties who could find that permission has been granted for a proposal different from that about which they were told.[34] Accordingly it has been suggested that it would not be proper, after the steps required in respect of publicity and consultation have been taken, for an application to be amended so as to make it substantially different from the original application.[35]

(3) Number of applications

A landowner is entitled to make any number of applications for planning permission which his fancy dictates, even though the development referred to is quite different when compared with others. It is open to a landowner to test the market by putting in a number of applications and seeing

---

33 As e.g. in *McClurg and Spiller v Department of the Environment for Northern Ireland* [1990] 2 NIJB 68.
34 See for example *R v Monmouth DC, ex p Jones* (1985) 53 P & CR 108 where Woolf J considered that the planning authority is under a duty to consider an application fairly, not only from the point of view of the applicant but also from that of persons entitled to object, and that the only way the authority could comply with the requirement of fairness in the circumstances of the case was to enable the objectors to make representations with regard to the amended plans. See also *Wessex Regional Health Authority v Salisbury DC and anor* [1984] JPL 344 and *Bernard Wheatcroft Ltd v Secretary of State for the Environment* (1982) 43 P & CR 233.
35 Purdue et al, *Planning Law and Procedure*, London: Butterworths 1989, p. 173. See e.g. *Breckland DC v Secretary of State for the Environment* (1993) 66 P & CR 34 where the decision of an inspector to allow an amendment to an application by increasing the size of the site from 0.47 ha to 0.6 ha was quashed by the court. The effect of the amendment was to bring the proposed development closer to nearby residences and to increase

what the attitude of the planning authority is to his proposals.[36] The authority is required to deal with the applications even though they are inconsistent one with the other, although there may be special cases where one application deliberately and expressly refers to or incorporates another.[37] In the absence of any such complication it is the duty of the planning authority to regard each application as a separate proposal, and to apply its mind to each application, asking itself whether the proposal therein is consistent with good planning in the factual background against which the application is made.[38] It is not part of the authority's duty to relate one application to another to see if they are contradictory: each application should be regarded as a proposal for separate and independent development, the merits of which should be considered on that basis.[39]

Nor is the applicant restricted in making successive applications, as the *res judicata* principle appears to have no application as circumstances can and do change materially from year to year or month to month.[40]

(4) Effect of application

As we have seen, where it appears to the Department that carrying out the operations specified in the application for planning permission or making the change of use proposed would not amount to development, or that an application for planning permission is not required, the Department may treat the application for planning permission as an application under Art. 41 of the 1991 Order and may make an appropriate determination (1991 Order, Art. 4(3)).[41]

(5) *Special cases*

Applications for planning permission in the following circumstances should be noted:

(a) *Development which has already taken place*

An application may be made for planning permission for retention of buildings or works constructed or carried out, or continuance of a use of land instituted, before the date of the application (1991 Order, Art. 29(1)). This may occur in three instances: (1) where the development was carried

---

the number of gipsy pitches on the site. The point made by Professor Purdue would appear all the more valid in Northern Ireland where the cases where publicity for the application is required are more extensive than in England and Wales.

36 *Pilkington v Secretary of State for the Environment* [1974] 1 All ER 283, 286 *per* Lord Widgery CJ. See also *Heron Corp. Ltd v Manchester CC* [1978] 3 All ER 1240, 1246 *per* Bridge LJ.
37 *Pilkington v Secretary of State for the Environment* [1974] 1 All ER 283, 286.
38 Ibid., 287.   39 Ibid.
40 *In re Kane's application* [1984] 17 NIJB *per* Macdermott J. See however *Thrasyvoulou v Secretary of State for the Environment* [1988] 2 All ER 781 for the application of the principle to appeals against enforcement notices and refusal of planning permission.
41 See Chapter 10.

out without planning permission; (2) where the development was carried out under a permission granted for a limited period; or (3) where the development would otherwise be in breach of a condition in an earlier planning permission (Art. 29(1)(a) and (b)). Any planning permission granted pursuant to such an application may be granted so as to take effect from the date on which the buildings or works were constructed or carried out, or the use was instituted, or, in the case of development under a limited planning permission, from the end of the limited permission (Art. 29(3)). An application under Art. 29(1)(b) must be in writing and give sufficient information to identify the previous grant of permission and any condition in question (GDO, Art. 7(3)).

(b) Applications for dispensation with conditions

Where planning permission has been granted subject to conditions it is possible to make an application for planning permission for development of the land without complying with those conditions (1991 Order Art. 28(1)). *Quaere* however if such an application is possible where the condition (being invalid) renders the permission void.[42]

An application must be made not later than the expiration of the period within which development was required to have been begun under the permission (1991 Order Art. 28(4)), and must be in writing. It must give sufficient information to identify the previous grant of permission and any condition in question (GDO, Art. 7(3)). On such an application the Department will consider only the question of the conditions (1991 Order, Art. 28(3)). If it decides that permission should be granted subject to conditions differing from those subject to which the original permission was granted, or that permission should be granted unconditionally, the Department is required to grant permission accordingly (Art. 28(3)(a)). If, however, the Department decides that permission should be granted subject to the same conditions, it is required to refuse the application (Art. 28(3)(b)). The form and content of applications under Art. 28 are provided for in the GDO.

(c) Applications for renewal of permission

It will be recalled that Arts 34 and 35 provide that planning permission is granted or deemed to be granted subject to conditions specifying the time within which development must be commenced and, in the case of outline planning permission, providing that an application for approval of reserved matters must be made within a certain period.[43] Art. 7(3) of the GDO provides for renewal of such permissions. Where the development has not commenced, and the time limit for commencing development or

---

42 See *Swale BC v Secretary of State for the Environment* [1994] JPL 236.
43 See Chapter 10 and above.

making an application for approval of reserved matters has not expired, an application may be made for planning permission for the same development. All that is required is for the application to be in writing and to give sufficient information to enable the Department to identify the previous grant of planning permission (GDO, Art. 7(3)). Where the Department is of opinion that further information is necessary to enable it to deal with the application it may require the applicant to submit such information.

(d) Applications affecting the environment

Applications for certain types of development are subject to the provisions of the Planning (Assessment of Environmental Effects) Regulations (NI) 1989. These are considered in Chapter 22.

(e) Enforcement appeals

Where an enforcement notice has been served on a developer[44] the developer has the right to appeal against the notice on various grounds (1991 Order, Art. 69). One of these grounds is that planning permission ought to be granted for the development to which the notice relates, or that a condition or limitation alleged in the notice not to have been complied with ought to be discharged (Art. 69(3)(a)). There is therefore a deemed application for planning permission where the developer appeals on this ground, though the application is dealt with by the Planning Appeals Commission rather than by the Department.

(f) Major applications

There is a special procedure provided in Art. 31 of the 1991 Order for dealing with applications for planning permission to which the Article relates. The Article relates to applications for development where, in the opinion of the Department, the development would, if permitted: (a) involve a substantial departure from the development plan for the area to which it relates; or (b) be of significance to the whole or a substantial part of Northern Ireland; or (c) affect the whole of a neighbourhood; or (d) consist of, or include the construction, formation, laying out or alteration of, a means of access to a trunk road or of any other development of land within 67 metres of the middle of such a road, or of the nearest part of a special road (Art. 31(a) to (d)).[45]

Where the Department considers that the development for which planning permission is sought falls within the foregoing circumstances,

---

44 See generally Chapter 15.
45 For the meaning of 'means of access' see 1991 Order, Art. 2(2). For the meaning of 'road', 'special road', 'trunk road', and 'proposed road' see ibid., Art. 31(6), applying the meanings of the terms in the Roads (NI) Order 1980. See now however Roads (NI) Order 1993, Arts 14 and 15.

it may apply the provisions of Art. 31 to the application. To do so it must serve a notice on the applicant within two months of the date of the application (Art. 31(2)).[46] Where the Department does apply Art. 31 to the application, it may cause a public local enquiry to be held by the Planning Appeals Commission for the purpose of considering representations made in respect of the application (Art. 31(2)),[47] and where this is done the Department is required to take the report of the Commission into account in determining the application (Art. 31(4)).[48] The decision on the application is made by the Department, not the Commission.

The Department is not obliged to call an enquiry: Art. 31(2) uses the permissive 'may' rather than 'shall'.[49] Where the Department does not cause an enquiry to be held, it is required before determining the application to serve a notice on the applicant indicating the decision it proposes to make. If within the time specified in the notice[50] the applicant so requests in writing, the Department is required to afford the applicant an opportunity of appearing before and being heard by the Planning Appeals Commission (Art. 31(3)).

Whether or not an enquiry is held or the applicant is heard by the Planning Appeals Commission, the decision of the Department on an application to which Art. 31 has been applied is final (Art. 31(5)).

(g) Disposal of Crown land

It is a principle of the interpretation of statutes that the Crown is not bound by an enactment unless the enactment expressly or by necessary implication provides that it is to be bound.[51] This principle applies to the 1991 Order as it does to any other enactment.[52] The 1991 Order does, however, make provision for the application of certain of its provisions to Crown land,[53] and makes special provision for certain situations.[54]

---

46 For the form of notice see GDO, sch. 3.
47 It seems that the fact that the Department causes an enquiry to be held under one of the circumstances specified in Art. 31(1) rather than another will not matter unless this causes prejudice to anyone seeking to quash the Department's decision: In re Blair's application [1985] NI 68.
48 The Department is not bound to follow the recommendation of the Commission: the subsection merely requires the Department to take the report into account. For an instance where the Department declined to follow the recommendation of the Commission see In re Blair's application [1985] NI 68.
49 See In re Bangor Flagship Developments Ltd's application (No 2) (HC) Carswell J, 21 August 1992 unrep.; In re McCann's application (HC) Carswell J, 10 July 1992 unrep.
50 Not being less than twenty eight days from service of the notice.
51 Minister of Agriculture, Fisheries and Food v Jenkins [1963] 2 All ER 147, 149 per Lord Denning MR.
52 Ibid., in relation to the Planning Acts in England and Wales. The same is the case in Scotland: Lord Advocate v Dumbarton DC [1990] 1 All ER 1.
53 Defined in Art. 118(1) as land in which there is an estate belonging to Her Majesty in right of the Crown, or belonging to a government department or held in trust for Her Majesty for the purposes of a government department.
54 The provisions e.g. in relation to listed buildings and tree preservation orders affecting Crown land are considered in the chapters dealing with those matters.

At the risk of stating the obvious, the value of land with planning permission will be greater than that of the same land without permission. Certainly, the land should be more attractive in the market. The same should be true in the case where the land is for sale with the benefit of any consents which may be needed in certain circumstances under the Order, e.g. listed building consent. Art. 114 accordingly contains provisions for the purpose of enabling Crown land or an estate in Crown land to be disposed of with the benefit of planning permission, listed building consent, hazardous substances consent, conservation area consent, or a determination whether planning permission is required, or listed building consent is needed (Art. 114(1)). The Article provides that notwithstanding the estate of the Crown in the land, an application for planning permission or the consents or determinations mentioned in Art. 114(1) may be made by various specified persons.[55] Any such planning permission, consent or determination applies only to development or work (or in the case of hazardous substances consent, presence of the substance on the land) after the land has ceased to be Crown land. So long as the land remains Crown land, the consent applies to such matters taking place by virtue of a private estate in the land (see Arts 114(3) to (5)).[56]

(h) Permission for continuance of use instituted by Crown

Finally, the Order provides for cases where the Crown has made or proposes to make a material change in the use of Crown land. The Department has power to make a direction in respect of the use resulting from such change, the effect of which is that on the land ceasing to be used by the Crown for that purpose, the use is to be treated as having been authorised by planning permission subject to a condition requiring its discontinuance at that time (Art. 117(2)). Accordingly any continuance of the use by someone other than the Crown will require that person to make an application for planning permission.

2 *Matters required to accompany applications*

In addition to the application form, drawings and plans required by the GDO, an applicant for planning permission will have to provide the Department with several other matters before the Department will deal with the application.

---

55 The Commissioner for Valuation for Northern Ireland, the Crown Estate Commissioners, relevant government departments, or persons authorised by the foregoing, depending on the circumstances: see Arts 114(2) and 118(1).
56 For the meaning of 'private estate' see Art. 118(1).

(1) Neighbour information

We have seen already that the Department may require the applicant to supply further information to enable it to deal with the application (GDO, Art. 7(4)). Since 1985 the Department has required that applications for planning permission be accompanied by the addresses of occupiers of neighbouring land. 'Neighbouring land' is land which adjoins the boundary of the application site and land which would adjoin the boundary but for an entry of a road less than 20 metres wide. Only the addresses of occupiers of buildings on such land which are within 90 metres of the boundary of the application site have to be provided. This is to enable the Department to notify certain occupants of such land of the application for permission.[57]

(2) Article 22 certificates

Art. 22(1) of the 1991 Order provides that the Department shall not entertain an application for planning permission unless it is accompanied by one of the four certificates mentioned in the subsection. This requirement does not apply (1) to applications made by the Northern Ireland Housing Executive in pursuance of a redevelopment scheme approved or proposed by the Executive (Art. 22(2)(a)); (2) to applications by an electricity undertaker to place an electricity line above or below ground across any land (Art. 22(2)(b) (as amended by Electricity (NI) Order 1992)); or (3) to applications for approval of reserved matters.[58] The submission of a certificate is a requisite to the jurisdiction of the Department to entertain an application for planning permission, and any decision made on an application without a certificate will be a nullity.[59]

(a) Alternative certificates

The certificates specified in Art. 22(1), one of which must accompany an application for planning permission (save in the cases mentioned) are as follows:[60]

(i) A certificate stating that the application is made by or on behalf of a person who at the date of the application is in the actual possession of all the land, and who is entitled to a legal or equitable fee simple absolute estate, a legal or equitable fee tail, a legal or equitable life estate, or a tenancy of which not less than forty years remain (Art. 22(1)(a)).

---

57 See below.
58 R v Bradford-on-Avon UDC and ors, ex p Boulton [1964] 2 All ER 492.
59 Horner v Department of the Environment for Northern Ireland [1971] NIJB.
60 For the form of each certificate see 1991 Order, Art. 22(7) and GDO, sch. 2.

(ii) A certificate stating that the application is made by or on behalf of the trustees of a trust or settlement which affects all the land and that at the date of the application a beneficiary under the trust or settlement is in the actual possession of the land, and no person other than a beneficiary under the trust or settlement is entitled to enter into the actual possession of the land within a period of forty years (Art. 22(1)(b)).[61]

(iii) A certificate stating that notice of the application has been given by or on behalf of the applicant to each person who at the beginning of the period of twenty one days ending with the date of the application was (a) a person described in Art. 22(1)(a) or (b); or (b) in actual possession of the land; or (c) was entitled to enter actual possession within a period of forty years (Art. 22(1)(c)).

(iv) A certificate stating (a) that the applicant has been unable to issue certificates (i) or (ii) above; (b) that he has made due enquiries and is of opinion for the reasons specified in the certificate that he is unable to issue certificate (iii) above; and (c) that he has given notice to any person who at the beginning of the period of twenty one days ending with the date of the application was in the actual possession of any part of the land (Art. 22(1)(d)).

In the case of certificates (iii) and (iv), the certificate must set out the names and addresses of the persons to whom notice of the application was given and the date on which notice was served (Art. 22(3)), and the Department is precluded from determining the application for a period of fourteen days beginning on the date of service, or, in the case of service on different persons, the latest date of service (Art. 22(4)).

(b) *Inaccurate certificates*

If a person issues a certificate which contains a statement which he knows to be false or misleading in a material particular, or recklessly issues a certificate which contains a statement which is false or misleading in a material particular, he is guilty of an offence (Art. 22(6)). Whether or not an offence is committed however, the question arises whether an inaccurate certificate means that any grant of planning permission issued on the strength of the certificate is invalid. In R v *Bradford-on-Avon* UDC *and ors, ex p Boulton*[62] Widgery J thought not, saying that the planning authority does not lose jurisdiction to deal with the application if the application is accompanied by a genuine certificate issued by a genuine applicant merely because there is some factual error in the contents of

---

61 For determining whether any person is entitled to enter into actual possession in certain circumstances see Art. 22(5).
62 [1964] 2 All ER 492.

the certificate.[63] However, in *Main v Swansea CC*[64] Parker LJ appeared to distinguish three possible grades of error which might be contained in a certificate, each having different consequences. First, the error may be no more than a mere irregularity 'which does not go to jurisdiction or anywhere like it'.[65] Second, at the other end of the scale are errors which make the certificate no certificate at all.[66] The inference seems to be that any permission granted on the strength of such a certificate will be void.[67] In between the two come errors which are more than mere irregularities but not so gross as to render the certificate no certificate at all.[68] Despite the concern expressed by Widgery J in *Boulton*[69] such a defect renders any planning permission granted following the certificate liable to be set aside on an application for judicial review, as happened in *Main v Swansea CC*. In considering whether the defect is of such a nature as to warrant quashing the planning permission the court will look not only at the nature of the defect but also at such matters as the identity of the applicant for relief, the lapse of time, and the effect on other parties and on the public.[70]

(3) Fees

Save in the cases noted below, where an application is made to the Department for planning permission or for approval of reserved matters, a fee must be paid to the Department.[71] A fee is payable also where there is a deemed application for planning permission in consequence of an appeal against an enforcement notice on the ground that planning permission ought to be granted for the development alleged in the notice to have taken place (Reg. 11(1)). No fee is payable, however, in

---

63 Ibid., 496. The references to genuine certificates and genuine applicants would seem to suggest that his Lordship's comments would not apply where the certificate is issued otherwise than in good faith.
64 (1985) 49 P & CR 26.
65 Ibid., 33.
66 Ibid.
67 Ibid., 38, where his Lordship said that the defects *in the present case* were not such as to render the permission a complete nullity.
68 Ibid., 33.
69 [1964] 2 All ER 492, 496.
70 *Main v Swansea CC* (1985) 49 P & CR 26, 37. Thus in *Main* the court had no doubt that a planning permission issued following a certificate which wrongly stated that notice of the application had been served on all owners of the application site could be quashed at the instance of the owner who had not been served. Whether such a defect could be relied on by someone other than the owner is doubtful (see *R v Secretary of State for the Environment, ex p Kent* (1989) 57 P & CR 431, where relief was refused) though in *Main* the court said that relief might be available to a local residents' association.
71 Planning (Fees) Regulations (NI) 1992, Reg. 3(1). See also Planning (Fees) (Amendment) Regulations (NI) 1993 and Planning (Fees) (Amendment) Regulations (NI) 1994. The power to make regulations regarding fees is contained in Art. 127 of the 1991 Order, which provides also that the application must *be accompanied* by the prescribed fee.

respect of applications where the Department is satisfied that the application relates solely to the carrying out of certain operations for the purpose of providing means of access to buildings for disabled persons (Reg. 4(1) and (2)), or for the change from one use to another within the same class in the UCO, the application being necessary only because of a condition imposed in an existing permission (Reg. 5).

The legislation does not specify what is to happen if the fee is not paid, but the GDO now provides that the period within which the Department is required to determine the application does not begin to run until the fee is paid (GDO, Art. 11(3)(c)).

Where a fee is payable, it is calculated in accordance with the provisions of sch. 1 of the Regulations (Reg. 3(2)) save in the case of certain applications (see Regs 6 to 9 and 18) which attract a flat fee (Regs 10 and 18). Any fee paid must be refunded by the Department if the application is rejected as invalidly made (Regs 3(3) and 10(2)).[72]

---

[72] There is no corresponding provision for fees paid in connection with the types of application mentioned in Reg. 18(1). A fee paid in connection with a deemed application for planning permission must be refunded in the circumstances set out in Reg. 13.

CHAPTER TWELVE

Determining Applications for Planning Permission

In this chapter we consider the process of decision making which follows the submission of an application for planning permission. It will be convenient to deal with this in two stages: first, a consideration of the procedural steps which must be taken in connection with the application; and second, an examination of the principles applicable to, and criteria adopted in, deciding whether to grant or refuse permission. In the next chapter we will consider the consequences which may flow from the decision taken by the Department.

1 *Mechanics of decision-making*

(1) **Notification of the application**

As we said earlier, an applicant for planning permission is required to inform the Department of the addresses of occupiers of neighbouring land. This is to enable the Department to notify certain occupiers of such land that an application for planning permission has been made and where the application may be inspected. The system of neighbour notification was introduced in 1985, when the government intended that the arrangements introduced would operate for two years, after which they would be replaced by a statutory scheme imposing the responsibility for notifying neighbours on the applicant rather than the Department. This replacement has not been made and the position remains that it is the Department which notifies neighbours of the application.[1]

Not all occupiers of neighbouring land[2] are notifiable occupiers. Only occupiers of buildings on neighbouring land which are within 90 metres of the boundary of the application site will be notified. Further, the Department exercises a discretion to decline to notify all such occupiers, e.g. occupiers at the rear of a building where the proposed development

---

1 For the background to the scheme see Thompson, 'Neighbour notification: recent developments in Scotland and Northern Ireland' [1985] JPL 530; see also Berry, Fitzsimmons and McGreal, 'Neighbour notification: the Scottish and Northern Ireland Models' [1988] JPL 804.
2 I.e. land which adjoins the boundary of the application site or which would adjoin the boundary but for an entry or a road less than 20 metres wide.

lies wholly to the front, or to notify occupiers in addition to those whose addresses have to be supplied.[3]

(2) Publication of the application

The Department is required to publish notice of an application for planning permission in at least one newspaper circulating in the locality in which the application site is situated (1991 Order, Art. 21(1)(a)). The requirement of a proper notice is mandatory as the giving of such notice is an essential part of the scheme of the 1991 Order[4] and a condition precedent to the Department granting planning permission.[5] Accordingly any planning permission granted following a defective notice is void and not merely voidable.[6]

To be a valid notice under Art. 21 the notice must bring home to the mind of a reasonably intelligent and careful reader both (1) the nature of any building, engineering, mining or other operations for which permission is sought in the application and (2) any material change in use for which permission is sought in the application.[7] Accordingly where the application is for structural alterations to a building and a change of use of the building, a notice which makes no reference to the change of use will be bad.[8] A minor inaccuracy on the other hand which does not mislead the public as to the nature of the application will not render the notice a nullity.[9]

If the notice is inaccurate and misleading, it makes no difference that the inaccurate and misleading nature of the notice is derived from the application itself being inaccurate, especially if the Department should have realised that the application was inaccurate.[10]

The Department has power to provide that the requirement of publication of notice of applications for planning permission shall not apply to applications for certain types of development (1991 Order, Art. 21(2)). In the exercise of this power the Department has exempted development consisting of the enlargement, improvement or alteration of a dwelling house; or the provision within the curtilage of a dwelling house of any

---

3   See the Department's neighbour notification form NN1, Advice Notes for Applicants.
4   Morelli v Department of the Environment for Northern Ireland [1976] NI 159, 166 per Murray J.
5   R (Thallon) v Department of the Environment for Northern Ireland [1982] NI 26, 46 per Hutton J.
6   R (Thallon) v Department of the Environment for Northern Ireland [1982] NI 26.
7   Ibid.
8   Morelli v Department of the Environment for Northern Ireland [1976] NI 159. See also Wilson v Secretary of State for the Environment [1974] 1 All ER 428 and R v Lambeth LBC, ex p Sharp (1985) 50 P & CR 284 and compare the position in the Republic: Crodaun Homes Ltd v Kildare CC [1983] ILRM 1; Monaghan UDC v Alf-a-Bet Promotions Ltd [1983] ILRM 64; Keleghan v Corby (1977) 111 ILTR 144; Electrity Supply Board v Gormley [1985] IR 129; Dooley v Galway CC [1992] 2 IR 136.
9   R (Thallon) v Department of the Environment for Northern Ireland [1982] NI 26, 45.
10 Ibid.

building or enclosure for a purpose incidental to the enjoyment of the dwelling house, or the enlargement, improvement or alteration of such a building or enclosure.[11]

Apart from the publicity afforded to applications for planning permission by Art. 21, information as to applications for permission is recorded in the planning register maintained by the Department under Art. 124 of the 1991 Order. The Department is required to enter in the register such information as may be specified with respect *inter alia* to applications made or deemed to be made for planning permission, and the manner in which such applications have been dealt with (Art. 124(1)(a) and (b)). The register is open to public inspection (Art. 124(2)), and a copy of the register or an extract from it may be obtained from the Department on payment of a fee (Art. 124(3)). Details of applications for planning permission and how they have been dealt with will also appear on the property certificate obtained from the Department by solicitors in the course of the purchase of land.

(3) *Consultations*

Before determining an application for planning permission the Department is required to consult the district council for the area where the land covered by the application is situated. In determining the application the Department must take into account any representations received from the council (GDO, Art. 15(a)).[12] Where the development is within or adjacent to an area where toxic, highly explosive or inflammable substances are present the Department is required to consult also the Department of Economic Development (GDO, Art. 15(b)).[13] While these are the only consultations which the Department is obliged to carry out, the Department may undertake further consultations, and in practice will consult with its own Roads Service and Water Service and the public health authority.

(4) *Representations*

As we have noted, the Department is required to take into account any representations made by the district council in determining an application for planning permission (GDO, Art. 15(a)). Apart from such representations, the Department is required to take into account also any representations received by it within fourteen days from the date on which notice of the application is first published in a newspaper in cases where such publication is required under Art. 21(1) of the 1991 Order

---

11 Planning Applications (Exemption from Publication) Order (NI) 1991.
12 For the meaning of 'consult' see Chapter 2.
13 For the meaning of 'hazardous substance' and 'notifiable quantity' see GDO, Art. 2. For the provisions of the 1991 Order dealing with hazardous substances see Chapter 18.

(1991 Order, Art. 25(2)). And where an application for planning permission is accompanied by a certificate such as those mentioned in Art. 22(1)(c) or (d)[14] the Department is required to take into account any representations made by any person falling within the descriptions in Art. 22(1)(c) (Art. 25(3)(a)).[15]

(5) *Time for determining applications*

The 1991 Order prescribes a mimimum period before the expiration of which the Department is prevented from determining an application for planning permission, and the GDO prescribes a period within which notification of the decision of the Department is required to take place.

Where an application for planning permission is publicised in accordance with Art. 21(1)(a) of the 1991 Order, the Department is prevented from determining the application before the expiration of fourteen days from the date on which notice of the application is first published in a newspaper (1991 Order, Art. 21(1)(b)). Where the application does not have to be publicised, the period is twenty one days from the date on which the application is received by the Department (Art. 21(3)). The Order does not specify the effect of a determination made before the expiration of the specified period, but insofar as the provisions of Art. 21 appear to be mandatory it is thought that any permission granted by the Department in such circumstances must be void.

Where the 1991 Order provides a date before which the Department is prevented from determining the application, the GDO provides a date by which notification of the Department's decision must be given to the applicant. Art. 11 of the GDO provides that notice of the Department's decision is to be given within two months of the date of receipt of the application form, supporting documents and the fee required or such extended period as may be agreed in writing between the applicant and the Department. As we have seen, it has been held that notice is 'given' when it is received.[16] The comparable provisions of the GDO in England have been held to be directory only[17] so that any determination made after the expiry of the two month period is not void but at most voidable.[18] If permission is granted after the two month period it is good, at any rate if it is accepted and acted on or if an appeal is made against it, for then it is too late to avoid it.[19] If permission is refused after the two month period the applicant can appeal as indeed he can at the expiration of the

---

14 See above.
15 Thus e.g. on an application by someone other than the owner of the application site the Department is required to take into account representations made by the owner.
16 *Freeney* v *Bray UDC* [1982] 2 ILRM 29.
17 *James* v *Secretary of State for Wales* [1966] 3 All ER 964, 987 *per* Lord Wilberforce.
18 *James* v *Minister of Housing and Local Government* [1965] 3 All ER 602, 606 *per* Lord Denning MR.
19 Ibid.

period (see 1991 Order, Art. 33). If he does not appeal he cannot afterwards say that the grant or refusal was bad because it was made after the two months.[20]

2   Considerations in decision-making

(1) General principles

(a) Duty to act fairly

In dealing with an application for planning permission the Department is under a duty to act fairly.[21] In that sense the rules of natural justice apply,[22] though this does not mean that the applicant for permission is entitled to a hearing. Whether or not the Department does act fairly is a question of fact in each individual case.[23] The duty may require the Department to afford third parties an opportunity of making representations e.g. following amendment of the application[24] or following a request for the decision to be deferred.[25] If the complaint is that the planning authority has an interest in the outcome of the decision, the sole test is whether the authority has genuinely and impartially exercised its discretion.[26] Once this is found or conceded to be the case there is no requirement to pose some further test by which the decision may be impugned as unlawful or void, whether by what a reasonable man would suspect, or by reference to whether, viewed through some other eyes such as those of the court, there was a real likelihood of bias.[27] The Department does not breach its duty to act fairly if one of its officers attends the application site for consultations with the applicant.[28] Nor is there any rule that the officer cannot advise the applicant as to the general policy of the Department and the considerations which the Department applies to certain types of development, provided that the officer does not commit the Department

---

20 James v Minister of Housing and Local Government [1965] 3 All ER, 602, 606. The statement of the law in James was accepted as correct by Carswell J in In re Bangor Flagship Developments Ltd's application [1991] 5 NIJB 57.
21 R v Amber Valley DC, ex p Jackson [1984] 3 All ER 501, 508 per Woolf J; R v Monmouth DC, ex p Jones (1987) 53 P & CR 108, 115 per Woolf J.
22 R v Amber Valley DC, ex p Jackson [1984] 3 All ER 501, 508.
23 R v Great Yarmouth BC, ex p Botton Brothers Arcades Ltd (1988) 56 P & CR 99, 109 per Otton J.
24 R v Monmouth DC, ex p Jones (1987) 53 P & CR 108. See also Stratford-on-Avon DC v Secretary of State for the Environment [1993] EGCS 131 (natural justice requiring the Secretary of State to afford applicant opportunity of making representations where Secretary of State taking into consideration change in national policy).
25 R v Great Yarmouth BC, ex p Botton Brothers Arcades Ltd (1988) 56 P & CR 99.
26 R v St Edmundsbury BC, ex p Investors in Industry Commercial Properties Ltd [1985] 3 All ER 284, 255 per Stocker J.
27 The court declining to follow Steeples v Derbyshire CC [1984] 3 All ER 468 which had put forward the 'reasonable man' test. See also R v Sevenoaks DC, ex p Terry [1985] 3 All ER 226.
28 R (Thallon) v Department of the Environment for Northern Ireland [1982] NI 26.

to approving a proposed development, and makes it clear that the application will be considered by the Department in accordance with its statutory duties, and that the Department will have to take into account any objections which may be received.[29]

(b) A duty of care?

As we will see, an applicant for planning permission may appeal to the Planning Appeals Commission if the Department refuses permission or grants permission subject to conditions (1991 Order, Art. 32(1)) or fails to notify the applicant of its decision within the period prescribed by the GDO (Art. 33). Persons other than the applicant have no such right of appeal, but may challenge the decision of the Department (whether to grant permission or refuse it) by way of judicial review in appropriate circumstances. It appears from the authorities in England that neither an applicant for planning permission nor a third party has any cause of action against the planning authority arising from any negligence of the authority in handling the application.[30] In *Ryeford Homes Ltd v Sevenoaks DC*[31] Judge Newey said that despite the foreseeability of damage, there is no sufficient proximity between the planning authority and an individual landowner for the authority to owe him a duty of care. Even if this existed it would be contrary to public policy for the authority to be liable in negligence. The judge went on to say that even if he were wrong and there was a duty in negligence, breach of that duty would result in economic loss only.[32] The courts in the Republic have also considered the question of damages both in relation to the local council as planning authority and the minister of state.[33] In *McInerney Properties Ltd and ors v Department of the Environment for Northern Ireland and ors*[34] following the revocation of planning permission the plaintiffs issued proceedings against *inter alios* the Department alleging negligence in the consideration and granting of planning permission in the first place. In the event the proceedings were held to be statute-barred so that the question of the liability of the Department for negligence did not have to be considered. However, in *Chambers v Department of the Environment for Northern Ireland*[35] (a case not concerning planning) the Court of Appeal considered the principles relevant to the liability of a public body arising out of the

---

29 Ibid., 54 *per* Hutton J.
30 *Strable* v *Dartford BC* [1984] JPL 329 (action by applicant); *Ryeford Homes Ltd* v *Sevenoaks DC* [1990] JPL 36 (action by third party). See also *Dunlop* v *Woollahra MC* [1981] 1 All ER 1202.
31 [1990] JPL 36.
32 Ibid., 39.
33 *O'Neill* v *Clare CC* [1983] 3 ILRM 141; *Pine Valley Developments Ltd* v *Minister of the Environment* [1987] 7 ILRM 747.
34 [1984] 2 NIJB.
35 [1985] NI 181. See also *McKernan* v *McGeown* [1983] 4 NIJB.

exercise of a statutory power or discretion. Gibson J said that if a statute confers on a public body the power to choose how it will exercise a particular function it cannot be liable if it properly exercises that power. Negligence is the breach of a duty and there cannot be a duty to do something which the body has a discretion to refrain from doing. It is only where the act occasioning damage is not authorised by statute that there is any scope for a claim at common law. The permitted scope of claims at common law begins where the permitted range of statutory discretion ends, and there is no overlapping of boundaries.[36] Any liability however, which may exist from the application of these principles to the exercise of the Department's discretion to refuse planning permission must be considered in the light of the points made in *Ryeford Homes* that the applicant for planning permission has a right of appeal against the Department's decision,[37] and that any damage he suffers will be economic only. The most recent case in which the liability of a planning authority in negligence has been considered is *Tidman v Reading BC*[38] in which the court dismissed the plaintiff's action for alleged negligent advice, on the ground that the planning authority owed no duty of care to him.

(2) Specific considerations

Art. 25(1) of the 1991 Order provides that in dealing with an application for planning permission the Department shall have regard to the development plan, so far as material to the application and to any other material considerations.

(a) The development plan

The obligation imposed on the Department by Art. 25(1) is *to have regard to* the development plan, so far as material to the application. The Department is not obliged slavishly to adhere to the development plan: it is obliged to consider the plan but not necessarily to follow it. The Article requires the Department to consider all material considerations, of which the development plan is one.[39]

(b) Other material considerations

The 'material considerations' to which the Department is required by Art. 25(1) to have regard in dealing with an application for planning permission

---

36 Ibid.
37 Though this is of no relevance to a claim by someone other than the applicant himself who claims to have suffered loss due to the Department's decision, e.g. a neighbour.
38 [1994] EGCS 180.
39 *Simpson v Edinburgh Corp.* 1960 SC 313 *per* Lord Guest; followed in *London Borough of Enfield v Secretary of State for the Environment* [1975] JPL 155.

must be considerations of a planning nature.[40] Such considerations, however, are not limited to matters of amenity: any consideration which relates to the use and development of land is capable of being a planning consideration.[41] Similarly in *Great Portland Estates plc v Westminster CC*[42] Lord Scarman said that the test of a material consideration is whether it serves a planning purpose and a planning purpose is one which relates to the character and use of land. Whether a particular consideration within the class of planning considerations is a material consideration in any given case will depend on the circumstances.[43] Whether a consideration is material has been likened to the test of validity of a condition attached to a planning permission, *viz.* the consideration must fairly and reasonably relate to the development for which permission is sought.[44] The most recent pronouncement on what amount to material considerations is by Hoffmann LJ in R v *Plymouth CC ex p Plymouth and South Devon Co-Operative Society Ltd*.[45] There his Lordship said that the question of what is a material consideration could be answered by reference to the tests propounded in *Newbury* for the validity of a planning condition, *viz.* that the condition must have a planning purpose; that it must be related to the development proposed; and that it is not unreasonable in the *Wednesbury* sense. The court in *Plymouth* was considering whether benefits offered by a developer were material considerations to be taken into account in determining an application for planning permission. In holding that they were material considerations the court rejected the argument that the benefits had to be necessary to the development proposed in the sense of overcoming some planning objection.

It is not possible to give an exhaustive list of 'material considerations' but the following have been considered by the courts:

(i) Policy

Art. 3(1) of the 1991 Order requires the Department to formulate and co-ordinate policy for securing the orderly and consistent development of land and the placing of that development. In determining any application for planning permission it is relevant for the Department to have regard to the policy it has formulated.[46] Likewise the Planning Appeals Commission is obliged to take such policy into account when determining an appeal against refusal of permission, or in considering whether

---

40 Stringer v Minister of Housing and Local Government [1971] 1 All ER 65, 77 per Cooke J; Clyde & Co. v Secretary of State for the Environment [1977] 3 All ER 1123, 1126 per Sir David Cairns.
41 Ibid. See also Mitchell v Secretary of State for the Environment [1994] EGCS 111.
42 [1984] 3 All ER 744, 750.
43 Stringer v Minister of Housing and Local Government [1971] 1 All ER 65, 77.
44 R v Westminster CC, ex p Monahan [1989] 2 All ER 74, 104 per Staughton LJ.
45 (1993) 67 P & CR 78.
46 McGuigan's application, In re (unrep. 5 July 1990) (Campbell J).

permission should be granted in an enforcement appeal.[47] In *Wycombe DC v Secretary of State for the Environment*[48] Graham Eyre QC set out the following as propositions which could be gleaned from the authorities: (1) the policy being examined or being ruled on has to be a lawful policy related to proper planning considerations.[49] (2) If the policy relates to development or land use or other proper planning considerations, regard must be had to it by the determining authority, either at first instance or on appeal. (3) The determining authority must correctly interpret and understand the nature and content of the policy.[50] (4) Whether the policy is contained in a development plan or elsewhere, provided proper regard has been had to it, there is no requirement that it should be slavishly followed. (5) Assessing the relevance and weight to be attached to other material considerations is a matter for the determining authority in a particular case and the determining authority alone. (6) If the determining authority departs from the policy contained in the development plan in a particular case, it must set out its reasons for so doing and such reasons must be sound, clear-cut and intelligible. (7) Nonetheless the reasons can be briefly stated. (8) There can be no challenge of the reasons for departing from a policy or treating a particular case as an exception unless in that particular case they are substantially wrong or irrelevant. In *Gransden & Co. Ltd v Secretary of State for the Environment*[51] Oliver LJ pointed out that a policy cannot make a matter which is otherwise a material consideration an irrelevant consideration.[52]

Where proper regard is not given to the policy, the court will quash the decision of the determining authority unless the situation is an exceptional case where the court can be quite satisfied that the failure to have proper regard to the policy has not affected the outcome in that the decision would in any event have been the same.[53]

---

47 In re Magill's application [1968] 7 NIJB 37. The Commission must take its decision in the light of considerations at the time of its decision, so that any new policy statement coming into existence after the hearing conducted by the appointed member must be taken into account: JA Pye (Oxford) Estates Ltd v West Oxfordshire DC (1984) 47 P & CR 125, 132 per David Widdicombe QC; Newham LBC v Secretary of State for the Environment (1987) 53 P & CR 98, 104 per Webster J.
48 (1989) 57 P & CR 177, 180.
49 I.e. the policy must not go beyond the proper role of a policy by seeking to do more than indicate the weight which should be given to relevant considerations: Gransden & Co. Ltd v Secretary of State for the Environment (1987) 54 P & CR 86, 95 per Oliver LJ.
50 See Niarchos v Secretary of State for the Environment (1978) 35 P & CR 259; Bell and Colvill Ltd v Secretary of State for the Environment [1980] JPL 823.
51 (1987) 54 P & CR 86, 94. See also Horsham DC v Secretary of State for the Environment [1992] JPL 334 and South Somerset DC v Secretary of State for the Environment [1993] 26 EG 121.
52 For recent examples of departing from stated policy see R v Plymouth CC ex p Plymouth and South Devon Co-Operative Society Ltd (1993) 67 P & CR 78 and Tescos Stores Ltd v Secretary of State for the Environment [1994] JPL 227.
53 Gransden & Co. Ltd v Secretary of State for the Environment (1987) 54 P & CR 86, 94 per Oliver LJ.

(ii) Draft plans and policy: prematurity

We have seen that the authority determining an application for planning permission, be it the Department or the Planning Appeals Commission, is obliged by Art. 25(1) to take into account the development plan, and as a material consideration, any policy issued by the Department. We have seen also that the preparation of a development plan requires publication first of the Department's proposals (Art. 5(3)).[54] Is a *draft* development plan or draft policy statement a material consideration to which the determining authority is required to have regard in determining an application for planning permission? In *J A Pye (Oxford) Estates Ltd v Secretary of State for the Environment*[55] Sir David Cairns took the view that a draft *circular* is not a material consideration, but in *Richmond upon Thames LBC v Secretary of State for the Environment*[56] Glidewell J did not accept that a draft circular could never be a material consideration. In *Wyre Forest DC v Secretary of State for the Environment*[57] Slade LJ said that the provisions of an emerging plan or the fact that the report of a local plan inspector was shortly to be made must clearly be capable of being a material consideration to be taken into account.[58] Accordingly it is open to the determining authority to refuse permission on the ground that the application is premature. This, however, is a matter of discretion and the existence of an emerging plan or pending report does not necessarily prevent the determining authority from determining the application.[59] While the absence of a development plan is not a reason for refusal of permission, there may be circumstances where the public interest requires that the implications of the development for which permission is sought should be investigated in the context of the formulation of a plan, and accordingly permission may be refused on the ground that the application is premature.[60]

(iii) Compatibility

It is a proper consideration for the Department to take into account whether the proposed development is compatible with the proper and desirable use of other land in the area.[61] The duty of the Department is to plan the area concerned, and an essential feature of planning is the separation of different uses or activities which are incompatible with one another.[62]

---

54 See Chapter 3.
55 (1982) 47 P & CR 125, 130.
56 [1984] JPL 24.
57 (1984) 58 P & CR 291, 294.
58 See also *Allen v City of London Corp.* [1981] JPL 685 and *Davies v London Borough of Hammersmith & Fulham* [1981] JPL 682.
59 *Wyre Forest DC v Secretary of State for the Environment* (1989) 58 P & CR 291, 294.
60 *Arlington Securities Ltd v Secretary of State for the Environment* (1989) 57 P & CR 407. See also *High Peak BC v Secretary of State for the Environment* [1992] JPL 446.
61 *Stringer v Minister of Housing and Local Government* [1971] 1 All ER 65, 77.
62 *Fitzpatrick Development Ltd v Minister of Housing and Local Government* (1965) unrep. *per* Widgery J (cited by Cooke J in *Stringer* at 77.)

(iv) Alternative sites

The availability of other sites where the development could take place may be a material consideration. In *Trusthouse Forte Ltd v Secretary of State for the Environment*[63] Simon Brown J said that the authorities established the following principles:[64] (1) The fact that other land exists upon which the development would be more acceptable for planning purposes would not justify refusal of permission on the application site. (2) Where, however, there are clear planning objections to development on a particular site then it may well be relevant and indeed necessary to consider whether there is a more appropriate alternative site elsewhere. This is particularly so when the development is bound to have significant adverse effects and where the major argument advanced in support of the application is that the need for the development outweighs the planning disadvantages inherent in it. (3) Instances of this type of case are developments, whether of national or regional importance, such as airports, coalmining, petrochemical plants, nuclear power stations and gipsy encampments. (4) In contrast to these situations are cases where permission is being sought for dwelling houses, offices and superstores. (5) There may be cases which would otherwise give rise to the need to consider other sites, where it could properly be regarded as unnecessary to go into questions of comparability. This would be so particularly if the environmental impact is relatively slight and the planning objections not especially strong. (6) Compulsory purchase cases[65] are *a fortiori* to planning cases. In *Trusthouse Forte* Simon Brown J referred to the 'helpful though expressly not exhaustive' approach to the problem of determining whether consideration of alternative sites is material, given in *Greater London Council v Secretary of State for the Environment and anor.*[66] There Oliver LJ said that comparability is appropriate generally to cases having the following characteristics: (1) the presence of a clear public convenience or advantage, in the proposal under consideration; (2) the existence of inevitable adverse effects or disadvantages to the public or some section of the public in the proposal; (3) the existence of an alternative site for the same project which would not have those effects, or would not have them to the same extent; and (4) a situation in which there can be only be one permission granted for such development, or at least only a very limited number of permissions.[67]

(v) Previous planning decisions

The planning history of the application site may be a material consideration to be taken into account by the Department in determining an application

---

63 (1987) 53 P & CR 293.
64 Ibid., 299.
65 E.g. *Brown v Secretary of State for the Environment* (1980) 40 P & CR 285.
66 (1986) 52 P & CR 158, 172.
67 See also *Edwards (PG) v Secretary of State for the Environment* [1994] EGCS 60.

for planning permission.[68] So in *Spackman v Secretary of State for the Environment*[69] the decision of an inspector was quashed on the ground that the inspector had failed to take into account when determining the application the fact that a valid planning permission was in existence, a matter described by Willis J as a 'vitally material consideration'.[70] If, however, the Department does take into account a previous permission, treating it as valid, and it turns out that the earlier permission is void, the decision of the Department may be set aside.[71] The fact that a previous planning permission has expired will not automatically prevent it from being a material consideration, though the Department is not bound to follow the previous decision.[72] If the previous decision is taken into account it must not be given more weight than appropriate. Ironically, when in *South Oxfordshire DC v Secretary of State for the Environment*[73] the Secretary of State did take into account a previous expired permission, describing it as a 'vitally material consideration', his decision was quashed.[74]

(vi) Effect of the decision as a precedent

The effect of a decision as a precedent is a consideration which may be taken into account by the Department. 'In all planning cases it must be of the greatest importance when considering a single planning application to ask oneself what the consequences in the locality will be—what are the side effects which will flow if such a permission is granted. Insofar as an application for planning permission on site A is judged according to the consequence on sites B, C and D, . . . no error of law is disclosed but only what is perhaps the most elementary principle of planning practice is being observed.'[75]

(vii) Preservation of an existing use

Where an application is made for permission for a material change of use, the planning authority is entitled to take into account the desirability of preserving the existing use of the property,[76] a proposition which was considered so self-evident by Forbes J that he was surprised that it should have been necessary for there to be authority.[77] Indeed, his Lordship

---

68 For recent examples see *North Wiltshire DC v Secretary of State for the Environment* [1992] EGCS 65 and *Barnet LBC v Secretary of State for the Environment* [1992] JPL 540.
69 [1977] 1 All ER 257.
70 Ibid., 261.
71 *R (Thallon) v Department of the Environment for Northern Ireland* [1982] NI 26.
72 *South Oxfordshire DC v Secretary of State for the Environment* [1981] 1 All ER 954.
73 [1981] 1 All ER 954. 74 Ibid.
75 *Collis Radio Ltd v Secretary of State for the Environment* (1975) 29 P & CR 390, 396 per Lord Widgery CJ. See also *Dibben v Secretary of State for the Environment* [1991] JPL 260; *Poundstretcher Ltd v Secretary of State for the Environment* [1989] JPL 90 and *Witherspoon v Secretary of State for the Environment* [1992] JPL 547.
76 *Clyde & Co. v Secretary of State for the Environment* [1977] 3 All ER 1123.
77 *Granada Theatres Ltd v Secretary of State for the Environment* (1980) 257 EG 1154, 1155.

thought that he was not going too far in considering that the desirability of preserving the existing use *must always* be a material consideration in determining an application for permission for change of use.[78] The correct proposition according to Forbes J is that the desirability of preserving an existing use is always a material consideration when planning permission is sought to change it. There may, however, be facts which make it unnecessary to consider it, e.g. where there is no possibility that refusal of permission will result in its retention, as where both parties agree that continuation of the existing use is undesirable, or impossible.[79] Consequently, in a contest between the planning merits of two competing uses, to justify refusal of permission for use B on the sole ground that use A ought to be preserved, it must be necessary to show a balance of probability that, if permission is refused for use B, the land will be put to use A.[80]

While the desirability of preserving an existing use may be a material consideration, this does not mean that the Department is obliged to apply a competing needs test of whether in planning terms the desirability of preserving the existing use outweighs the merits of the proposed new use, since this would result in the presumption in favour of development being overriden and planning permission being necessarily refused in any case where there is some desirability, however slight, of the existing use being retained and no demonstrable need or desirability for the proposed new use.[81]

(viii) Adequacy of infrastructure

The adequacy of the existing infrastructure to serve the proposed development is a material consideration. In R *(Thallon)* v *Department of the Environment for Northern Ireland*[82] the adequacy of the roads in the area of the application site was described as a crucial question in deciding whether or not to grant permission, so that when the Department granted permission, in the mistaken belief that its own Roads Service considered the roads were adequate when instead the Roads Service was opposed to the development proposed, the permission was quashed.

(ix) Development which has already taken place

We have already seen that it is possible to apply for planning permission for retention of buildings or works already constructed or a use already instituted (Art. 29(1)). Is the fact that the development for which permission is sought has already taken place a material consideration to be

---

78 Ibid., author's emphasis.   79 Ibid.
80 *Westminster CC* v *British Waterways Board* [1984] 3 All ER 737, 742 per Lord Bridge. See also *Christchurch BC* v *Secretary of State for the Environment* [1993] EGCS 217.
81 *London Residuary Body* v *Lambeth LBC and ors* [1990] 2 All ER 309.
82 [1982] NI 26.

taken into account by the Department in altering the application? In *Chris Fashionware (West End) Ltd v Secretary of State for the Environment*[83] the court held that the Secretary of State had been entitled to hold that the fact that the development for which permission was sought had been carried out was irrelevant. If, however, the existing development has become immune from enforcement action by the Department, this will be a material consideration to be taken into account by the Department in determining the application, because to ignore the fact that the development can remain would be to ignore reality entirely.[84]

(x) Private interests

In *Stringer v Minister of Housing and Local Government*[85] an application was made to quash the decision of a planning authority to refuse planning permission on the ground *inter alia* that the authority had taken into account the effect of the proposed development on the Jodrell Bank telescope; that this was a private interest; and that the authority was not entitled to consider private interests. Cooke J had no reluctance in rejecting this submission, saying that while the scheme of the planning legislation is to restrict development for the benefit of the public at large, the protection of the interests of individual occupiers is one aspect, and an important one, of the public interest as a whole. The distinction between public and private interests was a false distinction in this context.[86] While an individual might have no right to maintain proceedings in the courts he might yet be a person whose interests may very properly be considered at an anterior stage when the question whether to grant permission or not is being dealt with.[87]

(xi) Financial considerations[88]

The argument has been advanced that the circumstances of the applicant (his ability financially to carry out the development) or the economic viability of the development are not material considerations which may be taken into account by the Department in considering whether to grant or refuse planning permission. The proposition is that the proposed development is independent of the ability or otherwise of the applicant to carry it into effect. So in *J Murphy & Sons Ltd v Secretary of State for the Environment*[89] Ackner J held as a matter of law that the Minister was not entitled to have regard to the cost of developing a site in determining

---

83 [1980] JPL 678.
84 *In re Kane's application* [1984] 17 NIJB *per* MacDermott J.
85 [1971] 1 All ER 65.
86 Ibid., 77. 87 Ibid., 78.
88 See Robinson, 'Commercial Viability in Planning—a Lawyer's View' (1993) JPL Occasional Papers No 121.
89 [1973] 2 All ER 26.

whether planning permission should be granted.[90] The planning authority, he said, is concerned with how the land is to be used, not whether the development proposed is going to be a wise commercial venture: 'the planning authority exercises no paternalistic or avuncular jurisdiction over would-be developers to safeguard them from their financial follies'.[91] The view that cost can never be a material consideration was rejected by Forbes J in *Sovmots Investments Ltd v Secretary of State for the Environment*[92] and in *Hambledon and Chiddingfold PC v Secretary of State for the Environment*[93] Ackner J said that while he still thought that the general proposition was correct, he might have stated it too widely. Despite this it seems now to be accepted that cost can be a material consideration. In *R v Westminster CC, ex p Monahan*[94] Kerr LJ pointed out that financial constraints on the economic viability of a desirable planning development are unavoidable facts of life in an imperfect world, and it would be unreal and contrary to common sense to insist that they must be excluded from the range of considerations which may properly be regarded as material in determining planning applications. Provided an ultimate determination is based on planning grounds and not on some ulterior motive, and that it is not irrational, there would be no basis for holding it to be invalid in law solely on the ground that it has taken account of, and adjusted itself to, the financial realities of the overall situation.[95] In *Monahan* the court held that the planning authority had been entitled to take into account as a material consideration the fact that part of the development proposed would generate finance which would allow another part of the development to take place. A similar conclusion was reached in *Northumberland CC v Secretary of State for the Environment*[96] when the court said that it was now well settled that economic considerations may amount to planning considerations to be borne in mind when granting or refusing permission.[97]

(xii) Applicant's personal circumstances

The argument that whether development should be permitted is separate from the applicant's financial ability to carry it out applies no less strongly to other personal circumstances of the applicant. Nonetheless, it has been said recently that personal circumstances of an occupier, personal hardship, the difficulties of businesses which are of value to the character of a community are not to be ignored in the administration of planning

---

90 Ibid., 32.
91 Ibid., 31.
92 [1976] 3 All ER 178. For appeals see [1976] 3 All ER 720 (CA) and [1977] 2 All ER 385 (HL).
93 [1976] JPL 502.
94 [1989] 2 All ER 74.
95 Ibid., 96.
96 (1990) 59 P & CR 468.
97 Ibid., 475 *per* Malcolm Spence QC.

control.[98] However, personal circumstances must be considered as exceptional: if the Department is to give effect to them, a specific case has to be made and the Department must give reasons for accepting it.[99] In cases where the decision is evenly balanced personal circumstances may be relevant.[100] The applicant's personal circumstances are frequently advanced in cases where planning permission is sought for development which would otherwise be contrary to the Department's rural policy.

(xiii) Avoidance of compensation

It is open to the Department to take into account in determining an application for planning permission the fact that by its decision it may bring about a state of affairs which could otherwise be brought about only with the consequence that it would be liable to pay compensation either to the applicant or a third party. In *Westminster Bank Ltd v Minister of Housing and Local Government*[101] an application for planning permission for development near a road was refused by the local council which was both planning authority and roads authority. The applicant objected that the council could not use its power as planning authority to achieve without payment of compensation a result which it could have obtained as roads authority only on payment of compensation. The House of Lords rejected this objection, Lord Reid saying that even if the sole reason of the authority proceeding in the way it did had been the desire to save public money, it did not follow that they were not entitled to do that.[102] In *R v Exeter CC, ex p Terry*[103] an application for residential development was granted by the local planning authority. The application site was near sites occupied by two companies for animal waste processing and steel fabricating. The companies were concerned that the residents of the new development might be able to sue the companies for nuisance and accordingly the companies would have to relocate their activities. The companies sought to have the grant of permission quashed, arguing that if the planning authority wanted the companies to cease their activities it had to use discontinuance proceedings which carried a consequential liability to pay compensation, and that the authority had granted permission for an ulterior motive, the avoidance of compensation. Simon Brown J held that provided planning permission was granted out of a genuine desire to see the application site developed as permitted, not simply as a device to create trouble for existing users adjoining or

---

98 *Great Portland Estates plc v Westminster CC* [1984] 3 All ER 744, 750 *per* Lord Scarman.
99 Ibid.
100 *New Forest DC v Secretary of State for the Environment* [1984] JPL 178. See also *Tameside MBC v Secretary of State for the Environment* [1984] JPL 180.
101 [1970] 1 All ER 734.
102 Ibid., 739. See also *Hoveringham Gravels Ltd v Secretary of State for the Environment* [1975] 2 All ER 931.
103 [1990] 1 All ER 413.

near the site in order to force them out without the planning authority having to use its discontinuance powers, the fact that the authority hoped that the grant of permission would cause an existing user to relocate did not render the permission invalid or unreasonable or disentitle the authority from granting permission. Since this test was satisfied the authority's decision was not invalid or unreasonable even if a substantial part of the authority's motivation was the hope that it would avoid payment of compensation.

CHAPTER THIRTEEN

The Decision and its Consequences

In this chapter we consider the various decisions open to the Department following an application for planning permission and the consequences which flow from each.

1 *Decisions possible*

The Department is required to make one of three possible decisions on the application. It may grant planning permission unconditionally; it may grant permission subject to conditions; or it may refuse permission (1991 Order, Art. 25(1)). Each will be considered in turn.

(1) **Grant of planning permission unconditionally**

Where planning permission is granted unconditionally the applicant gets what he has asked for and goes away (presumably) happy. Other parties, e.g. neighbours, may not be so pleased: their position is considered below. Subject to the decision being upset by way of judicial review, the effect of the Department granting planning permission unconditionally is as follows:

(a) *Permission enures for benefit of the land*

Except insofar as the permission otherwise provides, planning permission enures for the benefit of the land and of all persons for the time being having an estate therein (1991 Order, Art. 30(1)). Thus, the permission attaches to the land itself and may be utilised by e.g. a purchaser of the land to which the permission relates.

(b) *Implementation of permission*

We have seen that any number of different and mutually inconsistent applications for planning permission may be made for the same site and that each must be decided on its own merits. The consequence of this is that various permissions may exist for the same land. While the *existence* of planning permission may have certain consequences e.g. in making the land more attractive commercially, it is the *implementation* of a permission which has consequences from a planning standpoint. In *Pilkington* v *Secretary of State for the Environment*[1] planning permission had been granted

---

1 [1974] 1 All ER 283.

in 1953 to build a house on the northern part of a piece of land. In 1954 permission was granted to build a house on another part of the site and this was implemented. Later the owner began to build a second house on the northern part of the site, relying on the earlier permission. The planning authority issued enforcement proceedings saying that by implementation of the 1954 permission the 1953 permission had ceased to be capable of implementation. The court upheld this view, saying that where one planning permission had been implemented it was not thereafter possible to implement another permission which could not be carried out consistently with the permission that had been implemented. If, therefore, planning permission is granted for the erection of a house on a site showing one acre of land as that to be occupied with the house, and later permission is granted for a house on a different part of the same acre which is again shown as to be occupied with the house, it would not be possible to construe the two permissions as permitting two houses on the same acre.[2]

(c) Judicial review

The decision of the Department or the Planning Appeals Commission on an application for planning permission, whether to grant permission unconditionally, subject to conditions, or to refuse permission, is open to judicial review by the court in appropriate circumstances.[3] This is considered below.

(d) Miscellaneous

In contrast to granting permission subject to conditions or refusing permission, there is no right of appeal from the decision of the Department to grant planning permission unconditionally (see Art. 32(1)) as the applicant has got what he asked for. Nor is there any duty on the Department to give reasons for its decision, as there is in the other two cases (GDO, Art. 13). There is, however, a duty on the Department to draw the attention of the person to whom permission is granted to the provisions of the Chronically Sick and Disabled Persons (NI) Act 1978 and the Code of Practice for Access for the Disabled to Buildings when granting permission for development which will result in provision of certain buildings or premises (1991 Order, Art. 26(1)).

---

2 Ellis v Worcestershire CC (1961) 12 P & CR 178, 183 per Erskine Simes QC. See also Hoveringham Gravels Ltd v Cheshire DC (1977) 76 LGR 533; Pioneer Aggregates Ltd v Secretary of State for the Environment [1984] 2 All ER 358; Durham CC v Secretary of State for the Environment (1990) 60 P & CR 507; In re Bangor Flagship Developments Ltd's application (No 2) (HC) Carswell J, 21 August [1992] 8 BNIL 91.
3 In R (Thallon) v Department of the Environment for Northern Ireland [1982] NI 26, 34 Hutton J considered it to be clear that certiorari could issue in appropriate cases to quash the decision of a planning authority.

The grant of planning permission may have consequences in other areas of law. In *Gillingham BC v Medway (Chatham) Dock Co. Ltd*[4] planning permission had been granted for the use of a former naval dockyard as a commercial port. This resulted in heavy traffic using roads in a residential area at all times of the day and night. The council later sought a declaration that use of the roads at night would constitute a public nuisance. Dismissing the action Buckley J held that where planning permission had been granted for a development or change of use the question of nuisance would thereafter fall to be decided by reference to a *changed* neighbourhood.

(2) Grant of permission subject to conditions

The second option open to the Department in dealing with an application for planning permission is to grant permission subject to conditions. The imposition of conditions on the grant of permission by planning authorities in England and Wales and the question of the validity of the conditions, have resulted in a substantial body of case law, though surprisingly the courts here have not been similarly troubled to date.

Before considering the rules applicable to the imposition and validity of conditions, two preliminary points should be noted: first there is apparently no principle of law preventing the imposition of conditions which would have the effect of reducing the permitted development below that for which permission had been applied unless the effect of the conditional permission would be to allow development which is in substance different from that for which permission had been applied.[5] In answering whether the conditional permission would be to allow development in substance different from that for which permission had been applied, the main, but not the only, criterion is whether the development is so changed thereby that it would deprive those who should have been consulted of the opportunity of consultation[6] on the changed development. Second, while it is open to the planning authority to impose conditions whose effect is to reduce the development below that for which permission was sought, the planning authority is not under any obligation to consider whether a more restricted application than that submitted would be acceptable. In *Garbutt v Secretary of State for the Environment*[7] an application for permission was made for siting a permanent residential caravan on certain land. Following refusal of permission the applicant sought to quash the decision on the ground *inter alia* that the inspector had failed to consider granting permission subject to conditions as to its

---

4   (1992) 63 P & CR 205.
5   *Bernard Wheatcroft Ltd v Secretary of State for the Environment* (1982) 43 P & CR 233.
6   Ibid.
7   (1989) 57 P & CR 234.

duration. The court rejected the application on this ground, saying that the applicants had not sought permission in those terms. The duty of the authority is to consider the application made: if the authority considers it is a proper case in which to grant permission, the authority can go on to consider whether conditions should be attached to this permission. There is no obligation on the authority to try to make an unacceptable use acceptable by the imposition of conditions.[8]

(a) *Power to impose conditions*

As we have seen Art. 25(1) empowers the Department to grant planning permission subject to such conditions as it thinks fit. Apart from this, Art. 27(1) provides that conditions may be imposed on the grant of planning permission (a) for regulating the development or use of any land under the control of the applicant (whether or not it is land in respect of which the application was made)[9] or requiring the carrying out of works on such land, so far as appears to the Department to be expedient for the purposes of or in connection with the development authorised by the permission (Art. 27(1)(a)), or (b) for requiring the removal of any buildings or works authorised by the permission, or the discontinuance of any use of land so authorised, at the end of a specified period, and the carrying out of any works required for the reinstatement of land at the end of that period (Art. 27(1)(b)). The provisions of Art. 27(1) are expressly 'without prejudice to the generality of Art. 25(1)' so that it would seem that the Department has an unrestricted power to impose such conditions 'as it thinks fit'.[10] Nonetheless, the courts have taken unto themselves a supervisory role and have evolved their own tests which a condition must satisfy in order to be valid. These are as follows:

(i) The condition must have a planning purpose

The first test which must be satisfed if a condition is to be valid is that it must have a planning purpose.[11] The condition may have other purposes as well, but if it is imposed solely for some other purpose or purposes it will not be valid as a planning condition.[12] The planning authority is not at liberty to use its powers for an ulterior object, however desirable that

---

8 *Mason* v *Secretary of State for the Environment* [1984] JPL 332.
9 There is no power to impose a condition requiring the carrying out of work on land not within the application site or under control of the applicant: *Medina* BC v *Proberun Ltd* (1991) 61 P & CR 77, 84 *per* Glidewell LJ.
10 Note that there appear to be three separate provisions for the conditions which the Department may impose: under Art. 25(1), when the test is such conditions as the Department thinks fit; under Art. 27(1)(a), when the test is 'so far as appears to the Department to be expedient for the purposes of or in connection with the development authorised'; and under Art. 27(1)(b) where there is no test at all.
11 *Newbury DC* v *Secretary of State for the Environment* [1980] 1 All ER 731, 745 *per* Lord Fraser.
12 Ibid.

object might be in the public interest.[13] Thus in R v Hillingdon LBC, ex p Royco Homes Ltd[14] conditions imposed by the council (which was both planning authority and housing authority) on the grant of permission which required that the residential accommodation permitted should be occupied first by persons on the housing authority's waiting list and rented for a specified period were held to be invalid. Bridge J said that it was difficult to see how any authority could go further towards unburdening itself and placing on the shoulders of the applicant for planning permission the duty to provide housing accommodation which Parliament had said in the relevant Housing Act should be performed by the local authority.

(ii) The condition must relate to the permitted development

To be valid, the condition must relate to the permitted development to which it is annexed.[15] So in Newbury DC v Secretary of State for the Environment[16] a condition requiring removal of certain buildings was held to be invalid on this ground, the permission to which it was attached being merely a permission for a change of use of the buildings for a limited period. There was nothing about the change of use which required or justified a condition for removal of the buildings: the reason why the planning authority had ordered their removal was to impose or restore amenity and, while that might be a very proper object, it had nothing particularly to do with the use permitted.[17] On the other hand, the court in R v St Edmundsbury DC, ex p Investors in Industry Commercial Properties Ltd[18] upheld a condition requiring three independent retail units in a permission for development of a site as a supermarket: the condition was within the general ambit of the permission sought and the purpose of the condition was to improve the facilities that the development would afford.[19]

(iii) The condition must be 'reasonable'

The third test which a condition must satisfy in order to be valid is that it must be 'reasonable' in the sense of Associated Provincial Picture Houses Ltd v Wednesbury Corp.[20] The condition will be invalid if it is so clearly unreasonable that no reasonable planning authority could have imposed it.[21] If

---

13 Pyx Granite Co. Ltd v Minister of Housing and Local Government [1959] 1 All ER 625, 633 per Lord Denning. (Decision reversed on appeal to the House of Lords: see [1959] 3 All ER 1).
14 [1974] 2 All ER 643.
15 Newbury DC v Secretary of State for the Environment [1980] 1 All ER 731, 745 per Lord Fraser; Pyx Granite Co. Ltd v Minister of Housing and Local Government [1959] 1 All ER 625, 633 per Lord Denning.
16 [1981] 1 All ER 731.   17 Ibid., 747 per Lord Fraser.
18 [1985] 3 All ER 234.   19 Ibid., 250.
20 [1947] 2 All ER 680.
21 Kingston-upon-Thames Royal LBC v Secretary of State for the Environment [1974] 1 All ER 193, 196 per Lord Widgery CJ; Newbury DC v Secretary of State for the Environment [1981] 1 All ER 731, 746 per Lord Fraser.

the condition is unreasonable in this sense it is beyond the power of the planning authority to impose it and this is so even if the developer consents to the condition. The willingness of the developer is irrelevant as *vires* cannot be conferred by consent.[22] But the fact that the developer has suggested a condition or agreed to its terms is likely to be powerful evidence that the condition is *not* unreasonable on the facts, since the parties are usually the best judges of what is reasonable.[23]

Until recently a number of cases stressed that a condition would not satisfy the test of reasonableness unless there was a reasonable prospect that the condition would be fulfilled. In *Jones v Secretary of State for Wales*[24] Glidewell LJ explained that it cannot be reasonable to impose a condition where there is no reasonable prospect of its fulfilment since this would inevitably stultify the permission.[25] Accordingly, the authority was required to ask itself 'what are the prospects that the problem [which the condition is intended to deal with] can be overcome within the life of the permission?' If the answer to that was 'there is no reasonable prospect', it would not be reasonable to impose the condition.[26] This 'reasonable prospects' test was rejected by the House of Lords in *British Railways Board v Secretary of State for the Environment*,[27] which held also that *Jones v Secretary of State for Wales* had been wrongly decided.

We saw in Chapter 12 that it is not an abuse of power by the planning authority to refuse permission if this will produce a result which could not otherwise be produced without payment of compensation.[28] Likewise, it is no objection to the imposition of a condition on the grant of planning permission that the effect of the condition is to require cessation of lawful activities which could otherwise be brought about only upon payment of compensation.[29]

Difficulties arise with conditions which seek to impose an obligation on the developer to pay for works which would otherwise have to be met out of the public purse, e.g. conditions requiring the developer to widen a road. In *Hall & Co. Ltd v Shoreham-by-Sea UDC*[30] the Court of Appeal held that a condition which required a developer to construct a road at the developer's expense and to give right of passage over it to adjoining land was unreasonable and therefore *ultra vires*, on the ground that the authority

---

22 *City of Bradford MC v Secretary of State for the Environment* (1987) 53 P & CR 55, 64 *per* Lloyd LJ.
23 Ibid.
24 (1991) 61 P & CR 238.
25 Ibid., 248. See also *Medina BC v Proberun Ltd* (1991) 61 P & CR 77, 86 and *Pedgrift v Oxfordshire CC* (1992) 63 P & CR 246.
26 (1991) 61 P & CR 238, 248.
27 [1994] JPL 32
28 *R v Exeter CC, ex p Terry* [1990] 1 All ER 413, *ante* Chapter 12.
29 *Kingston-upon-Thames Royal LBC v Secretary of State for the Environment* [1974] 1 All ER 193, disapproving dicta to the contrary in *Allnatt London Properties Ltd v Middlesex CC* (1964) 15 P & CR 288.
30 [1964] 1 All ER 1.

was in effect taking away the developer's rights of property without compensation.[31] *Hall & Co.* was recently followed in *City of Bradford MC v Secretary of State for the Environment*,[32] where the court was asked to say (1) that a planning condition which requires the developer to carry out or fund a public function of a planning authority as the price of getting planning permission is always unlawful, and (2) that the degree of acquiescence by the developer in the condition so imposed is wholly irrelevant.[33] Lloyd LJ expressed doubt about the principle so stated saying that the true principle was simply that the condition must not be manifestly unreasonable.[34]

(iv) The condition must not be uncertain

A condition will be invalid if it is uncertain, i.e. if it can be given no meaning or no sensible or ascertainable meaning.[35] Merely because the condition is ambiguous or leads to absurd results does not mean the condition is void for uncertainty as it is the function of the courts to resolve ambiguities.[36] The true question is whether the language of the condition makes sense, i.e. is capable of a reasonable construction, and not whether the developer is left uncertain how the condition will operate, though that may be relevant in considering whether the condition is reasonable.[37] A recent example is *Alderson v Secretary of State for the Environment*[38] where the court had to consider a condition restricting occupancy of a dwelling to a person employed locally in agriculture. The court held that the word 'locally' did not render the condition void for uncertainty.[39]

(b) Enforceability and validity

The validity of a condition imposed on the grant of planning permission is to be tested by reference to the matters just considered. In *Bromsgrove DC v Secretary of State for the Environment*[40] it was argued that in addition to these matters a further test applied, namely that a condition would be invalid if it was incapable of enforcement. Mann J held that there was no such principle.[41] The practical difficulties of enforcing a condition are a separate issue from the validity of the condition. If, however, enforcement

---

31 Ibid., 10 *per* Willmer LJ.
32 (1987) 53 P & CR 55.
33 Ibid., 64.
34 Ibid.
35 *Fawcett Properties Ltd v Buckinghamshire CC* [1960] 3 All ER 503, 517, *per* Lord Denning.
36 Ibid.
37 *Hall & Co. Ltd v Shoreham-by-Sea UDC* [1964] 1 All ER 1, 5 *per* Willmer LJ.
38 (1985) 49 P & CR 307.
39 See also *Ashford BC v Secretary of State for the Environment* [1992] JPL 362.
40 (1988) 56 P & CR 221.
41 Ibid., 227.

is *impossible* rather than a matter of practical difficulty, it may be that the condition would fail as being absurd.[42]

The relationship between the validity of a condition and the ability of the planning authority to enforce it can be seen also in *Grampian Regional Council v City of Aberdeen DC*.[43] There planning permission for development of land was refused on the ground of traffic safety. It was found at an enquiry that the problem of safety could be resolved if a public road were to be closed. The reporter conducting the enquiry concluded it would not be competent to grant permission subject to a condition requiring closure of the road, as closure did not lie wholly within the powers of the developer to bring about. The reporter's decision was quashed, the court holding that it would be competent to frame the condition in the negative, i.e. that no development should be carried out until the road was closed. In the House of Lords it was argued that there was no difference between a condition requiring a result which it was not within the power of the developer alone to bring about and a condition prescribing that no development should begin until the result had been achieved. Lord Keith held that there was a crucial difference between the two types of condition, in that the latter is enforceable whereas the former is not.[44]

(c) *Effect of invalid conditions*

Where a condition fails to satisfy the tests the courts have evolved for determining its validity, it is void and of no effect. The question arises, however, as to the validity of the permission to which it is attached: if the condition is invalid, does this mean that the whole permission is invalid, or can the condition be severed from the remainder of the permission so that the development permitted can go ahead without the condition? The view has been taken that planning permission is *sui generis* and entire, so that if a condition is invalid the whole permission fails.[45] It appears now to be clearly established however that severance is possible in appropriate cases. In *Kent CC v Kingsway Investments (Kent) Ltd*[46] Lord Reid thought that a condition which had nothing to do with planning considerations but which was calculated to achieve some ulterior object thought to be in the public interest would be severable, whereas a condition, although invalid, which limited the manner in which the land could be developed would not.[47] In the same case Lord Morris distinguished conditions

---

42 Ibid., 225.
43 (1984) 47 P & CR 633.
44 Ibid.
45 *Kent CC v Kingsway Investments (Kent) Ltd* [1970] 1 All ER 70, 89 *per* Lord Guest; see also *Pyx Granite Co. Ltd v Minister of Housing and Local Government* [1958] 1 All ER 625, 637 *per* Hodgson LJ.
46 [1970] 1 All ER 70.
47 Ibid., 75.

which were unimportant or incidental from those which were part of the structure of the planning permission. The former would be severable whereas the latter would not.[48] Similarly, in the Court of Appeal Davies LJ had said that an invalid condition which related to matters fundamental to the development would render the whole permission void, while a condition which related to matters preparatory or introductory to the permission or its final form would be severable.[49]

(d) *Duty to give reasons*

Where the Department decides to grant permission subject to conditions it is obliged to state its reasons for such decision in the decision notice (GDO Art. 13). While the requirement to state the Department's reasons is mandatory, failure to do so will not render the decision void.[50] Failure to give reasons or the giving of inadequate reasons may however justify the court quashing the decision on an application for judicial review. This will be the case only if the court is satisfied that the interests of the applicant for judicial review have been substantially prejudiced.[51] Normally prejudice will arise from one of three causes: (1) where the reasons for the decision are so inadequately or obscurely expressed as to raise a substantial doubt whether the decision was taken within the powers of the statute; (2) where the policy considerations on which the decision is based are not explained sufficiently clearly to enable the developer reasonably to assess the prospects of success in an application for some alternative form of development; and (3) an opponent of development may be substantially prejudiced by a decision to grant permission in which the planning considerations on which the decision is based, particularly if they relate to planning policy, are not explained sufficiently clearly to indicate what, if any, impact they may have in relation to the decision of future applications.[52]

(e) *Effect of permission subject to conditions*

As with the grant of permission unconditionally, the grant of planning permission subject to conditions enures for the benefit of the land and of all persons for the time being having an estate therein (1991 Order, Art. 30(1)). In *Brayhead (Ascot) Ltd v Berkshire CC*[53] the court raised the question how far the doctrine that someone who takes the benefit of a grant

---

48 Ibid., 86.
49 [1969] 1 All ER 601, 618. For an example of conditions fundamental to the permission see R v *Hillingdon LBC, ex p Royco Homes Ltd* [1974] 2 All ER 643.
50 *Brayhead (Ascot) Ltd v Berkshire CC* [1964] 1 All ER 149.
51 *Save Britain's Heritage v Secretary of State for the Environment* [1991] 2 All ER 10, 24 *per* Lord Bridge.
52 Ibid.
53 [1964] 1 All ER 149, 154.

must also bear its burdens operates to carry with a planning permission its attached burdens, limitations and conditions. This, however, may be a mistaken translation of principles of private law into a public law context,[54] and certainly no doubt was expressed in *Times Investment Ltd v Secretary of State for the Environment*[55] that conditions would continue to bind the land in the hands of any successor in title to the original applicant.

(f) Appeals

Where planning permission has been granted subject to conditions, the applicant has the right to appeal against the decision to the Planning Appeals Commission ((1991 Order, Art. 32(1)), except where the application is one to which the provisions of Art. 31 have been applied (Art. 32(2)).[56] The provisions of the 1991 Order as to appeals are considered later.

(g) Purchase notices

The grant of planning permission subject to conditions allows the owner of land to serve a purchase notice on the Department requiring the Department to purchase his estate in the land under Art. 94 of the 1991 Order, provided that the conditions set out in Art. 94(1) are satisfied (1991 Order, Art. 94(1)(a)). The owner must show (1) that the land has become incapable of reasonably beneficial use in its existing state; (2) that the land cannot be rendered capable of reasonably beneficial use by the carrying out of the permitted development in accordance with the conditions subject to which permission was granted; and (3) that the land cannot be rendered capable of reasonably beneficial use by the carrying out of any other development for which planning permission has been granted (Art. 94(1)).[57]

(h) Compensation

The grant of planning permission subject to conditions may entitle the applicant to compensation under ss 14 or 29 of the Land Development Values (Compensation) Act (NI) 1965. S. 14(1) of the Act provides that compensation is payable in respect of a compensatable estate[58] following the grant of planning permission subject to conditions on an application for planning permission made after 25 February 1963 for carrying out what the Act defines as 'new development', i.e. development[59] other than

---

54 See *Pioneer Aggregates (UK) Ltd v Secretary of State for the Environment* [1984] 2 All ER 358.
55 (1991) 61 P & CR 98.
56 For the provisions of Art. 31 see Chapter 11.
57 Purchase notices are considered in Chapter 24.
58 As defined in s. 43(1).
59 As defined in s. 9(1) of the Planning (Interim Development) Act (NI) 1944: see 1965 Act, s. 43(1). The definition is not identical to the definition of development in the 1991 Order.

that specified in sch. 1 of the Act (1965 Act, s. 43(1)). Compensation is payable if at the time that permission is granted (1) the land has a balance of development value;[60] (2) the value of the compensatable estate is depreciated by the decision on the application for permission; and (3) compensation under the Planning (Interim Development) Act (NI) 1944 has not been paid and is not payable in respect of the decision.

Compensation is not payable in respect of the grant subject to conditions of permission to display advertisements (s. 15(3)), or where planning permission is granted subject to conditions relating to (1) the dimensions, design, structure or external appearance of any building, or the materials to be used in its construction; (2) the number of any buildings included in the development or the disposition of any building so included; (3) the character or user of any building or other land included in the development; (4) the position in which caravans may be stationed on a caravan site at any one time or the number of caravans which may be so stationed; (5) the net annual value of any building included in the development; (6) the manner in which any land is to be laid out for the purposes of the development, including the provision of facilities for the parking, loading, unloading or fuelling of vehicles on the land; (7) the width, position or arrangement of streets or the materials to be used in the construction of streets; (8) the width, position or arrangement of any means of access to a highway or the materials to be used in the construction of any such means of access; or (9) the getting of minerals or any operations incidental thereto (s. 15(4)). Nor is compensation payable where the conditions subject to which permission has been granted are those contained in Arts 34 or 35 of the 1991 Order,[61] or if any development permitted by the decision is initiated before the date on which an appeal is determined under Art. 32 of the 1991 Order.[62]

Where compensation is payable under s. 14, the amount of the compensation is the amount by which the compensatable estate is depreciated by the planning decision, or the amount of the balance of development value[63] immediately before the decision, whichever is the less (s. 17(1)).[64]

S. 29 provides for compensation to be payable in respect of decisions on applications for planning permission for development of any class specified in sch. 1 of the Act, i.e. development other than 'new development' to which s. 14 applies (s. 29(1)).[65]

If it can be shown that the value of a compensatable estate in the land is less than it would have been had planning permission been granted unconditionally, compensation of an amount equal to the difference is

---

60 See below, p. 142.
61 1972 Order, Art. 69A(1) (as inserted by the 1991 Order, Art. 133 and sch. 5).
62 1965 Act, s. 15(5), as amended by the 1991 Order, sch. 5.
63 See below.
64 For calculation of depreciation see ss 18 and 19.
65 S. 29(1). Compensation under s. 29 is payable once only in relation to any estate in land: s. 29(3A) (inserted by Planning (Amendment) (NI) Order 1982, Art. 18(c)).

payable unless compensation under the Planning (Interim Development) Act (NI) 1944 has been paid or is payable (1965 Act s. 29(2)). Compensation is not payable under s. 29 in respect of the grant of permission subject to conditions for the use as two or more separate dwelling houses of a building which at a material date[66] was used as a single dwelling house, unless the lower value of the compensatable estate is not reasonable having regard to the value of any other comparable dwelling houses in the area (s. 29(3)). For the purposes of s. 29 the conditions contained in Arts 34 and 35 of the 1991 Order are disregarded (1972 Order, Art. 69A(2)).

Special provision is made under both s. 14 and s. 29 for cases where the compensatable estate is held by a public body (1965 Act, s. 14(2); s. 30). The procedure for making claims is considered later.

Finally, compensation is payable by virtue of Art. 68 of the 1972 Order if planning permission is granted subject to conditions in respect of certain types of development which were permitted under the 1944 Act.[67]

(i) *Judicial review*

As with any other decision on an application for planning permission, the grant of permission subject to conditions is open to challenge by way of judicial review in appropriate circumstances.

(j) *Getting rid of conditions*

Finally, assuming planning permission is granted subject to conditions which satisfy the tests for validity outlined above, what can be done to get rid of the conditions? There are several possibilities. To begin with, the condition may of course expire naturally, e.g. where it prohibits use of property in a particular way for a specified period only. Again, the condition will cease to be applicable once it has been fulfilled, e.g. a condition prohibiting development until adequate sightlines have been provided. Thirdly, it appears that a condition may cease to apply if it becomes incapable of fulfilment. In R *Bell & Co. (Estates) Ltd* v *Department of the Environment for Northern Ireland*[68] planning permission was granted subject to conditions requiring that the developer should submit a layout co-ordinating development on the application site with the overall detailed layout proposals (which had yet to be prepared) for the area, and that such submission should take place within three years. By the end of the three year period such overall proposals had still not been prepared by the Department. The Court of Appeal held that the condition requiring submission of proposals by the developer within three years

---

66 As defined in sch. 1 of the Act.
67 Development by mining undertakers and erection of certain buildings for the purposes of agriculture.
68 [1982] NI 322.

did not apply as it had become impossible for the developer to comply with it due to the acts and omissions of the Department.

A condition will not cease to apply merely because the activity prohibited in the condition is permitted in some other way. In R v *Tunbridge Wells BC, ex p Blue Boys Development Ltd*[69] planning permission had been granted for self-catering holiday units subject to a condition that the accommodation would be used only for short-term lettings and not for permanent occupation. The developer later obtained a determination under the equivalent of Art. 41 of the 1991 Order stating that a change of use from holiday units to residential units would not constitute development. The developer sought a declaration that the condition in the planning permission no longer applied. Popplewell J accepted that the effect of the determination was to grant permission for use as residential units but held that this did not abolish the condition in the original permission.

Where the condition does not cease to apply through one of the above occurrences, it may be possible for the developer to take action to have the condition in effect removed. We have already seen that an applicant to whom planning permission is granted subject to conditions may appeal to the Planning Appeals Commission (1991 Order, Art. 32(1)). Such an appeal, however, must be made within six months of the decision of the Department, or such longer period as the Commission allows (Art. 32(3)). If the developer wishes to have the condition removed after that period has elapsed he may apply for planning permission for development of the site without compliance with the conditions under Art. 28(1).[70] As we have seen, on such an application the Department will consider only the question of the conditions (Art. 28(3)). Again, it will be recalled that planning permission may be applied for to retain buildings or works already constructed or a use of land already instituted without compliance with conditions subject to which a previous planning permission was granted (Art. 29(1)).[71] It seems that it is not possible to make use of the provisions of the Property (NI) Order 1978 which empowers the Lands Tribunal or the court to modify or extinguish impediments to the enjoyment of land, as the impediments which may be modified do not include obligations imposed under statutory provisions of a public general character, e.g. conditions attached to planning permissions.[72]

---

69 (1990) 59 P & CR 315.
70 See Chapter 11.
71 Ibid.
72 Property (NI) Order 1978, Article 3(1)(b); Dawson, 'Modification and extinguishment of land obligations under the Property (NI) Order 1978' (1978) 29 NILQ 223, 225.

(3) Refusal of planning permission

The third decision open to the Department on an application for planning permission is a refusal of permission. As with the grant of permission subject to conditions, if the Department refuses permission it is required to give its reasons for so doing (GDO, Art. 13). Likewise, the applicant has a right of appeal to the Planning Appeals Commission under Art. 32 of the 1991 Order, and the provisions of Art. 94 as to service of a purchase notice apply. Again, as with any decision of the Department on an application for planning permission, the decision may be challenged by way of judicial review in appropriate circumstances.

As with the grant of planning permission subject to conditions, the refusal of planning permission may entitle the owner of a compensatable estate in the land the subject of the decision to compensation under s. 14 or s. 29 of the Land Development Values (Compensation) Act (NI) 1965, or under Art. 68 of the 1972 Order.[73] There are, however, certain differences in the case of compensation payable under s. 14 of the 1965 Act between the grant of permission subject to conditions and the refusal of permission. Compensation is not payable under s. 14 following the refusal of planning permission (a) where the development consists of a change in the use of a building; or a change in the use of any land other than buildings, unless the development consists of the carrying out of any building operations or the getting of minerals or the stationing of caravans on the land; (b) if the reason or one of the reasons stated for the refusal is that development of the kind proposed would be premature having regard to the order of priority, if any, contained in a development plan for the area, or any existing deficiency in the provision of water supplies, sewerage services or roads and the period within which any such deficiency may reasonably be expected to be made good (1965 Act, s. 15(1) (a) and (b)). The restriction on compensation by virtue of (b) above does not apply if the application was made more than seven years after a previous refusal for the same reason (s. 15(1)). Nor is compensation payable under s. 14 following a refusal of planning permission if the reason, or one of the reasons, for refusal is that the land is unsuitable for the proposed development on account of its liability to flooding or subsidence (s. 15(2)), or if permission is available for development of the land of a residential, commercial or industrial character being development which consists wholly or mainly of houses, flats, shop or office premises, or industrial buildings or any combination thereof (s. 16(1) and (3)).

In the case of a refusal of permission for certain classes of development which is not 'new development', compensation is not payable under s. 29 of the 1965 Act if, by virtue of a previous planning permission, it remains a condition that the building to which the refusal relates be demolished or cease to be used as a dwelling house.[74]

---

73 See above.
74 S. 29(2A) (as inserted by Planning (Amendment) (NI) Order 1982, Art. 18(b)).

(4) Failure to make a decision

We have seen that the period within which the Department is required to give notice of its decision on an application for planning permission is two months from the date of receipt of the application or such longer period as may be agreed (GDO, Art. 11(2)). If the Department fails to give notice of its decision within that period the applicant has various options open to him. He may of course decide to do nothing and simply await the decision which will come sooner or later. He is not obliged to do so. Art. 33 of the 1991 Order empowers the applicant to appeal to the Planning Appeals Commission as if the Department had refused permission and he had received notification of refusal at the end of the two month period, or of any extended period agreed in writing between him and the Department. The Article enables the applicant to take the matter out of the hands of the Department and put it in the hands of the Commission. But this may not always be in the applicant's best interests. As we have seen, if the Department refuses permission, it is obliged to give its reasons for doing so (GDO, Art. 13). The applicant may appeal to the Planning Appeals Commission, and will go to the Commission with knowledge of the Department's objections to his proposals. If, however, the applicant appeals under Art. 33 where the Department has failed to make any decision, he will not know whether the Department objects at all and, if so, what its objections are. Therefore, he will not be able to focus the preparation of his case on known issues of contention, which would be the situation should he choose to await a formal refusal from the Department. There is a third option open to the applicant. The Department is under a duty to determine an application for planning permission. As with any other duty imposed on a public authority, failure to carry out the duty is actionable by way of judicial review. Mandamus is available to compel an authority to carry out its duties, and would seem to be available against a planning authority where it has failed to determine an application for planning permission.[75]

2 Appeals

As we have seen, an appeal lies to the Planning Appeals Commission against the decision of the Department to grant planning permission subject to conditions, or to refuse permission (1991 Order, Art. 32(1)), or where the Department fails to make any decision within the time specified in the GDO (1991 Order Art. 33). Only the applicant may appeal for permission (Art. 32(1)). Third parties have no right of appeal, and are

---

75 Bovis Homes (Scotland) Ltd v Inverclyde DC 1982 SLT 473.

therefore limited to challenging the decision by way of judicial review. An appeal is made by notice in writing which must be served on the Commission within six months from the date of notification (or deemed notification in the case of appeals in default of a decision under Art. 33) of the decision of the Department to which it relates, or such longer period as the Commission may allow (Art. 32(3)). The provisions of Arts 21 to 28 of the 1991 Order apply in relation to appeals as they apply to applications for planning permission (Art. 32(6)). Thus, e.g. publication of the appeal will take place in a local newspaper, and the criteria for determining applications for planning permission *viz.* the development plan and other material considerations are applicable to determination of appeals by the Commission.

As we have noted, appeals to the Commission are heard by a member of the Commission appointed by the Chief Commissioner for that purpose, who then makes a report to the Commission which as a whole determines the appeal (1991 Order, Art. 111).[76] Appeals may be dealt with either by a hearing at which the appellant and the Department (and possibly third parties) present their cases, or they may be dealt with on the basis of written representations. There are no rules of procedure governing either method. Art. 32(5) of the 1991 Order provides that the Commission shall, if either the appellant or the Department so desires, afford to each of them an opportunity of appearing before and being heard by the Commission, so that the disposal of an appeal by way of written representations can take place only where neither the appellant nor the Department requests a hearing. Where a hearing is requested, conduct and procedure are determined by the Commission. The Commission is bound to observe the rules of natural justice both in reaching its decision and in the conduct of any hearing held by one of its members.[77] Insofar as hearings are concerned, there are two questions: first, who is entitled to appear and take part in the hearing, second, what do the rules of natural justice require in the particular case?[78] On the first question it has been said that a person is entitled to object to a planning matter if he has a *bona fide* reason. He does not have to be a ratepayer, nor does he have to be a resident, but he must not be an officious bystander or an officious busybody. He must have what any reasonable person would have said was a legitimate interest in being heard in objection.[79] In *In re North Down BC's application*[80] it was accepted by the Planning Appeals Commission that a district council would normally be regarded as having a legitimate interest in a planning appeal relating to land within its

---

76 See Chapter 2.
77 *In re North Down BC's application* [1986] NI 304, 321 *per* Carswell J.
78 Ibid.
79 *R v Hammersmith & Pulham LBC, ex p People Before Profit Ltd* [1981] JPL 869, 870 *per* Comyn J.
80 [1986] NI 304.

district.[81] Insofar as the conduct of the hearing is concerned, Carswell J in the same case noted the comments of Lord Diplock in Bushell v Secretary of State for the Environment[82] warning against 'over-judicialising' enquiries, and Viscount Dilhorne's comments in the same case that the procedure does not have to be the same as that of a court of law, so long as objectors are given a full opportunity of being heard in support of their objection.[83] A tribunal such as the Planning Appeals Commission must give each of the parties the opportunity of adequately presenting his case, and it falls short of that standard if it fails to give him a fair chance of effective participation in the proceedings.[84] Thus, the decision of a Commission conducting a hearing to refuse an application for an adjournment has twice justified relief by way of judicial review on the application of the party seeking the adjournment.[85]

The procedure adopted at appeals against refusals of planning permission or grants subject to conditions is that the Department presents its case, is then cross-examined by the other parties, followed by the third party objectors who present their case and are cross-examined, followed finally by the appellant. After the conclusion of the appeal the commissioner appointed to hear it will report his findings and recommendations to the Commission which will make the decision on the appeal. The provisions of the 1991 Order in this regard have already been noted.[86] When determining an appeal the Commission has a wider task than that of a judge determining a civil action. The Commission has to consider material considerations, whether canvassed by the parties or not. It is not obliged however to cast about trying to think of every issue which may be relevant.[87] The issues raised by the parties are a good indication of what they consider relevant.[88] It appears that the Commission will be entitled to differ from the appointed member on an inference of fact, provided there is material sufficient for it to do so.[89] If it is a matter of planning policy the Commission is entitled to disagree with the conclusions or recommendations of the appointed member, but the

---

81 Ibid., 320.
82 [1980] 2 All ER 608.
83 [1986] NI 304, 322.
84 Ibid.
85 In re Johnston's application [1984] 10 NIJB; In re North Down BC's application [1986] NI 304.
86 See Chapter 2.
87 Compare *Top Deck Holdings Ltd v Secretary of State for the Environment* [1991] JPL 961; *Pehrsson v Secretary of State for the Environment* (1990) 61 P & CR 266; *Murphy v Secretary of State for Wales* [1994] JPL 156 (whether decision-maker obliged to consider whether planning objection could be overcome by imposition of planning conditions). See also *Elmbridge BC v Secretary of State for the Environment* [1994] JPL 242 on the duties of an inspector hearing an appeal.
88 *Secretary of State for the Environment v Cambridge CC* [1992] EGCS 16.
89 *Coleen Properties Ltd v Minister of Housing and Local Government* [1971] 1 All ER 1049, 1053 per Lord Denning, MR. See also *Secretary of State for the Environment v Cambridge CC* [1992] EGCS 16.

Commission will have to make clear what the policy is and its relevance to the issues raised at the hearing.[90] If there has been conflicting evidence at the enquiry the Commission may prefer one piece of evidence to another provided there is material to entitle it to do so and the Commission gives its reasons for doing so. The courts will of course interfere with the Commission's decision if it acts *ultra vires*, and the materials on which they will base their decisions are the report of the appointed member and the decision notice of the Commission,[91] though the decision notice will not be subjected to the kind of scrutiny appropriate to the determination of a contract or a statute.[92]

3 Compensation: the Land Development Values (Compensation) Act (NI) 1965

As we have noted, the grant of planning permission subject to conditions or the refusal of planning permission may entitle the applicant to compensation under the provisions of the Land Development Values (Compensation) Act (NI) 1965. We have seen that in the case of 'new development' i.e. development of a kind not mentioned in sch. 1 of the Act, compensation is payable only if the land to which the decision of the Department relates has a balance of development value (s. 14(1)(a)). In the case of development other than new development, no such requirement exists. It is therefore necessary to know whether the development which is the subject of the decision of the Department is new development or not and, if so, whether the application site has a balance of development value.

(1) New development

As already noted, 'new development' means development[93] which is not of a class specified in sch. 1 of the Act (1965 Act, s. 43(1)). The types of development which are specified in the schedule—and which therefore do not constitute new development—comprise certain works of rebuilding or enlargement of buildings in existence at the passing of the Act (paras 1 and 3); certain works in connection with mineral excavation (para. 5); and certain changes of use (paras 2 and 6).[94] Most types of development, however, will constitute 'new development' for the purposes of the Act.

---

90 *Seddon Properties Ltd* v *Secretary of State for the Environment* (1978) 42 P & CR 26.
91 Ibid.
92 Ibid.; *Save Britain's Heritage* v *Secretary of State for the Environment* [1991] 2 All ER 10, *per* Lord Bridge.
93 As defined in s. 9(1) of the Planning (Interim Development) Act (NI) 1944.
94 See also sch. 2.

(2) Development value

In cases of new development, compensation is payable only if the application site has a balance of development value (s. 14(1)(a)). To understand when this will exist it is necessary to understand the scheme of the Act. S. 1 of the Act provides that land has a development value where the unrestricted value of the land, i.e. the value that a fee simple absolute in possession in the land would have had on 25 February 1963 (s. 2(1)(a)), exceeds the restricted value of that land, i.e. the value that such a fee simple would have had on that date if computed on the assumption that planning permission would have been granted for development other than 'new development' (s. 2(1)(b)). The development value of the land in other words represents the difference in value which planning permission for 'new development' makes to the land. However, for the purposes of the provisions of s. 14 as to compensation, land is taken as having a development value only if a development value has been determined to exist following an application for that purpose made under s. 5 of the Act (s. 8). In determining whether land has a balance of development value, any compensation paid under the Planning (Interim Development) Act (NI) 1944 and any compensation paid under s. 14 of the 1965 Act are deducted from that development value (s. 9), as is the value[95] of any new development[96] which has been initiated (s. 10(1)). The Act contains provisions for enabling anyone to obtain a certificate from the Department stating whether any land has a development value and if so the amount of that value (s. 13(1)).[97]

(3) Procedure for obtaining compensation

The procedure for making a claim for compensation under s. 14 or s. 29 is set out in s. 20(2),[98] and Regulations made under the Act.[99] A claim must be made before the end of six months beginning with the date of the planning decision to which it relates, but the Department may allow an extended period for making a claim (s. 20(2)). Where the Department disputes a claim under s. 14 on the grounds (1) that the development to which the planning decision relates was not new development, (2) that at the time of the decision no part of the land to which the claim relates had a balance of development value, or (3) that compensation is excluded by

---

95 Determined in accordance with sch. 3 of the Act.
96 Other than development taken to have been completed at 4 November 1965 or initiated in pursuance of a decision made before 4 November 1965 on an application made before 26 February 1963: s. 10(2).
97 See also Land Development Values (Ascertainment and Certificates) Regulations (NI) 1965.
98 Applied to cases under s. 29 by s. 29(9).
99 Land Development Values (Compensation) Regulations (NI) 1965.

s. 15 or s. 16, the Department is required to notify the claimant accordingly, stating on which of these grounds it appears that compensation is not payable (s. 20(4)(a)). The claimant may within three months refer the matter to the Lands Tribunal which is then required to confirm or vary the Department's findings.[100] If the dispute is not referred to the Tribunal within that time the Department's findings are treated as conclusive.[101]

Where compensation is payable under s. 14 or s. 29, the Department is required to pay the compensation to the person who was entitled to the compensatable estate at the date of the relevant decision, unless that person does not make a claim in which case the Department may pay the compensation to the person (being a person entitled to an equitable interest) who, as against the person in whom the equitable estate is vested, is entitled absolutely to that estate (s. 22(1)).[102] If the Department is unable to determine to whom compensation is payable, the compensation may be paid into court (s. 22(5)).

(4) Repayment of compensation

Where compensation has been paid under s. 14, s. 24(1) provides that a condition applies by which no 'relevant development' is to be initiated on the land to which the planning decision relates until the amount of the compensation repayable under s. 24 has been paid to or secured to the Department. 'Relevant development' means new development which is development of a residential, commercial or industrial character and consists wholly or mainly of the construction of houses, flats, shop or office premises, or industrial buildings (including warehouses), or any combination thereof; or which, having regard to the probable value of the development, the Department determines should constitute relevant development (s. 24(14)). The amount repayable is the whole of the compensation if the land on which the 'relevant development' is to be carried out is identical with or includes the land to which the decision relates (s. 24(3)(a)); or a proportion of the amount of the compensation[103] where the land to be developed is part of the land to which the decision relates or includes part of the land together with other land (s. 24(3)(b)). The amount repayable is to be paid as a single capital payment without interest[104] to the Department and is recoverable as a civil debt (s. 24(10) and (11)).[105]

---

100 Land Development Values (Compensation) Regulations (NI) 1965, Reg. 6(1) and (3).
101 Ibid., Reg. 6(4).
102 For application to claims under s. 29 see s. 29(9). For cases where the compensatable estate is comprised in a settlement, see s. 22(2).
103 Calculated in accordance with s. 24(4).
104 Though the Department has power to direct that the amount shall be paid as a single capital payment with interest at a specified time or by instalments: s. 24(10)(a) and (b).
105 See also s. 24(12). Where relevant development is initiated without the developer complying with the condition as to repayment of compensation the Department may serve

144 Development Control

The Department has power to remit the whole or part of the amount repayable under s. 24 where it is satisfied that development which it considers desirable for serving the most appropriate planning of the area in question is unlikely to be carried out unless the condition as to repayment is modified (s. 24(6)).

4 Judicial review

We have already noted that a decision of a planning authority on an application for planning permission is open to challenge by way of judicial review.[106] An application for judicial review is an application in which the applicant seeks relief by way of an order of mandamus, certiorari, or prohibition; a declaration, or an injunction (Judicature (NI) Act 1978, s. 18(1)). The procedure for an application for judicial review is contained in Order 53 of the Rules of the Supreme Court (NI) 1980. A detailed examination of the ambit of the remedy of judicial review is outside the scope of this book; what follows is a brief examination of the remedy with reference to its application to planning matters.[107]

To begin with, judicial review may be granted in respect of decisions of the Department in relation to the exercise of its powers under the 1991 Order[108] and the Planning Appeals Commission in relation to appeals to the Commission.[109] The remedy is concerned with a review of the decision-making process of the body against whom the remedy is sought: it is not concerned with the merit of the decision itself. The remedy is to ensure that the applicant has been given fair treatment by the body in question, rather than to enquire if the court would have come to a different decision on the facts. The function of the court is therefore supervisory rather than appellate. Furthermore, the remedy is discretionary and may be refused if a more appropriate remedy exists. We have seen that an applicant for planning permission has a right of appeal against a refusal of permission or grant of permission subject to conditions, but this will not of itself prevent the court granting relief by way of judicial review at the suit of an applicant for planning permission in appropriate circumstances.[110]

---

notice on the developer specifying the amount to be repaid and requiring him to repay it within the time specified in the notice, not being less than three months: s. 24(5).
106 See e.g. R (Thallon) v Department of the Environment for Northern Ireland [1982] NI 26; In re Blair's application [1985] NI 68.
107 For fuller examination of the remedy see Hadfield, 'Judicial Review in Northern Ireland: A primer' (1991) 42 NILQ 332.
108 R (Thallon) v Department of the Environment for Northern Ireland [1982] NI 26.
109 In re Johnston's application [1984] 10 NIJB; In re North Down BC's application [1986] NI 304; In re Magill's application [1988] 7 NIJB 37.
110 R v Hillingdon LBC ex p Royco Homes Ltd [1974] 2 All ER 643. See Hadfield, op. cit., p. 341 n. 33. Where the applicant for judicial review is someone other than the applicant for planning permission the problem does not arise. On the availability of judicial review where an appeal procedure exists see R v Birmingham CC ex p Ferrero Ltd [1993] 1 All ER 530.

(1) Grounds for review

In *Council of Civil Service Unions* v *Minister for the Civil Service*[111] Lord Diplock said that the grounds on which administrative action is subject to control by way of judicial review may be classified under three heads:

(a) Illegality

A decision may be quashed on the ground of illegality. The decision-maker must understand correctly the law which regulates his decision-making power and must give effect to it.[112] A decision may be quashed under this heading when the decision-maker has for example purported to exercise a power which he does not in law possess,[113] or when he takes into account irrelevant factors or fails to take into account relevant factors.[114] Thus, the decision of the Department to grant planning permission was quashed when the Department had failed to take into account the opposition of the Department's Roads Service to the proposed development and had taken into account a matter which should not have been, *viz.* the purported grant of planning permission at an earlier date which was in fact void.[115] Similarly, a decision of the Planning Appeals Commission was quashed on the ground that the Commission had incorrectly applied the Department's rural policy.[116]

(b) Irrationality

The second ground identified by Lord Diplock as one on which a decision of an administrative body will be open to judicial review is that of irrationality, or 'Wednesbury unreasonableness'.[117] A decision will be unreasonable in this sense if it is 'so outrageous in its defiance of logic or of accepted moral standards that no sensible person who had applied his mind to the question to be decided could have arrived at it.'[118] A decision of the planning authority is a decision on policy involving a consideration of what is the best thing to do, and not just an assessment of the facts, so that it is possible for the Department to reach a different decision from that of the Planning Appeals Commission. Accordingly, the fact that the Commission recommends refusal of planning permission following a public local enquiry held by it and the Department later grants permission will not of itself mean that the Department has acted

---

111 [1984] 3 All ER 935, 950.
112 Ibid.
113 Ibid., 953 *per* Lord Roskill.
114 Hadfield, *op. cit.*, 348.
115 R (*Thallon*) v *Department of the Environment for Northern Ireland* [1983] NI 26.
116 *In re Magill's application* [1988] 7 NIJB 37. See also *In re McGuigan's application* (1991) unrep.
117 *Associated Provincial Picture Houses Ltd* v *Wednesbury Corp.* [1947] 2 All ER 680.
118 *Council of Civil Service Unions* v *Minister for the Civil Service* [1984] 3 All ER 935, 951.

unreasonably.[119] If, however, the report of the Commission shows that there is no demand or need for the development proposed and the Department grants permission, the basis for the grant of permission would have disappeared.[120] When the Department's decision is based on the application of a policy, adherence to that policy can be condemned only by showing that circumstances render it wholly unreasonable to persist with that policy, or that a wholly unwarrantable use or disregard of evidence has occurred to prop up that policy.[121]

(c) *Procedural impropriety*

Lord Diplock's 'procedural impropriety' is traditionally expressed as failure to observe the rules of natural justice, but this expression has been criticised as being widely misunderstood and misused.[122] Likewise, speaking of a duty to act fairly may not be accurate.[123] The expression 'procedural impropriety' includes failure to observe applicable procedural rules, even though such failure does not amount to denial of natural justice.[124] Whichever expression is used, the two elements of the obligation on the decision-maker are the rule against bias and the right to be heard.[125] We have already described the duty of the Department to act fairly on the consideration of an application for planning permission[126] and noted the obligation of the Planning Appeals Commission to observe the rules of natural justice.

(2) Standing

On an application for judicial review the court is precluded from granting any relief unless it considers that the applicant has a sufficient interest in the matter to which the application relates.[127] Clearly an applicant for planning permission has a sufficient interest in the decision the Department makes on the application,[128] as would, it is suggested, a successor in title to the applicant,[129] but what of third parties e.g. neighbours? As we have seen such parties do not have any right to appeal against the decision of the Department on an application for planning

---

119 In re Blair's application [1985] NI 68.
120 Ibid., 83.
121 Ibid.
122 *Council of Civil Service Unions v Minister for the Civil Service* [1984] 3 All ER 935, 954 *per* Lord Roskill.
123 Ibid.
124 Ibid., 951 *per* Lord Diplock.
125 Hadfield, *op. cit.*, 352.
126 Chapter 12.
127 Judicature (NI) Act 1978, s. 18(4).
128 In re Magill's application [1988] 7 NIJB 37.
129 See *Times Investment Ltd v Secretary of State for the Environment* (1991) 61 P & CR 98.

permission, nor can they bring an action in private law for a declaration that the planning authority has acted *ultra vires*, as the decision does not affect any of their legal rights, as opposed to their amenity,[130] assuming that a private law action would be available after O'Reilly v Mackman,[131] so that their only remedy is by way of judicial review. The courts have granted relief to individual neighbours,[132] to the chairman of an unincorporated local residents' association[133] and to an incorporated residents' association,[134] although the fact that many people join together and assert they have an interest does not create an interest if the individuals did not have one, nor does the fact of incorporation create an interest if the corporators did not have one.[135] In R v Great Yarmouth BC, ex p Botton Brothers Arcades Ltd[136] relief was granted to local traders, even though there was no duty on the local planning authority to hear the applicants before determining the application, nor did the applicants have a legitimate expectation of being heard, having no enforceable right being affected by the decision of the authority or promise that their view would be taken into account.[137] A more restrictive approach to standing was taken in R v *Secretary of State for the Environment, ex p Rose Theatre Trust Co.*[138] when the court held that a company formed to preserve an archaeological site did not have standing to obtain relief against the decision of the Secretary of State not to schedule the site under the Ancient Monuments and Archaeological Areas Act 1979. Finally, the local council has a sufficient interest in a planning application to entitle it to apply for relief.[139]

(3) Time limits

Before an application for judicial review can be made, leave of the court must be obtained (Judicature (NI) Act 1978, s. 18(2)). An application for leave must be made promptly and in any event within three months from the date when grounds for the application first arose unless the court considers there is good reason for extending the period (RSC (NI), O53 r4).

---

130 *Gregory v Camden LBC* [1966] 2 All ER 196.
131 [1982] 3 All ER 1124: see discussion below.
132 R v *North Hertfordshire DC, ex p Sullivan* [1981] JPL 752; R v *Monmouth DC, ex p Jones* (1987) 53 P & CR 108.
133 *R (Thallon) v Department of the Environment for Northern Ireland* [1982] NI 26.
134 *Covent Garden Community Association Ltd v GLC* [1981] JPL 183; R v *Hammersmith & Fulham LBC, ex p People Before Profit Ltd* [1981] JPL 869.
135 R v *Secretary of State for the Environment, ex p Rose Theatre Trust Co.* [1990] 1 All ER 754, 766 *per* Schiemann J.
136 (1988) 56 P & CR 99.
137 See however R v *Canterbury CC ex p Springimage Ltd* [1994] JPL 427 (persons with commercial interests likely to be affected by planning decision have locus standi).
138 [1990] 1 All ER 754.
139 *In re North Down BC's application* [1986] NI 304.

(4) Private law actions

We have seen that, apart from the old prerogative orders of certiorari, mandamus and prohibition, the court may, on an application for judicial review, grant relief by way of a declaration or an injunction (Judicature (NI) Act 1978, s. 18(1)). These latter forms of relief are of course available also in actions in private law. It seems, however, that where an individual has rights to which he is entitled to protection under public law, he may not generally defend those rights by way of an ordinary action in private law.[140]

---

140 O'Reilly v Mackman [1982] 3 All ER 1124. For the extent of the the principle see *Buckley v Law Society* [1983] 2 All ER 1039; *Davy v Spelthorne BC* [1983] 3 All ER 278; *Gillick v West Norfolk and Wisbech Area Health Authority* [1985] 3 All ER 403; *R v Crown Court at Reading, ex p Hutchinson* [1988] 1 All ER 333; *Roy v Kensington and Chelsea FPC* [1992] 1 AC 624.

CHAPTER FOURTEEN

Termination of Lawful Development Rights

In this chapter we consider a number of concepts and procedures whose common element is that they require a landowner to cease to do something which he is entitled otherwise to do. We will see, for example, that the Department has power to require the removal of buildings or works which are lawfully erected or constructed on land and to require the discontinuance of a use lawfully carried on by a landowner. Apart from such cases of interference by the Department, a landowner may find that he has lost the right to carry on a use of land through his own actions, as where he has abandoned a use of land. To complete the picture of how a landowner may find that he has lost his rights, we consider how he may find that certain rights he may have to carry out development in the future can cease to exist.

It will be convenient to consider this under three headings: (1) cases where the rights cease to exist automatically; (2) cases where they cease to exist by reason of some action or inaction on the part of the owner himself; and (3) cases where they cease to exist because of some action on the part of the Department.

(1) Automatic termination: expiry of planning permission for a limited period

We have seen that the Department has power to grant planning permission subject to conditions requiring the removal of buildings or works authorised by the permission, or the discontinuance of a use authorised by the permission, at the end of a specified period (1991 Order, Art. 27(1)(b)). Such permission is known as planning permission for a limited period (Art. 27(2)) and, as its name implies, the permission will come to an end at the end of that period. The continued existence of the buildings or works, or the continuance of the use, after the period specified in the permission expires, will be a breach of the condition in the permission and therefore unlawful.

(2) Termination by action/inaction of the landowner

There are several ways in which a landowner's rights may come to an end through his own action or inaction.

(a) Abandonment of use

Where a landowner is entitled to carry on a particular use of land (otherwise than a use for which planning permission exists), he may lose that right if he abandons the use. The doctrine applies to established uses,[1] i.e. uses immune from enforcement action, but is inappropriate to describe the loss of the right to carry on a use where that use is one for which planning permission has been granted.[2] There is no general principle of 'abandonment' in planning law.[3]

'Abandonment' signifies a situation in which a landowner has stopped the activities constituting the use of the land, not merely for a temporary period, but with no view to their being resumed. If that has happened, then as a matter of fact the use has ceased.[4] The significance is that once the use is abandoned it cannot be resumed without planning permission.[5] The question is whether the cessation of the use has been merely temporary, or whether it has been abandoned: in the former case it can be resumed without planning permission, in the latter it cannot.[6] Abandonment implies the cessation of a use of land followed by a period in which the land is put to no use.[7] In *Young v Secretary of State for the Environment*[8] Watkins LJ followed Glidewell J in *Balco Transport Services Ltd v Secretary of State for the Environment*[9] in saying that the concept of abandonment is not apt to describe a change from one use to another use. The use of the word 'abandonment' in such circumstances is inappropriate and potentially misleading: all that has happened is that one use has been supplanted by another.[10]

In *Trustees of the Castell-y-Mynach Estate v Secretary of State for Wales*[11] the following factors were identified as being the principal factors to be considered in answering whether cessation of a use is merely temporary or amounts to abandonment: (1) the physical condition of the building; (2) the period of non-use; (3) whether there has been any other use; and (4) the intentions of the owner of the property.[12] The intentions of the owner

---

1 Hartley v Minister of Housing and Local Government [1969] 3 All ER 1658; White v Secretary of State for the Environment (1989) 58 P & CR 281. See also Smith v Secretary of State for the Environment [1994] JPL 640.
2 Pioneer Aggregates (UK) Ltd v Secretary of State for the Environment [1984] 2 All ER 358.
3 Ibid.
4 Hartley v Minister of Housing and Local Government [1969] 3 All ER 1658, 1661 per Widgery LJ.
5 Ibid., 1660 per Lord Denning MR.
6 Ibid.
7 Ibid.
8 (1983) 47 P & CR 165, 184 CA (on appeal [1983] 2 All ER 1105 HL).
9 (1981) 45 P & CR 216, 222.
10 (1983) 47 P & CR 165, 184: see below.
11 [1985] JPL 40. See also Northavon DC v Secretary of State for the Environment [1990] JPL 579.
12 On this last point see Wheatfield Inns (Belfast) Ltd v Croft Inns Ltd [1978] NI 83, where the evidence e.g. the fact that fixtures and fittings remained in the premises, showed that the cessation of use was due to poor trading, the intention of the owner being to recommence.

are however only one factor to be considered and may be established both from direct evidence and from the conduct and behaviour of the owner. Whatever the owner says about his intentions may be contradicted by the facts and circumstances so that his intention can be rejected.[13]

(b) By change of use

We saw above that where one use is followed by another without there being any period in which the land is put to no use, there is no abandonment of the earlier use, as abandonment necessarily implies a period of non-use following the cessation of the use which has been abandoned. Where there is no intervening period of non-use all that has happened is that the former use has been supplanted by the latter.[14] In such a case the earlier use cannot be revived without planning permission[15] and this is so whether the latter use is lawful or not.[16]

(c) By implementation of planning permission

The right to carry on an existing use of land may be lost if the landowner implements a planning permission. This will happen only if implementation of the permission leads to the creation of a new planning unit, or a new chapter in the planning history. Where the evidence fails to establish the creation by development actually carried out of a new planning unit, the grant of permission does not preclude a landowner from relying on existing use rights, such rights being 'hardy beasts with a great capacity for survival.'[17] The likely application of these principles is where planning permission is granted for erection of a building on a site. If the building is constructed, does this result in the termination of the right to use the site for its previous purposes? In *Petticoat Lane Rentals Ltd v Secretary of State for the Environment*[18] Widgery LJ held that where formerly open land becomes part of, or is merged with, a building the previous planning unit

---

13 Nicholls v Secretary of State for the Environment [1981] JPL 890, 891 per McNeill J.
14 Young v Secretary of State for the Environment (1983) 47 P & CR 165, 184 per Watkins LJ. In JL Engineering Ltd v Secretary of State for the Environment [1994] JPL 453 the idea of a use being supplanted was considered wholly apposite. There, an industrial use had been supplanted by a change of use to agriculture and was therefore lost, even though the agricultural use did not amount to development. For appeal, see EGCS 110.
15 There is no equivalent in the 1991 Order to the provisions of s. 23(9) of the Town and Country Planning Act 1971 mentioned in Young (see now s. 57(4) of the Town and Country Planning Act 1990) by which a landowner may revert to the previous use of land following an enforcement notice without planning permission.
16 Young v Secretary of State for the Environment (1983) 47 P & CR 165, 184. The decision of the House of Lords in Young ([1983] 2 All ER 1105) was considered by Balcombe LJ in Cynon Valley BC v Secretary of State for Wales (1987) 53 P & CR 68, 76 to have endorsed the views of Watkins LJ on this point.
17 Pioneer Aggregates (UK) Ltd v Secretary of State for the Environment [1984] 2 All ER 358, 365 per Lord Scarman. See also Newbury DC v Secretary of State for the Environment [1980] 1 All ER 731, 739 per Viscount Dilhorne; 744 per Lord Fraser.
18 [1971] 2 All ER 743.

ceases to exist and its rights of use disappear.[19] However, in *Jennings Motors Ltd v Secretary of State for the Environment*[20] the Court of Appeal emphasised that the new building will not automatically mean that the previous use rights are extinguished, this being a matter of fact and degree in each case. To bring existing use rights to an end there must be such a radical change in the nature of the building or the use to which it is put as to amount to a fresh start in the character of the site.[21]

The implementation of a planning permission may also have the effect of bringing to an end rights which have been conferred by another planning permission. We have seen that any number of mutually inconsistent permissions may exist in connection with the same land. Implementation of one may mean that it becomes impossible to implement the other, thereby extinguishing the rights authorised by the other permission.[22] Impossibility, however, is different from incompatibility, which is not sufficient to bring about extinguishment of the other permission.[23]

Even when it is not impossible to implement the former permission, the rights created by that permission may be lost if the permission is 'spent'. This will be the case when a change of use is involved: a change of use necessarily involves a change *from* use A *to* use B, the consequence of which is that while it may nevertheless remain possible to re-implement use A, it is not permissible to do so as the right to carry on use A is spent.[24] The 'permission spent' principle applies only when the permission to which it is sought to revert is for a change of use. Where the question is whether a landowner may resume operational development for which permission was granted, following the implementation of a permission for change of use, the relevant test is whether it is possible to do so having regard to the change of use which has taken place.[25]

---

19 See also *Prosser v Minister of Housing and Local Government* (1968) 67 LGR 109 and *Leighton and Newman Car Sales Ltd v Secretary of State for the Environment* (1976) 32 P & CR 1. In *Petticoat Lane Rentals* Bridge J posed the question whether, in the absence of an express condition prohibiting the former use, the erection of a building on part only of a site would automatically extinguish the existing use rights in relation to the remainder of the site: [1971] 2 All ER 793, 791.
20 [1982] 1 All ER 471.
21 Ibid., 476 *per* Lord Denning MR.
22 *Pioneer Aggregates (UK) Ltd v Secretary of State for the Environment* [1984] 2 All ER 358; *Ellis v Worcestershire CC* (1961) 12 P & CR 178; *Pilkington v Secretary of State for the Environment* [1974] 1 All ER 283.
23 *Prestige Homes (Southern) Ltd v Secretary of State for the Environment* [1992] EGCS 66. Contrast *Wealdon DC v Taylor* [1992] JPL 1036. See also *In re Bangor Flagship Developments Ltd's application (no 2)* [1992] 8 BNIL 91 (also reported *sub nom In re Genova Ltd's application* [1992] 10 NIJB 1).
24 *Cynon Valley BC v Secretary of State for Wales* (1987) 53 P & CR 68.
25 *Durham CC v Secretary of State for the Environment* (1990) 60 P & CR 507, applying *Pilkington v Secretary of State for the Environment* [1974] 1 All ER 283. See also *Regent Lion Properties Ltd v Westminster CC* (1990) 4 EG 131 and *Camden LBC v McDonald's Restaurants Ltd* (1992) 65 P & CR 423.

(c) By agreement

We will see later[26] that a landowner may enter an agreement with the Department under Art. 40 of the 1991 Order for the purpose of facilitating, regulating or restricting the development or use of land. Such an agreement may provide for the landowner to give up rights he may have e.g. to carry on a use of land.[27]

(3) Termination by action by the Department

There are various ways in which a landowner's rights to carry out development or to continue his present activities may be terminated by the Department.

(a) Completion orders

When planning permission has been granted for development subject to a condition that the development must be begun by the expiration of a particular period, the right to carry out the development lapses if it is not begun by that time. Once it has begun within the specified period the condition is complied with, even though no further action is taken by the developer. The consequence may be that the developer begins work to keep the permission alive, but takes no further steps, for example because of financial restraints or because he is awaiting a purchaser for the property. This may result in a site lying partially developed for some time. The Department has power to remedy such a situation by means of a completion order under Art. 37 of the 1991 Order, which terminates the planning permission at the end of a specified period.

Art. 37 applies when development has been begun within the time required by a condition imposed by Art. 34 or Art. 35, but has not been completed by the expiration of that period (Art. 37(1)). In such a case if the Department is of opinion that the development will not be completed within a reasonable period it may make a completion order whereby the planning permission authorising the development will cease to have effect at the expiration of a further period specified in the order, which may not be less than twelve months after the order takes effect (Art. 37(2)). The effect of the order is to make invalid the planning permission at the expiration of the period specified in the order, but any development carried out under the permission until that time remains lawful (Art. 37(4)).

The procedure for making a completion order requires the Department to serve notice of its intention to make the order on the owner and occupier of the land affected and any other person who in the opinion of the

---

26 Chapter 16.
27 *West Oxfordshire DC* v *Secretary of State for the Environment* (1988) 56 P & CR 434, 445.

Department would be affected by the order (Art. 37(3)). Any person served with such notice may within a period to be specified in the notice (not less than twenty one days from service) request the Department in writing to afford him an opportunity of appearing before and being heard by the Planning Appeals Commission, and if he makes such a request, the Department is required to afford him such an opportunity (Art. 37(3)). Once a completion order is made a notice stating the general effect of the order must be served on the persons served with the notice of intention to make an order (Art. 37(5)). Finally, a completion order may be withdrawn at any time before the expiration of the period at the end of which the planning permission ceases to have effect (Art. 37(6)). If an order is so withdrawn, notice of the withdrawal has to be served on the persons on whom notice of the making of the order was served (Art. 37(6)).

(b) *Revocation and modification of planning permission*

The Department has power to revoke or modify a planning permission already granted if it considers it expedient to do so having regard to the development plan and to any other material considerations, and to the extent it considers expedient having regard to those matters (Art. 38(1)). The power to revoke or modify a permission may be exercised, in the case of permission for operational development, at any time before the operations have been completed (Art. 38(3)(a)); and in the case of permission for a change of use, at any time before the change has taken place (Art. 38(3)(b)). In the case of revocation or modification of a permission relating to operational development, this does not affect any operations carried out (Art. 38(3)), nor, in the case of mining operations by surface working, will it prevent the continuation of those operations on any land in use for the purpose of those operations at the date on which the revocation or modification order comes into operation (Art. 38(4)).

As with completion orders, before an order revoking or modifying a permission is made, the Department has to serve notice on the owner and occupier of the land affected and on any other person who in its opinion would be affected by the order (Art. 38(2)). Such persons may within the period specified in the order request the Department in writing to afford them an opportunity to appear before and be heard by the Planning Appeals Commission (Art. 38(2)). Once an order is made revoking or modifying a permission, a notice stating the general effect of the order must be served on the persons on whom the preliminary notice was served (Art. 38(5)).

Where the Department does make an order revoking or modifying a planning permission, it is obliged to pay compensation to any person interested in the land[28] to which the permission related who has paid for

---

28 See *Pennine Raceway Ltd v Kirklees MC* [1982] 3 All ER 628.

work which is rendered abortive by the revocation or modification, or who has otherwise sustained loss or damage which is directly attributable to the revocation or modification.[29] Compensation is not payable for any work carried out before the permission was granted or for any other loss or damage[30] arising out of anything done or omitted to be done before the permission was granted (1965 Act, s. 26(3)). Expenditure incurred in the preparation of plans or similar preparatory matters is taken as spent in carrying out the work rendered abortive by the revocation or modification and is therefore compensatable (1965 Act, s. 26(2)).

Nor is compensation payable following revocation of planning permission in the circumstances set out in Art. 3 of the Planning (Amendment) (NI) Order 1978. These are: (1) planning permission is revoked with the consent of a person entitled to a compensatable estate in the land to which the permission related; (2) planning permission is granted on or after the revocation, for other land, for development similar to that permitted by the revoked permission; and (3) the new permission specifies that it is in substitution for the revoked permission. In such cases compensation is not payable to the person who consented to the revocation.

In the case of the revocation or modification of planning permission for development consisting of the winning and working of minerals, a claim for expenditure or loss will not be entertained in respect of buildings, plant or machinery unless the claimant shows that he is unable to use the buildings, plant or machinery or to use them except at the loss claimed (1972 Order, Art. 97(1)). Claims for compensation which include claims for such matters are severable and the claim in respect of the buildings, plant or machinery may be dealt with after the remainder of the claim (1972 Order, Art. 97(2)).

Claims for compensation must be made within six months of the date of the order revoking or modifying the permission, unless the Department allows a longer period.[31]

Finally, where planning permission is revoked or is modified by the imposition of conditions, an owner of the land may serve a purchase notice requiring the Department to purchase his estate in the land (1991 Order, Art. 94(1)(b)). He must show (1) that the land has become incapable of reasonably beneficial use in its existing state; (2) in cases where the permission has been modified by the imposition of conditions, that the land cannot be rendered capable of reasonably beneficial use by the carrying

---

29 Land Development Values (Compensation) Act (NI) 1965, s. 26(1).
30 Not being loss or damage consisting of depreciation of the value of a compensatable estate in the land: s. 26(3)(b). For the meaning of 'compensatable estate' see s. 43(1). For compensation in respect of claims based on depreciation of compensatable estates a distinction has to be made between cases where the permission revoked or modified was for 'new development' as defined in s. 43(1) and other cases: see ss 26(4) and (5).
31 1965 Act, s. 20(2), as applied by s. 26(6). See also Land Development Values (Compensation) Regulations (NI) 1965.

out of the permitted development in accordance with those conditions; and (3) that the land cannot be rendered capable of reasonably beneficial use by the carrying out of any other development for which planning permission has been granted (Art. 94 (1)).[32]

(c) *Discontinuance orders*

The Department has various powers under Art. 39 of the 1991 Order to interfere with or terminate planning rights of a landowner which it may exercise when it considers it expedient to do so in the interests of the proper planning of an area, including the interests of amenity, regard being had to the development plans and other material considerations (Art. 39(1)). The Department may (1) require the discontinuance of any use of land; (2) impose such conditions as it may specify[33] on the continuance of a use; (3) require such steps as are specified to be taken for the alteration of buildings or works; or (4) require such steps as are specified to be taken for the removal of buildings or works (Art. 39(1)). Where the requirements of an order made by the Department under Art. 39 involve the displacement of persons residing in any premises, it is the duty of the Northern Ireland Housing Executive (insofar as there is no other residential accommodation suitable to the reasonable requirements of such persons available on reasonable terms) to secure the provision of such accommodation in advance of the displacement (Art. 39(6)).

An order made under Art. 39 may grant planning permission for any development of the land to which the order relates, subject to such conditions as may be specified in the order (Art. 39(2)), including conditions for the retention of buildings or works constructed or carried out before the date on which the order was made (Art. 39(3)(a)), or for the continuance of a use of the land instituted before that date (Art. 39(3)(b)).

(i) Procedure

The procedure for making an order under Art. 39 is similar to that for making completion orders or orders revoking or modifying planning permission. Before making the order the Department is required to serve notice on the owner and occupier of the land and on any other person who, in the Department's opinion, would be affected by the order (Art. 39(4)). Such persons may request the Department within the period specified in the order to afford them an opportunity to appear before and be heard by the Planning Appeals Commission (Art. 39(4)). Once an order is made a copy of the order has to be served on the owner and occupier of the land to which the order relates and on any other person who in the Department's opinion would be affected by the order (Art. 39(5)).

---

32 For purchase notices generally see Chapter 24.
33 Subject to those conditions satisfying the tests for validity considered in Chapter 13.

(ii) Non-compliance with the order

The consequences which flow from non-compliance with an order made by the Department under Art. 39 depend on whether the order requires the discontinuance of a use of land or its continuance subject to conditions, or requires the alteration or removal of buildings or works.

Where an order requires the discontinuance of a use, or imposes conditions on the continuance of a use, any person who uses the land for that use, or in breach of the conditions imposed by the Department on the continuance of that use, is guilty of an offence (Art. 83(1)).[34] It is a defence to show that the defendant took all reasonable measures and exercised due diligence to avoid commission of the offence by himself or by any person under his control (Art. 83(3)).[35]

In the case of non-compliance with an order requiring steps to be taken for alteration or removal of buildings or works, a person authorised in writing by the Department may enter the land and take the steps required and the Department may recover from the person who is then the owner of the land any expenses reasonably incurred by it in so doing (Art. 83(5)). That apart, a person who was served with a copy of the order, and who was at that time the owner of the land, is guilty of an offence (Art. 83(6)), unless at some time before the period allowed for compliance with the order he ceased to be the owner and he proves that failure to take the steps required by the order was attributable in whole or in part to the default of the new owner, and that he (the original owner) took all reasonable steps to secure compliance with the order. In such a case the new owner may be convicted of the offence (Art. 83(7) and (8)).

In the case of non-compliance with an order requiring discontinuance of a use or its continuance subject to conditions and in the case of non-compliance with an order requiring alteration or removal of buildings or works, non-compliance with the order following conviction for an offence under Art. 83 is a further offence (Art. 83(2) and (9)).

(iii) Compensation

As with an order revoking or modifying planning permission, the making of an order under Art. 39 renders the Department liable to pay compensation. Any person who suffers damage in consequence of the order by depreciation of the value of an interest in the land to which he is entitled or by being disturbed in his enjoyment of the land is entitled to compensation from the Department in respect of that damage.[36] Furthermore,

---

34 No offence is committed if the person has in the meantime obtained planning permission so to use the land: ibid.
35 See also Art. 83(4) precluding the defendant from relying on the defence without leave of the court in certain circumstances.
36 1972 Order, Art. 65A(2) as inserted by Planning and Building Regulations (Amendment) (NI) Order 1990, Art. 21.

any person who carries out any works in compliance with an order under Art. 39 is entitled to recover from the Department compensation in respect of any expenses reasonably incurred by him in that behalf (1972 Order, Art. 65A(3)). No compensation is payable however, if a purchase notice is served in consequence of the order and the land is purchased by the Department (1972 Order, Art. 65A(5)). If compensation is payable, the amount of compensation is reduced by the value of any timber, materials or apparatus removed by the claimant for the purpose of complying with the order (1972 Order, Art. 65A(4)).

A claim for compensation in consequence of an order under Art. 39 must be made within six months from the date of the order, or within such extended period as the Department allows (1972 Order, Art. 65A(6)). If the parties cannot agree on the amount of compensation the matter will be determined by the Lands Tribunal (1972 Order, Art. 65A(7)).

(iv) Purchase notice

Any person entitled to an estate in land in respect of which an order has been made under Art. 39 may serve a purchase notice on the Department requiring the Department to purchase his estate in the land where he can show that by reason of the order the land is incapable of reasonably beneficial use in its existing state and that it cannot be rendered capable of reasonably beneficial use by the carrying out of any development for which planning permission has been granted, whether by the order under Art. 39 or otherwise (1991 Order, Art. 94(3)).[37]

(d) GDO directions

It will be recalled that the permission granted by the GDO for the classes of development set out in the schedule to the GDO may be rendered inapplicable to development in any particular area or to any particular development by directions made by the Department (GDO, Art. 4).[38]

(e) Conditions

A condition attached to a planning permission may withdraw the right to carry on a particular use of land or to carry out other development. Thus, conditions taking away rights which would normally exist by reason of the UCO or GDO are lawful.[39]

---

37 For purchase notices generally see Chapter 24.
38 See Chapter 10.
39 See *Carpet Decor (Guildford) Ltd v Secretary of State for the Environment* (1982) 261 EG 56 and *City of London Corp. v Secretary of State for the Environment* (1971) 71 LGR 28 (UCO); *Gill v Secretary of State for the Environment* [1985] JPL 710, *Dunoon Developments Ltd v Secretary of State for the Environment* (1992) 65 P & CR 101 and *Mirai Networks Ltd v Secretary of State for the Environment* [1994] JPL 337 (GDO).

CHAPTER FIFTEEN

Enforcement Powers

The 1991 Order maintains the system of development control based on the requirement of planning permission for development which was introduced by the 1972 Order. Unfortunately not all developers abide by the rules. The 1991 Order contains various provisions enabling the Department to enforce the system of development control contained in the Order. These provisions are considered in this chapter. As we will see, the procedures provided in the 1991 Order for enforcement may not be the only means available for the prevention of unlawful development.

1 Who can take enforcement action?

The first matter to be considered is who can take action to ensure that the rules contained in the 1991 Order are complied with.

(1) Members of the public

In the absence of proof that breach of the provisions of a statute will constitute an infringement of an individual's private rights or inflict special damage on him, an individual cannot bring an action to restrain unlawful activity.[1] This applies to the 1991 Order as it applies to any other statute. The scheme of the planning legislation is to restrict development for the benefit of the public at large and not to confer new rights on any individual members of the public, whether they live close to or far from the proposed development.[2] Accordingly, it has been held that a ratepayer has no cause of action entitling him to an injunction to restrain unlawful development by a district council, though individual members of the council stand in a different position.[3] In *Mahon v Sharma*[4] Campbell J held that the operator of a market had no cause of action to restrain a potential competitor from holding a market where the latter had not obtained planning permission.[5] In the absence then of a right to take action himself,

---

1 Gouriet v Union of Post Office Workers [1977] 3 All ER 70; In re Cook's application [1986] NI 242.
2 Buxton v Minister of Housing and Local Government [1960] 3 All ER 408, 411 per Salmon J.
3 In re Cook's application [1986] NI 242.
4 [1990] 2 NIJB 76.
5 Note that in the Republic the court may prohibit unlawful development on the application of the planning authority *or any other person*: Local Government (Planning and Development) Act 1976, s. 27. See e.g. *Stafford v Roadstone Ltd* [1980] 1 ILRM 1. A proposal that third parties

a member of the public who wishes to see unlawful development restrained is limited to seeking to provoke appropriate action by the Department or the Attorney-General in the manner considered below.[6]

(2) The Attorney-General

The Attorney-General as law officer of the Crown has power to act to enforce the provisions of a statute, either at his own instigation or at the request of a member of the public, the latter case being known as a relator action. The only difference between an action instituted by the Attorney-General *ex officio* and one instituted at the relation of a third party is that in the latter the relator is responsible for costs.[7] Actions have been successfully brought by the Attorney-General at the relation of local planning authorities to restrain unlawful development[8] and it would seem that the procedure is equally open to members of the public.[9] It has been suggested that the Attorney-General will interfere only in the most extreme and blatant cases.[10] It seems also that if the Attorney-General refuses to give his consent to a relator action there may be no power of the court to review his decision.[11]

(3) The Department

As it is the Department which is entrusted with the duty of formulating and co-ordinating planning policy (1991 Order, Art. 3(1)) and determining applications for planning permission (Art. 25), not surprisingly it is the Department which is given various powers to enforce planning control. The nature of these powers, and the powers available to the Department outside the 1991 Order, are the subject of the remainder of this chapter.

2 The discretion to enforce

Apart from the cases of special control considered at 4 below, unlawful development is not itself an offence.[12] Rather the Department has the

---

should have a similar right in England and Wales has recently been rejected: see *Enforcing Planning Control* (Carnwath Report), London, HMSO 1989, ch. 6, para. 5.5.

6 One commentator suggests that planning authorities are not likely to be short of such attempts: Millichap, *The Effective Enforcement of Planning Controls*, London: Butterworths 1991, p. 21.

7 *Attorney-General v Logan* [1891] 2 QB 100; *Stoke-on-Trent CC v B & Q (Retail) Ltd* [1984] 2 All ER 332.

8 *Attorney-General ex rel Hornchurch UDC v Bastow* [1957] 1 All ER 497; *Attorney-General ex rel Egham UDC v Smith* [1958] 2 All ER 557.

9 Alder, *Effective Enforcement of Planning Control*, Oxford: BSP Professional Books (1989), p. 119.
10 Ibid., 120.
11 *Gouriet v Union of Post Office Workers* [1977] 3 All ER 70.
12 The suggestion that it should be was rejected in the Carnwath Report on the ground

discretion to take enforcement action or let matters rest as they are.[13] While the Department may therefore choose not to take action against a developer who has broken the rules it is thought that such a decision, like any other decision of a public authority, would be open to judicial review by the court. As we will see, the 1991 Order contains a provision whereby the Department can bring unlawful development under proper control in circumstances where the Department does not consider enforcement proceedings appropriate (Art. 23).[14]

3 Gathering information

As well as giving the Department the various powers to enforce planning control considered later in this chapter, the 1991 Order confers on the Department powers to obtain information which the Department may need in order to decide whether it should exercise its powers of enforcement.[15] Art. 121 entitles any person authorised in writing by the Department to enter land at any reasonable time for the purpose of surveying it in connection with various matters, including any proposal by the Department to issue a notice under Part VI of the Order, which relates to enforcement (Art. 121(1)(a)). Such a person must, if required, produce evidence of his authority (Art. 122(1)(a)). The effectiveness of this right of entry is limited as the person exercising it cannot demand admission as of right to any land which is occupied unless three days' notice of the intended entry has been given to the occupier (Art. 122(1)(b)).[16] Any person who wilfully obstructs a person acting in the exercise of the power under Art. 121 is guilty of an offence (Art. 122(2)).

Apart from the power to enter land conferred by Art. 121, the Department may by notice in writing require the occupier of premises and any person who directly or indirectly receives rent in respect of premises to give the Department information which may be of assistance

---

that the margins between lawful and unlawful development were not sufficiently clear-cut to form an acceptable basis of a new criminal offence: Carnwath Report, ch. 6, para. 2.7.

13 See 1991 Order, Arts 68(1), 73(1) and 23(1), all using the permissive 'may' rather than 'shall'.

14 See below.

15 It has been said however of the situation in England and Wales that aggrieved neighbours are the primary source of information regarding breaches of planning control: Millichap, *op. cit.*, p. 21.

16 The comparable provisions of the Town and Country Planning Act 1971 (s. 280) were seen as too narrow, and the requirement of giving notice before entering occupied land was thought to weaken its power by affording sufficient time to destroy any evidence that might come to light when entry has been made, a criticism all the more pertinent to the situation here, as s. 280 required only twenty four hours notice to be given, rather than the three days required under Art. 122. See Carnwath Report, ch. 7, para. 2.1 and now Town and Country Planning Act 1990, s. 196A.

in taking enforcement action (Art. 125(1)). The information required must be given in writing within twenty one days of the date on which the notice requiring the information is served, or such longer period as is specified in the notice or as the Department may allow (Art. 125(1)). The matters about which the Department can require information are (1) the nature of the estate in the premises of the recipient of the notice; (2) the name and address of any other person known to the recipient of the notice as having an estate in the premises; (3) the purpose for which the premises are being used; (4) the time that use began; (5) the name and address of any person known to the recipient of the notice as having used the premises for that purpose; and (6) the time when any activities carried out on the premises began (Art. 125(2)). Failure to give the information required without reasonable excuse is an offence (Art. 125(3)), as is knowingly making a misstatement (Art. 125(4)). In addition, failure to give the required information or making a misstatement will be taken into account in the assessment of any compensation which may be payable if a stop notice is served (1972 Order, Art. 67(5).[17]

4   Notices requiring planning permission

Where it appears to the Department[18] that development has been carried out without the grant of planning permission or without the grant of any approval of the Department required under a development order, the Department may issue a notice requiring the making of an application for planning permission or approval to the Department (1991 Order, Art. 23(1)). The existence of this power enables the Department to require developers to comply with the requirement of obtaining planning permission for development which has been carried out and is appropriate where the development is not objectionable in principle, so that an enforcement notice is not appropriate. The procedure has two notable advantages: first, it requires the developer to pay the appropriate fee for the application for planning permission and thus prevents the developer profiting from unlawful development,[19] second, it enables the Department to impose conditions, if it considers this appropriate, on the development when permission is granted.[20]

---

17 For stop notices see below.
18 For the significance of the same expression in Art. 68(1) of the 1991 Order see below.
19 Payment of the fee is assured by Art. 23(12) which provides that for the purposes of Art. 23 an application for planning permission or approval is not made unless it is accompanied by the prescribed fee.
20 A statutory power to require an application for planning permission does not exist in England and Wales. A suggestion that it should was rejected in the Carnwath Report, ch. 7, para. 2.10.

(1) Contents of notice and limitation period

A notice under Art. 23 must specify the matters alleged to constitute the development to which the notice relates (Art. 23(3)). The notice can be issued only within a period of four years from the date on which the development was begun (Art. 23(2))[21] and in this regard the provisions of Art. 36(1) of the 1991 Order[22] apply to determine when the development is taken to have begun. If four years have elapsed since the development began the power to serve a notice requiring an application for planning permission no longer exists, though other powers of the Department in relation to enforcement may still be available to it.

(2) Issue, service and withdrawal of the notice

As with enforcement notices and stop notices, Art. 23(1) provides that the Department may *issue* a notice requiring an application for planning permission.[23] In contrast to enforcement notices and stop notices, notices under Art. 23 are not included in the matters which must be entered by the Department in the planning register maintained by the Department under Art. 124.

Once a notice under Art. 23 has been issued, a copy of it must be served on the owner and on the occupier of the land to which it relates (Art. 23(4)).[24]

A notice under Art. 23 may be withdrawn by the Department at any time before the end of the period allowed for compliance with the notice (Art. 23(9)). That period is the period of twenty eight days from service of a copy of the notice or such extended period as the Department may allow (Art. 23(1) and (11)). If the notice is withdrawn, notice of the withdrawal must be served on the persons who were served with a copy of the notice requiring the making of the application for permission (Art. 23(10)).

(3) Appeals

Before the period allowed for compliance with a notice under Art. 23 expires, a person who has been served with a copy of the notice[25] may

---

21   Note the difference between the four year rule under Art. 23 and that under Art. 68. In the former time runs from the date on which the development was *begun*, while in the latter time runs in the case of operational development from the date on which the development was substantially *completed*: see below.
22   See Chapter 13.
23   For the meaning of 'issue' see below.
24   Service on the owner and on the occupier are the same as in the case of enforcement notices, and reference should be made to the discussion below in this regard. Art. 23 does not, however, provide for service on other persons having an estate in the land, as in the case of enforcement notices (Art. 68(5)(b)).
25   Note the difference between the persons entitled to appeal against a notice under Art. 23 and those entitled to appeal against an enforcement notice (Art. 69).

appeal against the notice to the Planning Appeals Commission (Art. 24(1)). Where an appeal is made, the notice is of no effect pending the final determination or withdrawal of the appeal (Art. 24(5)). An appeal must be made by notice in writing (Art. 24(3)). The notice must indicate the grounds of appeal and state the facts on which the appeal is based (Art. 24(3)). The grounds on which an appeal may be brought are (1) that the matters alleged in the notice under Art. 23 do not constitute development; (2) that the development alleged in the notice under Art. 23 has not taken place; or (3) that the notice under Art. 23 was not issued within the period of four years from the date on which the development was begun (Art. 24(2)). Where it is one of these grounds that the recipient of a notice under Art. 23 relies on, the only way in which he can challenge the notice is by way of an appeal to the Planning Appeals Commission (Art. 24(7)). If, however, the recipient wishes to challenge the notice on some other ground, he may do so in the appropriate manner, e.g. by an application for judicial review.[26]

On an appeal under Art. 24 the Planning Appeals Commission is required to quash the notice under Art. 23, vary its terms, or uphold it (Art. 24(6)(a)). The Commission may correct any informality, defect or error in the notice or vary its terms if it is satisfied that the correction or variation can be made without injustice to the appellant or to the Department (Art. 24(6)(b)). Before determining an appeal the Commission is required to afford the appellant and the Department an opportunity of appearing before and being heard by the Commission (Art. 24(4)).

(4) Offences

If at the end of the period allowed for compliance with a notice under Art. 23 an application for planning permission or approval has not been made to the Department, any person who was served with a copy of the notice is guilty of an offence (Art. 23(5)). Where criminal proceedings are brought against someone who was the owner of the land to which the notice relates at the time when a copy of the notice was served on him, but ceased to be the owner by the end of the period allowed for compliance with the notice, that person (the original owner) is entitled to have the new owner brought before the court in the proceedings (Art. 23(6)). The new owner will be convicted instead of the original owner, where the latter shows that he took all reasonable steps to secure compliance with the notice and that failure to make the application for planning permission or approval was attributable in whole or in part to the default of the new owner (Art. 23(7)). Failure to make the application following conviction is a further offence (Art. 23(8)).

---

26 See the comparable provisions of Art. 69(9) in relation to enforcement notices, discussed below.

5 Enforcement notices

The principal method provided in the 1991 Order for the Department to take action against someone who has carried out unlawful development is the issue of an enforcement notice.[27]

(1) Power to issue enforcement notices

Art. 68(1) of the 1991 Order provides that where it appears to the Department that there has been a breach of planning control after 25 August 1974, the Department may, if it considers it expedient to do so, having regard to the provisions of the development plan and to any other material considerations, issue a notice requiring the breach to be remedied. Such a notice is known as an enforcement notice (Art. 68(2)).

(a) 'Where it appears'

The Department may issue an enforcement notice *where it appears to the Department* that there has been a breach of planning control. The power to issue an enforcement notice does not depend on the *existence* of a breach of planning control but merely on the *apparent existence* of a breach. If it appears to the Department that a breach has occurred, it may issue a notice, leaving it to the recipient to show on an appeal against the notice that a breach has not in fact occurred.[28] Illustrations of the point seem invariably to involve the holding of occasional markets. In *Tidswell v Secretary of State for the Environment*[29] an enforcement notice was served on someone who had operated a Sunday market on nine occasions. The operator of the market claimed that under the GDO he was entitled to hold a market on up to fourteen occasions,[30] accordingly there had been no breach of planning control and the enforcement notice was premature. Forbes J held, however, that this approach presumed that there was a duty on the planning authority before serving an enforcement notice to satisfy itself about whether a developer could bring himself within some exception or permission arising otherwise than from the authority's own records, which there was not. Once the authority had satisfied itself from looking at its own records that development had taken place without planning permission, it was entitled to say that it appeared to the authority that a breach of planning control had taken place.[31] In *Don and Don t/a Northern Markets v Department of the Environment for Northern Ireland*[32] Jones LJ referred to the 'possibly debateable [sic] territory of the decision

---

27 As we will see, the Order also empowers the Department to issue a stop notice, but only where an enforcement notice has already been issued.
28 See *Jeary v Chailey RDC* (1973) 26 P & CR 280; Alder, *op. cit.*, p. 34.
29 [1977] JPL 104.
30 See GDO, Sch. 1, Part 4, Class B.   31 [1977] JPL 104, 105.   32 [1981] 1 NIJB.

in *Tidswell*' and held that the Department had acted *ultra vires* in issuing an enforcement notice against an operator of a market which had been held on one or at most two occasions, that of itself not being sufficient justification for the Department issuing the enforcement notice. The most recent illustration is R v *Rochester upon Medway* CC, *ex p Hobday*[33] which again concerned an occasional market. There, the local planning authority resolved to issue an enforcement notice, but believing that the operator of the market was entitled to hold the market on fourteen occasions, the authority delayed issuing the notice until after the fifteenth occasion on which the market was held. The court held that the resolution to issue the enforcement notice was *ultra vires*: rather than it appearing to the authority that there had been a breach of planning control at the time of the resolution, the authority in fact believed that there *had not* been a breach, but that a breach *would occur* on the fifteenth occasion on which the market was held.

(b) '*Breach of planning control*'

There is a breach of planning control in either of the following cases: (1) if development has been carried out without the grant of planning permission; (2) if any conditions or limitations subject to which planning permission was granted have not been complied with (Art. 68(3)(a) and (b)). As we will see it is important for the Department to distinguish clearly between the two, and to decide which type of breach has occurred before issuing the notice (see Art. 68(6)).

(c) *25 August 1974*

The Department can issue an enforcement notice only in respect of breaches of planning control which have occurred after 25 August 1974.[34] This does not mean that any development which was carried out before that date is lawful, but merely that it is immune from enforcement action.[35] It will be recalled that the 1972 Order which introduced the requirement of planning permission for the carrying out of development came into operation on 1 October 1973.[36] Accordingly, any development carried out after that date,[37] whether without planning permission or in breach of conditions or limitations in a planning permission is unlawful,

---

33 (1989) 58 P & CR 424.
34 As we will see, in certain cases the Department is prevented from taking action even in respect of breaches occurring after that date.
35 See LTSS *Print & Supply Services Ltd* v *Hackney* LBC [1976] 1 All ER 659.
36 See Chapter 1.
37 Note that works or uses in existence on 1 October 1973 but for which permission under the Planning (Interim Development) Act (NI) 1944 had not been obtained became liable to enforcement action by the Department under the 1972 Order: see 1972 Order, Art. 109 and sch. 5, para. 2(1). Sch. 5 has now been repealed: see Planning and Building Regulations (Amendment) (NI) Order 1990, Art. 30(3).

but if carried out before 26 August 1974 is immune from enforcement action. The significance of the later date really only concerns development consisting of a material change in use because of the four year rule applicable to operational development considered below.[38]

(d) 'May'

We have alrady noted that the procedure established by the 1991 Order for enforcement is discretionary. Art. 68(1) provides that the Department *may* issue an enforcement notice, not that it *shall* do so. The Department must consider if it is expedient to do so having regard to the provisions of the development plan and any other material considerations. The fact that a developer has lodged an appeal against refusal of planning permission will not prevent the Department from issuing an enforcement notice.[39]

(2) Limitation period

Even where the breach of planning control has taken place after 25 August 1974, the Department may be prevented from taking enforcement action by the operation of what is known as the four year rule. Art. 68(4) of the 1991 Order provides that where an enforcement notice relates to one of the four types of breach of planning control specified in the subsection, the notice may be issued only within a period of four years from the date of the breach (Art. 68(4)(ii)).[40] In cases where the four year rule applies the effect of failure to issue an enforcement notice within that period is the same as where unlawful development took place before 26 August 1974, i.e. the development is immune from action but remains unlawful.[41]

The breaches of planning control which are subject to the four year rule are the following (Art. 68(4) (a) to (d)):

(i) Where the breach consists in the carrying out without planning permission of building, engineering, mining or other operations. Operational development in other words becomes immune from enforcement action after four years. This, however, is subject to two

---

38 To be accurate, a change of use to a dwelling house is also subject to the four year rule: see 1991 Order, Art. 68(4)(c).
39 *Davis v Miller* [1956] 3 All ER 109.
40 In the case of failure to comply with a condition or limitation relating to the carrying out of mining operations, the notice may be issued only within four years *from the date on which that failure came to the knowledge of the Department*: Art. 68(4)(i).
41 The significance of the difference between lawful development and development which is unlawful but immune from enforcement action has been reduced by the decision of the House of Lords in *Hughes v Doncaster* MBC [1991] 1 All ER 295 and the absence in any event of provisions equivalent to s. 57(4) of the Town and Country Planning Act 1990. Note that in England and Wales development which is immune from enforcement action is now *lawful*: Town and Country Planning Act 1990, s. 191(2) (substituted by Planning and Compensation Act 1991, s. 10).

caveats. First, if what has been done is a single operation, then the entire operation can be enforced against, even though part of it was carried out more than four years earlier. Thus, for example, an enforcement notice can require a building to be demolished completely even though part of the building was constructed more than four years before the notice was issued.[42] If the development consists not of a single operation but of a series of operations, as in the case of mining operations, where each shovelful is a separate operation, the enforcement notice can require only that the land be restored to the state it was in four years earlier.[43] Second, if the operational development is an integral part of unlawful development consisting of a material change in use, then the operational development can be enforced against by the authority taking action in respect of the change of use, even though the operational development was carried out more than four years earlier.[44] The exact extent of this principle has yet to be settled. It has recently been said that 'where what is built is substantial, obviously seen, it is unlikely . . . that one could come to the conclusion that it should lose the protection of [the four year rule] because it involved also a change of use'.[45]

(ii) Where the breach consists in the failure to comply with any condition or limitation which relates to the carrying out of building, engineering, mining or other operations and subject to which planning permission was granted.[46]

---

42 Ewen Developments Ltd v Secretary of State for the Environment [1980] JPL 404. See also Graham v Secretary of State for the Environment [1993] JPL 353 and Howes v Secretary of State for the Environment [1984] JPL 439.
43 Thomas David (Porthcawl) Ltd v Penybont RDC [1972] 1 All ER 733.
44 See Murfitt v Secretary of State for the Environment [1980] JPL 598 (notice requiring restoration of land to the state it was in before unlawful change of use took place not invalid though it required removal of hardcore laid more than four years earlier, as this was an integral part of the change of use). See, however, criticism of the decision at [1980] JPL 601. It may be that such operations can be enforced against by action in respect of an unlawful change of use even though the operations are not an integral part of the change of use: see Perkins v Secretary of State for the Environment [1981] JPL 755. For recent consideration of Murfitt and Perkins see Shephard & Love v Secretary of State for the Environment [1992] JPL 827 and Hertfordshire CC v Secretary of State for the Environment [1994] JPL 448. See also Somak Travel Ltd v Secretary of State for the Environment [1987] JPL 630 (planning authority entitled to require removal of internal staircase in enforcement proceedings for change of use, even though staircase not development).
45 Newbury DC v Secretary of State for the Environment [1995] JPL 329 (Roy Vandermeer QC).
46 See Peacock Homes Ltd v Secretary of State for the Environment (1984) 48 P & CR 20 and Harvey v Secretary of State for Wales (1990) 60 P & CR 152. The effect of Harvey has been the subject of differing views: see [1990] JPL 900; [1991] JPL 31, 232, 427, 625 and 853. See also Purdue, 'Rural Rides: an examination of agricultural occupancy conditions' (1991) 42 NILQ 229, 236, and Mitchell v Secretary of State for the Environment [1992] JPL 553. Harvey v Secretary of State has recently been distinguished by a majority in a differently constituted Court of Appeal, which held that the four year rule does not apply to the usual agricultural occupancy condition: see Newbury DC v Secretary of State for the

(iii) Where the breach consists in the making without planning permission of a change of use of any building to use as a single dwelling house.[47] Until recently it was not settled whether the four year rule applies where a single dwelling house is converted into two or more apartments. *Worthing BC v Secretary of State for the Environment*[48] held that it does, but *Doncaster BC v Secretary of State for the Environment*[49] and *Van Dyck v Secretary of State for the Environment*[50] were *contra*. The Court of Appeal has now held that the rule does apply in such instances.[51]

(iv) Where the breach consists of the failure to comply with a condition which prohibits or has the effect of preventing a change of use of a building to use as a single dwelling house.

The period of four years does not begin to run in cases of operational development until the operation is substantially completed,[52] in contrast, as we have seen, to the situation under Art. 23 when time runs from the date on which development begins. In cases of change of use, time runs from the date on which the change of use occurs.

(3) Contents of enforcement notice

Art. 68 requires that an enforcement notice shall specify the following matters:

(a) The matters alleged to constitute a breach of planning control

An enforcement notice must specify the matters alleged to constitute a breach of planning control (Art. 68(6)). It will be recalled that there is a breach of control if development is carried out without planning permission or in breach of any conditions or limitations in a planning permission (Art. 68(3)). The notice must make it plain what the developer has done wrong, i.e. the notice has to make it clear whether the developer has carried out development without permission or committed a breach of a condition subject to which permission was granted.[53] Subject to the power to

---

Environment (1993) 67 P & CR 68. The Planning Appeals Commission has followed *Harvey*; see PAC decisions 1993/A256 and 1993/A291.

47 See *Backer v Secretary of State for the Environment* (1982) 47 P & CR 149.
48 (1992) 63 P & CR 446.
49 (1992) 63 P & CR 437.
50 [1992] JPL 356.
51 *Doncaster BC v Secretary of State for the Environment* [1993] 21 EG 112.
52 Purdue et al, *Planning Law and Procedure*, London: Butterworths 1989, p. 323 and commentary on *Ewen Developments Ltd v Secretary of State for the Environment* [1980] JPL 404, 406. See also *Graham v Secretary of State for the Environment* [1993] JPL 353 and *Howes v Secretary of State for the Environment* [1983] JPL 439. The position has received statutory confirmation in England and Wales: Town and Country Planning Act 1990, s. 171(B)(1).
53 *Eldon Garages Ltd v Kingston-upon-Hull CBC* [1974] 1 All ER 358, 369 *per* Templeman J.

correct the notice if the planning authority 'puts the case in the wrong pigeon-hole' the notice will be set aside.[54]

A notice which specifies the wrong breach was described by Templeman J in Eldon Garages Ltd v Kingston-upon-Hull CBC[55] as null and void, but in Miller-Mead v Minister of Housing and Local Government[56] Upjohn LJ took the view that such a notice would not be a nullity, but merely set aside on appeal against the notice. However, it may be that a notice which specifies the wrong breach may be corrected by the Planning Appeals Commission on an appeal to it, as the power of the Commission to correct defects (Art. 70(2)) extends to *any* defect or error.[57]

Subject to this power to correct errors the Department must then be careful to identify correctly whether what is complained of is development without permission or breach of a condition or limitation in a permission. In certain cases the Department may have a choice, as the unlawful development may constitute both development without permission and also breach of a condition or limitation. In West Oxfordshire DC v Secretary of State for the Environment[58] planning permission had been granted for a specified use. The permission contained a condition that the premises should be used for no other purpose. The premises were later put to a different use and an enforcement notice was issued alleging breach of the condition in the planning permission. The question arose whether the breach had been correctly specified. The court held that in the circumstances the authority had a choice whether to allege development without permission or breach of condition. Such cases apart, the Department must take care to make it clear to the recipient of the notice what he is being accused of, but the magic words of the legislation are not required.[59] Nor is it necessary in cases where the unlawful development consists of a material change in use for the enforcement notice to specify the base use (i.e. the use from which the change is alleged to have been made).[60] In cases where the four year rule applies, there is some uncertainty as to whether the enforcement notice must specify that the breach took place within the preceding four years. In H T Hughes &

---

54 Kerrier DC v Secretary of State for the Environment (1980) 41 P & CR 284, 289; Whitley & Sons Ltd v Secretary of State for Wales (1990) 60 P & CR 185. See e.g. Francis v Yiewsley and West Drayton RDC [1957] 3 All ER 529. (Cp Postill v East Riding CC [1956] 2 All ER 685). The view that the notice must specify the type of breach complained of is not unanimous: see Rochdale MBC v Simmonds (1980) 40 P & CR 432, a decision recognised to be in conflict with Eldon Garages in Scott v Secretary of State for the Environment [1983] JPL 108. Unfortunately in Scott the court did not say which of the two decisions is correct.
55 [1974] 1 All ER 358, 369.
56 [1963] 1 All ER 459, 473.
57 R v Tower Hamlets LBC, ex p Ahern (London) Ltd (1990) 59 P & CR 133, 148 per Roch J.
58 (1988) 56 P & CR 434.
59 Eldon Garages Ltd v Kingston-upon-Hull CBC [1974] 1 All ER 358, 369.
60 Ferris v Secretary of State for the Environment (1988) 57 P & CR 127.

Sons Ltd v Secretary of State for the Environment[61] Hodgson J thought that the notice should do so, but this view was not accepted by Webster J in Harrogate BC v Secretary of State for the Environment[62] who pointed out that there was nothing in the comparable English legislation to require it.

Finally, while Art. 68 refers to a breach of planning control, it has recently been held that an enforcement notice may allege more than one breach of control, so that it is not necessary for the planning authority to issue a separate notice if more than one breach has occurred.[63]

(b) Any steps required to remedy the breach

In addition to specifying the breach of planning control, an enforcement notice must specify any steps which are required by the Department to be taken in order to remedy the breach (Art. 68(7)(a)).[64] This means steps for the purpose of restoring the land to its condition before the development took place or securing compliance with the conditions subject to which planning permission was granted, depending on the circumstances of the breach (Art. 68(9)).[65] Such steps may include the demolition or alteration of any building or works, the discontinuance of any use of land, or the carrying out of any building or other operations (Art. 68(9)).[66] In Miller-Mead[67] Upjohn LJ said that the recipient of an enforcement notice is entitled to say that he must find out from within the four corners of the document exactly what he is required to do or abstain from doing. The requirement of certainty is particularly important as the enforcement notice may lead to a criminal prosecution, and 'unless the notice states clearly what the recipient is required to do, he can hardly be convicted of not doing it'.[68] Thus, a notice which required the recipient to discontinue a use of land 'on such Sundays as fall within the period of summertime in any year' was held invalid, being hopelessly ambiguous.[69]

---

61 (1985) 51 P & CR 134, 135.
62 (1986) 55 P & CR 224, 231.
63 Valentina of London Ltd v Secretary of State for the Environment [1992] EGCS 77.
64 While the subsection refers to 'any' steps, this must mean 'the' steps, as Art. 68(1) provides for 'a notice requiring the breach to be remedied'.
65 There is some doubt whether an enforcement notice can require the recipient to carry out steps which, while satisfying the planning authority, would be less than would be required to remedy the breach of planning control (underenforcement): see Grant, Urban Planning Law, London: Sweet and Maxwell 1982, pp 412–13. This may no longer be relevant in Northern Ireland in view of the provisions of Art. 23. If the Department would be satisfied with the developer carrying out steps which would fall short of remedying the breach of control the appropriate action would seem to be to require the developer to submit an application for planning permission to retain the development in the form acceptable to the Department.
66 Ibid. Where an enforcement notice requires discontinuance of a use, this means discontinuance permanently: Art. 76(2).
67 [1963] 1 All ER 459, 469.   68 Carnwath Report, ch. 5, para. 1.2.
69 Dudley Bowers Enterprises Ltd v Secretary of State for the Environment (1985) 52 P & CR 365. For other examples see Metallic Protectives Ltd v Secretary of State for the Environment [1976] JPL 166 and London Borough of Hounslow v Secretary of State for the Environment [1981] JPL 510.

The view that the recipient of an enforcement notice should be able to find out from within the four corners of the document what he is required to do suggests that it is not possible for an enforcement notice to provide that what is to be done is to be found in a source outside the notice, yet in *Murfitt v Secretary of State for the Environment*[70] a notice which required that land should be restored in accordance with a scheme to be agreed with the planning authority or in default of agreement as should be determined by the Secretary of State was upheld.[71]

In specifying the steps to be taken to remedy the breach, the Department must not go too far. An enforcement notice cannot require the recipient to cease to exercise any existing use rights he may have. In *Mansi v Elstree UDC*[72] land was occupied as a nursery. From 1922 onwards part of the property was used for the sale of nursery produce.[73] This use intensified in 1959 and an enforcement notice was issued requiring the discontinuance of the sale of goods. The court considered that the notice went too far as it required the recipient's existing use rights to cease and should be amended so as to preserve those rights. It has recently been suggested that the problem illustrated by *Mansi* could be solved by inserting a statement in an enforcement notice to the effect that the notice does not affect any existing use rights or uses which are not development, thereby bringing the *Mansi* series of cases[74] to an end.[75] There is a presumption that enforcement notices are construed so as to retain any existing rights, so that where a notice required removal of vehicles from a site, this was construed as not to require removal of vehicles lawfully there as being ancillary to the use of the site.[76]

Two recent cases illustrate aspects of the requirement that the notice state what is required to be done by the recipient to remedy the breach. In *Bennett v Secretary of State for the Environment*[77] the court held that an enforcement notice issued following the change of use of a house to two dwellings could require the use as two dwellings to cease, but could not require the restoration of use as a single dwelling. In *McKay v Secretary of State for the Environment*[78] an enforcement notice was served requiring the

---

70 [1980] JPL 598.
71 Compare *Kaur v Secretary of State for the Environment* (1991) 61 P & CR 249 in which a notice requiring remedial action to be agreed with the planning authority was held invalid, there being no provision for what was to happen in the event that agreement could not be reached.
72 (1964) 16 P & CR 153.
73 This was therefore an existing use (see Chapter 14), i.e. one in existence at the coming into operation of the Town and Country Planning Act 1947.
74 A list of which is conveniently provided in *South Ribble BC v Secretary of State for the Environment* (1991) 61 P & CR 87.
75 *Swinbank v Secretary of State for the Environment* (1988) 55 P & CR 371, 378 per David Widdicombe QC.
76 *R v Harfield* [1993] JPL 914.
77 [1993] JPL 134.   78 [1994] JPL 806.

recipient to carry out works to land. The land was an ancient monument and the works required could not be lawfully carried out without consent under other legislation. The court held that the notice was a nullity.

(c) Any steps required for the purpose of making the development comply with planning permission

The notice must specify any steps required by the Department to be taken for the purpose of making the development comply with the terms of any planning permission which has been granted in respect of the land (Art. 68(7)(b) and (10(a)). Again, such steps must be specified with sufficient certainty.

(d) Any steps for the purpose of alleviating injury to amenity

The notice must also specify any steps required by the Department to be taken for the purpose of removing or alleviating any injury to amenity which has been caused by the development (Art. 68(7)(b) and (10)(b)). In the case of development which has involved the making of a deposit of refuse or waste materials on land, the enforcement notice may require that the contour of the deposit be modified by altering the gradient(s) of its sides in such manner as is specifed in the notice (Art. 68(11)).

(e) The period for taking the steps required

As well as prescribing the steps which the Department requires to be taken, an enforcement notice must specify the period within which those steps are to be taken (Art. 68(8)). Different periods may be prescribed for different steps (Art. 68(8)). Any period so prescribed must be reasonable, as one of the grounds on which an appeal may be brought to the Planning Appeals Commission against the notice is that such period falls short of what should reasonably be allowed (Art. 69(3)(h)).

(f) The date on which the notice will take effect

An enforcement notice must specify a date on which it will take effect (Art. 68(13)). The significance of this date is that it provides a reference point for the latest date on which a copy of the enforcement notice must be served (Art. 68(5)),[79] and for the bringing of an appeal to the Planning Appeals Commission against the notice (Art. 69(1)).[80]

(4) Issuing and serving the notice

Assuming that the Department has succeeded so far, in that it has been able to identify the breach correctly and has included in the notice the

---

79 See below.   80 See below.

required matters, and has not fallen foul of the limitation period prescribed by the legislation, the formal steps which the Department must take are to issue the notice (Art. 68(1)) and to serve a copy of it on the prescribed persons (Art. 68(5)). Issuing the notice means that the Department prepares a properly authorised document and retains it in its records.[81] After the notice is issued, a copy of it must be served on the owner and on the occupier of the land to which it relates, and on any other person having an estate in the land, being an estate which in the opinion of the Department is materially affected by the notice (Art. 68(5)). The 'owner' of land is the person, other than a mortgagee not in possession who, whether in his own right or as trustee for any other person, is entitled to receive the rack rent of the land, or where the land is not let at a rack rent, would be so entitled if the land were so let (Art. 2(2)).[82] While mortgagees not in possession are excluded from the definition of 'owner', they may be served with a copy of an enforcement notice as other persons having an estate in the land which in the opinion of the Department is materially affected by the notice (Art. 68(5)(b)).[83] It would seem that the requirement to serve a copy of the notice on *the* owner means that the Department must serve *all* owners.[84]

The requirement to serve a copy of an enforcement notice on the occupier of the land affected by the notice has been considered on a number of occasions by the courts.[85] In *Caravans & Automobiles Ltd v Southall BC*[86] the court held that the requirement to serve the occupier of the land was not satisfied unless all occupiers had been served. This, together with the absence of anything in the legislation to restrict the meaning of the word 'occupier' by reference to the nature of the occupier's right to be in occupation, means that the Department may have to make extensive enquiries to ensure that it has the names of all occupiers of the land, however transient their interest may be. An attempt was made in *Munnich v Godstone UDC*[87] to limit the persons who were occupiers for the purposes of service by excluding licensees, but in *Stevens v*

---

81 Bourne, *Enforcement and Stop Notices*, London: Sweet and Maxwell 1986, para. 6.14.
82 See *London Corp. v Cusack-Smith* [1955] 1 All ER 302 and Chapter 25. In connection with enforcement notices, see *Courtney-Southan v Crawley UDC* [1967] 2 All ER 346.
83 *Quaere* the position of lenders who have advanced money on security of registered land: being chargees only, they have no estate in the land: see Land Registration Act (NI) 1970, s. 41 and sch. 7. The question arises also in connection with the entitlement to appeal against an enforcement notice: see below.
84 See *Caravans & Automobiles Ltd v Southall BC* [1963] 2 All ER 533; and *Courtney-Southan v Crawley UDC* [1967] 2 All ER 246.
85 It should be noted that although there is a requirement to serve the occupier of land, and that the occupier may be guilty of an offence if the enforcement notice is not complied with (see Art. 72(5)) an occupier as such does not have any right to appeal against the notice to the Planning Appeals Commission: see below.
86 [1963] 2 All ER 533.
87 [1966] 1 All ER 930.

London Borough of Bromley[88] Munnich was distinguished, the court holding by a majority that the fact that occupants of land were licensees did not necessarily preclude them from being entitled to receive a copy of an enforcement notice. It seems that 'occupier' may in fact include squatters on the land.[89] Whether or not an occupant of land is an 'occupier' and entitled to be served with a copy of the notice depends on the facts of any particular case. A relevant factor will be the permanence of the occupation in question.[90]

Service must be effected not later than twenty eight days after the date the enforcement notice is issued, and not later than twenty eight days before the date specified in the notice as the date on which it is to take effect (Art. 68(5)).[91] No particular means of service is prescribed by the 1991 Order.

Failure to serve copies of an enforcement notice as required by Art. 68(5) whether within the time prescribed or on the persons specified does not render the notice a nullity[92] but is a ground on which an appeal can be made to the Planning Appeals Commission (Art. 69(3)(g)), though in the case of failure to serve a person required to be served the Commission may disregard this if neither the appellant nor that person has been substantially prejudiced by the failure to serve him (Art. 70(3)).

(5) Withdrawal of the enforcement notice

An enforcement notice may be withdrawn by the Department at any time before the notice takes effect (Art. 68(14)). If the notice is withdrawn, the Department must give notice of the withdrawal to every person who was served with a copy of the enforcement notice (Art. 68(15)). If an enforcement notice is withdrawn, this does not prevent the Department serving another enforcement notice at a later date (Art. 68(14)), subject however to a later notice being caught by the four year rule. Even if the first notice is not withdrawn, it is open to the Department to serve a second notice.[93]

(6) Effect of planning permission

If, following service of a copy of an enforcement notice, planning permission is granted for the retention on land of buildings or works, or for the continuance of the use of land, to which the enforcement notice relates, the notice ceases to have effect insofar as it requires steps to be taken for

---

88 [1972] 1 All ER 712.
89 *Scarborough BC v Adams and Anor* [1983] JPL 673.
90 Ibid.
91 See however *Porritt v Secretary of State for the Environment* [1988] JPL 414.
92 *R v Greenwich LBC, ex p Patel* (1985) 51 P & CR 282.
93 *Wychavon DC v Secretary of State for the Environment* [1992] JPL 753; *Mid-Glamorgan CC v Bargoed Coal Co. Ltd* [1992] JPL 832.

demolition or alteration of the buildings or works or the discontinuance of the use (Art. 75(1)).[94] Likewise, the notice ceases to have effect insofar as it requires steps to be taken for complying with a condition in a planning permission if planning permission is later granted permitting the retention of buildings or works or the continuance of the use of land without complying with that condition (Art. 75(2)). In both cases any liability of a person for an offence in respect of failure to comply with the notice before the relevant provisions of the notice ceased to have effect remains (Art. 75(3)).

(7) Challenging enforcement notices

The recipient of a copy of an enforcement notice who is not content to comply with its requirements may challenge the notice in a number of ways. Which method is appropriate depends on two factors: first, whether the notice is a nullity or merely invalid, and secondly, the operation of Art. 69(9).

(a) Nullity or invalidity?

A distinction must be made between an enforcement notice which is a nullity and a notice which is not a nullity but is for some reason invalid.[95] A notice which is a nullity is 'so much waste paper'.[96] It can in consequence be ignored completely by the recipient, though it may be more prudent for the recipient to take appropriate action to be sure of his position, i.e. by an application for judicial review for a declaration that the notice is a nullity. If the notice is a nullity the recipient may raise the issue as a defence to any prosecution the Department may later bring on foot of the enforcement notice, or by a civil action against the Department if the Department attempts to assert its rights to enter the land and carry out the steps required in the notice itself.[97]

The question which therefore arises is when will a notice be a nullity as opposed to merely being invalid? In *Miller-Mead v Minister of Housing and Local Government*[98] Upjohn LJ identified two situations where a notice would be a nullity: (1) where on its face the notice fails to contain the matters required by the legislation; and (2) where the notice is uncertain so that the recipient does not know what he has done wrong or what he is required to do. In addition a notice may be a nullity on the ground of *ultra vires*.[99]

---

94 See R v *Chichester Justices, ex p Chichester DC* (1990) 60 P & CR 342.
95 *Miller-Mead v Minister of Housing and Local Government* [1963] 1 All ER 459, 470 *per* Upjohn LJ.
96 Ibid.
97 Alder, *op. cit.*, p. 72. For the Department's right to enter the land and carry out work see Art. 74.
98 [1963] 1 All ER 454, 470.
99 E.g. where the decision to issue it was made for improper reasons: see Alder, *op. cit.*, p. 89; or because the authority did not believe there had been a breach of control at the time of the resolution: R v *Rochester upon Medway BC, ex p Hobday* (1989) 58 P & CR 424.

Such cases apart, an enforcement notice may be defective (to use a neutral expression) because, for example, it has been issued outside the period permitted by Art. 69(4), or because it alleges a breach of planning control when none has in fact taken place. Here the notice is not a nullity but the defect means that it is invalid. The notice cannot be ignored by the recipient, and appropriate action must be taken if the recipient is to avoid compliance with the notice. The nature of that action is considered below.

Before leaving the issue of whether a defective enforcement notice is a nullity or merely invalid, it will be recalled that in R v *Tower Hamlets* LBC *ex p Ahern (London) Ltd*[100] Roch J held that power now exists to amend *any* defect or error in an enforcement notice so long as this can be done without injustice to either party. In view of this it has been suggested that 'the number of occasions on which a vitiating flaw in an enforcement notice renders such a notice so flawed as to be a worthless scrap of paper will be considerably fewer than the traditional analysis would have accepted.'[101]

(b) Article 69(9)

Art. 69(9) of the 1991 Order provides that, with one exception, the validity of an enforcement notice shall not, except by way of an appeal to the Planning Appeals Commission, be questioned in any proceedings whatsoever on any of the grounds on which such an appeal may be brought. Such appeals and the grounds on which they may be brought are considered below. The effect of Art. 69(9) is that if the recipient wishes to challenge the validity of the notice on one of such grounds, the *only* way he can do so is by means of an appeal to the Planning Appeals Commission. He cannot challenge the notice in any prosecution which may later be brought by the Department on foot of the notice, whether the notice is valid or not.[102] The extent of the operation of the subsection may be seen in *Square Meals Frozen Foods Ltd v Dunstable BC*[103] where developers sought a declaration that their proposed use of premises did not require planning permission. The action was commenced after a letter had been received from the planning authority threatening enforcement proceedings should the proposed use commence, but *before* any enforcement notice was issued. After the action was instituted the proposed use was commenced and enforcement notices were issued. The court held that the developers' action for a declaration was one in which the validity of the enforcement notice was being challenged on one of the grounds on which an appeal

---

100 (1990) 59 P & CR 133.
101 Millichap, *op. cit.*, para 6.7.1.1.
102 *Department of the Environment for Northern Ireland v Thompson* [1992] 2 BNIL 126; R v *Smith* (1984) 48 P & CR 392; *Perrins v Perrins* [1951] 1 All ER 1075; *Epping Forest DC v Scott* (1985) 53 P & CR 79.
103 [1974] 1 All ER 441.

could be brought and so was barred by the equivalent of Art. 69(9),[104] notwithstanding that the action had been begun before enforcement notices had been issued.

Art. 69(9) applies only when the ground of challenge is one of the grounds on which an appeal can be brought to the Planning Appeals Commission. Where the recipient of a copy of an enforcement notice wishes to challenge the validity of the notice on some other ground, i.e. a ground not specified in Art. 69(3) of the 1991 Order[105] Art. 69(9) has no application.[106] The appropriate means of challenge in such circumstances will be an application for judicial review.

As we have noted, there is an exception to the rule in Art. 69(10). Where a criminal prosecution is brought under Art. 72(5) of the 1991 Order[107] against the holder of an estate in land the subject of an enforcement notice, which estate has been held since before the notice was issued, and that person was not served with a copy of the notice, then if he satisfies the court (1) that he did not know and could not reasonably have been expected to know that the notice had been issued and (2) his interests have been substantially prejudiced by the failure to serve him with a copy of the notice, Art. 69(9) does not prevent him from challenging the validity of the enforcement notice (Art. 69(10)).

(c) *Appeals to the Planning Appeals Commission*

The usual means by which an enforcement notice may be challenged is by way of an appeal to the Planning Appeals Commission on one or more of the grounds set out in Art. 69(3) of the 1991 Order.

(i) Who may appeal

An appeal may be made by any person having an estate in the land to which the enforcement notice relates (Art. 69(1)).[108] Whether a person has

---

104 Town and Country Planning Act 1971, s. 243.
105 E.g. because the resolution to issue the notice was *ultra vires*: R v *Rochester upon Medway CC, ex p Hobday* (1989) 58 P & CR 424.
106 *Davy v Spelthorne* BC [1983] 3 All ER 278.
107 See below.
108 This includes mortgagees of unregistered land, but would seem to exclude lenders who have advanced money on security of registered land, as such lenders are chargees only: Land Registration Act (NI) 1970, s. 41 and sch. 7, as amended by Registration (Land and Deeds) (NI) Order 1992, Art. 21. Such an anomaly cannot have been intended. Although para. 5(1) of sch. 7 to the 1970 Act provides that the owner of a charge shall have all the rights and powers of a mortgagee under a mortgage by deed such rights and powers arise from the agreement between the parties or statute, rather than from the existence in the mortgagee of an estate in the land. While in England and Wales all mortgages are in the form of charges, and it is not doubted that mortgagees there can appeal against an enforcement notice, the comparable provisions of the Town and Country Planning Act 1990 (s. 174) refer to a person having an *interest* rather than an *estate* in the land affected by the enforcement notice.

an estate is a matter which goes to the jurisdiction of the Commission and, accordingly, is a matter which may be determined by the court which is not limited to reviewing any decision on the matter by the Commission on grounds of perversity or unreasonableness.[109]

In addition to persons having an estate in the land affected by an enforcement notice, an appeal may be made by any person who at the date on which the enforcement notice is issued occupies the land to which the notice relates by virtue of a licence in writing and continues to occupy the land 'as aforesaid'.[110] Persons other than those having such rights in the property have no right of appeal.

(ii) Time for appeal

An appeal to the Commission must be made before the date specified in the enforcement notice as the date on which the notice is to take effect (Art. 69(1)). The notice of appeal must be *received* by the Commission before that date. In *Lenlyn Ltd v Secretary of State for the Environment*[111] an enforcement notice stated that it would take effect on 16 February. On 15 February notice of an appeal was posted, and was received the following day. The court held that the appeal was out of time. The rigour of the time limit can be seen in R v *Secretary of State for the Environment, ex p JBI Financial Consultants*[112] when an enforcement notice stated it would take effect on 1 June. Notice of appeal was delivered on that date, the previous day being a Sunday. The court held that the appeal could have been made on 31 May (despite this not being a working day) by inserting the notice in the letter box, and accordingly the appeal was out of time.

(iii) Mode of appeal

An appeal is made by notice in writing to the Commission (Art. 69(4)). The notice must indicate the grounds of appeal and state the facts on which it is based (Art. 69(4)). The requirement that the appeal should be made by notice in writing within the prescribed period is mandatory and goes to jurisdiction, but the requirements that the notice of appeal should specify the grounds of appeal and the facts on which the appeal is based is directory only and failure to comply with these requirements is not fatal; the defect can be remedied at a later date.[113]

---

109 R v *Secretary of State for the Environment, ex p Davies* (1990) 61 P & CR 481.
110 This presumably means 'by virtue of a licence in writing' rather than by virtue of *the* licence in writing and so would seem to allow someone to appeal in circumstances when he occupied the land under a licence in writing which determined after the enforcement notice was issued, but a new notice in writing was granted to him before the date of making the appeal.
111 (1984) 50 P & CR 129.
112 (1988) 58 P & CR 84.
113 Howard v *Secretary of State for the Environment* [1974] 1 All ER 644.

(iv) Grounds of appeal

An appeal may be made on one or more of the grounds set out in Art. 69(3). These are as follows:

(a) That planning permission ought to be granted for the development to which the enforcement notice relates or that a condition or limitation alleged in the enforcement notice not to have been complied with ought to be discharged.

This ground does not challenge the validity of the enforcement notice at all, but enables the appellant to ask for planning permission for the development which is complained of in the notice. Irrespective of whether the appellant includes this as one of his grounds of appeal or not, by his appeal against the enforcement notice he is deemed to have made an application for planning permission for the development to which the notice relates (Art. 71(3)).

(b) That the matters alleged in the enforcement notice do not constitute a breach of planning control.

This will cover the situation where the appellant claims that what is alleged in the enforcement notice does not amount to 'development' and where, although amounting to development, planning permission exists for what has been done, for example under the GDO.

(c) That the breach of planning control alleged in the notice has not taken place.

This is simply a matter of fact, the appellant claiming that what is alleged to have occurred has not in fact happened.

(d) That in cases where the four year rule applies, the notice has been issued out of time.

Where the appellant seeks to rely on the four year rule, the onus is on him to show that the notice was issued out of time.[114]

(e) That in any other case the breach of planning control took place before 26 August 1974.

(f) That copies of the enforcement notice were not served as required by Art. 68(5).

---

114 *Nelsovil Ltd v Minister of Housing and Local Government* [1962] 1 All ER 423.

The issue of the persons required to be served and the time when service must be effected have already been discussed. While it is a ground of appeal that service was not effected as required, this may be a limited success because of Art. 70(3) which provides that if it would otherwise be a ground for allowing an appeal that someone who should have been served was not served, the Commission may disregard that fact if neither the appellant nor that person has been substantially prejudiced by the failure to serve him.

(g) That the steps required by the enforcement notice exceed what is necessary to remedy any breach of planning control; to make the development comply with the terms of any planning permission which has been granted; or to remove or alleviate any injury or amenity which has been caused by the development.

(h) That the period specified in the enforcement notice as the period within which any step is to be taken falls short of what should reasonably be allowed.

(v) Duty of Planning Appeals Commission

When an appeal has been made to the Planning Appeals Commission, it is the duty of the Commission to quash the notice, vary the terms of the notice or uphold the notice (Art. 70(1)). Before it does so, however, the Commission is required to notify the district council for the district within which the land to which the enforcement notice relates (Art. 69(5)) and to afford the appellant and the Department an opportunity of appearing before and being heard by the Commission if either party so desires (Art. 69(6)). The Commission is also required to publish notice of the appeal in a local newspaper and to take into account any representations made to it following such publication in the same way as the Department is required to on an application for planning permission.[115] The time limits before the expiration of which the Department cannot determine such an application (Art. 21(1)(b) and (3)) also apply to appeals to the Commission (Art. 69(7)).

There is no duty on the Commission to consider ways in which an appeal might succeed when they have not been suggested on behalf of the appellant. In *Hobday v Secretary of State for the Environment*[116] an appeal was made against an enforcement notice on the grounds that planning permission ought to be granted for the development. The inspector appointed to hear the appeal concluded that suitable conditions to control the development could not be imposed and accordingly dismissed

---

115 Art. 69(7) applying Arts 21 and 25(2) with necessary modifications.
116 (1990) 61 P & CR 225.

the appeal. The appellant sought judicial review of the inspector's decision on the ground that he had failed to consider whether a planning agreement could be a solution to the problem. The court refused the application on this ground, as the issue of a planning agreement had not been raised at the appeal by the appellants.

(vi) Powers of Commission

In addition to the power already noted for the Commission in certain cases to disregard failure to serve someone who should have been served (Art. 70(3)), the Commission has power to correct any informality, defect or error in the enforcement notice, or to vary its terms, if the Commission is satisfied that the correction or variation can be made without injustice to the appellant or to the Department (Art. 70(2)).[117] In R v *Tower Hamlets* LBC, *ex p Ahern (London) Ltd*[118] Roch J thought the similar legislative provisions in England and Wales should be read so as to mean what they say, i.e. that *any* defect or error can be corrected so long as this can be done without injustice to either party, saying that the law had progressed 'to the point where pettyfogging has stopped, where artificial distinctions understood only by lawyers no longer prevail'.[119]

On the determination of an appeal against an enforcement notice, the Commission has power to grant planning permission for the development to which the notice relates; for part of that development; or for the development of part of the land to which the notice relates (Art. 71(1)(a)). In considering whether to grant permission the Commission is required to take into account any representations received by the Commission from the district council (Art. 69(5)) and to have regard to the development plan, so far as material to the subject matter of the enforcement notice, and to any other material considerations (Art. 71(2)). Any planning permission granted by the Commission may include permission to retain or complete any buildings or works on the land, or to do so without complying with a condition attached to a previous planning permission (Art. 71(2) (a)), and may be granted subject to such conditions as the Commission thinks fit (Art. 71(2)(b)).[120] Any planning permission granted by the Commission is treated as granted on the deemed application made by the appeal against the enforcement notice (Art. 71(3)(a)) and has the like effect as a permission granted by the Department (Art. 71(3)(c)), except that the decision of the Commission is final (Art. 71(3)(b)).

---

117 See *Wealden DC v Secretary of State for the Environment* (1983) JPL 234 and *Harrogate BC v Secretary of State for the Environment* (1986) 55 P & CR 224. It appears the Commission may be under a duty 'to try to get the enforcement notice in order': *Hammersmith LBC v Secretary of State for the Environment* (1975) 30 P & CR 19, 21 *per* Lord Widgery CJ; *Newbury DC v Secretary of State for the Environment* (1990) 61 P & CR 258.
118 (1990) 59 P & CR 133.
119 See also *Graham v Secretary of State for the Environment* [1993] JPL 353.
120 Doubtless, however, the usual tests for validity of conditions will apply.

The Commission has power also to discharge any condition or limitation in an existing planning permission (Art. 71(1)(b)). Before doing so the Commission must take into account any representations made by the district council, as in the case when the Commission grants planning permission (Art. 69(5)). Where the Commission does discharge a condition or limitation it may substitute another condition or limitation in its place, whether that new condition or limitation is more onerous or less (Art. 71(2)). As with a decision to grant planning permission, a determination to discharge a condition or limitation is final (Art. 71(3)(b)).

There appears unfortunately to be no power for the Commission to declare the lawful use of land affected by an enforcement notice, as exists in England and Wales.[121]

(vii) Effect of appeal

Once an appeal against an enforcement notice is brought, the notice is of no effect until the final determination or withdrawal of the appeal (Art. 69(8)).[122] Again, as we have noted, the making of an appeal against an enforcement notice is deemed to be an application for planning permission for the development to which the notice relates (Art. 71(3)).

While such are the effects of *making* an appeal against an enforcement notice, it is of course the effect of the *decision* on the appeal that will primarily concern the parties. We have seen that the Commission must either quash the notice, vary its terms, or uphold it (Art. 70(1)). The decision of the Commission is final, subject only to the possibility of judicial review. If the notice is varied or upheld by the Commission, the appellant must comply with it or risk prosecution.[123] If, however, the notice is quashed the appellant need not do anything. The quashing of a notice does not prevent the Department from issuing another one, subject to the principle of issue estoppel, or the possibility that a later notice may be caught by the four year rule. The House of Lords has recently held that the principle of *res judicata* applies to decisions on enforcement appeals, so that a determination of the Planning Appeals Commission in favour of the appellant in an enforcement appeal on grounds (b) to (e) of Art. 69(3) of the 1991 Order will estop the Department from alleging in any later enforcement notice that matters are otherwise than as found by the Commission.[124] A decision of the Commission on ground (a) of Art. 69(3)

---

121 Town and Country Planning Act 1990, s. 177(1)(c).
122 There are no provisions in the 1991 Order for appeals against the decision of the Planning Appeals Commission similar to those in s. 289 of the Town and Country Planning Act 1990, the only redress against such decision being judicial review. It has been thought unlikely that this would be considered part of the determination of an appeal and consequently the 'final determination' of the appeal takes place when the Commission makes its decision: see W D Trimble, in Alder, *op. cit.*
123 See Art. 72 and below.
124 *Thrasyvoulou v Secretary of State for the Environment* [1990] 1 All ER 65.

(i.e. that planning permission should or should not be granted) does not give rise to any estoppel as the decision is merely an application to the facts of planning policy at the time the decision is made.[125] An estoppel will arise only from a determination by the Commission on the merits, and not from a decision reached on procedural grounds only.[126] Whether findings of the Commission in relation to a ground of appeal against an enforcement notice would give rise to an estoppel, where those findings are not essential to the decision of the Commission, remains to be seen.[127]

(8) *Consequences of enforcement notice taking effect*

Once an enforcement notice takes effect, one of the consequences is that the permitted use of the land to which the notice relates is that for which the notice requires the land to be used. Any previous existing use or established use has gone.[128] It also becomes incumbent upon the recipient of the notice to comply with it or run the risk of a prosecution under Art. 72.[129]

Compliance with the notice does not discharge the notice (Art. 76(1)). Accordingly, if the notice requires discontinuance of a use and this is complied with, resumption of the use at a later date is contravention of the notice (Art. 76(2)). Similarly, if the notice requires demolition or alteration of buildings or works, and the notice is complied with, any development by way of reinstating or restoring the buildings or works at a later date is caught by the notice (Art. 76(3)). But where a notice issued in respect of development consisting of the erection of a building or the carrying out of works without planning permission and requiring steps to be taken for removing or alleviating injury to amenity has been complied with, planning permission for the retention of the buildings or works as they are following such compliance is deemed to be granted (Art. 68(16)).

If the steps required by an enforcement notice to be taken to remedy the breach of planning control (other than the discontinuance of a use) are not taken within the time allowed for compliance with the notice,[130] a person authorised in writing by the Department may enter the land and

---

125 Ibid.; R v *Wychavon DC, ex p Saunders* [1991] EGCS 122.
126 R v *Wychavon DC, ex p Saunders* [1991] EGCS 122. The procedural grounds with which the case was concerned have no equivalent provision in the 1991 Order.
127 *Young v Secretary of State for the Environment* (1990) 60 P & CR 560.
128 *Nash v Secretary of State for the Environment* (1985) 52 P & CR 261, 264, *per* Nourse LJ.
129 The expenses incurred by the owner or occupier of land in complying with an enforcement notice are deemed to be incurred for the use and at the request of the person by whom the breach of planning control was committed: Art. 74(2). Note also the power of the court to order the occupier of land to permit execution of work required by an enforcement notice: Art. 68(12).
130 I.e. the period specified in the notice for compliance or such extended period as may be allowed by the Department: Art. 72(6).

take those steps (Art. 74(1)).[131] The reasonable expenses in doing so are recoverable by the Department from the person who is then the owner of the land (Art. 74(1)),[132] and until recovered are a charge on the estate of the owner of the land and of any person deriving title under him (Art. 74(7)).[133] Any expenses incurred by the owner to the Department are deemed to be incurred at the request of the person by whom the breach of planning control was committed (Art. 74(2)). Any materials removed by the Department other than refuse may be sold unless within three days of removal they are claimed and taken away by their owner (Art. 74(3) and (5)). The proceeds of such sale after deduction of expenses must be paid to the owner of the materials (Art. 74(4)).

(9) Offences

The 1991 Order creates a number of offences based on failure to comply with the requirements of an enforcement notice.

First, where any steps required to be taken by an enforcement notice (other than discontinuance of a use) have not been taken within the period allowed for compliance with the notice, the person who at the time a copy of the enforcement notice was served on him was the owner of the land to which the notice relates is guilty of an offence (Art. 72(1)).[134] The offence is one of strict liability: the Department does not have to show the defendant was aware of the notice.[135] The Department is required to prove that the defendant was the owner at that time.[136] If the defendant was the owner at that time but ceased to be the owner before the time allowed for compliance with the notice, he may require the new owner to be brought before the court (Art. 72(2)) and if he shows that failure to comply with the notice was attributable in whole or in part to the default of the new owner, the new owner may be convicted (Art. 72(3)(a)). If the defendant also shows that he took all reasonable steps to secure compliance with the notice, he will be acquitted of the offence (Art. 72(3)(b)).

Second, a person convicted of the offence described in the preceding paragraph who fails to do everything in his power, as soon as practicable, to secure compliance with the enforcement notice, is guilty of a further offence and liable to a fine for each day following his conviction for the

---

131 See R v Greenwich LBC, ex p Patel (1985) 51 P & CR 282. The power conferred by Art. 74(1) includes power to take some only of the steps required by the enforcement notice: Arcam Demolition and Construction Co. Ltd v Worcestershire CC [1964] 2 All ER 286.
132 If that person is receiving rent from the land as agent or trustee, his liability is limited to the funds which he holds for his principal or beneficiary, but the Department may pursue the latter for the balance: Art. 74(6).
133 The charge is enforceable as if it were a mortgage by deed: Art. 74(8).
134 A prosecution may be brought within three years of commission of the offence: Art. 128.
135 R v Collett [1994] 2 All ER 372.
136 R v Ruttle, ex p Marshall (1988) 57 P & CR 299.

earlier offence on which any of the requirements of the enforcement notice remain unfulfilled (Art. 72(4)). This further offence has been described as a single offence, rather than a series of offences occurring each day following the initial conviction.[137] This, however, raises the question whether a person can be guilty of this 'further offence' on more than one occasion.[138]

These two offences, failure to comply with an enforcement notice within the period allowed and failure to comply after a conviction, have counterparts in notices which require the discontinuance of a use of land.[139] Any person using the land or causing or permitting the land to be used in contravention of an enforcement notice requiring discontinuance of a use is guilty of an offence (Art. 72(5)(a))[140] and of a further offence if after his initial conviction he continues to use the land in the way prohibited by the notice (Art. 72(5)(b)). Similarly, if the enforcement notice requires conditions or limitations to be complied with in respect of a use of land or in respect of the carrying out of operations on land, any person using the land or carrying out such operations or causing or permitting them to be carried out, is guilty of an offence (Art. 72(5)(a)).[141]

Finally, where buildings or works have been demolished or altered in compliance with an enforcement notice, it is an offence to carry out development by way of reinstating or restoring the buildings or works unless planning permission is obtained (Art. 76(5)).

(10) *Special enforcement notices*

Special provision is made for enforcement against unlawful development which has taken place on Crown land.[142] Where development of such land otherwise than by or on behalf of the Crown has been carried out at a time when no person was entitled to occupy the land by virtue of a private estate (Art. 118(1))[143] the Department may issue what is known as a special enforcement notice (Art. 116(1) and (2)). Various provisions of the 1991 Order applicable to enforcement notices apply to special enforcement notices (see Art. 116(7)), and the Department has power to apply other provisions also (Art. 116(7)).[144] Apart from this, certain specific provisions relating to enforcement notices are the same as those relating to ordinary enforcement notices. Thus, e.g. the Department must consider it expedient to issue a special enforcement notice, having regard to the provisions of

---

137 *Chiltern* DC v *Hodgetts* |1983| 1 All ER 1057.
138 See Alder, *op. cit.*, (1989) p. 102; Purdue *et al, op. cit.*, (1989) p.364.
139 'Desist notices' as opposed to 'do notices': *Chiltern* DC v *Hodgetts* |1983| 1 All ER 1057, 1060 *per* Lord Roskill.
140 Again a prosecution may be brought within three years: Art. 128.
141 A prosecution may be brought within three years: Art. 128.
142 As defined in Art. 118(1).
143 The example invariably given is the stationing of a hot-food bar on a road verge.
144 Ibid.; see Planning (Special Enforcement Notices) Regulations (NI) 1990.

the development plan and other material considerations (Art. 116(2)) and a copy of the notice must be served within the same period as is applicable to service of a copy of an ordinary enforcement notice (Art. 116(5)). There are however a number of differences, and these are noted here.

A special enforcement notice is required to specify the following matters (Art. 116(3) and (4)): (1) the matters alleged to constitute development of the kind mentioned in the preceding paragraph; (2) the steps which the Department requires to be taken for restoring the land to its condition before the development took place or for discontinuing any use of the land which was instituted by the development; (3) the date on which the notice is to take effect; and (4) the period within which any steps required to be taken are to be taken.[145]

A copy of a special enforcement notice must be served on the person who carried out the development to which the notice relates, unless the Department is unable after reasonable enquiry to identify or trace such person (Art. 116(5)). The Department is also required to serve a copy of the notice on any person who is occupying the land on the date on which the notice is issued, and 'the appropriate authority' (Art. 116(5)).[146]

An appeal against a special enforcement notice may be made to the Planning Appeals Commission by the person who carried out the development alleged in the notice or any person in occupation of the land on the date on which the notice is issued (Art. 116(6)). The appeal must be made before the date specified in the notice as the date on which the notice is to take effect (Art. 116(6)). There are only two grounds on which an appeal may be brought, *viz.* that the matters alleged in the notice have not taken place, or that they do not constitute development to which Art. 116 relates (Art. 116(6)).

6 Stop notices

While the mechanism of an enforcement notice may be effective either to deter the recipient from doing something which the notice requires him to cease doing, or to persuade him to do something the notice requires him to do, it suffers from the disadvantage that it cannot require immediate action to remedy a breach of planning control. The combined effect of Arts 68(5) and 69(3)(h) is that there may be a considerable delay between the date on which the notice is issued and the date on which non-compliance with the notice becomes a criminal offence. During that period the continuation of the unlawful development may cause damage to the land to which the notice relates or to amenity or both. While the

---

145 As with enforcement notices, different periods may be prescribed for different steps: Art. 116(4).
146 Ibid. For the meaning of 'the appropriate authority' see Art. 118(1).

notice once it takes effect may oblige the developer to restore the land to its former state, the intervening delay does nothing to encourage belief in the effectiveness of the system to prevent unlawful development.[147] The 1991 Order does provide a further means of enforcement action which can in part deal with the delayed-action effect of an enforcement notice, enabling the Department to require unlawful development to cease virtually immediately.

(1) *Power to serve stop notice*

Art. 73(1) of the 1991 Order empowers the Department to serve a stop notice, the effect of which is to prohibit the carrying out of activities on land as soon as the notice comes into effect, which may be three days after it has been served (Art. 73(3)). A stop notice cannot be served unless the Department has already served a copy of an enforcement notice (Art. 73(1)(a)). This does not, however, prevent the Department from serving a copy of an enforcement notice and a stop notice at the same time,[148] nor is the stop notice invalid because a copy of the enforcement notice to which it relates was not properly served if it is shown that the Department took all such steps as were reasonably practicable to effect proper service (1991 Order, Art. 73(9)). The Department must consider it expedient to prevent the activity in question before the expiry of the period allowed for compliance with the enforcement notice (Art. 73(1)(9b)), but a recital in the stop notice to this effect will be sufficient to satisfy this requirement in the absence of evidence to the contrary.[149]

(2) *Contents of stop notice*

A stop notice does not take effect until the date specified in it, which may not be earlier than three days nor later than twenty eight days from the date on which it is first served (Art. 73(3)). The notice must therefore specify such a date or it will never come into effect. The notice must also refer to the enforcement notice and a copy of the enforcement notice must be annexed to the stop notice (Art. 73(1)). Needless to say, the stop notice must also specify with sufficient certainty the activity which is required to cease.[150]

(3) *Activities which may be prohibited*

A stop notice may prohibit the carrying out of any activity which is, or is included in, a matter alleged by the enforcement notice to constitute the

---

147 See criticisms noted in Carnwath Report, Chapter 5.
148 R v *Pettigrove and Roberts* (1991) 62 P & CR 355.
149 Ibid.
150 See R v *Runnymede BC, ex p Sarvan Singh Seehra* (1986) 53 P & CR 281.

breach of planning control complained of in the enforcement notice (Art. 73(1)). There are, however, certain exceptions. A stop notice cannot prohibit a person from continuing to use any building, caravan or other structure situated on the land as his permanent residence,[151] nor can a stop notice prohibit a person from taking any steps necessary to comply, or secure compliance, with an enforcement notice (Art. 73(2)(b)).

(4) Service of stop notice

A stop notice may be served by the Department on any person who appears to it to have an estate in the land or be engaged in any activity prohibited by the notice (Art. 73(5)).[152] Once a stop notice has been served the Department can display on the land affected by the notice a site notice stating that a stop notice has been served and that any person contravening the stop notice may be prosecuted for an offence (Art. 73(5)). A site notice is required to give the date on which the stop notice takes effect and indicate its requirements (Art. 73(5)). Service of a stop notice on a person or the display of a site notice are prerequisite to the commission of an offence of contravening a stop notice (Art. 73(7)).[153]

(5) Withdrawal of stop notice

A stop notice may be withdrawn at any time by the Department, without prejudice to the power to issue another stop notice (Art. 73(6)). Withdrawal is effected by serving notice to that effect on persons who were served with the stop notice and, if a site notice was displayed, by displaying notice of the withdrawal in its place (Art. 73(6)).

(6) When notice ceases to have effect

A stop notice ceases to have effect when (1) the enforcement notice referred to in it is withdrawn or quashed; (2) the period allowed for compliance with the enforcement notice expires; (3) notice of withdrawal of the stop notice is served; or (4) if, or to the extent that, the activities prohibited by it cease (in cases where the enforcement notice is varied) to be included in the matters alleged in the enforcement notice to constitute a breach of planning control (Art. 73(4)(a) to (d)).

---

151 Whether as owner, occupier, tenant, patient, guest or otherwise: Art. 73(2)(a). See *Runnymede* BC v *Smith* (1986) 53 P & CR 132.
152 Note the difference in procedure between stop notices and enforcement notices. In the latter the notice is *issued* and *a copy* served.
153 See below.

(7) Offences

Any person contravening, or causing the contravention of, a stop notice after a site notice has been displayed or the stop notice has been served on him is guilty of an offence (Art. 73(7)). It is a defence, however, to show that the stop notice was not served on him and that he did not know and could not reasonably have been expected to know, of the existence of the stop notice (Art. 73(8)).[154] If a person is convicted of an offence and the offence is continued following conviction, he is liable to a further fine on a daily basis (Art. 73(7)).

(8) Appeals

There are no provisions for appeals against stop notices similar to those which exist in the case of enforcement notices. Any issue as to the validity of the stop notice may be raised in a prosecution brought by the Department for contravention of the notice,[155] or by way of an application for judicial review.[156]

(9) Compensation

While stop notices are potentially a very powerful means by which the Department can restrain unlawful development, they suffer from one notable disadvantage insofar as the Department is concerned. In certain cases following the service of a stop notice the Department is liable to pay compensation in respect of loss or damage directly attributable to the prohibition contained in the notice.[157]

Compensation is payable to a person who, at the time the stop notice is first served, had an estate in or occupied the land to which the notice relates,[158] in any of the following circumstances (1972 Order, Art. 67(2)):

(i) the enforcement notice to which the stop notice relates is quashed on any ground other than the ground that planning permission ought to be granted for the development complained of in the enforcement notice or that any condition or limitation alleged in the enforcement notice not to have been complied with ought to be discharged;

(ii) the enforcement notice is varied, otherwise than on such grounds, so that the matters alleged to constitute a breach of planning control cease to include one or more of the activities prohibited by the stop notice;

---

154 Note that stop notices are recorded in the register maintained by the Department under Art. 124 which is open to inspection by the public.
155 R v Jenner [1983] 2 All ER 40.
156 See e.g. R v Elmbridge DC, ex p Wendy Fair Markets Ltd [1994] EGCS 159.
157 1972 Order, Art. 67(1) (as substituted by 1991 Order, Art. 133 and sch. 5).
158 Ibid.

(iii) the enforcement notice is withdrawn by the Department otherwise than in consequence of the grant of planning permission for the development to which the notice related or for its retention or continuance without compliance with a condition or limitation subject to which a previous planning permission was granted; or
(iv) the stop notice is withdrawn.

The loss or damage sustained by a claimant includes any sum payable in respect of a breach of contract caused by the taking of action necessary to comply with the stop notice (1972 Order, Art. 67(4)), but in assessing the amount of compensation there will be taken into account the extent to which the claimant's entitlement to compensation is attributable to his failure to comply with a notice from the Department requiring information under Art. 125 of the 1991 Order, or any misstatement made by him in response to such a notice (1972 Order, Art. 67(5)). As usual, if the parties cannot agree on the amount of compensation, the amount will be determined by the Lands Tribunal (1972 Order, Art. 67(6)).

A claim for compensation must be in writing and made within six months from the service of the stop notice or such longer period as the Department allows (1972 Order, Art. 67(3); GDO, Art. 17)).

7 Injunctions

The mechanisms contained in the 1991 Order for enforcement of planning control may not be only means by which the Department can compel developers to obey the rules. It would seem that the Department may in certain circumstances be able to obtain an injunction to restrain a developer from acting unlawfully.[159] We have already seen that injunctions have been granted to the Attorney-General at the relation of planning authorities in England and Wales,[160] and in the case of members of a council wishing to prevent unlawful development by the council itself.[161] It is thought that the principles upon which the court might grant assistance to the Department are as follows:

(i) The jurisdiction to grant an injunction will be invoked and exercised exceptionally and with great caution,[162] an injunction in aid of the criminal law being a remedy of last resort which ought not to be

---

159 The principle is derived from the authorities in England and Wales, but it has been said that there is nothing to suppose that the practice of the courts here would be any different: see W D Trimble in Alder, *op. cit.* (1989), p. 143.
160 *Attorney-General, ex rel Hornchurch UDC v Bastow* [1957] 1 All ER 497; *Attorney-General, ex rel Egham UDC v Smith* [1958] 2 All ER 557.
161 *In re Cook's application* [1986] NI 242.
162 *London City Corp. v Bovis Construction Ltd* (1988) 86 LGR 660.

granted if other less draconian means of securing obedience to the law are available.[163] An injunction may be granted where for example an offence is frequently repeated in disregard of criminal penalties or in cases of emergency.[164]

(ii) As a general rule the Department will have to try the effect of the criminal proceedings available to it under the 1991 Order before seeking the assistance of the civil courts.[165] This is not an absolute rule, however, and there may be cases where the court will grant an injunction even though the Department has not brought prosecutions against the developer, e.g. where prosecutions would be too slow.[166] In *Doncaster BC v Green*,[167] however, the court refused to grant an injunction on the ground that the time allowed for compliance with an enforcement notice which had been served by the planning authority had not yet expired, the court saying that until it did the developer's conduct was not illegal.

It has been said that the duty of a planning authority is not limited to enforcing penalties for past offences,[168] suggesting that the Department may be able to obtain an injunction to prevent a threatened breach of planning control.[169]

(iii) To justify the grant of an injunction there must be more than a mere infringement of the criminal law[170] though it is not necessary to show that the developer is 'deliberately and flagrantly flouting the law'.[171] Other considerations may suffice such as whether the criminal penalties provided for under the 1991 Order are inadequate[172] though the fact that criminal penalties are substantial does not preclude the court from granting an injunction in appropriate cases.[173] Again, the fact that the developer's activities may cause irreparable damage may justify the court in granting an injunction.[174]

---

163 *Waverley BC v Hilden* [1988] 1 All ER 807, 823 *per* Scott J.
164 *Gouriet v Union of Post Office Workers* [1977] 3 All ER 70, 83 *per* Lord Wilberforce.
165 *Stoke-on-Trent CC v B & Q (Retail) Ltd* [1984] 2 All ER 332; *East Hampshire DC v Davies* (1991) 61 P & CR 481, where the absence of previous prosecutions was taken into account in weighing the balance of convenience in an application by a planning authority for an interlocutory injunction.
166 *Runnymede BC v Ball* [1986] 1 All ER 629, 634 *per* Fox LJ; See also *Stoke-on-Trent CC v B & Q Retail Ltd* [1984] 2 All ER 332.
167 [1991] EGCS 117.
168 *Runnymede BC v Ball* [1986] 1 All ER 629, 637 *per* Purchas LJ.
169 See Millichap, *op. cit* ., (1991) para. 9.7.3 referring to *London Borough of Southwark v Frow* noted at [1989] JPL 645.
170 *London City Corp. v Bovis Construction Ltd* (1988) 86 LGR 660.
171 *Runnymede BC v Ball* [1986] 1 All ER 629, 637 *per* Purchas LJ. The expression comes from *Stafford BC v Elkenford Ltd* [1977] 2 All ER 519.
172 *Runnymede BC v Ball* [1986] 1 All ER 629; cp *Stoke-on-Trent CC v B & Q plc* [1991] 4 All ER 224.
173 *Reigate and Banstead DC v Brown* [1992] EGCS 26.
174 *Runnymede BC v Ball* [1986] 1 All ER 629, 637 *per* Purchas LJ.

(iv) The essential foundation for the exercise of the court's jurisdiction is the need to draw the inference that the defendant's unlawful activities will continue unless and until effectively restrained by the law and nothing short of an injunction will be effective to restrain them.[175]
(v) Where the court does grant an injunction, the injunction will be limited to matters for which the Department needs the assistance of the court. If, for example, what the Department wants to do can be achieved under its powers under Art. 74 of the 1991 Order, an injunction will not be granted.[176]
(vi) Finally, it seems that a decision of the Department to seek an injunction may be open to challenge by way of judicial review.[177]

8 Prohibition

Prohibition is one of the orders which may be granted by the court on an application for judicial review (Judicature (NI) Act 1978, s. 18). As its name implies, it is an order prohibiting the body against whom the order is made from acting in the way prohibited. An order of prohibition was sought in In re Cook's application[178] by councillors seeking to restrain the unlawful display of an advertisement by a council, but was thought by the court to be an inappropriate remedy to stop a breach of planning control. The court granted an injunction instead.

---

175 London City Corp. v Bovis Construction Ltd (1988) 86 LGR 660.
176 Waverley BC v Hilden [1988] 1 All ER 807.
177 Ibid.
178 [1986] NI 242.

CHAPTER SIXTEEN

Planning by Agreement

We have seen in a previous chapter[1] that the Department has power to impose conditions on the grant of planning permission. This power enables the Department to regulate the development or use of land. It will be recalled that the power to impose conditions is exercisable not only in respect of the site which is the subject of the application for planning permission but extends to any land under the control of the applicant. The ability of the Department to control the development or use of land by means of the imposition of conditions is not, however, the only means by which the Department can control the development or use of land. Powers exist elsewhere to achieve this by means of agreements between the Department and landowners. The nature and form of such agreements are considered in this chapter.

1 *The* 1991 *Order*

Art. 40 of the 1991 Order empowers the Department to enter an agreement with any person having an estate in land for the purpose of facilitating, regulating or restricting the development or use of the land (Art. 40(1)).[2] 'Any person having an estate' would seem to include a person with an equitable estate, so enabling someone who has contracted to purchase land subject to planning permission to enter an agreement with the Department in the hope that this may facilitate the grant of permission. The reference in the subsection to facilitating the development of land indicates that agreements under the Order may be used to achieve a positive result rather than being intended merely to regulate or restrict such development.[3]

---

1 Chapter 13.
2 The power of planning authorities in England and Wales to enter agreements under similar statutory provisions has given rise to discussion of the ability of authorities to secure a 'planning gain' by means of such agreements. The concept of planning gain—i.e. the ability of a planning authority to extract some benefit from a would-be developer as 'the price of planning permission'—is controversial, and the term has been described as imprecise and misleading (Department of the Environment and Welsh Office Circular 16/91, para. B3). Policy on the use of planning agreements has recently been restated in England and Wales in the Circular mentioned. A discussion of such policy is outside the scope of this book. For recent judicial consideration of such policy see *Barber* v *Secretary of State for the Environment* [1991] JPL 559; *Safeway Properties Ltd* v *Secretary of State for the Environment* [1991] EGCS 68; *R* v *South Northamptonshire DC, ex p Crest Homes plc* (1994) 68 P & CR 187.
3 See Trimble, 'Planning Agreements come to Northern Ireland' (1990) 41 NILQ 185, 187.

An agreement may facilitate, regulate or restrict the development or use of land either permanently or during such period as may be prescribed by the agreement (Art. 40(1)). Although in contrast to the equivalent provisions of the legislation in England and Wales (Town and Country Planning Act 1990, s. 106(2)(a)) Art. 40 does not expressly provide that an agreement may be made conditional, it will usually be the case that a person entering an agreement under Art. 40 will do so on the basis that the Department will grant planning permission for development he wishes to carry out, and that any restrictions in the agreement will be applicable only if such permission is granted. There would seem to be no reason why such an agreement should not be made expressly conditional on permission being granted.[4]

(1) Relation of agreements to planning conditions

As we have noted, the ability to enter an agreement under Art. 40 gives the Department a second means of controlling the development or use of land, in addition to the power in that behalf to impose conditions. Conditions of course suffer from the requirement that they comply with the tests formulated in *Newbury DC v Secretary of State for the Environment*[5] viz. (1) that the condition must have a planning purpose; (2) that it must fairly and reasonably relate to the development authorised by the planning permission; and (3) that it satisfies the 'reasonableness' test of *Wednesbury Corp*.[6] It is tempting to suppose that agreements under Art. 40 need not comply with these tests, as otherwise there would be little point in having Art. 40 at all.[7] Nonetheless, it has been held on the comparable provisions of the Town and Country Planning Act 1971 (s. 52)[8] that an agreement must comply with the first and third of the *Newbury* tests, i.e. it must have a planning purpose and it must not be unreasonable in the sense of *Wednesbury Corp*.[9] This being so, the difference between a condition and an agreement is that the latter may deal with matters which do not relate to the development for which planning permission is sought.[10]

---

4 See also *Windsor Royal BC v Brandrose Investments Ltd* [1983] 1 All ER 818 indicating that an agreement which is not followed by the grant of permission may simply become irrelevant.
5 [1980] 1 All ER 731.
6 See generally Chapter 13.
7 See comments of Roch J in *R v Gillingham BC, ex p Parham Ltd* (1989) 58 P & CR 73, 81, echoed by Popplewell J in *R v Wealdon DC, ex p Charles Church South East Ltd* (1990) 59 P & CR 150, 159 and 162.
8 See now Town and Country Planning Act 1990, s. 106.
9 *City of Bradford MC v Secretary of State for the Environment* (1987) 53 P & CR 55; *R v Gillingham BC, ex p Parham Ltd* (1989) 58 P & CR 73; *R v Wealdon DC, ex p Charles Church South East Ltd* (1990) 59 P & CR 150; *Good v Epping Forest DC* [1994] 2 All ER 156.
10 *R v Gillingham BC, ex p Parham Ltd* (1989) 58 P & CR 73. For criticism see Trimble, *op. cit.*, 189.

However, the view that planning agreements need not comply with all the *Newbury* tests applicable to conditions is not unanimous. In R v *Westminster* CC, *ex p Monahan*[11] Kerr LJ said that if a particular condition were illegal on the ground of manifest unreasonableness *or otherwise*, it could not acquire validity by being embodied in a planning agreement. His Lordship referred to the earlier decision in *Bradford* MC v *Secretary of State for the Environment*[12] in which Lloyd LJ had observed that the use of planning agreements might have gone beyond what the legislation justified. To answer the question of the point of planning agreements if they are limited by the same restrictions as apply to planning conditions, Kerr LJ noted three advantages of an agreement over a condition. First, an agreement may simplify the procedural aspects of the planning process; second, an agreement has the advantage of flexibility in that it is negotiable in contrast to a condition which is imposed unilaterally; and, third, an agreement is less vulnerable to the risk of judicial review.[13] It has been pointed out too that an agreement is easier to enforce than a condition, the appropriate remedy being an injunction rather than an enforcement notice.[14] To this may be added that no appeal lies to the Planning Appeals Commission against the terms of an agreement under Art. 40, whereas an appeal lies against a condition.

The most recent discussion of the applicability of the *Newbury* tests to planning agreements is in *Good* v *Epping Forest* DC,[15] in which the Court of Appeal adopted the views of Roch J in *ex p Parham* in preference to those of Kerr LJ in *ex p Monahan*. The result therefore appears to be that conditions (1) and (3) from *Newbury* do apply to planning agreements, but that (2) does not, i.e. the agreement need not be fairly and reasonably related to the proposed development. However, in R v *Plymouth* CC *ex p Plymouth and South Devon Co-Operative Society Ltd*[16] a differently constituted Court of Appeal held that the tests applicable to planning conditions do apply to planning agreements, throwing the matter into confusion once again.[17]

If the Department chooses to proceed by way of an agreement rather than a condition, thus precluding any appeal, it will not be acting contrary to public policy.[18]

---

11   [1989] 2 All ER 74, 100.
12   (1987) 53 P & CR 55, 65.
13   R v *Westminster* CC, *ex p Monahan* [1989] 2 All ER 74, 100. See also Alder, 'Planning Agreements and Planning Powers' [1990] JPL 880.
14   Alder, *op. cit.*, 886. For injunctions see *Avon* CC v *Millard* (1985) 50 P & CR 275 and discussion below.
15   [1994] 2 All ER 156.
16   (1993) 67 P & CR 78.
17   See also *Tesco Stores Ltd* v *Secretary of State for the Environment* (1994) 68 P & CR 219.
18   *Good* v *Epping Forest* DC [1994] 2 All ER 156.

(2) Contents of the agreement

The contents of an agreement under Art. 40 will of course depend on the particular circumstances of each individual case. The legislation indicates that, within the limits imposed by such of the *Newbury* tests as are applicable to agreements, an agreement under Art. 40 may include provisions for securing the carrying out of works for facilitating, regulating or restricting the development or use of land (Art. 40(2)(b)) and such incidental and consequential provisions as appear to the Department to be necessary or expedient for the purposes of the agreement (Art. 40 (2)(c)). Most importantly, those incidental and consequential provisions may include 'provisions of a financial character'. Thus, within the confines of the 'reasonableness' requirement of *Wednesbury Corp.*, a developer can be bound by an agreement under Art. 40, for example, to make a financial contribution to the cost of infrastructure which will be needed to serve the development for which he seeks planning permission.[19] It is also envisaged that agreements under Art. 40 may include covenants on the part of the person with whom the Department enters the agreement, as provision is made for the enforcement of such covenants against successors in title to the covenantor.[20]

(3) Effect of the agreement

Once an agreement under Art. 40 is concluded, its effect is to create a means of control of development additional to that provided by Art. 12 of the 1991 Order (the requirement of planning permission).[21] The two regimes constitute different systems of control and each has and retains an independent existence.[22] That created by the agreement has the advantage for the Department that it is free from the appellate jurisdiction of the Planning Appeals Commission. Once an agreement under Art. 40 is concluded the developer is bound by it, subject only to the possibility of modification or discharge of the agreement under the Property (NI) Order 1978.[23]

Despite the fact that the agreement is made with the Department as the body responsible for administration of planning control in the public interest, an agreement under Art. 40 will not create a public right which would render the agreement enforceable by the Attorney-General.[24] As the agreement must be made under seal,[25] the agreement will be enforceable between the parties to it as a contract. Insofar as the Department is

---

19 For policy regarding the seeking of financial contributions from developers in England and Wales see Department of the Environment and Welsh Office Circular 16/91.
20 See below.
21 *Re Jones' and White & Co.'s application* (1989) 58 P & CR 512, 516.
22 *Re Martins' application* (1988) 57 P & CR 119, 124.
23 For modification and discharge see below.
24 *Attorney-General ex rel Scotland v Barratt Manchester Ltd* (1992) 63 P & CR 179.
25 See below.

concerned, obligations undertaken by the other party to the agreement will be enforceable against that party and, provided certain requirements are met,[26] against successors in title to that party. Similarly, any obligations undertaken in the agreement by the Department will be enforceable against the Department as a matter of contract. There is one overriding principle however, namely, that the agreement cannot restrict the Department in the exercise of any of its powers under the 1991 Order in relation to the land which is the subject of the agreement, so long as those powers are exercised in accordance with the provisions of the development plan (Art. 40(8)(a)), or require the Department to exercise any such powers otherwise than in accordance with the provisions of the development plan (Art. 40(8)(b)). The meaning of the similar provisions of the Town and Country Planning Act 1971 (s. 52(3)) was considered in *Windsor Royal BC v Brandrose Investments Ltd*.[27] There, a developer and a local planning authority entered an agreement so that each could develop their respective sites. Development of the developer's site involved demolition of existing buildings, as the authority was aware. After granting the developer planning permission for its intended development, the authority declared the area where the developer's site was located a conservation area, with the effect that specific consent was required from the authority for the developer to demolish the buildings. Such consent not having been obtained, the authority sought an injunction to restrain the developer from carrying out the demolition. The developer argued that the authority had bound itself not to exercise its power to declare a conservation area affecting the developer's site, the statutory prohibition against the authority binding itself not being relevant, as there was no development plan for the area. At first instance the developer succeeded, but an appeal by the authority was allowed, Lawton LJ saying 'Whatever s. 52(3)[28] means, and we share the bemusement of counsel for the plaintiffs, it cannot in our judgment be construed as empowering a local planning authority to bind themselves not to exercise powers given to them ... which they have a duty to exercise.'[29]

As the Department cannot bind itself by an agreement under Art. 40, the fact that the agreement has been made does not mean that planning permission for development of the land will be granted. The making of the agreement and the granting of permission are two separate issues, and the Department must consider any planning application made by the developer in the light of circumstances relevant at the time the application falls to be considered. Were it otherwise, an agreement under Art. 40 would be the equivalent of planning permission to the prejudice of those persons entitled to object to the grant of planning permission.[30] It

---

26 See below.
27 [1983] 1 All ER 818.
28 Compare Art. 40(8)(a).
29 [1983] 1 All ER 818, 823.
30 *Windsor Royal BC v Brandrose Investments Ltd* [1983] 1 All ER 818, 822.

is therefore possible that the Department might enter an agreement under Art. 40 and later refuse planning permission for development of the land which is the subject of the agreement, or grant permission subject to conditions inconsistent with the terms of the agreement. In such cases the agreement may simply become irrelevant.[31]

(4) Formalities

An agreement under Art. 40 must be made in an instrument under seal (Art. 40(2)(a)). Where the agreement contains a covenant on the part of the person entering the agreement, the agreement should define the land to which the covenant relates and should state that the covenant is one to which Art. 40 applies, to enable the Department to take advantage of the provisions as to enforcement contained in Art. 40(3)(b) and (c).[32]

In contrast to agreements made under the Nature Conservation and Amenity Lands (NI) Order 1985 considered later, there is no provision for registration of agreements under Art. 40 of the 1991 Order in the statutory charges register.[33] Nor are agreements under Art. 40 included in the matters which have to be registered in the planning register (see 1991 Order, Art. 124). However, an agreement under Art. 40, being made under seal, will be a 'deed... affecting land' and accordingly registrable in the Registry of Deeds if the land affected by the agreement is unregistered land.[34] If the land is registered land, any obligation undertaken by the person entering the agreement will be a 'covenant or condition relating to the use or enjoyment of the land' and registrable as a sch. 6 burden.[35]

(5) Enforcement

As an agreement under Art. 40 must be contained in an instrument under seal, each party to the agreement will have the usual remedies open to a party to a deed, e.g. damages, an injunction or specific performance. If the agreement is breached by the developer, an injunction will normally be the only appropriate remedy for the Department as the Department will not normally suffer damage if the agreement is breached and will not normally be in search of damages as a remedy.[36] Nor is it necessary

---

31 Ibid.
32 For enforcement see below. A covenant is an agreement by deed between two or more parties to do or refrain from doing something (*Termes de la Ley*). As an agreement under Art. 40 must be under seal it would appear that any obligation entered into by the person entering the agreement will be a covenant.
33 Land Registration Act (NI) 1970, Part X.
34 Registry of Deeds Act (NI) 1970, s. 1.
35 Land Registration Act (NI) 1970, s. 39 and sch. 6, para. 12.
36 *Avon CC v Millard* (1985) 50 P & CR 275, 279 *per* Fox LJ. Compare *Re Quartley's application* (1989) 58 P & CR 518.

before an injunction will be granted for the Department to exhaust any enforcement action which may be open to it if breach of the agreement also amounts to unlawful development.[37]

We have already noted that if the agreement contains a covenant on the part of the person entering it the agreement should define the land to which the covenant relates and should state that the covenant is one to which Art. 40 applies (Art. 40(3)(b) and (c)). The purpose of the agreement doing so is that the Department is then enabled to enforce the covenant at any time against any person deriving title from the original covenantor in respect of his estate and any person deriving title from him in respect of any lesser estate, as if that person had also been a covenanting party in respect of the estate held by him (Art. 40(3)).[38] Thus, the burden of the covenant will run not only to successors to the estate of the original covenantor, but also to persons holding derivative interests from the covenantor. Further, by the device of deeming successors to be covenanting parties themselves, the subsection enables the Department to enforce *positive* as well as *negative* covenants against successors.

The ability of the Department to enforce covenants against successors to the original covenantor is subject to any question of priorities which may arise under the Registration of Deeds Act (NI) 1970 or the Land Registration Act (NI) 1970.[39]

Apart from enforcing a covenant by action, the Department may itself carry out any work which was to be done under the covenant. Art. 40(4) of the 1991 Order provides that if there is a breach of covenant in relation to any of the land to which the covenant relates a person authorised in writing by the Department may enter on the land concerned and do anything the covenant requires to be done or remedy anything which has been done in breach of the covenant. Before exercising this power, however, the Department must give at least twenty one days notice in writing of its intention to do so to anyone having an estate in the land, and anyone against whom the covenant is enforceable (Art. 40(5)). If the Department does exercise its power to enter the land and carry out the work it can recover any expenses incurred as a civil debt from any person against whom the covenant is enforceable (Art. 40(6)).

(6) Modification and discharge

We have seen that an agreement under Art. 40 may affect land either permanently or during such time as the agreement provides (Art. 40(1)). The agreement may therefore come to an end naturally. Apart from such

---

[37] Ibid.
[38] Such persons are entitled on request to a copy of the agreement under Art. 40 from the Department, free of charge: Art. 40(7).
[39] For priorities see Wylie, *Irish Land Law*, Abingdon, Oxon: Professional Books, 2nd ed., 1986, chs 21 and 22.

cases however, as with any agreement, it is possible for the parties to the agreement to rescind or vary the terms of the agreement by a later agreement. A later agreement, although not expressly rescinding or varying the earlier agreement, may have that effect, though this is a matter of construction of the later agreement.[40] Even if the parties do not agree to rescind or vary the agreement, the developer or his successor may apply for modification or variation of the agreement under the Property (NI) Order 1978. Before considering this, however, it should be noted that an agreement under Art. 40 will not cease to apply merely because the Department later grants planning permission for development of the land in a manner inconsistent with the terms of the agreement. The agreement is not extinguished by the permission.[41]

A detailed discussion of the provisions of the Property (NI) Order 1978 will be found elsewhere.[42] Suffice here to note that the Lands Tribunal is empowered on the application of any person interested in land affected by an 'impediment' to make an order modifying or wholly or partially extinguishing the impediment if it is satisified that the impediment unreasonably impedes the enjoyment of the land or, if not modified or extinguished, would do so (Property (NI) Order 1978, Art. 5(1)). 'Impediment' includes a restriction under a covenant, condition or agreement contained in a deed (Art. 3(1)(a)(i)) and extends therefore to agreements made under Art. 40 of the 1991 Order.[43] In considering whether to modify or extinguish an impediment the Tribunal is required to take into account a number of matters, including any public interest in the land, particularly as exemplified by any adopted development plan and any trend shown by decisions on applications for planning permission (see Art. 5(5)(c) and (d)). These are merely matters which the Tribunal is required to take into account: they do not automatically determine the issue whether an impediment should be modified or discharged. Even if planning permission is granted for development on the land which is the subject of the Art. 40 agreement, this does not mean that the Tribunal is bound to

---

40 See *Attorney-General ex rel Scotland v Barratt Manchester Ltd* (1992) 63 P & CR 179 (agreement made in 1934 under statutory provisions similar to Art. 40 not rendered invalid by agreement in 1988 under replacement provisions, but planning authority estopped from enforcing earlier agreement).
41 *Re Martins' application* (1989) 57 P & CR 119, 124.
42 Dawson, 'Modification and discharge of land obligations under the Property (NI) Order 1978' (1978) 29 NILQ 223.
43 For applications to modify or discharge agreements under the equivalent provisions in England and Wales see *Re Cox's application* (1986) 51 P & CR 335; *Re Martins' application* (1988) 57 P & CR 119; *Re Towner and Goddard's application* (1989) 58 P & CR 316; *Re Jones' and White & Co.'s application* (1989) 58 P & CR 512; *Re Quartley's application* (1989) 58 P & CR 518; *Re Barclays Bank plc's application* (1990) 60 P & CR 354; *Bedwell Park Quarry Co. Ltd v Hertfordshire CC* [1993] JPL 349; *Re Poulton's application* (1992) 65 P & CR 319; *Re Wallace & Co.'s application* (1992) 66 P & CR 124; *Re Hopcraft's application* (1993) 66 P & CR 475; *Re O'Reilly's application* (1993) 66 P & CR 485. See now Town and Country Planning Act 1990, s. 106A(1).

modify or extinguish the agreement.[44] The Department is entitled to oppose modification or extinguishment of the agreement notwithstanding that it may have granted planning permission for development in a manner inconsistent with the agreement, even if its reasons for opposing have not been relied on before or on their face are contrary to the planning decision, so long as the reasons are real and not fanciful or vexatious.[45]

If the Tribunal does make an order modifying or extinguishing an impediment, it has power to award compensation to the person entitled to the benefit of the impediment for the loss or disadvantage he suffers in consequence of the modification or extinguishment (Property (NI) Order 1978, Art. 5(6)(b)). While this provision is applicable where the Tribunal modifies or extinguishes an agreement under Art. 40 of the 1991 Order, in practice it may be of little relevance, as it has been said that money is not adequate compensation for the loss sustained by a planning authority as custodian of the public interest.[46]

2 The Nature Conservation and Amenity Lands (NI) Order

Apart from the provisions of Art. 40 of the 1991 Order, the Department has various powers to enter agreements with landowners or occupiers restricting the use of their land under the Nature Conservation and Amenity Lands (NI) Order 1985.

(1) Article 8 agreements

The Department has power under Art. 8 of the Order to enter into an agreement with, or accept a covenant from, an owner[47] of land in an area which the Department considers to be one of natural beauty or amenity, restricting the use or development of the land in any manner (1985 Order, Art. 8(1)). Such agreement or covenant may have effect either permanently or for a specified period (1985 Order, Art. 8(1)). Consideration may be given by the Department for the agreement or covenant, but this is not essential (1985 Order, Art. 8(1)), nor, in contrast to the situation under the 1991 Order, is it essential that the agreement be made under seal. This raises the question whether an agreement not made for consideration, and not made in an instrument under seal, would be enforceable. The

---

44 Re Martins' application (1988) 57 P & CR 119; Re Hopcraft's application (1993) 66 P & CR 475.
45 Re Jones' and White & Co.'s application (1989) 58 P & CR 512.
46 Re Quartley's application (1989) 58 P & CR 518; compare Avon CC v Millard (1985) 50 P & CR 275 (damages inadequate remedy for breach of agreement).
47 I.e. any person (other than a mortgagee not in possession) who is the holder of or is for the time being entitled to sell or otherwise dispose of the fee simple (including a fee farm grant) of the land or any person entitled to possession of the land by virtue of any estate in the land other than a mere licence: 1985 Order, Art. 2(2).

answer may be that the agreement is a statutory agreement for a public purpose, and private law principles should not be imported, but this is not certain.[48]

Enforcement of the agreement or covenant against persons other than the person entering it is possible where (1) that person has power to make the agreement or covenant binding on his successors and (2) the agreement or covenant is expressed to be binding on those successors (1985 Order, Art. 8(2)). The device used in the Order is, however, the cumbersome one of deeming the Department to be possessed of, or entitled to, or interested in adjacent land and deeming the agreement or covenant to have been expressed to have been entered into for the benefit of that land.[49] The intention seems to be that the agreement or covenant is to be enforceable by the Department as a restrictive covenant.[50]

In contrast to agreements under Art. 40 of the 1991 Order, agreements under Art. 8 of the Nature Conservation and Amenity Lands Order are registrable in the statutory charges register.[51] Accordingly, the liability of successors in title to the person entering the agreement or the original covenantor will be subject to the provisions for priorities contained in s. 88 of the Land Registration Act (NI) 1970.

As with any agreement, on ordinary principles the agreement may be terminated by a later agreement between the parties, or on an application under the Property (NI) Order 1978.[52] This being so, the provisions of Art. 8(3) of the 1985 Order, which empower the Department to waive (either permanently or temporarily) any condition imposed by the agreement which is inconsistent with any provision of a development plan or development order seem unnecessary.[53]

(2) Management agreements

As well as the provisions of Art. 8, the Nature Conservation and Amenity Lands Order empowers the Department to enter agreements in certain circumstances with respect to the management of the land which is the subject of the agreement. These are noted briefly.

---

48 See *Pioneer Aggregates (UK) Ltd v Secretary of State for the Environment* [1984] 2 All ER 358; compare *Ransom and Luck v Surbiton BC* [1949] 1 All ER 185.
49 Compare Town and Country Planning Act 1971, s. 52(2) (now repealed).
50 This in turn raises the question whether a positive obligation in an agreement or a positive covenant under Art. 8 would be enforceable against successors to the person entering the agreement or the original covenantor. But it may be that a positive obligation or covenant is inconsistent with the nature of an agreement or covenant under Art. 8 in any case, as the Article refers merely to *restricting* the development or use of land.
51 Land Registration Act (NI) 1970, sch. 11 para. 39 (inserted by Nature Conservation and Amenity Lands (NI) Order 1985, Art. 34(1) and sch. 4).
52 See above in connection with applications regarding agreements under Art. 40 of the 1991 Order.
53 It is considered unlikely that the subsection could be used to argue that an agreement under Art. 8 could *not* be waived *except* on the ground in Art. 8(3).

First, the Department may make an agreement with any person having an estate in land for the purpose of enhancing the natural beauty or amenity of the land or promoting its enjoyment by the public (1985 Order, Art. 9(1)). Such an agreement may impose restrictions on the person making it as respects the method of cultivation of the land, its use for agricultural purposes or the exercise of rights over the land, and may impose obligations on such person to carry out works or agricultural or forestry operations or do other things on the land (Art. 9(2)(a)). The agreement may also contain such incidental or consequential provisions as appear to the Department to be expedient for the purposes of the agreement (Art. 9(2)(b)). Such incidental provisions may include provisions for payment of money by the Department to the person making the agreement (Art. 9(2)(b)). The agreement may be either for a limited period or permanent (Art. 9(1)) and unless it provides to the contrary, the agreement will bind persons deriving title under or from the person making the agreement and be enforceable against such persons (Art. 9(3)).

Second, the Department may enter an agreement with any person having an estate in land which the Department considers should be managed as a nature reserve, for securing that the land is so managed (Art. 17(1)). The agreement may impose restrictions on the exercise of rights over the land by persons who can be bound by the agreement (Art. 17(2)) and may require work to be carried out and may contain financial provisions (Art. 17(3)). An agreement may be made irrevocably or subject to provisions for revocation or variation (Art. 17(5)) and as with agreements under Art. 8, any provision of an agreement under Art. 17 may be waived by the Department if it is inconsistent with any provision of a development plan or order (Art. 17(6) applying Art. 8(3)). If the person making the agreement agrees to grant any right as respects the land, successors in title to that person are bound by that provision to the extent which the person making the agreement would be bound (Art. 17(4)).[54]

Finally, where the Department has declared an area to be an area of special scientific interest, it may enter an agreement with any owner or occupier of land in that area for securing that his land is managed as an area of special scientific interest (Art. 24(8)(a)).[55]

As with agreements under Art. 8, management agreements are registrable in the statutory charges register.[56]

---

54 There being no other provision for successors in title, *quaere* whether the burden of a management agreement under Art. 17 is personal to the person entering the agreement except in the case envisaged by Art. 17(4).
55 The provisions of the Order regulating agreements in respect of land to be managed as a nature reserve (Art. 17) apply: Art. 24(9).
56 Land Registration Act (NI) 1970, sch. 11, para. 39.

PART FOUR

Special Control

CHAPTER SEVENTEEN

Listed Buildings and Historic Monuments

We saw in Chapter 6 how the Department is able to protect areas of special or architectural interest by designating them conservation areas. Apart from this form of protection of *areas* of the province, the Department is able to protect *individual buildings* by including them in the list it is obliged to compile under Art. 42 of the 1991 Order. The criterion for inclusion of a building in the list is that the building is of special architectural or historic interest (for relevant considerations as to whether a building should be included in the list, see Art. 42(2) and below). As we will see, there are various consequences which flow from the listing of a building. To begin with, financial assistance may be available from the Department for maintenance of the building (Art. 106)). More importantly perhaps, it is an offence to alter or demolish the building without the consent of the Department (Art. 44(1)), and the Department has power to acquire the building in the interests of preservation (Art. 109). These matters are considered in detail below.

Apart, however, from the protection afforded to buildings either by their being within a conservation area or by their being included in the list compiled by the Department under Art. 42 of the 1991 Order, the Department is responsible for the protection of historic monuments under the Historic Monuments Act (NI) 1971. After considering the protection of listed buildings afforded by the 1991 Order, it is proposed to consider briefly the protection afforded to historic monuments under the 1971 Act.

1 Buildings of special architectural or historic interest

(1) Listed buildings

Art. 42(1) of the 1991 Order imposes a duty on the Department to compile lists of buildings of special architectural or historic interest. Any such list compiled by the Department may thereafter be amended (Art. 42(1)(b)). Any building for the time being included in the Department's list is known, not surprisingly, as a 'listed building'.[1] Before considering the

---

1 As at 31 March 1991 there were 7,809 listed buildings in Northern Ireland: Historic Buildings Council for Northern Ireland, Report for 1988–1991, (1991), p. 14.

criteria the Department takes into account in deciding whether to include any building in its list, the following points should be noted as to exactly what may be protected as a listed building. First, for the purposes of the 1991 Order, the word 'building' includes any structure or erection, and any part of a building, as so defined (Art. 2(1)), so that the definition of what may be listed is wider than might at first be thought. Second, the Order treats as part of a listed building (a) any object or structure within the curtilage of the building and fixed to the building, and (b) any object or structure within the curtilage of the building which, although not fixed to the building, forms part of the land and has done so since 1 October 1973 (Art. 42(7)). A building which is Crown land may be included in the list maintained by the Department under Art. 42 (Art. 113(1)(c)).

(a) 'Any object or structure'

In *Debenhams plc* v *Westminster* CC[2] the House of Lords had to consider whether a separate building, linked to a listed building by a footbridge over the tunnel under a street was 'any object or structure . . . fixed to the [listed] building' so as to grant exemption from rates for the hereditament, which comprised the two buildings (General Rate Act 1967, sch. 1 para. 2(c)). By a majority the court held that the non-listed building was not part of the listed building by virtue of being an object or structure fixed to the listed building, that expression signifying only a structure which was ancillary and subordinate to the listed building itself, and that the fact that one building was subordinate to another for the commercial purposes of the occupier was irrelevant. The concept implied by Art. 42(7) is that of principal and accessory.[3]

(b) 'within the curtilage of the building'

The curtilage of a building is a small area forming part or parcel with the building to which it is attached:[4] 'a garden, yard, field or piece of void ground, lying near and belonging to the messuage'.[5] Whether any given area is within the curtilage of a building is a question of fact and degree in each case.[6] In *Watson-Smyth* v *Secretary of State for the Environment*[7] the

---

2 [1987] 1 All ER 51 HL.
3 *Debenhams plc* v *Westminster* CC [1987] 1 All ER 51, 55 *per* Lord Keith. See also *Attorney-General (ex rel Suttcliff)* v *Calderdale BC* (1982) 46 P & CR 399. In that case the Court of Appeal held that a terrace of cottages was a structure fixed to a listed building (a mill) and formed part of the land within the curtilage of the mill. While not overruling the case, the House of Lords in *Debenhams plc* v *Westminster* CC did not accept the width of the reasoning of Stephenson LJ in *Calderdale BC*. For a recent consideration of *Debenhams* and *Calderdale BC* see *Watts* v *Secretary of State for the Environment* (1991) 62 P & CR 366.
4 *Dyer* v *Dorset BC* [1988] 3 WLR 213.
5 *Sheppard's Touchstone of Common Asssurances*, Abingdon Oxon: Professional Books, 2nd ed., Repr. of 1648 ed., p. 94.
6 *Methuan-Campbell* v *Walters* [1974] 1 All ER 606, 617 *per* Goff LJ.
7 [1992] JPL 451.

High Court in England refused to upset the finding of an inspector that a ha-ha or ditch or sunken fence forming a garden boundary so as not to interrupt the view was part of the curtilage of a listed building and therefore part of the building.[8]

(c) Fixed to the building or part of the land

The final requirement to make the structure or object part of the listed building by virtue of Art. 42(7) is that the object must be fixed to the building or if not, form part of the building and have done so since 1 October 1973. The word 'fixed' has the same connotation as in the law of fixtures, and what is intended by the legislative provisions is that the ordinary rule of the common law is applied so that any object or structure fixed to a building should be treated as part of it.[9]

(2) Criteria for listing

Obviously, as the list compiled by the Department is a list of buildings of special architectural or historic interest, the first consideration whether to include any particular building in the list will be the building itself. The Department has pointed to the following as relevant criteria in connection with listing: the age and style of the building; its appearance; its design; the condition of the building; any alterations to the building; any extensions to the building; the system of proportion; the system of ornamentation; the plan form of the building; its spacial organisation; its aesthetic quality; its present value; its authorship; the number of buildings of merit in the area; and the townscape value of the building.[10] There are several categories of listing: *Category* A (buildings of national importance); *Category* B+ (buildings which might have merited Category A status but for relatively minor detracting features such as impurities of design, lower quality additions or alterations; also buildings which stand out above the general mass of Category B buildings because of exceptional interiors, environmental qualities or some other feature); *Category* B (buildings of national or local importance or good examples of some period or style). Category B is subdivided into categories B1 and B2. *Category* C buildings are buildings which have positive architectural or historic interest, but not in such degree as to be called 'special'. The category includes structures which individually would not merit listing but which contribute to the value of other buildings or groups which may be integrated into new schemes.[11]

---

8 See also *James v Secretary of State for the Environment* [1991] JPL 550; *Lewis v Rook* [1992] EGCS 21; *Lambeth LBC v Secretary of State for the Environment* [1992] EGCS 17.
9 *Debenhams plc v Westminster CC* [1987] 1 All ER 51, 59 *per* Lord Mackay.
10 Department of the Environment for Northern Ireland Memorandum No 163 *Criteria and standards for listing* (23 July 1991).
11 Ibid.

However, the 1991 Order provides that in addition to the building itself, the Department may take into account in considering whether to include a building in the list (a) any respect in which the exterior of the building contributes to the architectural or historic interest of any group of buildings of which it forms part (Art. 42(2)(a)); and (b) the desirability of preserving, on the ground of its architectural or historic interest, any feature of the building which consists of a man-made object or structure fixed to the building or which forms a part of the land and which is comprised within the curtilage of the building (Art. 42(2)(b)). In *Iveagh (Earl) v Minister of Housing and Local Government*[12] Lord Denning MR said that it is open to the Minister to consider not only the intrinsic interest of the building by itself, but also the interest which it derives from its association with others.[13] In the same case Donovan LJ gave the example that a building in a terrace might have no special architectural interest if looked at through blinkers, yet regarded as part of the whole terrace might well acquire such an interest.[14]

(3) Procedure for listing

As with the exercise of many other powers and duties, the first step for the Department to take is consultation. Art. 42(3) requires the Department before it compiles and amends its lists to consult both the district council and also the Historic Buildings Council. Thereafter, unlike other provisions of the 1991 Order, there are no provisions for representations or objections to the listing. Presumably, however, the decision of the Department to include a building in its list would be open to challenge by judicial review on the usual grounds.

After the Department has compiled or amended its list, a copy of the relevant part of the list must be deposited by the Department with the appropriate district council (Art 42(4)), and the Department is required to give notice to every owner and occupier of any building included in the list either on its compilation or amendment, or excluded from the list on amendment (Art. 42(5)). Copies of the lists prepared by the Department must be made available for public inspection (Art. 42(6)) and once a building is listed, an entry is required to be made in the statutory charges register.[15]

(4) Consequences of listing

The 1991 Order provides that a number of consequences flow from the inclusion of a building in the list maintained by the Department.

---

12 [1963] 3 All ER 817.   13 Ibid., 822.   14 Ibid.
15 Land Registration Act (NI) 1970, sch. 11, entry 27(a), as provided by Art. 131 of the 1991 Order.

(a) Financial assistance towards maintenance

We will see below that the effect of listing a building is to prevent its alteration or demolition without consent of the Department. The 1991 Order thus prevents the owner from taking positive action to alter the building or to remove it altogether, but does not prevent the owner from allowing the building to fall into disrepair.[16] The Department is empowered, however, by Art. 106(1) of the 1991 Order to make grants or loans towards expenditure in the repair or maintenance of a listed building, objects ordinarily kept in the building, and the upkeep of land comprising, or contiguous or adjacent to, any listed building. Where a grant or loan is made, it is open to the Department to attach conditions for securing public access to the whole or part of the property (Art. 106(4)).

(b) Alterations and demolition

The demolition of a listed building, or its alteration or extension in any manner which would affect its character as a building of special architectural or historic interest, requires the consent of the Department, failing which any person excluding or causing such work to be carried out is guilty of an offence (Art. 44(1)). The consent of the Department which is required to render such work lawful is known as listed building consent (Art. 44(4)). In the case of demolition of a listed building, in addition to the consent of the Department being necessary, it is also necessary to afford someone authorised by the Department reasonable access to the building for at least one month following the grant of consent and before the works are begun, for the purpose of recording the building, save where the Department has said it has completed its recording or that it does not wish to record the building (Art. 44(2)(b)).

(i) When consent is required

Listed building consent is needed for any works for the demolition of a listed building or for its alteration or extension in any manner which would affect its character as a building of special architectural or historic interest (Art. 44(1)). It would seem therefore that any alteration or extension which does not so affect the building does not require consent.[17] It should not be assumed, however, that the question whether the alteration or extension affects the character of the building so as to require consent is one answerable by reference to the magnitude of the works involved. Painting or repairing the exterior of a listed building may affect the

---

16 Though the Department has power to acquire the building compulsorily if the owner fails to comply with a repairs notice served by the Department (Art. 109), and where urgent repairs are required, the Department has power to carry out the remedial work itself (Art. 80). For discussion of Arts 109 and 80, see below.
17 See *Royal Borough of Windsor and Maidenhead* v *Secretary of State for the Environment* (1988) 56 P & CR 427, 432 *per* Mann J.

character of the building so as to require consent,[18] and the removal of parts of a listed building will be an offence if consent is not obtained.[19] The erection of a fence not physically attached to a listed building is not an alteration of the building and does not therefore require listed building consent though, once erected, it becomes part of the listed building by virtue of Art. 42(7) and thereafter requires consent before it can be demolished or altered.[20]

Listed building consent is not required when the building in question is an ecclesiastical building which is for the time being used for ecclesiastical purposes or would be so used but for the works of demolition, alteration or extension (Art. 44(8)(a)); or where it is the subject of a guardianship or protection order under the Historic Monuments Act (NI) 1971 (Art. 44(8)(b)); or where the building is included in a schedule of historic monuments published by the Department under the 1971 Act (Art. 44(8)(c)).[21] 'Ecclesiastical building' does not include a building used or available for use by a Minister of Religion wholly or mainly as a residence from which to perform his duties (1991 Order, Art. 44 (8)). In *Attorney-General ex rel Bedford CC v Trustees of the Howard United Reformed Church, Bedford*[22] it was held that the word 'ecclesiastical' was not synonymous with 'Anglican', though the question whether 'ecclesiastical building' was limited to a Christian church, or could cover a synagogue or mosque was left open.[23]

To be exempt under Art. 44(8)(a) the building must not only be an ecclesiastical building, but must be used for the time being for ecclesiastical purposes, or be so used but for the works of demolition, alteration or extension. The relevant date at which to consider whether the building is being used for ecclesiastical purposes is the date when the works are being carried out and not any earlier period.[24] If on that date the building is not being used for ecclesiastical purposes, then the exemption created by Art. 44(8)(a) will not apply and listed building consent will be required, unless it can be shown that the building would be used for ecclesiastical purposes but for the works of demolition, alteration or extension. In the case of demolition works, a distinction must be drawn between total and partial demolition: in the case of total demolition of a listed ecclesiastical building it cannot be said that the building would be used for ecclesiastical purposes but for the works of demolition. The reason for the non-use of the building for those purposes is not the works of demolition, but the

---

18 *Royal Borough of Windsor and Maidenhead v Secretary of State for the Environment* (1988) 56 P & CR 427.
19 *R v Wells Street Stipendiary Magistrate, ex p Westminster CC* [1986] 3 All ER 4.
20 *Cotswold DC v Secretary of State for the Environment* (1986) 51 P & CR 139, when the anomaly presented by Art. 42(7) was noted.
21 For the provisions of the 1971 Act, see below.
22 [1975] 2 All ER 337.
23 Ibid., 345 *per* Lord Cross.
24 Ibid.

decision of the trustees of the building to demolish it.[25] Accordingly, where it is intended to demolish a listed ecclesiastical building totally, listed building consent will be necessary. If it is intended to demolish a listed ecclesiastical building only partially, then it may be able to claim the exemption granted by Art. 44(8)(a) if the works of demolition do not prevent the rest of the building being used once more for ecclesiastical purposes when the works have been completed.[26] Finally, Art. 44(a) provides that the exemption for ecclesiastical buildings will cease to have effect if an order to that effect is made by the Department.

In cases of doubt as to whether listed building consent is required, Art. 48 enables someone proposing to carry out work to a listed building to apply to the Department to determine whether consent is needed (Art. 48(1)) and provision is made for appeals from such determinations, and from failure to make a determination within the prescribed time.[27] The 1991 Order provides also that the Department may treat an application for listed building consent as an application under Art. 48(1) if it is satisfied that the exclusion of the work specified in the application for consent does not involve the alteration or extension of the building in a manner which would affect its character as a listed building (Art. 48(3)).

(ii) Procedure for obtaining consent

The procedure for obtaining listed building consent is contained in sch. 1 of the 1991 Order and the Planning (Listed Buildings) Regulations (NI) 1992.[28] Together these provide that an application for listed building consent is to be made on a form supplied by the Department, accompanied by a plan sufficient to identify the building and such other plans and drawings as are necessary to describe the works for which consent is sought (1991 Order, sch. 1, para. 1; 1992 Regulations, Reg. 2). In addition to the form and plans, the applicant must pay the prescribed fee for the application[29] and submit an ownership certificate.[30]

The Department is required to publish notice of the application for consent in at least one local newspaper (1991 Order, sch. 1, para. 2(a)) and to consult the district council for the area in which the listed building is situated before determining the application (1991 Order, sch. 1, para. 1(2); 1992 Regulations, Reg. 3(a)). The Department is also required to consult the Historic Buildings Council where the application would result in the need to amend any list of buildings of special architectural or historic

---

25 Ibid.
26 Ibid.
27 See Art. 48(2) and sch. 1, paras 7 and 8
28 Replacing Planning (Listed Buildings) Regulations (NI) 1973.
29 The 1973 Regulations (Reg. 3(4)) provided that the application form should *be accompanied by* the prescribed fee. The 1992 Regulations do not contain a similar provision but the Planning (Fees) Regulations (NI) 1992 provide a fee for listed building consent.
30 1991 Order, sch. 1, para. 3; 1992 Regulations, Reg. 6.

interest (1992 Regulations, Reg. 3(b)). In determining the application the Department is required to take into account any representations made within fourteen days following publication of the application (1991 Order, sch. 1, para. 4(1)) any representations made by the owner (where the application is not made by the owner) (1991 Order, sch. 1, para. 4(2)(a)); and any representations which are received from the district council or the Historic Buildings Council (1992 Regulations, Reg. 3).

Where the application for consent is granted subject to conditions, or refused, the Department is required to state its reasons in writing (1992 Regulations, Reg. 4(2)). In either case the applicant may appeal to the Planning Appeals Commission (1991 Order, sch. 1, para. 7). Such appeal must be made within six months from the date of notification of the decision or such longer period as the Commission allows (1991 Order, sch. 1, para. 7(2)). On an appeal both the appellant and the Department have a right to be heard by the Commission before it determines the appeal (1991 Order, sch. 1, para. 7(4)). The powers of the Commission are to allow or dismiss the appeal or reverse or vary any part of the decision whether the appeal relates to that part of the decision or not, and the Commission may deal with the application as if it had been made to the Commission initially (1991 Order, sch. 1, para. 7(3)).

Finally, the Department is required to give the applicant for consent notice of its decision within eight weeks from the date of receipt of the application, or such longer period as may be agreed between the parties (1992 Regulations, Reg. 4(1)). Where the Department fails to do so, the applicant may appeal to the Planning Appeals Commission as if consent had been refused (1991 Order, sch. 1, para. 8).

(iii) Granting or refusing consent

The Department has three options open to it in determining an application for listed building consent. It may grant consent unconditionally; it may refuse consent; or it may grant consent subject to conditions (Art. 45(2)). In considering whether or not to grant consent the Department is required to have special regard to the desirability of preserving the building or its setting or any features of special architectural or historic interest which it possesses (Art. 45(1)).

Of the three options open to the Department, refusal of consent and granting consent subject to conditions require further comment. To begin with, in both cases the Department must state its reasons for choosing the option selected (1992 Regulations, Reg. 4(2)), and in both cases an appeal will lie to the Planning Appeals Commission against the Department's decision (1991 Order, sch. 1, para. 7). Secondly, in both cases if the owner of the listed building claims (1) that the building has become incapable of reasonably beneficial use in its existing state; (2) (where consent has been granted subject to conditions) that the building cannot be rendered capable of reasonably beneficial use by carrying out the work in accordance with the conditions; and (3) that the building cannot be rendered capable of reasonably beneficial use by the carrying out of any other works for which consent has been granted; he can serve a purchase notice on the Department requiring it to purchase his estate in the building (Art. 94(2)).[31] Thirdly, in both cases compensation may be payable by the Department. To be entitled to compensation on the refusal of listed building consent or the grant of consent subject to conditions the owner must show (a) either that the works for which consent was sought do not constitute development, or if they do, that planning permission is granted for them by a development order (1972 Order, Art. 64(1)(a)); and (b) that the value of a compensatable estate[32] is less than it would have been if consent had been granted or granted unconditionally (1972 Order, Art. 64(2)). Claims for compensation must be made in writing and received by the Department within six months of the date of making of the decision to which the claim relates, or such extended period as the Department allows (1992 Regulations, Reg. 8).

In cases where the Department decides to grant listed building consent subject to conditions, Art. 45(3) provides that conditions which may be imposed *include* conditions with respect to (a) the preservation of particular features of the building, either as part of the building or after severance from the building; (b) the making good of any damage caused to the building by the works proposed; and (c) the reconstruction of the building or any part of it after the work to which the consent relates, with the use of original materials and with such alterations of the interior of the building as the conditions specify. In addition to the provisions of Art. 45(3), where the works for which consent is granted are for the demolition of the building, a condition may be imposed providing that the building shall not be demolished before a contract for carrying out redevelopment of the site has been made and planning permission for redevelopment granted (1991 Order, Art. 45(5)).

Finally, the Department may include a condition reserving specified details of the works for later approval by the Department (Art. 45(4)).

When the Department does grant consent subject to conditions, it is possible to apply thereafter for consent to execute the works for which consent was granted, without compliance with the conditions attached (1991 Order, sch. 1, para. 5). On any such application the Department will consider only the conditions attached to the consent and may dismiss the application; grant the application unconditionally; or grant the application but substitute other conditions (1991 Order, sch. 1, para. 5(3)).

---

31 In cases where the Department has served a repairs notice on the owner under Art. 109(4), the owner may not serve a purchase notice for three months: Art. 94(7). Purchase notices are discussed in Chapter 24.
32 For definition, see Land Development Values (Compensation) Act (NI) 1965, s. 43(1).

(iv) Duration of listed building consent

Where listed building consent is granted, the consent enures for the benefit of the listed building and of all persons for the time being having an interest in the building (1991 Order, sch. 1, para. 6). The works to which the consent relates must be started not later than five years beginning on the date on which the consent was granted, or such other period as the Department directs, being a period the Department considers appropriate having regard to any material considerations (Art. 46(1)). There is no provision that the works have to be completed by any given time, nor is there power to make any Order similar to a completion order in the case of development which has been commenced but not completed, as provided in Art. 37. Until the works have been completed, however, the Department has power to revoke or modify the consent (Art. 47(3)). The power to revoke or modify listed building consent exists when the Department considers it expedient to do so having regard to the development plan and other material considerations (Art. 47(1)).[33] Where the power is exercised, the revocation or modification does not affect any works which have already been carried out (Art. 47(3)).

Before making a revocation or modification order the Department is required to serve notice on the owner and occupier of the listed building and anyone else who in the Department's opinion would be affected by the revocation or modification order and to afford any of such persons who so request an opportunity of being heard by the Planning Appeals Commission (Art. 47(2)). After making an order, the Department is obliged to notify the same persons of the general effect of the order (Art. 47(4)).

When the Department does revoke listed building consent, or modifies such consent by imposing conditions, the owner of the building becomes entitled to serve a purchase notice on the Department, requiring it to purchase his estate in the building (Art. 94(2)(b)).[34] Apart from this, any person interested in the building who incurred expenditure in carrying out work which was rendered abortive by the relocation or modification, or who otherwise sustained loss or damage directly attributable to the relocation or modification is entitled to compensation from the Department in respect of his loss (1972 Order, Art. 65(1)). Again, claims for compensation must be made in writing and received by the Department within six months of the date of making of the decision to which the claim relates or such extended period as the Department allows (1992 Regulations, Reg. 8).

(v) Offences

The Order makes it an offence to carry out works requiring listed building consent without having obtained that consent and, where appropriate,

---

33 For 'material considerations' see Chapter 12.
34 The owner must of course show the requirements that the land has become incapable of reasonably beneficial use etc., noted above. For purchase notices generally, see Chapter 24.

having afforded the Department an opportunity of recording the building (Arts 44(1) and (2)). There are two offences: carrying out works without consent (Art. 44(1)), and failing to comply with any conditions in any consent which was granted (Art. 44(5)). The former is an offence of strict liability[35] but in either offence it is a defence to prove (a) that works to the building were urgently necessary in the interests of safety or health or for the preservation of the building; (b) that it was not practicable to secure safety or health or the preservation of the building by repairs or temporary support or shelter; (c) that the works carried out were the minimum measures immediately necessary; and (d) that notice in writing justifying in detail the carrying out of the works was given to the Department as soon as reasonably practicable (Art. 44(7)).

Where works have been carried out to a listed building without consent, it is possible to obtain consent from the Department for the retention of the works, and when such consent is obtained, the works are authorised from the grant of the consent (Art. 44(3)).

(c) Damage to listed buildings

In addition to the offences under Art. 44 relating to carrying out demolition, alterations or extensions to listed buildings without listed building consent, Art. 49 makes it an offence to do or permit any act to be done which causes, or is likely to result in, damage to the building, with the intention of causing such damage. There is no offence committed if the work carried out was authorised by planning permission or by listed building consent.

(d) Acquisition of listed buildings

The fourth consequence which ensues from the Department listing a building is that the Department becomes entitled to acquire the building from its owner. This may take place either by agreement or by compulsory purchase.

(i) Acquisition by agreement

Art. 107 provides that the Department may acquire by agreement,[36] or may accept the gift of, a listed building; any land comprising or contiguous or adjacent to a listed building; or any objects ordinarily kept in a listed building which is vested in the Department or under its control or management (Arts 107(1) and (2)). Where any such property is acquired by the Department, the Department may transfer the property to any body it thinks suitable if it considers that the property would be more expediently or efficiently preserved by such body (Art. 107(4)).[37]

---

35 R v *Wells Street Metropolitan Stipendiary Magistrate, ex p Westminster* CC [1986] 3 All ER 4.
36 Whether by purchase, lease or otherwise: Art. 107(1).
37 The subsection mentions in particular the National Trust, another government department, or a district council.

(ii) Compulsory acquisition

As a means of ensuring the preservation of listed buildings, the Department is given power to acquire buildings when reasonable steps are not being taken by the owners for preservation of the building. Art. 109(1) provides that where it appears to the Department that reasonable steps are not being taken to preserve a listed building, the Department may compulsorily acquire the building and any land comprising or contiguous or adjacent to it which is required to preserve the building or its amenities, or for affording access to it, or for its proper control or management. This power does not apply to listed buildings which are subject to a guardianship or protection order under the Historic Monuments Act (NI) 1971, or which are scheduled monuments under that Act (1991 Order, Art. 109(2)).

The procedure for acquisitions pursuant to Art. 109(1) is by way of vesting order, and the provisions of Arts 87–93 apply with appropriate modifications (Art. 109(3)).[38] Before any proceedings for acquisition can be taken, the Department must have served a repairs notice on the owner of the building and two months must have elapsed since service of the notice (Art. 109(4)). The repairs notice must specify the works which the Department considers reasonably necessary for the proper preservation of the building and explain the effect of Art. 109. In considering what works are reasonably necessary, no account is to be taken of the means of the owner of the building.[39] Construction of the provisions in England and Wales equivalent to Art. 109(4) fell to be considered by the House of Lords in *Robbins v Secretary of State for the Environment*.[40] The court held that 'preservation' was distinct from 'restoration' but that a repairs notice which included work which related to restoration rather than preservation was not invalid. Unless inextricably mingled in the repairs notice, the restoration works specified could be excised from the notice, leaving the notice valid as to the remainder.[41] The court also held that in referring to the preservation of the building, the legislation directed attention to the date on which the building was listed rather than the date on which the repairs notice is served, so that the repairs notice can include work required to return the building to its state on the date of listing, not merely on the date of service of the notice.

(e) Urgent works to preserve building

The scheme of the provisions of the 1991 Order as to listed buildings is to prevent the owner from taking positive action to alter the buildings without the Department's consent. The provisions do not prevent the

---

38 For procedure under Arts 87–93, see Chapter 7.
39 *Rolf v North Shropshire* DC (1988) 55 P & CR 242.
40 [1989] 1 All ER 878.
41 Ibid., 890 *per* Lord Ackner.

owner allowing the building to fall into disrepair. We have seen, however, that the Department has power under Art. 109 to acquire the building if it considers reasonable steps are not being taken for properly preserving the building. Apart from this power, the Department has power under Art. 30 to execute works which are urgently necessary for the preservation of the building (Art. 80(1)). The Department must give at least seven days notice of its intention to carry the works out and describe the works proposed (Art. 80(4)). Works may not, however, be carried out to any part of the building which is occupied (Art. 80(3)).

Apart from the Department being able to carry the works out, it may also recover the cost of the works from the owner of the building (Art. 80(5)–(10)). To do so the Department must give notice to the owner requiring payment (Art. 80(6)). The owner may appeal within twenty eight days to the Planning Appeals Commission on the grounds (1) that the works were unnecessary for the preservation of the building; (2) in the case of temporary repairs, the temporary arrangements have continued too long; and (3) that the amount sought to be recovered is unreasonable or that its recovery would cause the owner hardship (Art. 80(8)).

The power conferred on the Department to execute works applies not only to listed buildings, but also to buildings in conservation areas whose preservation is important for maintaining the character or appearance of the conservation area, and in respect of which the Department has given a direction under Art. 80(1)(b) that the provisions of the Article are to apply.

(5) *Enforcement*

The 1991 Order provides for enforcement of the provisions of the Order relating to listed buildings by means of listed buildings enforcement notices in much the same way as the Order provides for enforcement notices in relation to ordinary breaches of development control. By Art. 77(1) it is provided that the Department may serve a listed building enforcement notice where it appears that works have been, or are being, carried out to a listed building without listed building consent or, where consent has been granted, in breach of a condition in the consent.[42] The criterion for the Department deciding to issue a listed building enforcement notice is whether it is expedient to do so having regard to the effect of the works on the character of the building (Art. 77(1)).

As with an enforcement notice, a listed building enforcement notice is required to state a date on which it will take effect (Art. 77(4)).[43] Again,

---

42 A listed building enforcement notice cannot, however, be issued in respect of works executed by or on behalf of the Crown in respect of a building which was Crown land at the time the works were carried out: Art. 113(4).
43 Once the notice does take effect an entry must be made in the statutory charges register: Land Registration Act (NI) 1970, sch. 11, entry 27(d), as provided by Art. 131 of the 1991 Order.

the provisions of the Order as to service of a copy of an enforcement notice and withdrawal of an enforcement notice by the Department, also apply to a listed building enforcement notice, as do the provisions concerning non-compliance with an enforcement notice.[44] A listed building enforcement notice is also required to specify the alleged contravention of the provisions of the Order[45] and to specify the Department's requirements (1) for restoring the building to its former state;[46] (2) in cases where restoration is not reasonably practicable or is undesirable, for executing such works specified in the notice as the Department considers necessary to alleviate the effect of the unauthorised works; and (3) for bringing the building to the state it would have been in had the terms of any listed building consent been complied with (Art. 77(1)(i)(ii) and (iii)). If, after a listed building enforcement notice has been issued, listed building consent is granted for the unauthorised works which have taken place (see Art. 44(3)), the listed building enforcement notice ceases to have effect insofar as it requires steps to be taken for removal of the works which the consent authorises to be retained (Art. 79(1)), or, if applicable, for compliance with a condition which by the consent is dispensed with (Art. 79(2)).

As with enforcement notices the recipient of a listed building enforcement notice can appeal to the Planning Appeals Commission. The grounds on which he may do so are as follows (Art. 78(2)):

(a) that the matters alleged in the notice do not contravene Art. 44;
(b) that the alleged contravention has not taken place;
(c) that the contravention took place before 9 December 1978;[47]
(d) that (1) works to the building were urgently necessary in the interests of safety or health or for the preservation of the building; (2) it was not practicable to secure safety or health or the preservation of the building by repairs or temporary works; and (3) the works carried out were the minimum measures immediately necessary;
(e) that listed building consent ought to be granted, or that any condition be dispensed with or another condition substituted;

---

44 Art. 77(6), applying Arts 68(5), (12), (14) and (15), and 72 and 74.
45 I.e. whether work has been carried out without listed building consent or in breach of a condition contained in a consent, or, in the case of demolition works, without affording the Department an opportunity of recording the building: see Arts 44(1),(2) and (5).
46 Where the building has been demolished, either wholly or partially, the notice may require the building to be restored provided sufficient components of the building are extant to render restoration possible, this being a question of fact and degree: R v Leominster DC ex p Antique Country Buildings Ltd (1988) 56 P & CR 240. If after demolition there exists only rubble or ash restoration is not possible, as any constructional work would be only replication: at 246, per Mann J.
47 Art. 77(3) prevents the Department issuing a listed building enforcement notice in respect of breaches occurring before that date.

(f) that copies of the notice were not served as required;
(g) that the period specified in the notice for complying with the notice is less than should reasonably be allowed;
(h) that the requirements in the notice exceed what is needed to restore the building to its former state;[48]
(i) that the step required for restoration would not serve that purpose;
(j) that the steps required for alleviating the effect of the unauthorised works exceed what is necessary; and
(k) that the steps required for bringing the building to the state it would have been in had the terms of any consent been complied with exceed what is necessary.

On an appeal, the Planning Appeals Commission is required to quash, vary or uphold the listed building enforcement notice[49] and may grant listed building consent for all or part only of the works to which the listed building enforcement notice relates, or in the case of non-compliance with a condition in a consent, discharge the condition or substitute an alternative one (Art. 78(4)), and the decision of the Commission in relation to the grant of consent is final (Art. 78(6)), subject only to the possibility of judicial review.

Procedure in respect of appeals under Art. 78 is similar to that for appeals against enforcement notices[50] and as in the case of enforcement notices, it is provided that a listed building enforcement notice can be challenged only by way of an appeal to the Commission when the ground of appeal is one of the grounds in Art. 78(1) (Art. 78(7)).

(6) Certificates that building will not be listed

As will be apparent from the above discussion, the consequences of listing a building as being of special architectural or historic interest are significant, to say the least. Not only do they involve a restriction on the freedom of the owner to do what he wishes with the building, but they may have a significant impact on the value of the building and its marketability.[51] The risk of a building being listed is one which a purchaser runs, and does not entitle him to rescission of any contract on the ground of frustration.[52] Fortunately, there is a means of securing protection for a limited period

---

48 This does not apply to steps required in the notice to alleviate the effect of the unauthorised works, when the Department thinks restoration is not reasonably practicable or is undesirable (Art. 77(1)(b)(ii)); or to steps for bringing the building to the state it would have been in had the terms of any consent been complied with: (Art. 77(1)(b)(iii)).
49 Art. 70(1), as applied to listed building enforcement notices by Art. 78(3).
50 Art. 78(3), applying Arts 69(4) to (8) and 70.
51 For a chilling example, see *Amalgamated Investment and Property Co. Ltd v John Walker & Sons Ltd* [1976] 3 All ER 509 (building sold for £1,700,000 worth £200,000 in consequence of becoming listed).
52 Ibid.

against the risks of property being listed. Art. 43 provides that application may be made to the Department for a certificate stating that the Department does not intend to list the building. The effect of the certificate is to preclude the Department from listing the building for five years (Art. 43(1)).

An application for a certificate is required to be in writing, and must be accompanied by an ownership certificate.[53] Before determining the application the Department is required to consult both the Historic Buildings Council and the relevant district council (Art. 43(3)).

The important condition which must be met before an application for a certificate can be made, is that an application for planning permission must have been made for development involving the alteration, extension or demolition of a building, or that such planning permission has already been granted (Art. 43(1)).

(7) Endowments

Art. 108 of the Order makes provision for gifts of property to the Department when the income is to be used for the upkeep of a listed building. If the gift is not charitable, any rule of law or equity which would not have applied had the gift been charitable, does not apply to the gift (Art. 108(2)), and the Department has the same powers of management, disposition and investment of the property in the gift as are conferred on the tenant for life and the trustees of the settlement by the Settled Land Acts (Art. 108(3)).

2 Historic monuments

In addition to the protection afforded by the 1991 Order to buildings of special architectural or historic interest, protection is afforded to historic monuments by the Historic Monuments Act (NI) 1971. A detailed examination of the provisions of the Act is outside the scope of this book, but the main provisions of the Act are noted to indicate the restrictions on the owner of an historic monument in the enjoyment of his property. For the purposes of the Act a 'monument' includes any land on or in which there is any site, structure or erection, other than an ecclesiastical building, used for ecclesiastical purposes (s. 27), and an 'historic monument' includes any monument the protection of which is a matter of public interest by reason of the historic, architectural, traditional, artistic or archaeological interest attaching to the monument (s. 27). Historic

---

53 Art. 43(2), applying the provisions of Art. 2.
54 Originally the Ministry of Finance, whose functions in this regard were transferred to the Department in 1976: see Departments (Transfer of Functions) Order (NI) 1976.

monuments may be protected under the Act in various ways. Thus, the Department[54] may acquire the monument (s. 1) or remove it for preservation elsewhere (s. 6). The provisions as to scheduling monuments and making monuments the subject of preservation orders are of particular relevance.

Under s. 7 of the Act the Department is required to prepare schedules specifying such historic monuments as are reported to it by the Historic Monuments Council[55] as being in need of protection, and such other monuments as the Department thinks fit. One of the consequences of a monument being included in such schedules is that the owner is required to notify the Department if he intends to carry out any work which is likely to result in the demolition or removal of the monument, or in the addition or structural alteration to the monument, or which is likely injuriously to affect the monument (s. 7(4)). In addition, the owner is precluded from beginning such work for a period of six months from giving such notice, or such lesser period as the Department agrees (s. 7(4)). Failure to comply with these requirements is an offence (s. 7(6)).

Similar provisions apply in the case of monuments which are the subject of preservation orders under s. 9 of the Act. Protection orders may be made by the Department in respect of historic monuments which have been reported to the Department by the Historic Monuments Council as being in danger of destruction or removal, or damage from neglect or injurious treatment (s. 9(1)).[56] Where a protection order is in force, it is an offence to remove the monument, make additions or structural alterations to the monument, or carry out any work which injuriously affects or is likely injuriously to affect the monument without the consent of the Department (s. 10(1)).

3 Archaeological sites

Finally, in addition to any planning permission which may be required if the works intended to be carried out amount to operational development, the digging or excavating in or under any land for the purpose of searching generally for archaeological objects or of searching for, exposing or examining any particular structure or thing of archaeological interest requires a licence from the Department.[57] This is so whether the work involves the removal of the surface of the land or not.[58] Carrying out such work without a licence or in breach of the terms of a licence is an offence (s. 11(4)).

---

55 For the establishment of the Council and its constitution see s. 14.
56 For the procedure for making such orders see sch. 2 of the Act.
57 Historic Monuments Act (NI) 1971, s. 11(1).
58 Ibid.

CHAPTER EIGHTEEN

Tree Preservation

The second form of special control created by the 1991 Order is in relation to trees. The legislation seeks to secure preservation of trees by imposing a duty on the Department to ensure where appropriate that in granting planning permission adequate provision is made for the preservation of trees by the imposition of planning conditions (Art. 64(a)) and by the making of tree preservation orders (Art. 64(b)). Protection is not limited to existing trees, as the Order provides that the planting of trees may be required both by planning conditions (Art. 64(a)) and by preservation orders (Art. 65(1)(b)). The use of planning conditions has been considered earlier,[1] but before considering tree preservation orders it is necessary to consider what is meant by 'trees' in the Order.

(1) *Trees*

A distinction may be drawn between timber trees on the one hand and fruit or orchard trees on the other, so that at common law the word 'trees' meant wood applicable to buildings, and did not include orchard trees.[2] Again, in *Wyndham* v *Way*[3] it was said that an exception of 'trees' in a lease meant trees useful for their wood and did not extend to fruit trees. Early legislation also singled out particular types of tree for protection. A series of Acts known as the Irish Timber Acts[4] sought to encourage the planting of trees by a system of registration and by making it an offence to cut or injure such trees save in certain cases. These Acts applied only to the types of tree specified in the Acts. The question arises whether the 1991 Order makes any distinction between trees or whether it applies to all trees. 'Trees' is not defined in the Order. In *Kent CC* v *Batchelor*[5] Lord Denning MR suggested that to be a tree in woodland a plant would need to be over seven or eight inches in diameter.[6] This suggestion was not followed by Phillips J in *Bullock* v *Secretary of State for the Environment*,[7] who thought that anything which ordinarily would be called a tree is a tree for the purposes of the legislation,[8] though bushes, scrub and shrubs are not within the term.[9]

---

1   Chapter 12. 2   *Bullen* v *Denning* (1826) 5 B & C 851.
3   (1812) 4 Taunt 318.
4   The most important being the Land Improvement Acts (Ireland) 1765, 1775 and 1783.
5   (1976) 33 P & CR 185.
6   Ibid., 187. 7   (1980) 254 EG 1097.
8   Ibid., 1100. 9   Ibid.

(2) Tree preservation orders

Apart from encouraging the use of planning conditions as a means of protecting trees and providing for new planting, the 1991 Order provides that the Department may make tree preservation orders for individual trees, or for groups of trees or woodlands (Art. 65(1)). The criterion for making such an order is that it appears to the Department to be expedient in the interests of amenity to make provision for the preservation of the trees (Art. 65(1)). Any such order may provide for prohibiting the cutting down, topping, lopping or wilful destruction of the trees without the Department's consent, which may be given subject to conditions (Art. 65(1)(a)); for securing replanting of any part of a woodland area felled in the course of forestry operations permitted under the order (Art. 65(1)(b)); and for applying any of the provisions of the 1991 Order concerning development control in relation to the consent required to fell or injure protected trees (Art. 65(1)(c)).

A tree preservation order does not apply to the cutting down or injuring of trees which are dying or dead or which have become dangerous, or where such action is required to comply with any statutory provision or to prevent or abate a nuisance (Art. 65(3)). Where such action has been carried out the onus of proving that the action was lawful under Art. 65(3) is on the person carrying out the injury to the tree, and it is not the task of the prosecution in proceedings brought in respect of the injury to show that the defendant cannot rely on Art. 65(3).[10]

(a) Procedure for making orders

Art. 65(2) provides that the Department may make regulations as to the form of tree preservation orders and the procedure to be followed in connection with such orders, and provides for what may be included in such regulations (Art. 65(2)(a) to (d)). The regulations presently in force are the Planning (Tree Preservation Order) Regulations (NI) 1973 made under the 1972 Order. These provide that a tree preservation order is to be in the form set out in the schedule to the Regulations, and is to define the trees to which it relates by reference to a map (Regs 3(1) and (2)). Any order made by the Department takes effect immediately (Reg. 4(1)). The Department is required to serve notice of the making of the order on owners and occupiers of the land affected and anyone else whom the Department considers would be affected by the order (Reg. 4(1)). Any recipient of such notice may object within twenty eight days and require an opportunity of being heard by the Planning Appeals Commission (Reg. 4(1)). The Department is required to consider any objections or representations made and, if applicable, the report of the Commission, and to confirm the order with or without modifications, or to withdraw it

---

10 R v *Alath Construction Ltd and anor* (1990) 60 P & CR 533.

(Reg. 5(1)), and to notify those persons on whom notice of the making of the order was served of its decision (Reg. 5(2)). Finally, a tree preservation order must be registered in the statutory charges register.[11]

(b) Offences

Whenever a tree preservation order has been made, then, subject to the provisions of Art. 65(3) considered above, it is an offence to cut down or wilfully destroy the tree, or to top it or lop it in such a manner as to be likely to destroy it (Art. 66(1)).[12] In this context 'destruction' means that the tree has been rendered useless in the sense of having ceased to have any use as an amenity or as something worth preserving, and the offence of wilfully destroying the tree is committed if a person inflicts on the tree so radical an injury that in all the circumstances a competent forester, taking into account the situation of the tree, would decide that the tree ought to be felled.[13] It is not necessary for the prosecution to show that the defendant knew of the tree preservation order,[14] as the offence is one of strict liability.[15] If, however, the defendant did not cause the injury to the tree himself, he can only be guilty of an offence under the Article if he is vicariously liable for the person who caused the injury.[16] Where, therefore, the injury is caused by an independent contractor who has been told not to touch the tree, the defendant will not be guilty of an offence.[17]

(c) Enforcement regarding replanting

We have seen that a tree preservation order may enable the Department to impose conditions on the grant of consent to injure protected trees (Art. 65(1)(a)). If consent is given subject to conditions requiring replacement of trees, and these conditions are not complied with, the Department may issue a notice requiring the planting of such trees as are specified in the notice, within such time as is also specified in the notice (Art. 82(1)). Such a notice, however, may only be issued within a period of four years from the failure to comply with the conditions (Art. 82(1)). As with enforcement notices, a notice under Art. 82(1) takes effect on a date specified in the notice (Art. 82(3)) and the provisions regarding service of a copy of an enforcement notice (Art. 68(5)), withdrawal of an enforcement notice (Arts 68(14) and (15)) and offences (Arts 68(12), 72 and 74) apply with necessary modifications to notices under Art. 82(1) (Art. 82(2)). Again,

---

11 Land Registration Act (NI) 1970, sch. 11, entry 27, as provided by Art. 131 of the 1991 Order.
12 A prosecution may be brought within three years of commission of the offence: Art. 128.
13 *Barnet LBC v Eastern Electricity Board and anor* [1973] 2 All ER 319.
14 *Maidstone BC v Mortimer* [1980] 3 All ER 552.
15 *Groveside Homes Ltd v Elmbridge BC* (1988) 55 P & CR 214.
16 Ibid.
17 Ibid.

where a notice under Art. 82(1) has been served, a person having an estate in the land may appeal to the Planning Appeals Commission at any time before the date on which the notice is to take effect (Art. 82(4)) and the Commission is required to quash, vary or uphold the notice.[18] Until the final determination of the appeal or until the appeal is withdrawn the notice is of no effect (Art. 82(5)).

(d) Compensation

We have seen that a tree preservation order may provide for the consent of the Department being required for the cutting down or injuring of protected trees. Where any person suffers loss or damage in consequence of refusal of such consent, or the granting of consent subject to conditions, or the revocation or modification of such consent, he is entitled to compensation from the Department in respect of such loss or damage (1972 Order, Art. 66(1)). The amount of compensation is not limited to the commercial value of the timber which cannot be realised, but includes any diminution in the value of the land on which the trees are situated.[19] Compensation may be awarded to cover the cost of obtaining a specialist report on the effect of the trees on adjoining buildings,[20] and the cost of having work, permitted by the consent, carried out by an approved contractor, where this is a condition of the consent, if the claimant would otherwise have carried out the work himself.[21]

In assessing the amount of compensation, account is to be taken of any compensation paid to the claimant or any other person in respect of the same tree (1972 Order, Art. 66(2)(a)), and any injurious affect on to the land of the claimant which would result from the felling of the tree which is the subject of the claim (1972 Order, Art. 66(2)(b)). If the claimant and the Department cannot agree on the amount of compensation, the matter will be determined by the Lands Tribunal (1972 Order, Art. 66(3)).

(e) Crown land

A tree preservation order may be made in respect of trees on Crown land (1991 Order, Art. 115(1)) but the order is of no effect until the land ceases to be Crown land or becomes subject to a private estate, whichever happens first (1991 Order, Art. 115(2)).[22] When that happens notice must be given to the Department of the person who has become entitled to the land or an estate in it (Art. 115(3)) and the date on which such notice is received is treated as the date on which the tree preservation order is made for the purposes of service of notices and objections (Art. 115(4)).

---

18 Art. 70, as applied by Art. 82(6).
19 Bell v Canterbury CC (1988) 56 P & CR 211.
20 Fletcher v Chelmsford BC (1992) 63 P & CR
21 Deane v Bromley BC (1992) 63 P & CR 308.
22 For the meaning of 'private estate' see Art. 118(1).

CHAPTER NINETEEN

Hazardous Substances

Special provision is made in the 1991 Order for the control of what the Order terms 'hazardous substances'. These are substances specified by the Department in regulations made under the Order (Art. 53(3)(a)(i)).[1] The means of control provided in the Order is to make it a requirement that the consent of the Department be obtained for the presence of hazardous substances on land, unless the quantity of the substance is less than the amount specified in regulations made by the Department.[2]

(1) Applications for consent

The form and content of applications for hazardous substances consent is also determined by regulations (Art. 54(1)), which make provision for advertising and publicising the application (Arts 54(1) and (4); Regs 5–7), and the time within which the application is to be dealt with (Arts 54(1) and (4); Reg. 11). An ownership certificate similar to that required on an application for planning permission is necessary (Art. 54(2); Reg. 7). The Regulations also require the Department to consult with the Department of Economic Development, the relevant district council and such other bodies as may be specified before the application is determined (Art. 54(4)(b); Reg. 10) and provide for the manner and time in which such consultation is to take place (Art. 54(4)(c)). As with applications for planning permission, there is special provision for applications which (a) would involve a substantial departure from the development plan for the area in which the land is situated; (b) would be of significance to the whole or a substantial part of the country; or (c) affect the whole of a neighbourhood (Art. 56(1)), and for applications to dispense with consent subject to which a previous consent was granted (Art. 58(1)).

(2) Determining the application

In determining an application for hazardous substances consent, the Department is required to have regard to material considerations (Art. 55(1)), in particular (1) to any current or contemplated use of the application site; (2) to the way in which land in the vicinity is used or likely to be used; (3) to any planning permission which has been granted for

---

1 See Planning (Hazardous Substances) Regulations (NI) 1993.
2 See Arts 53(1) and 53(3)(a)(ii).

development of land in the vicinity; and (4) to the provisions of the development plan (Art. 55(2)). As with planning permission, the powers of the Department on an application for hazardous substances consent are to refuse consent; to grant consent unconditionally; or to grant consent subject to conditions (Art. 55(1)). Such conditions may be in respect of (1) how and where the substance to which the consent relates is to be kept or used; (2) the times between which the substance may be present; (3) the permanent removal of the substance to which the consent relates; and (4) the consent being conditional on the commencement or execution of development authorised by a specified planning permission (Art. 55(5)). Where the application for consent relates to more than one substance, the Department may make different determinations as to each (Art. 55(3)). An appeal against refusal of consent or the grant of consent subject to conditions lies to the Planning Appeals Commission (Art. 57(1)). The appeal must be made within six months of the notification of the Department's decision or such longer period as the Commission allows (Art. 57(3)).

(3) Contents of consent

A hazardous substances consent must contain (1) a description of the land to which the consent relates; (2) a description of the substance(s) to which it relates; (3) a statement of the maximum quantity of each substance permitted by the consent to be present at any one time; and (4) the conditions relating to the permitted substance subject to which the consent is granted (Art. 55(4)). And where a consent is continued on an application made pursuant to Art. 60(2)[3] the consent must contain a statement that it is unchanged in relation to the foregoing matters, or if applicable, a statement of what changes apply (Art. 60(8)).

(4) Duration of consent

As with planning permission, a hazardous substances consent enures for the benefit of the land to which it relates and all persons having an estate in such land (Art. 60(1)). Where, however, there is a change of the person in control of *part* of the land to which the consent relates, the consent ceases to have effect unless an application for continuation of the consent has previously been made to the Department (Art. 60(2)). Where such an application is made, the Department may revoke or modify the consent (Art. 60(4)) and, in particular, may modify consent by including the conditions specified in Art. 55(5).[4] Where the Department does revoke or modify consent on an application under Art. 60(2) for continuation of the consent, it is liable to pay compensation to the person in control of

---

3 See below.
4 As to which see above.

the whole of the land before the change of owner took place, in respect of any loss or damage sustained by him and directly attributable to the modification or revocation,[5] the amount of compensation being determined by the Lands Tribunal in the event of failure of the claimant and the Department to agree (1972 Order, Art. 66A(2)).

Apart from the power to revoke or modify consent on an application under Art. 60(2), the Department may revoke a hazardous substances consent (1) if there has been a material change of use of land to which the consent relates, or planning permission has been granted for development, the carrying out of which would involve a material change of use of the land and such development has been commenced (1991 Order, Art. 59(1)); where the substance has not been present on the land for at least five years (Arts 59(2)(a) and (b)); and (3) where it is expedient to revoke it (Art. 59(3)). Alternatively, the Department may modify a consent to such extent as it considers expedient if it considers it expedient to do so (Art. 59(3)). Where the Department wishes to revoke or modify consent, it is required first to serve notice on the owner of the land, anyone appearing to the Department to be in control of the land, and anyone whom the Department thinks will be affected by the revocation or modification (Art. 59(5)), and to afford such persons if they so request an opportunity of appearing before and being heard by the Planning Appeals Commission (Art. 59(5)). Any order then made revoking or modifying consent must specify the grounds on which it is made (Art. 59(4)) and a copy of it must be served by the Department on the persons who were served with notice of the intended order (Art. 59(6)).

(5) Offence

Contravention of the provisions of the 1991 Order relating to hazardous substances control is an offence (Art. 61(1)). Contravention takes place if a quantity of a hazardous substance equal to or in excess of the quantity specified in regulations made under Art. 53(3)(a)(ii) is present on land without hazardous substances consent, or where consent exists, the amount exceeds the amount permitted by the consent (Art. 61(2)(a)); or where consent has been granted subject to conditions, a condition has not been complied with (Art. 61(2)(b)). There is no contravention if a hazardous substance is present on land without consent in cases where the Department has issued a direction to that effect under Art. 62. This provision enables the Department to issue such a direction where (1) the community, or part of it, is being, or is likely to be, deprived of an essential service or commodity, or that there is likely to be a shortage of such; and (2) the presence of the hazardous substance is necessary for the

---

5   1972 Order, Art. 66A(1), as inserted by 1991 Order, Art. 133 and sch. 5.

effective provision of that service or commodity (Art. 62(1)).[6] Where a direction is made, a copy must be served on the relevant district council and the Department of Economic Development (Art. 62(3)).

In both cases where there is a contravention of hazardous substances control it is a defence to show that the defendant took all reasonable precautions to avoid commission of the offence; or that commission of the offence could be avoided only by taking action amounting to breach of a statutory duty (Art. 61(5)). In the case of contravention consisting of the presence of a hazardous substance on land without consent or in excess of the permitted amount, it is also a defence to show that the defendant did not know that the substance was present in an amount equal to or in excess of the amount specifed in regulations, or in excess of the permitted amount, as the case may be (Art. 61(6)). Where contravention consists in failure to comply with a condition in a hazardous substances consent, it is a defence to show that the defendant did not know and had no reason to believe that there was a failure to comply with the condition (Art. 61(7)).

Where the offence is presence on land of a hazardous substance without consent or in excess of the permitted amount, the persons guilty of the offence are anyone knowingly causing the substance to be present on the land; anyone allowing it to be present; and the person in control of the land (Art. 61(3)). In the case of failure to comply with a condition in a consent, the person guilty of the offence is the person in control of the land (Art. 61(3)).

(6) Enforcement

Although contravention of hazardous substances control is an offence, the Department has power to serve enforcement proceedings in respect of the contravention and thereby to require the recipient of the proceedings to take steps to remedy the contravention. Art. 81(1) of the 1991 Order provides that the Department may issue a hazardous substances contravention notice where it appears to the Department that there has been a breach of control and the Department considers it expedient to do so having regard to any material consideration. Where, however, contravention can only be avoided by the taking of action amounting to breach of a statutory duty, the Department is precluded from issuing a notice (Art. 81(2)).

A hazardous substances contravention notice is required to specify (1) the contravention of hazardous substances control (Art. 81(3)(a)); (2) a

---

6 A direction made under Art. 62 ceases to have effect after three months, but may be renewed: Art. 62(2)(b). The Department has power to withdraw the direction at any time: Art. 62(2)(a).

date on which the notice will take effect;[7] (3) the steps required to be taken to remedy the contravention (Art. 81(3)(b)); (4) the period in which such steps are to be taken (Art. 81(5)(b)); and (5) such other matters as may be prescribed in regulations made by the Department (Art. 81(12)(a)). The Hazardous Substances Regulations require a hazardous substances contravention notice to identify the land to which the notice relates by reference to a plan or otherwise (Reg. 17). The remedial action the Department may require to be taken in a hazardous substances contravention notice includes removal of the substance from the land (Art. 81(6)) and, where such action is required, the notice may also contain a direction that at the end of a specified time any hazardous substances consent shall cease to have effect (Art. 81(7)).

A copy of the contravention notice must be served on the owner and occupier of the land to which it relates, any other person in control of the land and any other persons prescribed (Art. 81(4)). The copy must be accompanied by a statement setting out the Department's reasons for issuing the notice and the right of appeal against it (Reg. 17(3)). Until the notice takes effect the Department may withdraw the notice at any time and, where it does so, the Department is obliged to give notice of the withdrawal to those persons who were served with a copy of the notice (Arts 81(8) and (9)).

The procedure for appeals against hazardous substances contravention notices is dealt with by the Regulations and where any appeal is made the notice is of no effect until the final determination of the appeal or until the appeal is withdrawn (Art. 81(11)).

Various amendments to Arts 69 to 71 of the 1991 Order are made by the Regulations. The amended form of these Articles as they apply to hazardous substances is conveniently set out in the Regulations.

---

[7] Such date may not be less than twenty eight days from the date of service of copies of the notice under Art. 81(4): see below.

CHAPTER TWENTY

Advertisements

The display of advertisements is potentially a matter of concern from the standpoint of planning control. The variety of forms of advertising, together with the ease and speed with which advertisements can be displayed, require that special control be provided for them. Art. 67 of the 1991 Order makes provision for the control of the display of advertisements by way of regulations to be made by the Department. The regulations in force since 1 December 1992 are the Planning (Control of Advertisements) Regulations (NI) 1992. The form of control established by the Regulations is to make the display of advertisements to which the advertisements apply an offence unless the consent of the Department is granted or deemed to be granted (1991 Order, Art. 84(2)).

(1) *Advertisements*

An 'advertisement' for the purposes of the 1991 Order and the Regulations is any word, letter, model, sign, placard, board, notice, device or representation, whether illuminated or not, in the nature of, and employed wholly or partly for the purpose of, advertisement, announcement or direction and includes any hoarding or similar structure used, or adapted for use, for the display of advertisements (1991 Order, Art. 2(2)). Words appearing on a canopy outside a building constitute the display of an advertisement for the purposes of the Regulations.[1]

Certain types of advertisements are however excepted from the main provision of the Regulations, and may be displayed without the consent of the Department. These are advertisements of the types mentioned in sch. 2 of the 1992 Regulations and which comply with the conditions set out in the schedule for the type of advertisement in question, and what the Regulations refer to as the 'standard conditions'.[2]

(2) *Consent*

As noted above, the Regulations require that the consent of the Department is required for the display of advertisements other than those in Sch. 2. The means by which consent can be obtained are considered below. Where consent is granted, either expressly or where it is deemed by the

---

1 *Westminster CC v Secretary of State for the Environment* (1990) 59 P & CR 496.
2 See below. Note, however, the exception in Reg. 4(2)(ii).

Regulations to be granted, such consent takes effect as consent for the use of the site for the purposes of the display, whether by the erection of structures or otherwise, and for the benefit of any person interested in the site (1992 Regulations, Reg. 3(4)).

(a) Express consent

Where the consent of the Department is not deemed to be granted by the Regulations[3] an application must be made for the express consent of the Department to be granted.[4] In particular express consent may be given for retention of advertisements displayed originally without consent (Reg. 9(2)(c)). An application is required to be made on a form supplied by the Department and to be accompanied by a plan sufficient to identify the site to which it relates and such other plans and drawings as are necessary to describe the advertisement which is the subject of the application (Reg. 7(3)). Before determining the application the Department is required to consult the relevant district council and to take into account any representations made by the council (Reg. 8).

Where the Department grants consent, such consent is subject to the conditions set out in sch. 1 of the Regulations, *viz.* (1) that the advertisement and the site used to display it are maintained in a clean and tidy condition to the reasonable satisfaction of the Department; (2) that any structure or hoarding for displaying the advertisement is maintained in a safe condition to the reasonable satisfaction of the Department; (3) where removal of the advertisement is required, that such removal is carried out to the reasonable satisfaction of the Department; (4) that no advertisement may be displayed without the permission of the owner of the site or any other person with an interest in the site entitled to grant permission; and (5) that no advertisement may be displayed so as to obscure or hinder the ready interpretation of any road or other sign or signal or render hazardous the use of any of the means of transport mentioned in the Regulations. In addition to the standard conditions, however, the Department may on the grant of consent impose such other conditions as it thinks fit (Reg. 9(1)(b)). In particular, it may impose conditions (1) for regulating the display of the permitted advertisement or (2) the use of the site for the display of the advertisement on any adjacent land controlled by the applicant or requiring the carrying out of works on such land, and (3) for requiring the removal of any advertisement at the end of a specified time and the carrying out of works of reinstatement (Reg. 9(3)). Unless it appears to the Department to be required in the interests of amenity or public safety, an express consent is not to

---

3 See below.
4 Various provisions of the 1991 Order governing applications for planning permission are adapted and made applicable to applications for consent to display advertisements: see Regs 7(1), 11(1), 12(1), 13(1) and sch. 4.

Advertisements

contain any limitation or restriction relating to the subject matter, content or design of what is to be displayed (Reg. 3(3)).

An application for express consent to display advertisements is required to be determined and notification of the decision given to the applicant within eight weeks (Reg. 10(1)). As with applications for planning permission, if the Department fails to determine the application within that period, the applicant may treat the failure as a refusal and appeal to the Planning Appeals Commission (Reg. 12(2)). In the case of refusal of consent or the grant of consent subject to conditions in addition to the standard conditions, the Department is required to give reasons for its decision (Reg. 10(2)).

The power of the Department to grant or refuse consent is exercisable in the interests of amenity or public safety (Reg. 3(1)). The Department is required to determine the suitability of the use of the land or building on which the advertisement is to be displayed for the display of advertisements in the light of the general characteristics of the locality (Reg. 3(1)(a)) and to have regard to the safety of users of transport routes affected by the display. In particular the Department must consider whether the display is likely to hinder the reading of any traffic signs (Reg. 3(1)(b)). The Department may also have regard to any material change in circumstances likely to occur within the period for which the consent is required or granted (Reg. 3(2)).

Where the Department's decision is to refuse consent or grant consent subject to conditions, the applicant may appeal to the Planning Appeals Commission (Reg. 12(1)).

If consent is granted on an application, the Department may later revoke it or modify it.[5] Where consent is revoked or modified, the Department is liable to pay compensation in accordance with s. 26 of the Land Development Values (Compensation) Act (NI) 1965 as modified by sch. 4 of the Regulations. A claim for compensation must be made within six months of the revocation or modification, or such extended period as the Department may allow (Reg. 14(3)).

(b) Deemed consent

An application for express consent to the display of advertisements is not required in all cases. The Regulations provide a number of situations where consent is deemed to be granted (Reg. 5(1)). These are contained in Part I of sch. 3. In such cases consent is deemed to be granted subject to the conditions and limitations specified for the particular type of advertisement in question and the standard conditions contained in sch. 1 of the Regulations (Reg. 5(1)).

---

5 Reg. 13(1), applying Art. 38 of the 1991 Order as modified by sch. 4 of the Regulations.

(c) Exclusion of Regulation 5

In the case of advertisements for which consent is deemed to be granted by Reg. 5, the Department has power under Reg. 6 to direct that the provisions of Reg. 5 shall not apply to advertisements either in any particular area, or in a particular case. The effect of such a direction is that the express consent of the Department is needed for the display of advertisements in that area, or in that case (Reg. 6(1)). When such a direction is given in relation to advertisements in a particular area, notice of the direction must be published in a local newspaper, giving a full statement of the effect of the direction and naming a place where a copy of the direction may be inspected (Reg. 6(2)). When a direction is made in a particular case, notice of the direction must be served on the owner and occupier of land to which the direction relates and to anyone else whom the Department knows proposes to display an advertisement of the type to which the direction relates (Reg. 6(3)).[6]

(3) Enforcement

The display of an advertisement in contravention of the Regulations is an offence (1991 Order, Art. 84(2)).[7] A person displays an advertisement if the advertisement is displayed on land of which he is the owner or occupier, or the advertisement gives publicity to his goods, trade, business or other concerns (Art. 84(3)). It is a good defence, however, to show that the advertisement was displayed without the person's knowledge or consent (Art. 84(3)). The expression 'knowledge or consent' is disjunctive, so that even though the defendant has or acquires knowledge of the advertisement it is still open to him to establish (the burden being on him) that he does not consent to it.[8]

Although there is power in Art. 84(1) of the 1991 Order for the Department to make provision in regulations for the application of the provisions of the Order as to enforcement notices to advertisements, the 1992 Regulations do not contain any such provision, in contrast to the 1973 Regulations.

(4) Areas of special control

Finally, provision is made for the designation of areas of special control for the purposes of regulations to be made under Art. 67 of the 1991 Order (1991 Order, Art. 67(3)).

---

6 For the effective date of directions under Reg. 6, see Reg. 6(4).
7 The provisions of Reg. 3, *viz.* that consent can be granted or refused only on the grounds of amenity or public safety, have no application in the decision of the Department to bring a prosecution for breach of the Regulations: *Kingsley v Hammersmith & Fulham LBC* (1991) 62 P & CR 589.
8 *Merton LBC v Edmonds, The Times* 6 July 1993; *Wycombe DC v Michael Shanly Group Ltd* [1994] 2 EG 112.

CHAPTER TWENTY ONE

Caravans

The use of land as a caravan site is controlled not only by the 1991 Order, but additionally by the Caravans Act (NI) 1963 and the Local Government (Miscellaneous Provisions) (NI) Order 1985.[1] Under these enactments, district councils are directly involved in the control of land use and are not merely entitled to be consulted, as is the extent of their function under the 1991 Order. As will be seen, councils are responsible for granting or refusing licences required under the 1963 Act for land to be used as a caravan site.

(1) *Meaning of 'caravan' and 'caravan site'*

For the purposes of the 1963 Act and the 1985 Order, a 'caravan' is any structure designed or adapted for human habitation[2] which is capable of being moved from one place to another (whether by being towed, or by being transported on a motor vehicle or trailer) and any motor vehicle so designed or adapted.[3] The term does not include railway rolling stock in use or a tent.[4] For the same purposes a 'caravan site' is land on which a caravan is stationed for the purposes of human habitation and land which is used in conjunction with land on which a caravan is so stationed.[5]

The relevance of these definitions for purposes other than the 1963 Act and the 1985 Order has recently been considered in *Hammond* v

---

1 Note the comments of Lord Denning MR: 'it is an unfortunate feature of the legislation about caravans that it is exceedingly complicated. It is very easy to get lost in the maze of procedure which it lays down. Even the most diligent of planning authorities must be discouraged from taking proceedings against infringers. There seems to be no end to the obstacles which the ingenuity of lawyers can place in their way': *James* v *Minister of Housing and Local Government* [1965] 3 All ER 602, 606; (reversed in part *sub nom. James* v *Secretary of State for Wales* [1966] 3 All ER 964).
2 To be adapted for human habitation the structure must be physically altered in some way. Merely making the structure suitable for habitation by e.g. furnishing it with a bed and other furniture does not amount to adapting it for habitation, in the absence of such physical alteration: *Backer* v *Secretary of State for the Environment* [1983] 2 All ER 1021.
3 1963 Act, s. 25(1); 1985 Order, Art. 11. See *Carter* v *Secretary of State for the Environment* [1994] 29 EG 124.
4 Ibid.
5 1963 Act, s. 1(4); 1985 Order, Art. 11. The word 'site' connotes a place habitually devoted for some purpose and caravans are not 'stationed' for the purposes of s. 1(4) on an area where one or two of them has or have casually stopped for a night or more even though other caravans may have stopped in the vicinity for several years: *Biss* v *Smallburgh* RDC [1964] 2 All ER 543, 554 *per* Harman LJ.

Horsham DC[6] and *Wyre Forest DC v Secretary of State for the Environment and anor.*[7] In *Hammond v Horsham DC* an enforcement notice prohibiting the use of land as a caravan site and requiring the removal of caravans was challenged on the ground that the structure to which the notice related was not a caravan within the meaning of the equivalent English legislation.[8] The Divisional Court remitted the case to the justices on the ground that it was wrong to assume that the statutory definition applied: there was nothing to show that the planning authority intended to use the expressions 'caravan' and 'caravan site' as terms of art. However, in *Wyre Forest DC v Secretary of State of the Environment* Lord Lowry referred to the 'close link' between the Planning Acts and the Caravan Sites and Control of Development Act 1960[9] and was of the opinion that the words 'caravan' and 'caravan site' when used in a formal document under the Planning Acts[10] *prima facie* have the same meaning which they are given by the Caravans Act.[11]

(2) Site licences

The means of control of caravan sites established by the 1963 Act is the requirement of a site licence while land is used as a caravan site (1963 Act, s. 1(1)). Land may be used as a caravan site even though the use is seasonal.[12] Use of land as a caravan site without a licence is an offence (1963 Act, s. 1(2)).

(a) Planning permission prerequisite

No licence can be issued unless at the time the licence is issued, the applicant for the licence is entitled to the benefit of planning permission for the use of the land as a caravan site (1963 Act, s. 3(3); 1991 Order, sch. 5).

(b) Applications for site licence

Applications for site licences are made to and licences are issued by the district council in whose district the land is situated (1963 Art. ss 3(1) and (3)). An application is required to be made in writing and to specify the land in respect of which the application is made (1963 Act, s. 3(2)).[13]

---

6   (1989) 59 P & CR 410.
7   (1990) 60 P & CR 195. See also *Carter v Secretary of State for the Environment* [1991] JPL 131.
8   Caravan Sites Act 1968.
9   S. 29(1) of which corresponds to the definition in s. 25(1) of the Caravans Act (NI) 1963.
10 In the case itself a planning permission.
11 (1990) 60 P & CR 195, 205. In reaching this view Lord Lowry noted the incorporation of the definitions of 'caravan' and 'caravan site' in the GDO. The same incorporation exists in the Northern Ireland GDO also.
12 *Biss v Smallburgh* RDC [1964] 2 All ER 543.
13 In *Chelmsford RDC v Powell* [1963] 1 All ER 150 the court held that a letter saying 'I am making application for fifty [caravans] as under the new Act' was sufficient to be an application for a site licence.

The applicant is required either at the time of making the application or within such period as the council determines, to give to the council such particulars as are prescribed by the Department.[14] Such matters are set out in the schedule to the Caravan Sites (Licence Applications) Order (NI) 1963[15] which also provides the form in which such particulars are to be given. If at the date such particulars are given the applicant for a site licence has planning permission for use of the land as a caravan site, the council is required to issue the licence within two months from that date, or such longer period as the applicant and the council agree (1963 Act, s. 3(4)). If at such date the applicant does not have planning permission, but obtains permission later, the licence is to be issued within six weeks of the date when he obtains planning permission, or such later date as may be agreed (1963 Act, s. 3(5)). In either case the applicant must first pay a fee of £10 (ss 3(4) and (5)). If the council fails to issue the licence within the specified time the applicant for the licence does not commit an offence under s. 1 of the Act if he uses the land as a caravan site during the period between the date the licence should have been issued and the date it is actually issued (s. 6).

A site licence cannot be issued to a person who has held a licence which has been revoked within the previous three years (s. 3(6)).

(c) Duration of licence

Save in the case where planning permission for the use of land as a caravan site has been granted for a limited period, a site licence cannot be issued for a limited period (s. 4(1)). Where planning permission has been granted for a limited period however, a site licence is required to expire and to state that it will expire, at the same time as the planning permission comes to an end (s. 4(1)).

If after a site licence has been issued the terms of the planning permission are varied by the Planning Appeals Commission on an appeal under Art. 32 of the 1991 Order, the council is required to make any alteration in the site licence required to ensure that its terms comply with s. 4(1) (s. 4(2)).

(d) Conditions

S. 5(1) of the 1963 Act provides that a site licence may be issued subject to such conditions as the council thinks necessary or desirable in the interests of persons dwelling on the site in caravans, any other class of

---

14 Originally the Ministry of Health and Local Government, whose functions in this regard were transferred to the Department: see Ministries of Northern Ireland (Transfer of Functions and Adaptation of Enactments) Orders (NI) 1964 and 1972 (SR & O 1964 No 205 and 1972 No 111); and Department of Housing, Local Government and Planning (Dissolution) (NI) Order 1976, Art. 3.
15 SR & O 1963 No 151.

persons, or the public at large. The section goes on to provide a list of various conditions which may be imposed, but the list is inclusive rather than definitive.[16] The specified conditions are conditions (1) restricting the occasions when caravans can be stationed; (2) restricting the number of caravans; (3) controlling the types of caravan;[17] (4) regulating the location of the caravans; (5) preserving amenity; (6) for fire prevention; and (7) securing adequate sanitary and other facilities (s. 5(1)(a)–(g)). In addition to these, s. 5(3) provides that a condition may be attached to a site licence corresponding to any condition subject to which planning permission was granted for use of the land as a caravan site under the 1991 Order.[18] In deciding what conditions to attach to a site licence, the council is required to have regard to any model conditions which may be specified by the Department (s. 5(7)).

Unless the site licence is subject to a condition restricting to three or less the total number of caravans which may be on the site at the same time, the licence must contain an express condition that where there are caravans on site, a copy of the licence must be displayed on the site (s. 5(4)). Finally, where a condition attached to a site licence requires works to be carried out on the site, the condition may prohibit or restrict the bringing of caravans onto the site until the council has certified that the works have been carried out to its satisfaction and that the works be completed within a specified period (s. 5(5)).

(i) Relation between planning conditions and site conditions

It will be recalled that in granting planning permission the Department has power to impose conditions (1991 Order, Arts 25 and 27). S. 5 of the 1963 Act empowers district councils to impose conditions on the grant of site licences, which, as has been seen, may correspond with conditions in a planning permission (1963 Act, s. 5(3)). The relation between the imposition of conditions relating to the use of land as a caravan site under the 1991 Order and under the 1963 Act may be seen in a number of cases on the equivalent English legislation.[19] In R v Kent Justices and anor, ex p Crittenden[20] Lord Parker CJ thought that the control of caravan sites effected by the 1963 Act operates only within the boundaries of the planning permission, rather than being a wholly independent control in the sense of being able to provide for the use of land as a caravan site outside the limitations imposed by planning control.[21] Accordingly,

---

16 The specified conditions are 'without prejudice to the generality' of s. 5(1).
17 The control of the type of caravan however cannot be by reference to the materials used in the construction of caravans: s. 5(2).
18 S. 5(3) as amended by the 1991 Order, sch. 5.
19 The problem is perhaps compounded in England, as the planning authority is the local council, which is also the body responsible for site licences.
20 [1963] 2 All ER 245.
21 Ibid., 247. 'To take an example, can it really be said that the scheme of legislation

where a planning permission restricts the number of caravans permitted on the site, it is not open to the council to permit a greater number in a site licence.[22] His Lordship admitted, however, that his view of the relation between the two statutes was not expressly stated in the legislation. In the same case Ashworth J expressed his view that it would be wrong to imply a provision that a condition in a site licence is not to conflict with a corresponding condition in the relevant planning permission, or alternatively, that a condition in a site licence is not to be less restrictive than the corresponding planning condition, on the basis that such an implication would be to legislate in a matter where Parliament has failed to do so.[23] The relation of the two regimes was considered further in Esdell Caravan Parks Ltd v Hemel Hempstead RDC.[24] Lord Denning MR thought that the matter was one of outline approval and detail and the planning authority should ask itself the broad question whether the land should be used as a caravan site at all. If the answer is yes, the authority should grant permission without going into details as to the number of caravans and the like, or imposing any conditions in that regard. Once planning permission is given, the site authority should deal with the details, saying how many caravans should be permitted; whether they should be residential or holiday caravans; or the like.[25]

It is clear that the power to impose conditions in a site licence under s. 5 of the 1963 Act cannot be exercised on the basis of planning considerations.[26] So in Babbage v North Norfolk DC[27] the court allowed an appeal against a condition in a site licence which required all caravans to be removed during the winter months. There was nothing to suggest the council had any reason for imposing the condition except to improve the aspect for the benefit of persons occupying or using other land, which was solely a planning consideration.[28] The grounds on which conditions can be imposed under s. 5 are grounds of public health and similar considerations.[29] However, in Esdell Caravan Parks Ltd v Hemel Hempstead RDC[30] such a distinction was said to be devoid of reality and certainty, as many considerations are both 'planning considerations' and 'site considerations' e.g. sewage, educational and traffic considerations.[31] Accordingly,

---

permits the local authority to impose a condition that the caravans be painted red when the planning permission provided that they shall be green?'
22 Ibid.
23 Ibid., 250.
24 [1965] 3 All ER 737.
25 Ibid., 741.
26 Esdell Caravan Parks Ltd v Hemel Hempstead RDC [1965] 3 All ER 737, 743 per Lord Denning MR.
27 (1990) 59 P & CR 248.
28 Ibid., 255 per Fox LJ.
29 Minister of Housing and Local Government v Hartnell [1965] 1 All ER 490, 493 per Lord Reid.
30 [1965] 3 All ER 737.
31 Ibid. 743 per Lord Denning MR.

the position seems to be that a site licence can impose conditions based on considerations which are site considerations and planning considerations, but cannot impose conditions which are based solely on planning considerations.

(ii) Validity of conditions

A condition attached to a site licence is valid nothwithstanding that it can be complied with only by the carrying out of works which the licence holder is not entitled to carry out as of right (1963 Act, s. 5(6)). That apart, the courts have indicated their willingness to declare the validity or otherwise of conditions imposed under s. 5 in the same way as they have done in connection with planning conditions.[32] In *Esdell Caravan Parks Ltd* v *Hemel Hempstead RDC*[33] Harman LJ said that conditions imposed under s. 5 must be such as concern the site looked at from the point of view of the people who live on it in caravans or of their neighbours, or the general public.[34] A condition which does not relate to the use of the site will be void.[35] Thus, conditions requiring that the site rents be agreed with the council; that security of tenure be granted to the caravan occupiers; that site rules be restricted to items normally covered in a tenancy agreement; that there be no restriction on occupiers as to who they purchase commodities from; that no premium be charged for occupiers entering the site; and that there be no restriction as to the functions of a tenants' association were *ultra vires* as relating to the site owner's freedom of contract.[36]

In addition to the requirement that a condition relate to the use of the site, it is necessary that the condition be expressed with sufficient certainty.[37] Finally, the condition must not be unreasonable.[38] Although not mentioned in *Chertsey* v *Mixman's Properties Ltd* this requirement of reasonableness would seem to be the same as that in connection with planning conditions, based on *Associated Provincial Picture Houses Ltd* v *Wednesbury Corp*.[39]

(iii) Appeal against conditions

When a site licence has been issued subject to a condition[40] any person aggrieved by the condition may appeal within twenty eight days to a

---

32 As to which see *Newbury DC* v *Secretary of State for the Environment* [1980] 1 All ER 731 and authorities discussed in Chapter 13.
33 [1965] 3 All ER 737.
34 Ibid., 746.
35 *Chertsey UDC* v *Mixman's Properties Ltd* [1964] 2 All ER 627.
36 Ibid.
37 Ibid., 629 *per* Lord Reid; 637 *per* Lord Guest; 638 *per* Lord Upjohn.
38 Ibid., 640 *per* Lord Upjohn.
39 [1947] 2 All ER 680. See *Newbury DC* v *Secretary of State for the Environment* [1980] 1 All ER 731, 739 *per* Viscount Dilhorne.
40 Other than the conditions mentioned in s. 5(1)(a), (3) or (4).

court of summary jurisdiction for the petty sessions district in which the site is situated, and the court may vary or cancel the condition if it is satisfied that the condition is unduly burdensome (s. 7(1)). In considering whether the condition is unduly burdensome the court is to have regard to any model conditions specified by the Department under s. 5(7) (s. 7 (1)).[41] A similar right of appeal exists in respect of conditions referred to in s. 5(1)(a), but in this case the appeal is to the Department rather than the court (s. 7(2)). The Department must, if the appellant wishes, afford him and the council an opportunity of appearing before and being heard by an independent person appointed by the Department (s. 7(3)) who then makes a report on the hearing to the Department (s. 7(4)). The power under s. 7 to vary a condition does not enable the court or the Department to extend the licence to any use beyond the scope of the planning permission.[42]

(iv) Alteration of conditions

Conditions attached to a site licence may be altered at any time, whether by the variation or cancellation of existing conditions or the addition of new conditions, or by a combination of such methods (s. 8(1)). Alteration may be pursuant to an application made by the holder of a site licence (see ss 8(2), (6) and (7)), but the section allows for alterations to be made at the instigation of the council itself.[43] Where an application for alteration has been made by the holder of a site licence, the application is deemed to have been refused at the end of the period of two months from the date the council receives the application, unless within that period the applicant has been notified of the council's decision (s. 8(6)). Where, following an application, the council does alter the conditions, a fee of £1 is payable (s. 8(7)) and the licence holder may be required to deliver up the licence to enable the council to enter in it any alterations of the conditions (s. 11(1)).

In determining whether to alter the conditions of a licence the council is to have regard to any model conditions specified by the Department under s. 5(7) (s. 8(9)). It is also required to afford the holder of the licence an opportunity of making representations (s. 8(1)).

Where the council does alter the conditions pursuant to s. 8(1), or where it refuses to alter the conditions following an application by the licence holder, the licence holder may appeal.[44] In the case of conditions

---

41 Ibid. Where an appeal has been made against a condition requiring the carrying out of works, the condition is of no effect while the appeal is pending: s. 7(5).
42 R v Kent Justices and anor, ex p Crittenden [1963] 2 All ER 245.
43 Peters v Yiewsley and West Drayton UDC [1963] 1 All ER 843, 845 per Lord Parker CJ.
44 The right of appeal is not limited to cases where the council refuses an application to alter a condition which has already been altered under s. 8(1), but extends also to cases where the council refuses an application to alter a condition in its original form: Peters v Yiewsley and West Drayton UDC [1963] 1 All ER 843.

other than conditions under s. 5(1)(a), the appeal is to the court of summary jurisdiction for the petty sessions district in which the site is situated (s. 8(2)), but in the case of conditions under s. 5(1)(a), the appeal is to the Department (s. 8(3)), which must, if the appellant wishes, afford him and the council an opportunity of appearing before and being heard by an independent person appointed by the Department (s. 8(4)), who then makes a report to the Department (s. 8(5)). In either case the appeal must be made within twenty eight days of the notification of the alteration or refusal (ss 8(2) and (3)) and, where the court or the Department allows the appeal, it may give the council such directions as may be necessary to give effect to its decision (ss 8(2) and (3)).[45]

Insofar as the alteration of a condition requires the licence holder to carry out works which he would not otherwise have had to carry out, the alteration is of no effect while an appeal is pending (s. 5(8)).

(v) Breach of conditions

Failure to comply with a condition attached to a site licence is an offence (s. 9(1)). If the offender has had two or more previous convictions, the court may, on an application by the council, revoke the site licence (s. 9(2)). Where the breach consists in failure to complete works required by the condition to be carried out, the council has power to carry out the works and recover the cost from the licence holder (s. 9(4)).

(e) Transfer of licences

Where a licence holder ceases to be the occupier of the site[46] he may transfer the licence to the new occupier (s. 10(1)). Notice must be given to the council and a fee of 50p paid (s. 10(1)). Once this is done the council endorses on the licence the name of the transferee and the date of transfer (s. 10(2)), but the council is prevented from endorsing the name of a person who has held a licence which has been revoked during the previous three years (s. 10(3)). Likewise, where a person becomes by operation of law the occupier of a site which has the benefit of a licence, the council is required on an application to endorse the name of the new occupier and the date on which he became such (s. 10(4)). When the council does endorse a site licence under ss 10(2) or (4), the information endorsed is to be recorded in the register of site licences (s. 22(2)).

---

45 Ibid. In the case, however, of appeals allowed by the court, the court has no power to give a direction requiring the alteration of a condition which corresponds to a condition subject to which planning permission was granted: s. 8(10); as amended by the 1991 Order, Art. 133 and sch. 5.

46 For the meaning of 'occupier' see s. 1(3). In cases where there is a licence or tenancy, see also s. 12.

(f) Cases where licence not required

A site licence is not required for use of land as a caravan site in the circumstances specified in the schedule to the Act (s. 2). These circumstances are:

(1) Where the use of the land as a caravan site is incidental to the enjoyment as such of a dwelling house within the curtilage of which the land is situated;
(2) the use of land as a caravan site by a person travelling with a caravan who brings the caravan onto the land for a period including not more than two nights;[47]
(3) the use as a caravan site of land comprising not less than 5 acres in specified circumstances;[48]
(4) the use as a caravan site of land occupied by an organisation holding an exemption certificate, for purposes of recreation;[49]
(5) the use as a caravan site of land in respect of which a certificate, stating that the land has been approved for recreation by an organisation holding an exemption certificate, has been issued by such organisation;
(6) the use of land as a caravan site when the use is for a meeting of an organisation holding an exemption certificate, and the meeting is to last not more than five days;
(7) the use as a caravan site of agricultural land for accommodation during a particular season of farm workers;
(8) the use of land as a caravan site for accommodation during a particular season of forestry workers;
(9) the use as a caravan site of land forming part of, or adjacent to, building or engineering sites, where the use is for accommodation of site workers or the site owner;
(10) the use of land as a caravan site by a travelling showman who is a member of an organisation of travelling showmen holding a certificate of recognition from the Department, and who is travelling for business purposes or who has taken up winter quarters during specified periods;
(11) the use as a caravan site of land occupied by a district council.

The exemption from the requirement of a site licence granted by paras 2–11 of the schedule may be withdrawn by the Department on an application by a district council, in respect of land situated within the district of the council (sch. para. 13(1)).[50]

---

47 Ibid., para. 2. There are conditions: see subparas (a) and (b).
48 Ibid., para. 3(1). For the specified circumstances see subparas (a) and (b). The Department has power to exclude the operation of the paragraph: see para. (2).
49 Ibid., para. 4. For exemption certificates see para. 12.
50 For the requirement for making and publicising such orders see sch. paras 13(2) and 14.

(g) Register of site licences

District councils are required by s. 22(1) of the 1963 Act to maintain a register of site licences issued in respect of land within their district. Every such register is to be kept open for inspection by the public at all reasonable times (s. 22(1)).

(3) Other powers of councils

In addition to their powers in respect of site licences, district councils have power, with the consent of the Department, to provide sites where caravans may be brought and to manage the sites or lease them to some other person (s. 21(1)).[51] In connection with such sites, councils may, with the consent of the Department, acquire land already in use as a caravan site (s. 21(2)(a)), or provide for the use of persons occupying sites any services or facilities for their health or convenience (s. 21(2)(b)). Councils may charge for the use of sites provided or managed by them, or services or facilities provided by them (s. 21(3)).

In order to enable them to carry out their functions under the Act, councils have a right of entry in respect of any land used as a caravan site or in respect of which an application for a site licence has been made (s. 23(1)). The right is exercisable at all reasonable hours for the purposes of (1) enabling the council to determine what conditions should be attached to a site licence, or whether any such conditions should be altered; (2) ascertaining whether there has been any contravention of the provisions of the Act; (3) ascertaining whether circumstances exist which would authorise the council to take any action or execute any work under the Act; or (4) taking any action or executing any such work (s. 23(1)). Admission cannot be demanded however as of right unless twenty four hours notice of the intended entry has been given to the occupier (s. 23(1)). Obstruction of the council in the exercise of its right under s. 23 is an offence (s. 23(5)).

(4) Travelling people

The Local Government (Miscellaneous Provisions) (NI) Order 1985 makes special provision regarding caravans of travelling people.[52] To begin with, when the powers of a district council under s. 21 of the 1963 Act are exercised to provide caravan sites for the accommodation of travelling people, the Department may make grants in respect of any expenditure incurred by the council of a capital nature (1985 Order, Art. 8(1)). Secondly, the Order provides that the powers of a council under s. 21

---

51 Councils have no power to provide caravans: s. 21(6).
52 For the definition of 'travelling people' see the 1985 Order, Art. 11.

include power to provide in connection with such sites working space and facilities for the carrying on of such activities as are normally carried on by travelling people (1985 Order, Art. 8(3)).

Additional control of caravans used by travellers[53] is provided by Arts 9 and 10 of the 1985 Order. Art. 9(4) provides that a district council may apply to the Department for an order designating the district of that council as a district to which Art. 9 applies. No order can be made by the Department unless it appears to the Department that adequate provision is made in that district for accommodation of travelling people or that it is not necessary or expedient to make such provision (Art. 9(5)). Where an order is made, then a traveller who stations a caravan on the locations prohibited by Art. 9(1) for the purposes of residing for any period is guilty of an offence (Art. 9(1)). The locations prohibited are (a) any land forming part of a road; (b) any other unoccupied land; or (c) any occupied land without the consent of the occupier (Art. 9(1)).[54]

Where there has been a contravention of Art. 9, a court of summary jurisdiction may, on a complaint made by the council, make an order requiring any caravan stationed on the land to be removed, together with any person residing in it (Art. 10(1)). Such an order may authorise the council to take such steps as are reasonably necessary to ensure that the order is complied with and, in particular, may authorise the council to enter the land specified in the order and take such steps for securing entry to any caravan to be removed and rendering it suitable for removal as may be specified (Art. 10(2)). Any person intentionally obstructing the exercise of the powers conferred by such an order is guilty of an offence (Art. 10(4)).

(5) Permitted development

Finally, the provisions of the GDO as to the uses of land as a caravan site should be noted. The Order provides that the use of land, other than a building, as a caravan site in any of the circumstances specified in paras 2, 3 and 6–10 of the schedule to the 1963 Act or in the circumstances (other than those relating to winter quarters) specified in para. 10 of the schedule is permitted by the Order, subject to the condition that the use shall be discontinued when the circumstances cease to exist, and all caravans on the site shall then be removed (GDO, Art. 3 and sch. 1, part 5).

---

53 For definition see 1985 Order, Art. 11.
54 Ibid. For construction of the similar provision in s. 10(1)(c) of the Caravans Sites Act 1968, see *Stubbings v Beaconsfield Justices and anor* (1987) 54 P & CR 327.

CHAPTER TWENTY TWO

Environmental Protection

Applications for planning permission for certain types of development are subject to the provisions of the Planning (Assessment of Environmental Effects) Regulations (NI) 1989.[1] The Regulations were made by the Department pursuant to the provisions of European Community Directive 85/337/EEC on the assessment of the effects of certain public and private projects on the environment. The Regulations provide that planning permission for development to which the Regulations apply is not to be granted unless the Department or the Planning Appeals Commission, as the case may be, shall first have taken into account environmental information, that is, the environmental statement required to be submitted in certain cases by the Regulations, any representations made by any body required by the Regulations to be consulted, and any representations made by any other person about the likely environmental effects of the proposed development (Regs 3(1) and 2(2)). The purpose therefore of the Regulations is to require such effects to be assessed before planning permission is granted.[2] It is also provided that when planning permission is granted pursuant to an application to which the Regulations apply, the permission must state that environmental information has been taken into account.[3]

(1) *Development to which the Regulations apply*

The Regulations apply to applications for development of the types specified in schs 1 and 2 of the Regulations, except development in respect of which the Department has issued a direction under Reg. 17.[4] The types of development specified in the schedules are, broadly, major constructional or industrial types of development, and are set out in Appendix C.

---

1 As amended by Planning (Assessment of Environmental Effects) (Amendment) Regulations (NI) 1994.
2 The Regulations do not specify the effect of the granting of planning permission where such information has not been taken into consideration, but presumably any such permission would be liable to be set aside on the ground of failure to comply with the requirements of the Regulations.
3 Reg. 3(1)(A), as inserted by Planning (Assessment of Environmental Effects) (Amendment) Regulations (NI) 1994.
4 Reg. 17 empowers the Department to direct that a specific development is not development in respect of which the consideration of environmental information is required before planning permission can be granted.

(2) Schedule 1 and Schedule 2 applications

The types of development to which the Regulations apply are specified in sch. 1 and sch. 2. The significance of the difference between the two schedules is that while planning permission for development specified in sch. 1 is not to be granted unless environmental information[5] has been taken into consideration, the same applies to development specified in sch. 2 only where the proposed development is likely to have significant effects on the environment by virtue of factors such as its nature, size or location (Regs 3 (1)(a) and (b)). This will be the case where the applicant and the Department agree that an environmental statement[6] is required and the Department has notified its agreement in writing, or the Department has determined that an environmental statement is required under Reg. 4, 5 or 6.[7]

To assist would-be developers in finding out whether the development proposed is subject to the Regulations, Reg. 4 provides that a developer may, before applying for planning permission, apply to the Department for a determination whether the proposed development falls within sch. 1 or sch. 2, and if it falls within sch. 2, whether it would be likely to have a significant effect on the environment (Reg. 4(1)). Such an application must be in writing (Reg. 4(1)) and accompanied by a plan sufficient to identify the land on which the proposed development is to be carried out; a brief description of the nature and purpose of the proposed development; and such further information or representations as the applicant wishes to provide or make (Reg. 4(2)).[8] Before making its determination on such an application, the Department may consult the district council and such other statutory bodies as appear to have an interest in the proposal (Regs 4(3) and 8(2)). If the Department determines that the proposed development requires an environmental statement, it is required to give the applicant the reasons for its determination (Reg. 4(6)), whereupon the applicant must, within four weeks (Reg. 4(8)), notify the Department in writing that he accepts the determination and proposes to provide an environmental statement, or that he does not and proposes to seek a hearing before the Planning Appeals Commission (Reg. 4(7)). Where a hearing takes place, the Department is required to consider the report of the Commission and to confirm, amend or withdraw its determination (Reg. 6(2)). The determination made by the Department under Reg. 4 is required to be notified to the applicant within four weeks from receipt of the application or such longer period as may be agreed (Reg. 4(4)) and a copy of the determination is to be kept on the planning register.[9]

---

5 As defined by Art. 2(2).   6 See definition in Art. 2(2) and below.
7 See *In re McCann's application* [1992] 7 NIJB 60.
8 If the Department has insufficient information to determine the application it must notify the applicant of the points on which further information is needed: Reg. 4(5).
9 See Reg. 7 (as substituted by Planning (Assessment of Environmental Effects) (Amendment) Regulations (NI) 1994) and 1991 Order, Art. 124.

Where an application for planning permission has been submitted without an environmental statement, and it appears to the Department that the application may be a sch. 1 or sch. 2 application, the Department is required to determine whether an environmental statement is required (Reg. 5(1)).[10] If the Department determines that an environmental statement is required and the applicant fails to notify the Department that he accepts the determination or that he proposes to seek a hearing before the Planning Appeals Commission, his application for planning permission is deemed to have been withdrawn (Reg. 5(4)). If an environmental statement is required it must be submitted within six months of the date of determination by the Department or the Commission (Reg. 5(5)) and failure to do so will result in the application for planning permission being deemed to have been withdrawn (Reg. 5(5)).

(3) The environmental statement

An environmental statement comprises a document or series of documents providing, for the purpose of assessing the likely impact on the environment of the proposed development, the information specified in para. 2 of sch. 3 to the Regulations, and such further information as may be included under para. 3 (sch. 3, para. 1). The information specified in para. 2 consists of (a) a description of the proposed development; (b) the data necessary to identify and assess the main effects the development is likely to have on the environment; (c) a description of the likely significant effects, direct and indirect, on the environment of the development, explained by reference to its possible impact on people, flora, fauna, soil, water, air, climate, the landscape, the interaction between any such material assets, and the cultural heritage; (d) a description of the measures envisaged to alleviate any identified significant adverse effects; and (e) 'a summary in non-technical language of the information specified in sub-paras (a) to (d).' Further information may be included in the environmental statement on various matters set out in para 3 of the schedule and, if such information is included, a non-technical summary of that information must be provided (sch. 3, para. 4).

When a developer informs the Department he intends to submit an environmental statement with an application for planning permission he is required to supply the Department with the information necessary to identify the land and the nature and purpose of the proposed development, and to indicate the main environmental consequences to which he proposes to refer in the statement (Reg. 8(1)). The Department is then required to notify the district council for the area in which the land is situated and such other statutory bodies as appear to it to have an interest in the proposal, of details of the proposed development. In each case the

---

10 The provisions of Regs 4(3)–(8) apply as modified by Reg. 5(3). See Reg. 5(2).

Department must inform the bodies concerned that they have a duty to make available to the developer any information relevant to the preparation of the environmental statement. The Department is also required to supply such further information as may be requested by the bodies notified and inform the developer of the bodies who have been notified (Reg. 8(2)). Reg. 9 provides for consultation between the bodies notified by the Department and the developer, at the instigation of either party, concerning the provision of relevant information to the developer.

Once an environmental statement is received[11] the Department is required to place a copy of the statement on the planning register (Reg. 10(1)(a)), and to consult the district council and other statutory bodies appearing to the Department to have an interest in the proposal about the statement, and to inform them they may make representations (Reg. 10(1)(b)). Such bodies must also be given notice of not less than four weeks that environmental information is to be taken into consideration in determining the application for planning permission. The statement must be made available to the public by the developer and when the Department receives the statement it is required to publish notice of the planning application, stating that the application is accompanied by the statement and giving an address from which copies of the statement can be obtained from the developer.[12]

In respect of applications for planning permission where an environmental statement is required, the period for determining the application is amended from two months to sixteen weeks, which runs from the date of receipt of the statement (Reg. 14(1)). In any event, an application with which an environmental statement is required is not to be determined before the end of four weeks from receipt of the statement (Reg. 14(2)).

In the case of applications to which Art. 31 of the 1991 Order has been applied, Art. 31 is amended by the substitution of a period of two months by sixteen weeks, which runs from the date of receipt of the environmental statement (Reg. 15).

Finally, where an appeal is made under Arts 32 or 33 the 1991 Order to the Planning Appeals Commission[13] in respect of an application with which an environmental statement was submitted, the appeal is to be accompanied by a copy of the statement and the Commission may require the appellant to provide such further information as it may specify concerning any matter which is required to be or which may be in the statement (Reg. 16).

---

11 The developer must submit enough copies of the statement or parts of it, to enable the Department to consult the council and other statutory bodies appearing to have an interest in the proposal, and three additional copies: Reg. 10(2). In addition, enough copies must be available for inspection pursuant to Reg. 11(c): Reg. 12.
12 Upon payment of a reasonable charge: Reg. 13(1).
13 Appeals against refusal of planning permission or in default of a decision by the Department.

PART FIVE

Miscellaneous

CHAPTER TWENTY THREE

Roads

The 1991 Order gives the Department various powers in relation to roads, exercisable on planning grounds. Thus, the Department may, to improve the amenity of any area, make an order for the extinguishment of any right which persons may have to use vehicles on a road, other than a trunk road or a special road (1991 Order, Art. 100(1)). Such an order may permit vehicles to use the road, notwithstanding the extinguishment of the right to use it, at specified times (Art. 100(2)) and for the preservation of the rights of statutory undertakers in respect of apparatus (Art. 100(7)). Where an order has been made under Art. 100, any person who at the time the order comes into force has an estate in land having lawful access onto a road to which the order relates is entitled to compensation from the Department in respect of any depreciation in value of his estate which is directly attributable to the order and of any other loss or damage which is so attributable.[1]

Again, where the Department makes an order, it has power to carry out such works on the road, or to place such objects or structures on the road, as appear to be expedient for *inter alia* enhancing the amenity or providing a service to the public (1991 Order, Art. 101(1)(a)(ii) and (iii)), or as appear to be otherwise desirable for a purpose beneficial to the public (Art. 101(1)(b)). The powers of the Department under Art. 101 extend to laying out lawns, trees, shrubs and flowerbeds, provision of toilet facilities, recreation and refreshment facilities, trading kiosks and directional maps or plans (Art. 101(2)).

Apart from the power to extinguish the right to use a road conferred by Art. 100, the Department may extinguish a public right of way over land which has been acquired or appropriated for planning purposes and is held for those purposes (Art. 102(1)).[2] The power is exercisable where the Department is satisfied that the extinguishment of the right of way is necessary for the proper development of the land (Art. 102(1)).[3]

The procedure for making an order under Art. 100 or Art. 102 is the same. Before making the order the Department is required to publish a notice in a local newspaper stating the general effect of the order, specifying a place where a copy of the draft order and any relevant map may

---

1 1972 Order, Art. 66B (as inserted by the 1991 Order, Art. 133 and sch. 5).
2 For acquisition or appropriation of land for planning purposes see Arts 87 and 89 and Chapter 7.
3 For the effect of an order on telecommunications apparatus see Art. 104.

be inspected during a period of twenty eight days following publication of the notice, and stating that objections may be made within that period (Art. 103(1)). A copy of the notice, the draft order and the map must be served on the relevant district council(s), any gas or electricity undertakers affected and the operator of any telecommunications code system (Art. 103(2)). Service must take place not later than the date on which the notice is published in the newspaper (Art. 103(2)). The Department may cause a public local enquiry to be held by the Planning Appeals Commission to hear objections (Art. 103(3)). After considering any objections and, if applicable, the report of the Planning Appeals Commission, the Department may make the order, with or without modifications (Art. 103(4)). Once the order is made, notice of it must be published stating that it has been made and naming a place where a copy of it may be seen (Art. 103(5)).

CHAPTER TWENTY FOUR

Purchase Notices

We have already noted that in certain cases following an order or decision made by the Department, the Department may be required to purchase the land affected by that order or decision upon receipt of a purchase notice. It is proposed in this chapter to consider in detail the circumstances in which such a notice may be served, the procedure involved and the consequences which flow from the service of such a notice.

(1) Circumstances in which a purchase notice may be served

The circumstances in which a purchase notice may be served, the persons by whom it may be served and the conditions which must be fulfilled by such persons, are as follows:

(a) *Following an application for planning permission*

A purchase notice may be served where, on an application for planning permission, permission is refused or is granted subject to conditions (1991 Order, Art. 94(1)(a)). The notice may be served by any owner of the land (Art. 94(1)). 'Owner' means a person (other than a mortgagee not in possession) who is entitled to receive the rack rent[1] of the land, or, where the land is not let at a rack rent, would be so entitled if the land were so let (1991 Order, Art. 2(2)). The meaning of the corresponding provision of the Town and Country Planning Act 1947 was considered in *London Corp.* v *Cusack-Smith*.[2] Lord Reid pointed out that the definition of 'owner' has two limbs, the first dealing with the case where a person is entitled to receive the rack rent, the second where the land is not let at a rack rent. In connection with the first limb, whether land is let at a rack rent has to be considered at the date of the lease. This means that more than one rack rent may be payable out of the same land. If A grants a lease to B at a rent at that time representing the rack rent and some time later B in turn makes a lease to C, at a rent then representing the rack rent, both A and B fulfil the description of 'owner'. If, of course, A lets to B at a rent less than the rack rent, and B lets to C at the then rack rent, B is the owner and A is not. The second limb of the definition covers two situations: first, where the land is not let at all and, second, where the land is let but

---

1 I.e. a rent equal to the full rental value of the land.
2 [1955] 1 All ER 302.

the rent payable is not a rack rent. If the land is not let at all the definition requires that it be supposed that the freeholder has made a lease to a hypothetical tenant at a rack rent. If, however, there is in existence a tenant paying a rent which is not a rack rent, the freeholder is excluded from the definition of 'owner', and the tenant is the owner for the purposes of Art. 94.

The owner must show that (1) the land has become incapable of reasonably beneficial use in its existing state; (2) in a case where planning permission was granted subject to conditions, that the land cannot be rendered capable of reasonably beneficial use by the carrying out of the permitted development in accordance with those conditions; and (3) in any case, that the land cannot be rendered capable of reasonably beneficial use by the carrying out of any other development for which planning permission has been granted (1991 Order, Art. 94(1)(i)–(iii)).[3]

The 'land' referred to in Art. 94 means all of the land which is the subject of the planning decision and, consequently, where it is found that the title of the person serving the purchase notice does not extend to the whole of the land, the purchase notice will not be valid.[4]

(b) Following revocation or modification of planning permission

The second instance in which a purchase notice may be served is where, by an order under Art. 38 of the 1991 Order, planning permission is revoked, or is modified by the imposition of conditions (1991 Order, Art. 94(1)(b)). Again, the notice may be served by any owner of the land who must show: (1) that the land has become incapable of reasonably beneficial use in its existing state; (2) in a case where planning permission has been modified by the imposition of conditions, that the land cannot be rendered capable of reasonably beneficial use by the carrying out of the permitted development in accordance with those conditions; and (3) in any case, that the land cannot be rendered capable of reasonably beneficial use by the carrying out of any other development for which planning permission has been granted (Art. 94(1)(i)–(iii)).

(c) Following a discontinuance order

A purchase notice may be served following the making of an order by the Department under Art. 39 of the 1991 Order, i.e. an order requiring the discontinuance of a use of land or imposing conditions on the continuance of a use, or requiring the alteration or removal of buildings or works on land. In such cases a purchase notice may be served by any person entitled to an interest in land in respect of which the order under Art. 39

---

[3] The meaning of the expression 'incapable of reasonably beneficial use' is considered below.
[4] *Smart and Courtney Dale Ltd* v *Dover RDC* (1972) 23 P & CR 408.

has been made (Art. 94(3)). That person must show: (1) that by reason of the order the land is incapable of reasonably beneficial use in its existing state; (2) that the land cannot be rendered capable of reasonably beneficial use by the carrying out of any development for which planning permission has been granted, whether by the order or otherwise (Art. 94(3)(a) and (b)).

(d) Following an application for listed building consent

Where, on an application for listed building consent[5] in respect of a building, consent is refused or is granted subject to conditions, a purchase notice may be served by any owner of the land (Art. 94(2)(a)). In the context of purchase notices following an application for listed building consent or an order revoking or modifying such consent (see below) the 'land' means the building in question together with any land comprising the building, or contiguous or adjacent to it, being land as to which the owner claims that its use is substantially inseparable from that of the building and that it ought to be treated, together with the building, as a single holding (Art. 94(8)). The owner must show: (1) that the land has become incapable of reasonably beneficial use in its existing state; (2) where consent was given subject to conditions with respect to the execution of the works for which it was sought, that the land cannot be rendered capable of reasonably beneficial use by the carrying out of the works in accordance with those conditions; and (3) in any case, that the land cannot be rendered capable of reasonably beneficial use by the carrying out of any other works for which listed building consent has been granted (Art. 94(2)(i)–(iii)).

(e) Following revocation or modification of listed building consent

Finally, a purchase notice may be served where, by an order under Art. 47 of the 1991 Order, listed building consent has been revoked or modified by the imposition of conditions (Art. 94(2)(b)). The notice may be served by any owner of the land (Art. 94(2)) who must show: (1) that the land has become incapable of reasonably beneficial use in its existing state; (2) where consent has been modified by the imposition of conditions, that the land cannot be rendered capable of reasonably beneficial use by the carrying out of the works in accordance with those conditions; and (3) in any case, that the land cannot be rendered capable of reasonably beneficial use by the carrying out of any other works for which listed building consent has been granted (Art. 94(2)(i)–(iii)).

---

5   See Art. 44 and Chapter 17.

(2) 'Incapable of reasonably beneficial use'

The issue, then, of whether the Department can be required to purchase land from someone affected by an adverse decision or order of the Department is whether the land is incapable of reasonably beneficial use. Before considering what is required for land to satisfy this test a preliminary point should be noted. In cases (a), (b), (c) and (e) above, where a purchase notice may be served, the requirement of Art. 94 is that the land *has become* incapable of reasonably beneficial use (Arts 94(1)(i) and 94(2)(i)). In case (c) however (i.e. where a purchase notice is served following an order under Art. 39) the requirement is that by reason of the order the land *is* incapable of reasonably beneficial use (Art. 94(3)). Despite the difference in wording, the result may be the same: what is required to be considered is the situation at the time of the decision or order in question. The expression 'has become' does not mean that there must be an identifiable change in circumstances, i.e. that land was once capable of reasonably beneficial use and has since ceased to be.[6] The legislation does not require an investigation of the state of the land at some stage in its history.[7] Accordingly, where it appears that the land is at the time of the decision or order incapable of reasonably beneficial use, it is irrelevant that the land had always been incapable of reasonably beneficial use in the past. Thus, an owner was able to serve a purchase notice in respect of marsh land following refusal of planning permission, it being irrelevant that the land had always been marsh land.[8]

The question whether land is incapable of reasonably beneficial use is not the same as the question whether land is of less value than it would be if planning permission had been granted unconditionally. The test is not whether the land is of less use, or substantially less use, in its present state than if developed, nor does it follow that because it is of substantially less use than if developed the test is satisfied.[9] The requirement of Art. 94 is that the land is 'incapable of reasonably beneficial use', 'reasonably beneficial use' being a straightforward expression made up of ordinary words, meaning 'not only beneficial, in the sense that a benefit of some kind is to be derived, but *reasonably* beneficial, in the sense that a

---

6 *Purbeck DC v Secretary of State for the Environment* (1982) 263 EG 261. The court did not, however, think it necessary to go as far as the Secretary of State who had simply read 'has become' as meaning 'is'.
7 Ibid.
8 Ibid. Contrast *General Estates Co. Ltd v Minister of Housing and Local Government* (1965) 194 EG 202 where a purchase notice was rejected on the ground that there was nothing to prevent the continued use of the land as playing fields, this being a reasonably beneficial use.
9 R v *Minister of Housing and Local Government, ex p Chichester* RDC [1960] 2 All ER 407, 410 *per* Lord Parker CJ.

reasonable degree of benefit is to be derived.'[10] Further, the test is whether the land is incapable of reasonably beneficial use *to the owner* of the land.[11]

In considering whether land is incapable of reasonably beneficial use the conditions referred to in Arts 34, 35 and 46 of the 1991 Order are to be disregarded (Art. 94(6)).

Consideration of whether land is capable of reasonably beneficial use begs the question what is a reasonably beneficial use? Some assistance, albeit negative, is provided by Art. 94(5). This provides that in answering what is a reasonably beneficial use, no account is to be taken of any prospective use of the land which would involve the carrying out of 'new development' as defined in the Land Development Values (Compensation) Act (NI) 1965, or of any works requiring listed building consent. It will be recalled[12] that most development of land will constitute 'new development' and consequently will be excluded from consideration in determining whether land is incapable of reasonably beneficial use. Development which is not 'new development', i.e. development of the classes mentioned in sch. 1 to the 1965 Act, may be taken into account in determining whether land is capable of reasonably beneficial use, but this is not conclusive. In *Brookdene Investments Ltd v Minister of Housing and Local Government*[13] evidence was given that the annual value of premises in their existing state following refusal of planning permission was £10,000, whereas if development (not being 'new development') were to be carried out the value would be over £53,000. The court was asked to rule that if there was a substantial difference in such values this would necessarily mean that the land was incapable of reasonably beneficial use in its existing state. The court, however, rejected this, holding that the difference was merely a relevant factor to be taken into account.

It has been held in England that if part only of the land which is the subject of a purchase notice is incapable of reasonably beneficial use, a purchase notice cannot be served in respect of the whole of the land.[14] In *Allen v Department of the Environment for Northern Ireland*[15] it was pointed out that the Northern Ireland legislation lacks provisions corresponding to those on which reliance was placed in reaching such decision, and in the event the court in *Allen* did not have to decide the point.

Assuming that the person serving a purchase notice can show that the land is incapable of reasonably beneficial use, does it matter that the reason the land is so is because of the claimant's own conduct? In

---

10 *Allen v Department of the Environment for Northern Ireland* [1985] NI 195, 202 *per* Lord Lowry LCJ.
11 Ibid. See also *Adams and Wade Ltd v Minister of Housing and Local Government* (1965) 18 P & CR 60. (Note, however, the provisions of Art. 96 dealing with the specific issue in *Adams and Wade*: see below.)
12 Chapter 13.   13 (1969) 21 P & CR 545.
14 *Wain v Secretary of State for the Environment* (1982) 44 P & CR 289.
15 [1985] NI 195.

Purbeck DC v Secretary of State for the Environment[16] Woolf J thought that the corresponding provisions of the Town and Country Planning Act 1971 excluded a situation where the land had become incapable of reasonably beneficial use because of unlawful activity, (i.e. activity in breach of planning control) on the land: a landowner who renders the land incapable of reasonably beneficial use by his own conduct should not be able to take advantage of his own wrong so as to foist the land on an unwilling planning authority.[17] These views were criticised, however, in *Balco Transport Services Ltd v Secretary of State for the Environment*.[18] Glidewell LJ thought that the maxim that a man cannot take advantage of his own wrong has no application to the question whether land has become incapable of reasonably beneficial use in its existing state. His Lordship went on to say that if at the time a purchase notice is served: (1) the land to which it relates is in a state which has been caused by development without planning permission; (2) a valid enforcement notice in respect of that development either has been served or could be served; (3) such an enforcement notice could require the owner or occupier of the land to take steps to restore the land to its condition before the development took place; and (4) in such a condition the land would be capable of reasonably beneficial use; then the conditions for service of an enforcement notice would not be fulfilled.[19] If, however, as in *Balco*, the unlawful development is immune from enforcement proceedings (because e.g. it is operational development carried out more than four years earlier) then the owner is not prevented from serving a purchase notice.

(3) Procedure

A purchase notice must be in writing and served within six months (or such longer period as the Department allows) of the decision or order of the Department giving rise to the power to serve a notice.[20] The Department is required within two months of the date on which the purchase notice was served (Art. 95(2)(b)) to serve a notice on the person who served the purchase notice (the claimant) responding to the purchase notice.[21] The Department's response must be one of three notices: (1) a

---

16 (1982) 263 EG 261, 264.
17 Ibid., 262.
18 [1985] 3 All ER 689.
19 Ibid., 698.
20 1991 Order, Art. 94(4)(a); GDO, Art. 17. Where a repairs notice under Art. 109(4) of the 1991 Order has been served by the Department (see Chapter 17) a purchase notice cannot be served in respect of the building in question until the expiration of three months beginning on the date of service of the repairs notice. If within that period the Department begins proceedings for the compulsory purchase of the building under Art. 109, a purchase notice cannot be served until those proceedings are discontinued: Art. 94(7).
21 Where an appeal under Arts 32, 69 or 78 or para. 7 of sch. 1 is pending at the time the purchase notice is served, or is made within two months of that date, the period within which the Department is required to respond to the purchase notice is two months from the date on which the appeal is disposed of: Art. 95(2)(a).

notice that the Department is willing to comply with the purchase notice; or (2) a notice objecting to the purchase notice, stating that for the reasons specified the Department is not willing to comply with the purchase notice;[22] or (3) a counternotice objecting to the purchase notice and stating that planning permission[23] or listed building consent,[24] as the case may be, might reasonably be expected to be granted for any other development or works which in the opinion of the Department would, if carried out, render the land capable of reasonably beneficial use (Art. 95(1)). The 1991 Order does not specify the consequence of the Department's failure to respond either within the time prescribed or at all.

If the Department serves a counternotice objecting to the purchase notice, the claimant may refer the matter to the Lands Tribunal (Art. 97 (1)). This must be done within two months of receipt of the Department's counternotice (Art. 97(1)). The Tribunal is required to consider the matters set out in the purchase notice and the reasons specified in the counternotice and determine whether the purchase notice or the counternotice should be upheld (Art. 97(2)). As with blight notices, the Tribunal cannot consider any objection to the purchase notice which has not been specified by the Department in its counternotice.[25] In the event that the Tribunal upholds the purchase notice, it will declare the purchase notice valid (Art. 97(3)).

(4) *Effect of valid purchase notice*

If the Department in responding to the purchase notice serves a notice stating that it is willing to comply with the purchase notice the claimant and the Department are deemed to have entered a contract for the sale of the claimant's estate in the land to the Department (Art. 98(1)). The same is the case where the Department serves a counternotice objecting to the purchase notice, but the Department later withdraws its objection, or the objection is not upheld by the Lands Tribunal (Art. 98(1)). The date on which the contract is deemed to come into existence is the date when the period in which the Department is required to respond to the

---

22 In this regard the Department may object to a purchase notice, notwithstanding that the land is incapable of reasonably beneficial use, if the land was part of a larger area for which a previous planning permission exists, and it was intended that the land should be preserved as amenity land, see Art. 96, intended to reverse the decision in *Adams and Wade Ltd v Minister of Housing and Local Government* (1965) 18 P & CR 60. Art. 96 applies only where the whole of the land which is the subject of a purchase notice has a restricted use by virtue of a previous planning permission. If part of the land which is the subject of the purchase notice is not so restricted, the purchase notice must be upheld: *Plymouth CC v Secretary of State for the Environment* [1972] 3 All ER 225.
23 In the case of purchase notices served under Art. 94(1) or (3).
24 In the case of purchase notices served under Art. 94(2).
25 *Allen v Department of the Environment for Northern Ireland* [1985] NI 195, following *Essex CC v Essex Incorporated Congregational Church Union* [1963] 1 All ER 326.

purchase notice expires, or, if the Department has served a notice stating that it will comply with the purchase notice, the date on which such response is served, whichever is the earlier (Art. 98(8)(b)). In a case where a disputed purchase notice has been referred to the Lands Tribunal and the Tribunal has not upheld the Department's objection to the purchase notice, the date on which the contract is deemed to come into existence is the date of the Tribunal's determination (Art. 98(8)(a)). The date for completion of the contract deemed to exist between the claimant and the Department is three months from the date on which the parties agree on the amount of compensation the Department is to pay the claimant, or, in default of agreement, three months from the date on which the Lands Tribunal determines that amount (Art. 98(5)). The parties may agree however that completion shall take place on some other date (Art. 98(5)). Whatever the date for completion is, if the Department fails on that date to pay the amount of compensation due, it becomes liable to pay interest from that date until the date of actual payment, unless the failure to pay arises from a cause other than the Department's act or default (Art. 98(6)).[26]

The amount of compensation to be paid by the Department for the estate of the claimant is the amount which the Department would have paid had the Department compulsorily acquired the estate of the claimant under Art. 87 of the 1991 Order on the date when the contract between the parties is deemed to come into existence (Art. 98(2)).[27] That amount, however, will be reduced where compensation is payable under s. 26 of the Land Development Values (Compensation) Act (NI) 1965 (Art. 99). In the event of the claimant and the Department failing to agree on the amount of compensation to be paid by the Department, the matter will be determined by the Lands Tribunal (Art. 98(3)).

(5) *Withdrawal of purchase notice*

Finally, a purchase notice may be withdrawn by the person serving it at any time before the compensation has been agreed between the claimant and the Department or determined by the Lands Tribunal, or at any time before the end of six weeks beginning on the date on which the compensation is agreed or determined (Art. 98(4)). Where a purchase notice is withdrawn, the contract deemed to have been made between the claimant and the Department is deemed not to have been made (Art. 98(4)).

---

26 The interest rate is the rate determined by the Department of Finance and Personnel under para. 18(2) of sch. 6 of the Local Government Act (NI) 1972: Art. 98(6)
27 See also Art. 98(7).

Appendices

Appendix A Planning (Use Classes) Order (NI) 1989

© HMSO

Schedule

Class 1: *Shops*
Use for all or any of the following purposes—
(a) for the retail sale of goods other than hot food,
(b) as a post office,
(c) for the sale of tickets or as a travel agency,
(d) for hairdressing,
(e) for the display of goods for retail sale,
(f) for the hiring out of domestic or personal goods or articles,
(g) for the reception of goods including clothes or fabrics to be washed, cleaned or repaired either on or off the premises
where the sale, display or service is to visiting members of the public.

Class 2: *Financial, professional and other services*
Use for the provision of services which it is appropriate to provide in a shopping area, where the services are provided principally to visiting members of the public including—
(a) financial services, or
(b) professional services.

Class 3: *Business*
Use as an office other than a use within Class 2 (financial, professional and other services).

Class 4: *Light Industrial*
Use for:
(a) research and development of products of processes, or
(b) any industrial process
being a use which can be carried out without detriment to amenity by reason of noise, vibration, smell, fumes, smoke, soot, ash, dust or grit.

Class 5: *General Industrial*
Use for the carrying on of any industrial process other than one falling within Class 4 or Classes 7[1] to 10.

---

1 Amendment introduced by Planning (Use Classes) (Amendment No 2) Order (NI) 1993.

Class 6: Special Industrial[2]

Class 7: Special Industrial
Use for any of the following processes, except where the process is ancillary to the getting, dressing or treatment of minerals and is carried on in or adjacent to a quarry or mine—
- (a) smelting, calcining, sintering or reducing ores, minerals, concentrates or mattes,
- (b) converting, refining, re-heating, annealing, hardening, melting, carburising, forging or casting metals or alloys other than pressure die-casting,
- (c) recovering metal from scrap or drosses or ashes,
- (d) galvanising,
- (e) pickling or treating metal in acid,
- (f) chromium plating.

Class 8: Special Industrial
Use for any of the following processes, except where the process is ancillary to the getting, dressing or treatment of minerals and is carried on in or adjacent to a quarry or mine—
- (a) burning bricks or pipes,
- (b) burning lime or dolomite,
- (c) producing zinc oxide, cement or alumina,
- (d) foaming, crushing, screening or heating minerals or slag,
- (e) processing pulverised fuel ash by heat,
- (f) producing carbonate of lime or hydrated lime,
- (g) producing inorganic pigments by calcining, roasting or grinding.

Class 9: Special Industrial
Use of any of the following processes—
- (a) distilling, refining or blending oils (other than petroleum or petroleum products),
- (b) producing or using cellulose or using other pressure sprayed metal finishes (other than in vehicle repair workshops in connection with minor repairs, or the application of plastic powder by the use of fluidised bed and electrostatic spray techniques),
- (c) boiling linseed oil or running gum,
- (d) processes involving the use of hot pitch or bitumen (except the use of bitumen in the manufacture of roofing felt at temperatures not exceeding 220°C and also the manufacture of coated roadstone),
- (e) stoving enamelled ware,
- (f) producing aliphatic esters of the lower fatty acids, butyric acid, caramel, hexamine, iodoform, napthols, resin products (excluding plastic moulding or extrusion operations and producing plastic sheets, rods, tubes, filaments, fibres or optical components produced by casting, calendering,

---

2 Class 6 omitted by Planning (Use Classes) (Amendment No. 2) Order (NI) 1993.

moulding, shaping or extrusion), salicylic acid or sulphonated organic compounds,
(g) producing rubber from scrap,
(h) chemical processes in which chlorphenols or chlorcresols are used as intermediates,
(i) manufacturing acetylene from calcium carbide,
(j) manufacturing, recovering or using pyridine or picolines, any methyl or ethyl amine or acrylates.

Class 10: *Special industrial*
Use for carrying on any of the following industries, businesses or trades—
(a) boiling blood, chitterlings, nettlings or soap,
(b) boiling, burning, grinding or steaming bones,
(c) boiling or cleaning tripe,
(d) breeding maggots from putrescible animal matter,
(e) cleaning, adapting or treating animal hair,
(f) curing fish,
(g) dealing in rags and bones (including receiving, storing, sorting or manipulating rags in, or likely to become in, an offensive condition, or any bones, rabbit skins, fat or putrescible animal products of a similar nature),
(h) dressing or scraping of fish skins,
(i) drying skins,
(j) making manure from bones, fish, offal, blood, spent hops, beans or other putrescible animal or vegetable matter,
(k) making or scraping guts,
(l) manufacturing animal charcoal, blood albumen, candles, catgut, glue, fish oil, size or feeding stuff for animals or poultry from meat, fish, blood, bone, feathers, fat or animal offal either in an offensive condition or subjected to any process causing noxious or injurious effluvia,
(m) melting, refining or extracting fat or tallow,
(n) preparing skins for working.

Class 11: *Storage or distribution*
Use for storage or as a distribution centre.

Class 12: *Guest houses and hostels*
Use as a boarding or guest house or as a hostel where, in each case, no significant element of care is provided.

Class 13: *Residential institutions*
Use—
(a) for the provision of residential accommodation and care to people in need of care (other than a use within Class 14 (dwellinghouses)),
(b) as a hospital or nursing home, or
(c) as a residential school, college or training centre.

Class 14: *Dwellinghouses*
   Use as a dwellinghouse (whether or not as sole or main residence)—
   (a) by a single person or by people living together as a family, or
   (b) by not more than 6 residents living together as a single household (including a household where care is provided for residents).

Class 15: *Non-residential institutions*
   Any use (not including a residential use)—
   (a) for the provision of any medical or health services except the use of premises attached to the residence of the consultant or practitioner,
   (b) as a creche, day nursery or day centre,
   (c) for the provision of education,
   (d) for the display of works of art (otherwise than for sale or hire),
   (e) as a museum,
   (f) as a public library or reading room, or
   (g) as a public hall or exhibition hall.

Class 16: *Assembly and leisure*
   Use as—
   (a) a bingo hall,
   (b) a cinema,
   (c) a concert hall,
   (d) a dance hall,
   (e) a swimming bath, skating rink, gymnasium or area for other indoor or outdoor sports or recreations, not involving motorised vehicles or firearms, or
   (f) a theatre.

Appendix B Planning (General Development) Order (NI) 1993

© HMSO

Schedule 1
Development permitted under Article 3[1]

Part 1
Development within the curtilage of a dwellinghouse

Class A.
Permitted development

A. The enlargement, improvement or other alteration of a dwellinghouse.

Development not permitted

A.1 Development is not permitted by Class A if—

(a) the design and external finishes are not in conformity with those of the original dwellinghouse;

(b) the cubic content of the resulting building exceeds the cubic content of the original dwellinghouse—

(i) in the case of a terrace house or in the case of a dwellinghouse in a conservation area, by more than 50 cubic metres or 10%, whichever is the greater;

(ii) in any other case by more than 70 cubic metres or 15%, whichever is the greater;

(iii) in any case by more than 115 cubic metres;

(c) the part of the building enlarged, improved or altered exceeds the height of the highest part of the roof of the original dwellinghouse;

(d) any part of the resulting building is nearer to any road which bounds its curtilage than the part of the original dwellinghouse nearest to that road;

(e) the part of the building enlarged, improved or altered is within 3 metres of the boundary of the curtilage of the dwellinghouse and exceeds 4 metres in height;

(f) the total area of ground covered by buildings within the curtilage (other than the original dwellinghouse) exceeds 50% of the total area of the curtilage (excluding the ground area of the original dwellinghouse);

---

1 Note however the restrictions contained in Art. 3 (4), (5), (6) and (7).

(g) it consists of or includes the installation, alteration or replacement of a satellite antenna (see Class G);

(h) it consists of or includes an alteration to any part of the roof (see Class B); or

(i) it would consist of or include the erection of a building within the curtilage of a listed building.

Interpretation of Class A

A.2 For the purposes of Class A—

(a) the erection within the curtilage of a dwellinghouse of any building with a cubic content greater than 10 cubic metres shall be treated as the enlargement of the dwellinghouse for all purposes including calculating cubic content where—

 (i) the dwellinghouse is in a conservation area; or

 (ii) in any other case, any part of that building is within 5 metres of any part of the dwellinghouse;

(b) where any part of the dwellinghouse is within 5 metres of an existing building within the same curtilage, that building shall be treated as forming part of the resulting building for the purpose of calculating the cubic content.

Class B Permitted development

B. The enlargement, improvement or other alteration of a dwellinghouse consisting of an addition or alteration to its roof.

Development not permitted

B.1 Development is not permitted by Class B if—

(a) the design and external finishes are not in conformity with those of the original dwellinghouse;

(b) any part of the dwellinghouse, as a result of the works, exceeds the height of the highest part of the existing roof;

(c) any part of the dwellinghouse, as a result of the works, extends more than 15 centimetres beyond the plane of any existing roof slope which fronts any road;

(d) it increases the cubic content of the dwellinghouse by more than 20 cubic metres, in the case of a terrace house, or 25 cubic metres in any other case; or

(e) the cubic content of the resulting building exceeds the cubic content of the original dwellinghouse—

 (i) in the case of a terraced house by more than 50 cubic metres or 10% whichever is the greater;

 (ii) in any other case by more than 70 cubic metres or 15% whichever is the greater; or

 (iii) in any case by more than 115 cubic metres;

(f) the dwellinghouse is in a conservation area.

Appendix B 273

**Class C
Permitted
development**

C. The erection or construction of a porch outside any external door of a dwellinghouse.

*Development
not permitted*

C.1 Development is not permitted by Class C if—
    (a) the design and external finishes are not in conformity with those of the original dwellinghouse;
    (b) the ground area (measured externally) of the structure exceeds 2 square metres;
    (c) any part of the structure is more than 3 metres above ground level; or
    (d) any part of the structure is within 2 metres of any boundary of the curtilage of the dwellinghouse with a road.

**Class D
Permitted
development**

D. The provision within the curtilage of a dwellinghouse of any building or enclosure, swimming or other pool required for a purpose incidental to the enjoyment of the dwellinghouse, or the maintenance, improvement or other alteration to such a building or enclosure.

*Development
not permitted*

D.1 Development is not permitted by Class D if—
    (a) any part of the building or enclosure to be constructed or provided is nearer to any road which bounds the curtilage than the part of the original dwellinghouse nearest to that road;
    (b) any building to be constructed or provided has a cubic content greater that 10 cubic metres and any part of it is within 5 metres of any part of the dwellinghouse;
    (c) the height of the building or enclosure to be constructed or erected exceeds—
        (i) 4 metres, in the case of a building with a ridged roof; or
        (ii) 3 metres, in any other case;
    (d) the total area of ground covered by buildings or enclosures to be constructed or erected within the curtilage (other than the original dwellinghouse) exceeds 50% of the total area of the curtilage (excluding the ground area of the original dwellinghouse); or
    (e) in the case of land within a conservation area, an area of outstanding natural beauty, a National Park, or land within the curtilage of a listed building, it consists of the provision, alteration or improvement of a building with a cubic content greater than 10 cubic metres.

Interpretation of Class D	D.2	For the purposes of Class D 'purpose incidental to the enjoyment of the dwellinghouse' includes the keeping of poultry, bees, pet animals, birds or other livestock for the domestic needs or personal enjoyment of the occupants of the dwellinghouse, but excludes the keeping of pigeons.

Class E Permitted development

E. **The provision, within the curtilage of a dwellinghouse, of a hard surface for any purpose incidental to the enjoyment of the dwellinghouse.**

Class F Permitted development

F. **The erection or provision, within the curtilage of a dwellinghouse, of a container for the storage of oil or liquefied petroleum gas for domestic purposes.**

Development not permitted

F.1 Development is not permitted by Class F if—
 (a) the capacity of the container exceeds—
   (i) 3,500 litres, in the case of oil; or
   (ii) 2,500 litres, in the case of liquefied petroleum gas;
 (b) any part of the container is above the level of the ground by more than—
   (i) 3 metres, in the case of an oil container; or
   (ii) 2 metres, in the case of a liquefied petroleum gas container;
 (c) any part of the container is nearer to any road which bounds the curtilage than the part of the original building nearest to that road.

Class G Permitted development

G. **The installation, alteration or replacement of a satellite antenna on a dwellinghouse or within the curtilage of a dwellinghouse.**

Development not permitted

G.1 Development is not permitted by Class G if—
 (a) the size of the antenna (excluding any projecting feed element) when measured in any dimension exceeds 90 centimetres;
 (b) there is any other satellite antenna on the dwellinghouse or within its curtilage;
 (c) the highest part of the antenna to be installed on a dwellinghouse is higher than the highest part of the roof on which it is installed;
 (d) any part of the antenna projects beyond the forward-most part of any wall of the original dwellinghouse which fronts on to a road;

(e) the antenna extends beyond the plane of any existing roof slope which fronts on to a road;

(f) the dwellinghouse is in a conservation area, an area of outstanding natural beauty, or a National Park.

Interpretation of Part 1

For the purposes of Part 1—
'resulting building' means the dwellinghouse as enlarged, improved or altered, taking into account any enlargement, improvement or alteration to the original dwellinghouse, whether permitted by this Part or not.

Part 2
Minor Operations

Class A Permitted development

A. The erection, construction, maintenance, improvement or alteration of a gate, fence, wall or other means of enclosure.

Development not permitted

A.1 Development is not permitted by Class A if—

(a) the height of any gate, fence, wall or means of enclosure erected or constructed adjacent to a road used or designed to be used by vehicular traffic exceeds 1 metre above ground level;

(b) the height of any other gate, fence, wall or means of enclosure erected or constructed exceeds 2 metres above ground level;

(c) the height of any gate, fence, wall or means of enclosure maintained, improved or altered exceeds its former height or the height referred to in sub-paragraph (a) or (b) as the height appropriate to it if erected or constructed, whichever is the greater;

(d) it involves development within the curtilage of, or to a gate, fence, wall or other means of enclosure, surrounding a listed building; or

(e) it involves development on land determined by the Department as a private street in accordance with Article 3(1) of the Private Streets (Northern Ireland) Order 1980.

Class B Permitted development

B. The formation, laying out and construction or alteration of a means of access to a road which is not a special, trunk or classified road, where that access is required in connection with development permitted by any class in this Schedule (other than by Class A of this Part).

*Development
not permitted*

B.1 Development is not permitted in Class B if it is within a site of archaeological interest.

**Class C
Permitted
development**

C. The painting of the exterior of any building or work.

*Development
not permitted*

C.1 Development is not permitted by Class C where the painting is for the purpose of advertisement, announcement or direction.

*Interpretation of
Class C*

C.2 In Class C 'painting' includes any application of colour.

*Part 3
Changes of Use*

**Class A
Permitted
development**

A. Development consisting of a change of use of a building to a use falling within Class 1 (shops) or Class 2 (financial, professional and other services) of the Schedule to the Use Classes Order from a use as a betting office or from a use for the sale of food or drink for consumption on the premises or of hot food for consumption off the premises.

**Class B
Permitted
development**

B. Development consisting of a change of the use of a building—
  (a) to a use falling within Class 4 (light industrial) of the Schedule to the Use Classes Order from a use falling within Class 5 (general industrial);
  (b) to a use falling within Class 4 (light industrial) of that Schedule from a use falling within Class 11 (storage and distribution);
  (c) to a use falling within Class 11 (storage and distribution) of that Schedule from a use falling within Class 4 (light industrial) or Class 5 (general industrial).

*Development
not permitted*

B.1 Development is not permitted by Class B where the change is to or from a use falling within Class 11 of the Schedule to the Use Classes Order if the change of use relates to more than 235 square metres of floorspace in the building.

Class C Permitted development

C. Development consisting of a change of use of any building with a display window at ground floor level to a use falling within Class 1 (shops) to the Schedule to the Use Classes Order from a use falling within Class 2 (financial, professional and other services).

Class D Permitted development

D. Development consisting of a change of use of a building to a use falling within Class 14 (dwellinghouses) of the Schedule to the Use Classes Order from a use falling within Class 12 (guest houses and hostels) or Class 13 (residential institutions).

Part 4
Temporary Buildings and Uses

Class A Permitted development

A. The provision on land of buildings, moveable structures, works, plant or machinery required temporarily in connection with and for the duration of operations being or to be carried out on, in, under or over that land or on land adjoining that land.

Development not permitted

A.1 Development is not permitted by Class A if—
 (a) the operations referred to are mining operations;
 (b) planning permission is required for those operations but is not granted; or
 (c) it is within a site of archaeological interest.

Conditions

A.2 Development is permitted by Class A subject to the conditions that, when the operations have been carried out—
 (a) any building, structure, works, plant or machinery permitted by this Class shall be removed; and
 (b) any adjoining land on which development permitted by this Class is carried out shall as soon and so far as practicable, be reinstated to its condition before that development was carried out.

Class B Permitted development

B. The use of any land for any purpose for not more than 28 days in total in any calendar year, of which not more than 14 days in total may be for any purpose referred to in paragraph B.2, and the provision on the land of any moveable structure for the purposes of the permitted use.

Development not permitted	B.1 Development is not permitted by Class B if— (a) the land in question is a building or is within the curtilage of a building; (b) the use of the land is for a caravan site; or (c) the land is within a site of archaeological interest.
Interpretation of Class B	B.2 The purposes mentioned in Class B are— (a) the holding of a market; (b) motor car and motorcycle racing including trials of speed, and practising for these activities.

Part 5
Caravan Sites

Class A Permitted development	A. **The use of land, other than a building, as a caravan site in any of the circumstances referred to in paragraph A.2.**
Conditions	A.1 The use permitted by Class A shall be discontinued when the circumstances specified in paragraph A.2 cease to exist and all caravans on the site shall then be removed.
Interpretation of Part 5	A.2 The circumstances mentioned in this Part are those specified in paragraphs 2, 3 and 6 to 10 of the Schedule to the Caravans Act (Northern Ireland) 1963, but in relation to those mentioned in paragraph 10 do not include use for winter quarters.

Part 6
Agricultural Buildings and Operations

Class A Permitted development	A. **The carrying out on agricultural land comprised in an agricultural unit of—** **(a) works for the erection, extension or alteration of a building; or** **(b) any excavation or engineering operations;** **reasonably necessary for the purposes of agriculture within that unit.**

Development not permitted

A.1 Development is not permitted by Class A if—
  (a) the development is on agricultural land less than 0.5 hectares in area;
  (b) it consists of or includes the erection, extension or alteration of a dwelling;
  (c) a building, structure or works not designed for the purposes of agriculture is provided on the land;
  (d) the nearest part of any building or structure so erected or extended is—
     (i) more than 75 metres from the nearest part of a group of principal farm buildings; and
     (ii) where the building or structure is over 300 square metres in ground area is less than 75 metres from a dwellinghouse (other than the dwellinghouse of any person engaged in agricultural operations on the said unit);
  (e) the ground area to be covered by—
     (i) any works or structure (other than a fence) for the purposes of accommodating livestock or any plant or machinery arising from engineering operations; or
     (ii) any building erected or any building as extended or altered, other than a building to which paragraph A.1(d) applies, by virtue of Class A;
     exceeds 300 square metres, calculated as described in paragraph A.2;
  (f) the height of any part of the building, structure or works within 3 kilometres of the perimeter of an aerodrome exceeds 3 metres, or 12 metres in any other case;
  (g) any part of the development is within 24 metres from the nearest part of a special road, or within 24 metres of the middle of a trunk or a first or second-class road or 9 metres from the middle of other classes of road.

Interpretation of Class A

A.2 For the purposes of Class A—
  (1)(a) the area of 0.5 hectares shall be calculated without taking into account any separate parcels of land;
  (b) the ground area referred to in paragraph A.1(e) is the ground area which the proposed development covers together with the ground area of any building (other than a dwellinghouse), or any structure, works, plant or machinery within the same unit which is being provided or has been provided within the preceding 2 years and any part of which is within 75 metres of proposed development.

(2) 'agricultural land' has the meaning assigned to it by the Agriculture Act (Northern Ireland) 1949;

'agricultural unit' means land which is occupied as a unit for the purposes of agriculture other than fish farming but includes any dwellinghouse or other building occupied by the same person for the purpose of farming the land by the person who occupies the same unit;

'building' does not include anything resulting from engineering operations.

Class B
Permitted development

B. The winning and working on land held or occupied with land used for the purposes of agriculture of any minerals reasonably necessary for agricultural purposes within the agricultural unit of which it forms part.

Development not permitted

B.1 Development is not permitted by Class B if any excavation is within 24 metres of the nearest part of a special road or within 24 metres of the middle of a trunk or a first or second-class road or 9 metres from the middle of other classes of road.

Conditions

B.2 Development is permitted by Class B subject to the conditions—

(a) that no mineral extracted during the course of the operation shall be moved to any place outside the land from which it is extracted, except to land which is held or occupied with that land and is used for the purposes of agriculture;

(b) the surface of the land shall be levelled and any topsoil replaced as the uppermost layer;

(c) the land shall so far as practicable be restored to its former condition before the extraction took place.

Interpretation of Class B

B.3 For the purposes of Class B the expression 'purposes of agriculture' includes fertilizing the land used for the purposes of agriculture, and the maintenance, improvement or alteration of any buildings, structures or works occupied or used for such purposes on land so used.

Class C
Permitted development

C. The construction, formation, laying out or alteration of a means of access to a road.

*Development
not permitted*

C.1 Development is not permitted in Class C if—
   (a) it is required in connection with development for which a planning application is necessary under Part IV of the 1991 Order; or
   (b) the land is within a site of archaeological interest.

Part 7
Forestry Buildings and Operations

**Class A
Permitted
development**

A. The carrying out on land used for the purposes of forestry, including afforestation, of development reasonably necessary for those purposes consisting of—

   (a) works for the erection, extension or alteration of a building;

   (b) the formation, alteration or maintenance of private ways;

   (c) operations on that land, or on land held or occupied with that land, to obtain the materials required for the formation, alteration or maintenance of such ways;

   (d) other operations (not including engineering or mining operations).

*Development
not permitted*

A.1 Development is not permitted by Class A if—
   (a) it consists of or includes the provision or alteration of a dwelling;
   (b) the height of any building or works within 3 kilometres of the perimeter of an aerodrome exceeds 3 metres in height; or
   (c) any part of the development is within 24 metres of the nearest part of a special road or within 24 metres of the middle of a trunk or a first or second-class road or 9 metres from the middle of other classes of road.

Conditions

A.2 Development is permitted in Class A(c) subject to the following conditions—
   (a) the surface of the land shall be levelled and any topsoil replaced as the uppermost layer; and
   (b) the land shall, so far as practicable, be restored to its condition before the development took place.

Part 8
Industrial and Warehouse Development

Class A
Permitted development

A. The extension or alteration of an industrial building or a warehouse.

Development not permitted

A.1 Development is not permitted by Class A if—
   (a) the building as extended or altered is to be used for purposes other than those of the undertaking concerned;
   (b) the building is to be used for a purpose other than—
      (i) in the case of an industrial building, the carrying out of an industrial process or the provision of employee facilities;
      (ii) in the case of a warehouse, storage or distribution or the provision of employee facilities;
   (c) the height of the building as extended or altered exceeds the height of the original building;
   (d) the cubic content of the original building is exceeded by more than 20%;
   (e) the floorspace of the original building is exceeded by more than 750 square metres;
   (f) it materially affects the external appearance of the premises of the undertaking concerned;
   (g) any part of the development is within 5 metres of any boundary of the curtilage of the premises;
   (h) any part of the development is carried out within any boundary of the curtilage of the premises which adjoins the curtilage of any dwellinghouse or flat;
   (i) the development leads to a reduction in the space available for the parking or turning of vehicles;
   (j) the development is in a conservation area, an area of outstanding natural beauty or a National Park.

Conditions

A.2 Development is permitted in Class A subject to the conditions that any building extended or altered shall not be used to provide employee facilities—
   (a) between 7.00 p.m. and 6.30 a.m. for employees other than those present at the premises of the undertaking for the purposes of their employment;
   (b) if a notifiable quantity of a hazardous substance is present at the premises of the undertaking.

Interpretation of Class A

A.3 For the purposes of Class A—

(a) the erection of any additional building within the curtilage of another building (whether by virtue of this category or otherwise) and used in connection with it is to be treated as the extension of that building, and the additional building is not to be treated as an original building;

(b) where two or more original buildings are within the same curtilage and are used for the same undertaking, they are to be treated as a single original building in making any measurement;

(c) 'employee facilities' means social care or recreational facilities provided for employees of the undertaking, including creche facilities provided for the children of such employees.

Class B Permitted development

B. Development carried out on industrial land for the purposes of an industrial process consisting of—

(a) the installation of additional or replacement plant or machinery or structures or erections of the nature of plant or machinery;

(b) the provision, rearrangement or replacement of a sewer, main, pipe, cable or other apparatus; or

(c) the provision, rearrangement or replacement of a private way, private railway, siding or conveyor.

Development not permitted

B.1 Development is not permitted in Class B(a) if—

(a) it materially affects the external appearance of the premises of the undertaking concerned; or

(b) any plant or machinery exceeds a height of 15 metres above ground level or the height of anything replaced, whichever is greater.

Interpretation of Class B

B.2 In Class B 'industrial land' means land used for the carrying out of an industrial process, including land used for the purpose of an industrial undertaking as a dock, harbour or quay, but does not include land in or adjacent to and occupied together with a mine.

Class C Permitted development

C. The creation of a hard surface within the curtilage of an industrial building or warehouse to be used for the purpose of the undertaking concerned.

Development not permitted

C.1 Development is not permitted in Class C category if it would involve the removal of trees.

Interpretation of Part 8

D. For the purposes of Part 8,
In Classes A and C of this Part—

'industrial building' means a building used for the carrying out of an industrial process and includes a building used for the carrying out of such a process on land used as a dock, harbour or quay for the purpose of an industrial undertaking but does not include a building on land in or adjacent to and occupied together with a mine;

'warehouse' does not include a building on land in or adjacent to and occupied together with a mine.

Part 9
Repairs to Unadopted Street and Private Ways

Class A Permitted development

A. The carrying out on land within the boundaries of an unadopted street or private way of works required for the maintenance or improvement of the street or way.

Part 10
Repairs to services

Class A Permitted development

A. The carrying out of any works for the purposes of inspecting, repairing or renewing any sewer, main, pipe, cable or other apparatus, including breaking open any land for that purpose.

Part 11
Development under Local or Private Acts or Orders

Class A Permitted development

A. Development is authorised by—
 (a) any local or private Act of Parliament; or
 (b) by any order approved by both Houses of Parliament;
which designates specifically the nature of the development authorised and the land upon which it may be carried out.

Conditions

A.1 Development is not permitted by Class A if it consists of or includes—

(a) the erection, construction, alteration or extension of any building, bridge, aqueduct, pier or dam; or

(b) the construction, formation, laying out or alteration of a means of access to any road used by vehicular traffic;

unless the prior approval of the detailed plans and specifications is first obtained from the Department.

Part 12
Development by District Councils

Class A
Permitted development

A. The erection or construction and the maintenance, improvement or other alteration by a district council of—

(a) any small ancillary building, works or equipment on land belonging to or maintained by it required for the purposes of any function exercised by it on that land;

(b) lamp standards, information kiosks, public shelters and seats, public drinking fountains, refuse bins or baskets, and similar structures or works required in connection with the operation of any public service administered by it.

Interpretation of Part 12

A.1 For purposes of this Part a reference to any small building, works or equipment is a reference to building, works or equipment not exceeding 4 metres in height or 200 cubic metres in capacity.

Part 13
Development by Statutory and Other Undertakers

Class A

Railway undertakings

Permitted development

A. Development by railway undertakers on their operational land, required in connection with the movement of traffic by rail.

Development not permitted

A.1 Development is not permitted by Class A if it consists of or includes—

(a) the construction of a railway;

(b) the construction or erection of a hotel, railway station or bridge;

(c) the construction or erection otherwise than wholly within a railway station of a residential building, an office, or a building used for manufacturing or repair work; or

(d) the land is within a site of archaeological interest.

Interpretation of Class A

A.2 For the purposes of Class A references to the construction or erection of any building or structure includes references to the reconstruction or alteration of a building or structure where its design or external appearance would be materially affected.

Class B

Dock, pier, harbour or water transport undertakings

Permitted development

B. Development on operational land by statutory undertakers or their lessees in respect of dock, pier, harbour or water transport undertakings, required—

(a) for the purposes of shipping; or

(b) in connection with the embarking, disembarking, loading, discharging or transport of passengers, livestock or goods at a dock, pier or harbour, or the movement of traffic by any railway forming part of the undertaking.

Development not permitted

B.1 Development is not permitted by Class B if—

(a) it consists of or includes the construction or erection of a bridge or other building not required in connection with the handling of traffic; or

(b) the land is within a site of archaeological interest.

Interpretation of Class B

B.2 For the purposes of Class B references to the construction or erection of any building or structure includes references to the reconstruction or alteration of a building or structure where its design or external appearance would be materially affected.

Class C

Electricity undertakings

Permitted development

C. Development by electricity undertakers for the generation, transmission, distribution and supply of electricity for the purposes of the undertaking consisting of—

(a) the laying underground of pipes, cables or any other apparatus, and the construction of shafts and tunnels reasonably necessary in connection with such pipes, cables or apparatus;

(b) the installation in an electric line of—

(i) **feeder or service pillars; or**

(ii) **sub-stations enclosed in a chamber not exceeding 40 cubic metres in capacity; or**

(iii) **sub-stations enclosed in an underground chamber;**

(c) **the installation of service lines for individual consumers from an electric line;**

(d) **the addition or replacement of a single fibre optic telecommunications cable to an existing overhead line;**

(e) **the sinking of boreholes to ascertain the nature of the subsoil and the installation of any plant or machinery reasonably necessary in connection with such boreholes;**

(f) **the extension or alteration of buildings on operational land;**

(g) **the erection on operational land of the undertaking of a building solely for the protection of plant or machinery;**

(h) **any other development carried out in, on, over or under the operational land of the undertaking.**

Development not permitted

C.1 Development is not permitted by Class C if—

(a) in the case of any Class C(*b*) development involving the installation of a chamber for housing apparatus exceeding 40 cubic metres in capacity, that installation is carried out at or above ground level, or under a road used by vehicular traffic;

(b) in the case of Class C(*c*) development, the length of the line exceeds 100 metres;

(c) in the case of any Class C(*f*) development—

(i) the height of the original building is exceeded;

(ii) the cubic content of the original building is exceeded by more than 20%;

(iii) the floorspace of the original building is exceeded by more than 750 square metres;

(iv) it materially affects the external appearance of the buildings concerned;

(v) the development is in a conservation area, an area of outstanding natural beauty or a National Park;

(d) in the case of any Class C(*g*) development, the building exceeds 15 metres in height;

(e) in the case of any Class C(*h*) development, it consists of or includes—

(i) the erection of a building, or the reconstruction or alteration of a building where its design or external appearance would be materially affected; or

(ii) the installation or erection by way of addition or replacement of any plant or machinery exceeding 18 metres in height or the height of any plant or machinery replaced, whichever is the greater; or

(f) the land is within a site of archaeological interest.

Conditions

C.2 Development is permitted by Class C subject to the following conditions—

(a) in the case of any Class C(e) development, on the completion of that development, or at the end of a period of 6 months from the beginning of that development (whichever is the sooner) any such plant or machinery shall be removed and the land shall be restored as soon and so far as practicable to its condition before the development took place;

(b) in the case of any Class C(g) development, approval from the Department of details of the design and external appearance of the building shall be obtained before development is begun.

Class D

Gas undertakings

Permitted development

D. Development by a gas undertaker required for the purposes of its undertaking consisting of—

(a) the laying underground of mains, pipes or other apparatus;

(b) the installation in a gas distribution system of apparatus for measuring, recording, controlling or varying the pressure, flow or volume of gas, and structures for housing such apparatus;

(c) any other development carried out in, on, over or under the operational land of the gas undertaking.

Development not permitted

D.1 Development is not permitted by Class D if—

(a) in the case of Class D(b) development involving the installation of a structure for housing apparatus exceeding 29 cubic metres in capacity, that installation is carried out at or above ground level, or under any road used by vehicular traffic;

(b) in the case of Class D(c) development—

Appendix B 289

  (i) it consists of or includes the erection of a building, or the reconstruction or alteration of a building where its design or external appearance is materially affected;
  (ii) it involves the installation of any plant or machinery or structures or erections of the nature of plant or machinery, exceeding 15 metres in height, or capable without addition of being extended to a height exceeding 15 metres; or
  (iii) it consists of or includes the replacement of any plant or machinery, by plant or machinery exceeding 15 metres in height or exceeding the height of the plant or machinery replaced, whichever is the greater;
(d) the land is within a site of archaeological interest.

Conditions

D.2 Development is permitted by Class D(c) subject to the condition that approval from the Department of details of the design and external appearance of any building shall be obtained before the development is begun.

Interpretation of Class D

D.3 For the purposes of Class D—
 'Gas undertaker' means an undertaker established under Article 14(1) of the Gas (Northern Ireland) Order 1977.

Class E   **Road passenger transport undertakings**

Permitted development

E. **Development required for the purposes of the undertaking consisting of—**
 (a) the installation of telephone cables and apparatus, huts, stop posts and signs required in connection with the operation of public service vehicles;
 (b) the erection or construction and the maintenance, improvement or other alteration of passenger shelters and barriers for the control of people waiting to enter public service vehicles;
 (c) any other development on operational land of the undertaking.

Development not permitted

E.1 Development is not permitted by Class E(c) if it consists of—
 (a) the erection of a building or the reconstruction or alteration of a building where the design or external appearance would be materially altered;

(b) the installation or erection by way of addition or replacement of any plant or machinery which exceeds 15 metres in height or the height of any plant or machinery it replaces, whichever is the greater; or

(c) the land is within a site of archaeological interest.

Class F   **Lighthouse undertakings**

Permitted development

F. **Development required for the purposes of the functions of a general or local lighthouse authority under the Merchant Shipping Act 1894 and any other statutory provision made with respect to a local lighthouse authority, or in the exercise by a local lighthouse authority of rights, powers or duties acquired by usage prior to that Act.**

Development not permitted

F.1 Development is not permitted by Class F if—

(a) it consists of or includes the erection of offices, or the reconstruction or alteration of offices where their design or external appearance would be materially affected; or

(b) the land is within a site of archaeological interest.

Class G   **Post Office**

Permitted development

G. **Development required for the purpose of the Post Office consisting of—**

(a) the installation of posting boxes or self-service machines;

(b) any other development carried out in, on, over or under the operational land of the undertaking.

Development not permitted

G.1 Development is not permitted by Class G if—

(a) it consists of or includes the erection of a building, or the reconstruction or alteration of a building where its design or external appearance is materially affected;

(b) it consists of or includes the installation or erection by way of addition or replacement of any plant or machinery which exceeds 15 metres in height or the height of any existing plant or machinery, whichever is the greater; or

(c) the land is within a site of archaeological interest.

Part 14
Development by Civil Aviation Authority

Class A	**Development by the Civil Aviation Authority within an aerodrome**
Permitted development	A. The carrying out by the Civil Aviation Authority or its agents, within the perimeter of an aerodrome at which the authority provides air traffic control services, of development in connection with— (a) the provision of air traffic control services; (b) the navigation of aircraft using the aerodrome; or (c) the monitoring of the movement of aircraft using the aerodrome.
Class B	**Development by the Civil Aviation Authority for air traffic control and navigation**
Permitted development	B. The carrying out on operational land of the Civil Aviation Authority by the authority or its agents of development in connection with— **(a) the provision of air traffic control services;** **(b) the navigation of aircraft; or** **(c) monitoring the movement of aircraft.**
Development not permitted	B.1 Development is not permitted by Class B if— (*a*) any building erected is used for a purpose other than housing equipment used in connection with the provision of air traffic control services, assisting the navigation of aircraft or monitoring the movement of aircraft; (*b*) any building erected exceeds a height of 4 metres; or (*c*) it consists of the installation or erection of any radar or radio mast, antenna or other apparatus which exceeds 15 metres in height, or, where an existing mast, antenna or apparatus is replaced, the height of that mast, antenna or apparatus, if greater; (*d*) the development is in a conservation area, an area of outstanding natural beauty, a National Park, or within a site of archaeological interest.
Class C	**Development by the Civil Aviation Authority in an emergency**

Permitted development	C. The use of land by or on behalf of the Civil Aviation Authority in an emergency to station moveable apparatus replacing unserviceable apparatus.
Condition	C.1 Development is permitted by Class C subject to the conditions that on or before the expiry of a period of 6 months beginning with the date on which the use began, the use shall cease, and any apparatus shall be removed, and the land shall be restored so far as practicable to its condition before the development took place.
Class D	**Development by the Civil Aviation Authority for air traffic control etc.**
Permitted development	D. The use of land by or on behalf of the Civil Aviation Authority to provide services and facilities in connection with— (a) the provision of air traffic control services; (b) the navigation of aircraft; or (c) the monitoring of aircraft; and the erection or placing of moveable structures on land for the purpose of that use.
Development not permitted	D.1 Development is not permitted in Class D if the land is within a site of archaeological interest.
Condition	D.2 Development is permitted by Class D subject to the condition that on or before the expiry of the period of 6 months beginning with the date on which the use began, the use shall cease, and any structure shall be removed, and the land shall be restored to its condition before the development took place.
Class E	**Development by the Civil Aviation Authority for surveys etc.**
Permitted development	E. The use of land by or on behalf of the Civil Aviation Authority for the stationing and operation of apparatus in connection with the carrying out of surveys or investigations.
Condition	E.1 Development is permitted by Class E subject to the condition that on or before the expiry of 6 months beginning with the date on which the use began, the use shall cease, and any apparatus shall be removed, and the land shall be restored to its condition before the development took place.

Part 15
Aviation Development

Class A		**Development at an aerodrome**
Permitted development	A.	The carrying out on operational land by an aerodrome undertaking of development (including the erection or alteration of an operational building) in connection with the provision of services and facilities at an aerodrome.
Development not permitted	A.1	Development is not permitted by Class A if—

(1) It consists of or includes—
  (a) the construction or extension of a runway;
  (b) the construction of a passenger terminal;
  (c) the extension or alteration of a passenger terminal, where the floorspace of the building as existing at the date of coming into operation of this Order or, if built after that date, of the building as built, is exceeded by more than 15%;
  (d) the erection of a building other than an operational building;
  (e) the alteration or reconstruction of a building other than an operational building, where its design or external appearance is materially affected; or

(2) It is within a conservation area, an area of outstanding natural beauty, a National Park, or a site of archaeological interest.

Condition   A.2 Development is permitted by Class A subject to the condition that the aerodrome undertaking consults the Department before carrying out any development unless the development—
  (a) is urgently required for the efficient running of the aerodrome; and
  (b) consists of the carrying out of works, or the erection or construction of a structure or of an ancillary building, or the placing on land of equipment, and the works, structure, building or equipment do not exceed 4 metres in height or 200 cubic metres in capacity.

Interpretation of Class A   A.3 For the purposes of Class A—
  (a) floorspace shall be calculated by external measurement and without taking account of the floorspace in any pier or satellite;

(b) 'operational building' means a building, other than a hotel, required in connection with the movement or maintenance of aircraft, or with the embarking, disembarking, loading, discharge or transport of passengers, livestock or goods at an aerodrome.

Class B — **Air navigation development at an aerodrome**

Permitted development

B. **The carrying out on operational land within the perimeter of an aerodrome by an aerodrome undertaking of development in connection with—**
   (a) the provision of air traffic control services;
   (b) the navigation of aircraft using the aerodrome; or
   (c) the monitoring of the movement of aircraft using the aerodrome.

Class C — **Air navigation development near an aerodrome**

Permitted development

C. **The carrying out on operational land outside but within 8 kilometres of the perimeter of an aerodrome, by an aerodrome undertaking, of development in connection with—**
   (a) the provision of air traffic control services;
   (b) the navigation of aircraft using the aerodrome; or
   (c) the monitoring of the movement of aircraft using the aerodrome.

Development not permitted

C.1 Development is not permitted by Class C if—
   (a) any building erected is used for a purpose other than housing equipment used in connection with the provision of air traffic control services, with assisting the navigation of aircraft, or with monitoring the movement of aircraft using the aerodrome;
   (b) any building erected exceeds a height of 4 metres;
   (c) it consists of the installation or erection of any radar or radio mast or antenna or other apparatus which exceeds 15 metres in height, or, where an existing mast, antenna or apparatus is replaced, the height of that mast, antenna or apparatus if greater;
   (d) the development is in a conservation area, an area of outstanding natural beauty, a National Park or a site of archaeological interest.

Class D	**Use of aerodrome buildings managed by an aerodrome undertaking**
Permitted development	D. **The use of buildings within the perimeter of an aerodrome managed by an aerodrome undertaking for purposes connected with air transport services or other flying activities at that aerodrome.**
Interpretation of Part 15	E. For the purposes of Part 15— 'undertaking' in relation to an aerodrome has the meaning assigned to it by section 19(1) of the Aerodromes Act (Northern Ireland) 1971.

Part 16
Mineral Exploration

Class A **Permitted development**	A. **Development on any land during a period not exceeding 4 months consisting of—** **(a) the drilling of boreholes;** **(b) the carrying out of seismic surveys; or** **(c) the making of other excavations;** **for the purpose of mineral exploration, and the provision or assembly on that land or adjoining land of any structure required in connection with any of those operations.**
Development not permitted	A.1 Development is not permitted by Class A if— (a) the developer has not previously notified the Department in writing giving details of the location of the proposed development, target minerals, details of plant and operations and anticipated timescale; (b) any operation is within an area of special scientific interest or site of archaeological interest; (c) any explosive charge of more than 1 kilogram is used; (d) any structure assembled or provided would exceed 3 metres in height where such structure would be within 3 kilometres of an aerodrome.
Conditions	A.2 Development is permitted by Class A subject to the following conditions— (a) the development shall be carried out in accordance with the details contained in the developer's written notification to the Department referred to in paragraph A.1(a), unless the Department otherwise agrees in writing;

(b) no trees on the land shall be removed, felled, lopped or topped and no other thing shall be done on the land likely to harm or damage any trees, unless the Department so agrees in writing;

(c) before any excavation (other than a borehole) is made, any topsoil and any subsoil shall be separately removed from the land to be excavated and stored separately from other excavated material and from each other;

(d) within a period of 28 days from the cessation of operations unless the Department, in a particular case, agrees otherwise in writing—

   (i) any borehole shall be adequately sealed;
   (ii) any excavation shall be filled from material from the site;
   (iii) any structure permitted by Class A and any waste material arising from development permitted by Class A shall be removed from the land;
   (iv) the surface of the land on which any operations have been carried out shall be levelled and any topsoil replaced as the uppermost layer; and
   (v) the land shall, so far as is practicable, be restored to its condition before the development took place.

Interpretation of Part 16

A.3 For the purposes of this Part—

'mineral exploration' means ascertaining the presence, extent or quality of any deposit of a mineral with a view to exploiting that mineral;

'structure' means a building, plant or machinery or other structure.

Part 17
Development by Telecommunications Code System Operators

Class A Permitted development

A. Development by or on behalf of a telecommunications code system operator for the purposes of the operator's telecommunication system in, on, over or under land controlled by that operator or in accordance with his licence, consisting of—

(a) **the installation, alteration or replacement of any telecommunications apparatus;**

(b) **the use of land in an emergency for a period not exceeding 6 months to station and operate**

Appendix B

moveable telecommunications apparatus required for the replacement of unserviceable telecommunications apparatus, including the provision of moveable structures on the land for the purposes of that use;

(c) the use of land for a period of 6 months for the purpose of erecting temporary buildings for housing moveable telecommunications apparatus all in connection with development authorised by a grant of planning permission; or

(d) any building, works or equipment not exceeding 4 metres in height or 200 cubic metres in capacity.

Development not permitted	A.1 Development is not permitted by Class A(a) if—

    (a) in the case of the installation of apparatus (other than on a building or other structure) the apparatus exceeds a height of 15 metres above ground level;

    (b) in the case of the alteration or replacement of apparatus already installed (other than on a building or other structure), the apparatus, when altered or replaced exceeds the height of the existing apparatus or a height of 15 metres above ground level, whichever is the greater;

    (c) (i) subject to sub-paragraph (ii), in the case of the installation, alteration or replacement of apparatus on a building or other structure, the height of the apparatus (taken by itself) exceeds—

        (aa) 15 metres, where it is installed, or is to be installed, on a building or other structure which is 30 metres or more in height; or

        (bb) 10 metres in any other case;

    (ii) the highest part of the apparatus when so installed, altered or replaced exceeds the height of the highest part of the building or structure by more than—

        (aa) 10 metres, in the case of a building or structure which is 30 metres or more in height;

        (bb) 8 metres, in the case of a building or structure which is more than 15 metres but less than 30 metres in height;

        (cc) 6 metres in any other case;

    (d) in the case of the installation or replacement of any apparatus other than—

        (i) a mast or tower;

        (ii) any kind of antenna;

        (iii) a public call box; or

(iv) any apparatus which does not project above the level of the surface of the ground,

where the ground or base area of the structure exceeds 1.5 square metres;

(e) in the case of the installation, alteration or replacement on a building or structure of a microwave antenna or apparatus which includes or is intended for the support of such an antenna—

(i) the size of the antenna when measured in any dimension exceeds 1.3 metres (excluding any projecting feed element);

(ii) the development results in more than 2 microwave antennae on a building or 10 microwave antennae or any other structure; or

(iii) the building is a dwellinghouse;

(f) in the case of development in a conservation area, an area of outstanding natural beauty or a National Park, it consists of—

(i) the installation or alteration of a microwave antenna or of any apparatus which includes or is intended for the support of such an antenna; or

(ii) the replacement of such an antenna or such apparatus by an antenna or apparatus which differs from that which is being replaced,

unless the development is carried out in an emergency.

Conditions A.2 (1) Development is permitted by Class A(*a*) subject to the condition that any antenna or supporting apparatus installed, altered or replaced on a building in accordance with that permission shall, so far as is practicable, be sited so as to minimise its effect on the external appearance of the building.

(2) Development is permitted by Class A(*b*) subject to the condition that any apparatus or structure provided in accordance with that permission shall at the expiry of the relevant period be removed from the land and the land restored to its condition before the development took place.

(3) Development consisting of the installation of apparatus on, over or under land controlled by the operator is permitted by Class A in a conservation area, an area of outstanding natural beauty or a National Park subject to the condition that in the case of the installation of apparatus that operator shall—

(*a*) except in a case of emergency, give notice in writing to the Department not less than eight weeks before

Appendix B

development is begun of his intention to carry out such development; or

(b) in a case of emergency, give written notice of such installation not later than 3 days after the emergency begins.

Interpretation A.3 For the purposes of Class A—

'the 1984 Act' means the Telecommunications Act 1984;

'land controlled by an operator' means land occupied by the operator by virtue of a legal freehold interest or a lease granted or extended for a term not less than 10 years;

'development in accordance with a licence' means development carried out by an operator in pursuance of a right conferred on that operator under the telecommunications code, and in accordance with any conditions relating to the application of that code imposed by the terms of his licence;

'public call box' means any kiosk, booth, acoustic hood, shelter or similar structure which is erected or installed for the purpose of housing or supporting a public telephone and at which call box services are provided (or are to be provided) by a telecommunications code system operator;

'relevant period' means a period which expires either six months from the commencement of the use permitted by paragraph A.2 or when the need for that use ceases, whichever occurs first;

'telecommunications apparatus' means any apparatus falling within the definition of that term in paragraph 1 of Schedule 2 to the 1984 Act;

'the telecommunications code' means the code contained in Schedule 2 to the 1984 Act;

'telecommunications code system operator' means a person who has been granted a licence under section 7 of the 1984 Act which applies the telecommunications code to him in pursuance of section 10 of that Act;

'telecommunication system' has the meaning assigned to that term by section 4(1) of the 1984 Act.

Part 18
Other Telecommunications Development

**Class A
Permitted
development**

A. The installation, alteration or replacement on any building or other structure of a microwave antenna and any structure intended for the support of a microwave antenna.

*Development
not permitted*

A.1 Development is not permitted by Class A if—
   (a) the building is a dwellinghouse;
   (b) the development is permitted by Part 17;
   (c) the building or structure is less than 15 metres in height;
   (d) the development results in the presence on the building or structure of more than two microwave antennae;
   (e) in the case of a satellite antenna, the size of the antenna, including its supporting structure but excluding any projecting feed element, exceeds 90 centimetres;
   (f) in the case of a terrestrial microwave antenna—
      (i) the size of the antenna, when measured in any dimensions but excluding any projecting feed element, exceeds 1.3 metres; and
      (ii) the highest part of the antenna or its supporting structure is more than 3 metres higher than the highest part of the building or structure on which it is installed or is to be installed; or
   (g) it is in a conservation area, an area of outstanding natural beauty or a National Park.

Conditions

A.2 Development is permitted by Class A subject to the following conditions—
   (a) the antenna shall so far as is practicable, be sited so as to minimise its effect on the external appearance of the building or structure on which it is installed;
   (b) an antenna no longer needed for the reception or transmission of microwave radio energy shall be removed from the building or structure as soon as reasonably practicable.

Part 19
Development at Amusement Parks

**Class A
Permitted
development**

A. Development on land used as an amusement park consisting of—

(a) the erection of booths or stalls or the installation of plant or machinery to be used for or in connection with the entertainment of the public within the amusement park; or

(b) the extension, alteration or replacement of any existing booths or stalls, plant or machinery so used.

*Development
not permitted*

A.1 Development is not permitted by Class A if—

(a) in the case of any plant or machinery installed, extended, altered or replaced pursuant to this permission, that plant or machinery exceeds a height of 15 metres or the height of the highest existing structure (whichever is the lesser);

(b) in the case of an extension to an existing building or structure, that building or structure as a result of the extension exceeds 5 metres above ground level or the height of the roof of the nearest building or structure, whichever is the greater; or

(c) in any other case, the height of the building or structure erected, extended, altered or replaced would exceed 5 metres above ground level;

(d) the land is within 3 kilometres of the perimeter of an aerodrome.

*Interpretation of
Part 19*

A.2 For the purposes of this Part—

'amusement park' means an enclosed area of open land, or any part of a seaside pier, which is principally used (other than by way of a temporary use) as a funfair or otherwise for the purpose of providing public entertainment by means of mechanical amusements and side-shows; but, where part only of an enclosed area is commonly so used as a funfair or for such public entertainment, only the part so used shall be regarded as an amusement park;

'booths or stalls' includes buildings or structures similar to booths or stalls.

Part 20
Development required under the Roads (Northern Ireland) Order 1980

Class A
Permitted development

A. Development required by a notice served under the following provisions of the Roads (Northern Ireland) Order 1980—

(a) Article 30 and Schedule 2; and
(b) Article 44(1).

Appendix C Planning (Assessment of Environmental Effects) Regulations (NI) 1989

© HMSO

Schedule 1

Descriptions of Development

(1) The carrying out of building or other operations, or a material change of use of buildings or other land to provide any of the following—

1. A crude-oil refinery (excluding an undertaking manufacturing only lubricants from crude oil) or an installation for the gasification and liquefaction of 500 tonnes or more of coal or bituminous shale per day.

2. A thermal power station or other combustion installation with a heat output of 300 megawatts.

3. An integrated works for the initial melting of cast-iron and steel.

4. An installation for the extraction of asbestos or for the processing and transformation of asbestos or products containing asbestos:—

    (a) where the installation produces asbestos-cement products, with an annual production of more than 20,000 tonnes of finished products; or

    (b) where the installation produces friction material, with an annual production of more than 50 tonnes of finished products; or

    (c) in other cases, where the installation will utilise more than 200 tonnes of asbestos per year.

5. An integrated chemical installation that is to say, an industrial installation or group of installations where two or more linked chemical or physical processes are employed for the manufacture of olefins from petroleum products, or of sulphuric acid, nitric acid, hydrofluoric acid, chlorine or fluorine.

6. A special road; a line for long-distance railway traffic; or an aerodrome with a basic runway length of 2100 m or more.

7. A trading port, an inland waterway which permits the passage of vessels of over 1350 tonnes or a port for inland waterway traffic capable of handling such vessels.

8. A waste-disposal installation for the incineration or chemical treatment of special waste.

(2) The carrying out of operations whereby land is filled with special waste, or a material change of use of land to use for the deposit of such waste.

Schedule 2

Descriptions of Development

Development for any of the following purposes—
1. *Agriculture*
   (a) water-management for agriculture
   (b) poultry-rearing
   (c) pig-rearing
   (d) a salmon hatchery
   (e) an installation for the rearing of salmon
   (f) the reclamation of land from the sea.

2. *Extractive industry*
   (a) extraction of peat
   (b) deep drillings, including in particular:
      (i) geothermal drilling,
      (ii) drilling for the storage of nuclear waste material,
      (iii) drilling for water supplies,
   but excluding drillings for investigating the stability of the soil;
   (c) extracting minerals (other than metalliferous and energy-producing minerals) such as marble, sand, gravel, shale, salt, phosphates and potash
   (d) extracting of coal or lignite by underground mining or opencast mining
   (e) extracting petroleum
   (f) extracting natural gas
   (g) extracting ores
   (h) extracting bituminous shale
   (i) extracting minerals (other than metalliferous and energy-producing minerals) by open-cast mining
   (j) a surface industrial installation for the extraction of coal, petroleum, natural gas or ores or bituminous shale
   (k) a coke oven (dry distillation of coal)
   (l) an installation for the manufacture of cement.

3. *Energy industry*
   (a) an industrial installation for the production of electricity, steam and hot water (unless falling within Schedule 1)

(b) an industrial installation for carrying gas, steam or hot water; or the transmission of electrical energy by overhead cables
(c) the surface storage of natural gas
(d) the underground storage of combustible gases
(e) the surface storage of fossil fuels
(f) the industrial briquetting of coals or lignite
(g) an installation for hydroelectric energy production.

4. *Processing of metals*
   (a) an iron works or steelworks, including a foundry, forge, drawing plant or rolling mill (not being a works falling within Schedule 1)
   (b) an installation for the production (including smelting, refining, drawing and rolling) of non-ferrous metals, other than precious metals
   (c) the pressing, drawing or stamping of large castings
   (d) the surface treatment and coating of metals
   (e) boilermaking or manufacturing reservoirs, tanks and other sheet-metal containers
   (f) manufacturing or assembling of motor vehicles or manufacturing motor-vehicle engines
   (g) a shipyard
   (h) an installation for the construction or repair of aircraft
   (i) the manufacture of railway equipment
   (j) swaging by explosives
   (k) an installation for the roasting or sintering of metallic ores.

5. *Glass making*

   the manufacture of glass.

6. *Chemical industry*
   (a) the treatment of intermediate products and production of chemicals, other than development falling with Schedule 1
   (b) the production of pesticides or pharmaceutical products, paints or varnishes, elastomers or peroxides
   (c) the storage of petroleum or petrochemical or chemical products.

7. *Food industry*
   (a) the manufacture of vegetable or animal oils or fats
   (b) the packing or canning of animal or vegetable products
   (c) the manufacture of dairy products
   (d) brewing or malting
   (e) confectionery or syrup manufacture
   (f) an installation for the slaughter of animals
   (g) an industrial starch manufacturing installation
   (h) a fish-meal or fish-oil factory
   (i) a sugar factory.

8. *Textile, leather, wood and paper industries*
   (a) a wool scouring, degreasing and bleaching factory
   (b) the manufacture of fibre board, particle board or plywood
   (c) the manufacture of pulp, paper or board
   (d) a fibre-dyeing factory
   (e) a cellulose-processing and production installation
   (f) a tannery or a leather dressing factory.

9. *Rubber industry*

   the manufacture and treatment of elastomer-based products.

10. *Infrastructure projects*
    (a) an industrial estate development project
    (b) an urban development project
    (c) a ski-lift or cable-car
    (d) the construction of a road, or a harbour, including a fishing harbour, or an aerodrome, not being development falling within Schedule 1
    (e) canalisation or flood-relief works
    (f) a dam or other installation designed to hold water or store it on a long-term basis
    (g) a tramway, elevated or underground railway, suspended line or similar line, exclusively or mainly for passenger transport
    (h) an oil or gas pipeline installation
    (i) a long-distance aqueduct
    (j) a yacht marina.

11. *Other projects*
    (a) a holiday village or hotel complex
    (b) a permanent racing or test track for cars or motor cycles
    (c) an installation for the disposal of controlled waste or waste from mines or quarries, not being an installation falling within Schedule 1
    (d) a waste water treatment plant
    (e) site for depositing sludge
    (f) the storage of scrap iron
    (g) a test bench for engines, turbines or reactors
    (h) the manufacture of artificial mineral fibres
    (i) the manufacture, packing, loading or placing in cartridges of gunpowder or other explosives
    (j) a knacker's yard.

12. The modification of a development which has been carried out, where that development is within a description mentioned in Schedule 1.

13. Development within a description mentioned in Schedule 1, where it is exclusively or mainly for the development and testing of new methods or products and will not be permitted for longer than one year.

Index

abandonment of use, 150–51
access to open country, 12
acquisition of land, 44. *see also* blight notices; compulsory acquisition; purchase notices
  consultation requirements, 14, 45
  dealing with land acquired, 48–9
  development schemes, 32
  powers of, 4, 10, 44
  procedure, 45
    acquisitions by agreement, 45
    compulsory acquisition, 45–8
acquisition of listed buildings, 217–19
administration of planning control, 9–22. *see also* Department of the Environment; district councils; Planning Appeals Commission
  centralisation, 7–8
  Council for Nature Conservation and the Countryside, 20–21
  Department of the Environment, 9–12
  European Community, 22
  Historic Buildings Council, 21
  Laganside Corporation, 21–2
  local councils, 7, 12–16
  Northern Ireland Housing Executive, 22
  Planning Appeals Commission, 16–20
  reform (1972), 6
adoption of development plan, 29, 30
advertisements, display of, 75, 233–6
  areas of special control, 236
  consent, 233–4
    conditions, 234
    consultation of District Council, 14
    deemed consent, 233, 235
    exclusion of regulation 5, 236
    express consent, 234–5
    powers of Department, 235
    revocation or modification, 235
  enforcement, 236
  material change in use, as, 75
  meaning of 'advertisement', 233

advertisements regulations
  planning permission under, 84
advisory bodies, 9
aerodromes, 303
  permitted development (GDO, art. 3), 291–2, 293–5
afforestation. *see* forestry
agreements
  facilitating, regulating or restricting development or use. *see* planning agreements
  nature conservation
    article 8 agreements, 202–3
    management agreements, 203–4
agricultural buildings and operations
  environmental assessment, 304
  permitted development (GDO, art. 3), 278–81
    erection, extension or alteration of buildings, 278–80
    excavation or engineering operations, 278–80
    means of access to road, 280–81
    minerals, winning and working of, 280
agricultural purposes
  use of land for
    not 'development', 76–7
agricultural unit
  blighted land, 58
  meaning, 280
air navigation
  permitted development (GDO, art. 3), 291–2, 294
air traffic control services
  permitted development (GDO, art. 3), 291–2, 294
alterations to development plan, 30–31
alterations to dwellinghouse. *see* dwellinghouses
alternative sites, 117
amusement arcades, 77

amusement parks
   permitted development (GDO, art. 3), 301
ancient monuments. *see* historic monuments
ancillary uses of land, 73
animals and birds, keeping of
   domestic purposes, for, 274
appeals, 138–41. *see also* Planning Appeals Commission
   conditions, grant subject to, 133, 136
   conflicting evidence, 141
   criteria for determination, 139, 140
   determinations under article 41, against, 80
   enforcement notices, 178–84
   hazardous substances contravention notices, 232
   hearings, 139–40
   judicial review, 140, 141
   listed buildings enforcement notices, 220–21
   material considerations, 140
   natural justice, rules of, 139
   notice in writing, 139
   notices requiring planning permission (article 23), against, 163–4
   objectors, 139
   procedure, 19, 139–41
   publication of, 139
   site conditions, against, 242–3
   standing, 139–40
   stop notices, against, 190
applications for determinations (article 41), 79
applications for judicial review. *see* judicial review
applications for planning permission, 10, 11, 83, 91–102
   accompanying matter, 102
   article 22 certificates, 103–5
   false or misleading statements, 104
   inaccurate certificates, 104–5
   neighbouring land, information concerning, 102
   amendment, 97
   approval of reserved matters, 90, 92–7, 103. *see also* approval of reserved matters
   approval or consent, for, 97
   consultations, 12, 13, 109
   cases where consultation required, 13–14, 109
   continuance of use instituted by Crown, 102
   decisions, 124
      appeals. *see* appeals
      conditions, grant subject to, 126–36; *see also* conditions
      considerations in decision-making, 111–23
      failure to make a decision, 138
      grant of permission, 124–6
      refusal of permission, 137
   deemed application, 100, 183
   determination of. *see* determination of planning applications
   development which has already taken place, 98–9, 119–20
   dispensation with conditions, 99
   disposal of Crown land, 101–2
   effect of, 98
   enforcement appeals, 100
   environment, affecting, 100
      environmental assessment, 248–50
      environmental statements, 250–51
   failure to make a decision, 138
   fees, 105–6
   form and content, 91–7
   full permission, 91–2
   information to be recorded in planning register, 109
   major applications, 100–101
   minerals, extraction of, 10
   neighbour notification, 107–8
   notices requiring (article 23). *see under* enforcement of development control
   notification of, 107–8
   number of, 97–8
   outline permission, 92
   publication of notices, 108–9
   renewal of permission, for, 99–100
   representations, 109–10
   separate proposals, 98
   special cases, 98–102
   successive applications, 98
   time for determining, 110–11
   waste disposal, 10
appropriation of land, 48
   powers of Department of the Environment, 44

Index

approval of reserved matters, 85, 86, 90
  applications, 90, 92–7, 103
  different applications, 96
  form and content of application, 96
  must be within ambit of outline permission, 94–5
  time limit, 90, 93
approval or consent
  applications for, 97
archaeological interest
  sites of, 223
    development within, 276, 277, 278, 281, 286, 288, 289, 290, 291, 292, 294
  historic monuments, 222–3
  mineral exploration works, 295
architectural or historic interest
  areas of, 3, 14. *see also* conservation areas; environmentally sensitive areas
  buildings of. *see* conservation areas; listed buildings
  monuments. *see* historic monuments
Area Plans, 10, 25, 27
areas of outstanding natural beauty, 11, 33, 43
  development within, 291, 294, 298, 300
areas of special architectural or historic interest, 3, 14. *see also* conservation areas; environmentally sensitive areas
areas of special control. *see* green belts
areas of special scientific interest, 11, 33, 43, 204
  mineral exploration in, 295
assembly and leisure uses (class 16), 269
Attorney-General
  enforcement of development control, 160
aviation
  permitted development (GDO, art. 3), 293–4
    Civil Aviation Authority, development by, 291–2

bees, keeping of, 274
Belfast Gazette, 30, 34
Belfast Harbour Commissioners, 3
betting offices, 77

blight, 32, 50–60. *see also* blight notices
  agricultural units, affecting, 58
  compensation, 50
  counternotices, 54–5
  development schemes, land acquired for, 32
  instances of land affected by, 50–51
  mortgaged land, 59
  part only of property, acquisition of, 56–7
  partnership, land occupied by, 60
  personal representatives, service of notices by, 59–60
blight notices, 50
  article 9 notices, 58–9
  conditions, 50–53
    blighted land, 51–2
    premises saleable only at substantial undervalue, 53
    qualifying interest, 52–3
    reasonable endeavours to sell interest, 53
  counternotices, 54–5
  death of owner after service of, 60
  effect of valid notice, 57–8
  entitlement to serve, 50–53
  mortgaged land, 59
  objections, 54–7
    article 6(2)(c), under, 56–7
    grounds, 54
    not raised in counternotice, 55
    onus of proof, 55
    reference to Lands Tribunal, 55–6
  part only of property, acquisition of, 56–7
  partnerships, land occupied by, 60
  personal representatives, served by, 59–60
  procedure, 53–4
  purchase price, 57
  second notices, 54
  special cases, 58–60
  withdrawal, 58
breach of planning control, 166
  apparent existence of, 165–6
  enforcement notice. *see* enforcement notices
  'four year rule', 167–9
  stop notices. *see* stop notices
building operations, 64–7
  demolition of buildings, 65–7
  meaning of, 64–5

building operations (*contd.*)
  operational development, as, 63; *see also* operational development test, 65
buildings
  architectural or historic interest, of. *see* conservation areas; listed buildings
  change of use. *see* change of use
  demolition of. *see* demolition of buildings
  maintenance, improvement or alteration of interior not 'development', 75
  painting of exterior, 276
  planning permission
    construction of permission, 89
    temporary, 277–8
business uses (class 3), 267

caravan sites, 237–47
  definitions, 237–8
  permitted development (GDO, art. 3), 247, 278
  powers of district councils, 237, 238, 246
  rights of entry, 246
  site licences, 238
    alteration of conditions, 243–4
    appeal against conditions, 242–3
    applications, 238–9
    breach of conditions, 244
    cases where not required, 245
    conditions, 239–44
    duration, 239
    offences, 244
    planning permission prerequisite, 238
    register of, 246
    relation between planning conditions and site conditions, 240–42
    transfer of licences, 244
    validity of conditions, 242
  travelling people, 246–7
centralisation of planning administration, 7
certiorari. *see* judicial review
cessation of use
  abandonment, 150–51
  change of use, 151, 152
  material. *see* material change in use
  permitted development (GDO, art. 3), 276–7

Channon, Paul, 7
chemical industry
  environmental assessment, 305
  chemical installations, 303
civil aviation authority
  permitted development (GDO, art. 3), 291–2
classes of use. *see* Use Classes Order
Committee for Nature Conservation, 20
compatibility of proposed development, 116–17
compensation, 4, 6, 141–4. *see also* blight notices; purchase notices
  avoidance of, 122–3
  claims, 142–3
  development value, 142
  discontinuance orders, 157–8
  grant subject to conditions, 133–5
    exclusions, 134
  listed building consent
    refusal or conditional grant, 215
  'new development', 141, 142
  persons to whom payable, 143
  procedure for obtaining, 142–3
  references to Lands Tribunal, 143
  refusal of planning permission, 137
    exclusions, 137
  repayment of, 143–4
  revocation or modification of permission, 154–5
  stop notices, 190–91
  tree preservation orders, 227
completion orders, 153–4
compulsory acquisition
  blighted land. *see* blight; blight notices
  challenge to validity of vesting order, 46–7
  compensation provisions, 47–8
  contents of vesting order, 46
  effect of vesting order, 46
  listed buildings, 218–19
  operative date, 46
  persons aggrieved, rights of, 46–7
  planning blight, 51. *see also* blight notice
  powers of, 4
  Department of the Environment, 44
  procedure, 45–8
  public inspection of vesting order, 46
  publication of notices, 45, 46
  representations, 45–6

suspension of order, 47
vesting orders, 45–8
conditions, grant subject to, 86, 126–7, 194
  appeals, 133, 136, 138–41; *see also* appeals
  compensation, 133–5
  conditions incapable of fulfilment, 135
  dispensation with conditions, application for, 99
  duty to give reasons, 132
  effect of, 132–3
  enforceability, 130–31
  expiry of conditions, 135
  getting rid of conditions, 135–6
  invalid conditions, 131–2
    severability, 131–2
  judicial review of decisions, 135
  Newbury tests, 195
  planning agreements, and, 195–6
  power to impose conditions, 127–30
  purchase notices, 133, 257–8
  termination of lawful development rights, 158
  time limit for commencement of development, 153
  validity, 130–31
    effect of invalid conditions, 131–2
    planning purpose, 127–8
    reasonableness, 128–30
    relation to permitted development, 128
    uncertain conditions, 129
consent
  advertisements. *see* advertisements
  applications for, 97
  hazardous substances. *see* hazardous substances
  listed buildings. *see* listed building consent
conservation. *see* conservation areas; environmentally sensitive areas; historic monuments; listed buildings; nature conservation
conservation areas, 39–42, 207
  cancellation of designation, 39
  consultation requirements, 40
  development proposals affecting, 40–41
  development within, 291, 294, 298, 300
  district council's entitlement to consultation, 14
  effect of designation, 40
    control of demolition, 42
    effect on exercise of other powers, 40–41
    financial assistance, 40
    grants or loans, 40
    land in, 33
    power to designate, 39
    variation of designation, 39
considerations in decision-making. *see* determination of planning applications
consultation of district councils
  cases where consultation is required, 13–14
    acquisition of land, 45
    conservation areas, designation of, 40
    planning applications, 109
  meaning of 'consult', 14–16
Council for Nature Conservation and the Countryside, 20–21
countryside. *see also* countryside policy areas; nature conservation
  access to open country, 12
  Council for Nature Conservation and the Countryside, 20–21
  functions of Department of Environment, 11
countryside policy areas, 42
Crown land
  continuance of use instituted by Crown
    application for planning permission, 102
  disposal of
    application for planning permission, 101–2
  tree preservation orders, 227
  unlawful development
    special enforcement notices, 186–7
crude oil refineries, 303
curtilage of dwellinghouse. *see* dwellinghouses

dangerous substances. *see* hazardous substances
de minimis principle, 68, 69
dealing with land acquired, 48–9

declaratory relief, 148
definitions. *see* words and phrases
demolition of buildings
　conservation areas, in, 42
　development, whether, 65–7
　listed buildings, 67, 211; *see also* listed building consent
Department of Economic Development
　consultation, entitlement to, 109
Department of the Environment
　consultation of district councils
　　cases where consultation required, 13–14
　　meaning of 'consult,' 14–16
　Planning Directorate, 10, 11
　Planning Service, 10
　　Divisional Planning Offices, 10
　　organisation, 10–11
　　Planning Headquarters, 10
　powers and duties
　　1991 Planning Order, under, 9–10, 25, 33, 35, 39, 44, 79, 156, 194
　　access to the countryside, 12
　　acquisition of land, 44–8
　　agreements for development of land, 49
　　appropriation of land, 48
　　conservation areas, 39–40
　　determinations under art. 41, 79–80
　　development of land, 49
　　development plans, 25–6
　　development schemes, 32
　　discontinuance orders, 156
　　disposal of land, 48
　　enforcement of development control, 160
　　enterprize zone schemes, 35
　　general duties, 9
　　historic monuments, 11
　　Laganside development, 12
　　management agreements, 203–4
　　national parks, designation of, 42
　　nature conservation, 202, 203
　　nature conservation and amenity, 11, 42–3
　　new towns, 11
　　planning agreements, 194–5
　　redevelopment schemes, 11–12
　　roads, 255
　　simplified planning zone schemes, 33

determination of planning applications, 107–23
　appeal, right of, 112
　challenge to validity of decision, 112
　considerations in decision-making, 111–23
　　adequacy of infrastructure, 119
　　alternative sites, availability of, 117
　　applicant's personal circumstances, 121–2
　　avoidance of compensation, 122–3
　　compatibility, 116
　　development plan, regard to be had to, 113
　　development which has already taken place, 119–20
　　draft development plans, 116
　　draft policy statements, 116
　　duty of care?, 112–13
　　duty to act fairly, 111–12
　　effect of decision as precedent, 118
　　financial considerations, 120–21
　　general principles, 111–13
　　material considerations, 113–23
　　policy considerations, 114–15
　　preservation of existing use, 118–19
　　previous planning decisions, 117–18
　　private interests, 120
　　specific considerations, 113–23
　consultations, 12, 13, 109
　decisions, 124
　　failure to make a decision, 138
　　grant of permission, 124–6
　　grant subject to conditions. *see* conditions
　　refusal of permission, 137
　mechanics of decision-making, 107–11
　　neighbour notification, 107–8
　　publication of application, 108–9
　　representations, 109–10
　　rules of natural justice, 111
　　time for, 110–11
　　where environmental statements required, 251
determinations as to development (article. 41), 79–80
　appeals against, 80
　applications, 79
　estoppel, 81–2
　informal applications, 80

waiver of procedural requirements, 80–81
development
  acts expressly 'development', 74–5
  acts expressly not 'development', 75–8
    use classes, 77–8
  building operations, 63, 64–7. *see also* operational development
  classes of, 63–4
  demolition of buildings, 65–7
  determinations under article 41, 79–82
  engineering operations, 63, 67; *see also* operational development
  material change in use, 63, 69–73; *see also* material change in use
  meaning of, 63–82
  mining operations, 63, 67–8; *see also* operational development
  operational, 63, 64–8. *see also* operational development
  'other operations', 63, 68
  permitted development
    acts expressly not 'development', 75–8
    General Development Order (article 3), 84–5, 271–302
    powers of Department of Environment, 49
development orders, 13, 84–5. *see also* General Development Order
  district council's entitlement to consultation, 13
development plans, 9, 25–31
  adoption or rejection, 29, 30
  alterations, 30–31
  Area Plans, 25, 27
  challenge to validity of, 31
  departure from
    planning applications, 100–101
    public enquiries, 18
  determination of planning applications to have regard to, 113
  draft plans, 28, 116
    public inspection of proposals, 28–9
    publication of, 28
    representations, 28
  form and content, 26–7
    explanatory matter, 27
  incorporation of orders and schemes, 27
  maps, 26
  written statements, 26
  Local Plans, 27
  making of
    district council's entitlement to consultation, 13
    modifications, 29–30
    objections, 17, 29
    operative date, 30
    power to make, 25–6
    procedure, 28–30
    public enquiries, 17
    public local enquiries, 29
  repeal, 30–31
  replacement, 30–31
  Subject Plans, 27
  types of, 27
development rights
  termination of. *see* termination of lawful development rights
development schemes, 32
  acquisition of land, 32
  adoption, 32
  amendment, 32
  district council's entitlement to consultation, 14
  effect of, 32
  objections, 32
  procedure for making, 32
development value, 142
disabled persons
  access to buildings, 106, 125
discontinuance orders, 156
  compensation, 157–8
  non-compliance, 157
  procedure, 156
  purchase notice, power to serve, 158, 258
disposal of land, 48
  Crown land, 101
  letting, 48
district councils, 7, 12
  consultative functions, 13
    cases where consultation is required, 13–14
    meaning of 'consult', 14–16
  development by
    permitted development (GDO, art. 3), 285
  duties and powers

district councils (contd.)
  advertisements, 14
  caravan sites, 16, 237, 238, 246; see also caravan sites
  conservation areas, 14
  consultation, 13–14
  development plans, in relation to, 13
  development schemes, 14
  environmental protection, 16
  hazardous substances, 14
  land acquired for planning purposes, in relation to, 14
  listed buildings, 13
  other enactments, 16
  planning applications, 7, 13
  local government reform (1972), 12–13
  maintenance of services not 'development', 75–6
  planning functions, 13, 16
Divisional Planning Offices
  circulars and manuals, 10
  powers and duties, 10
dock or pier undertakings
  permitted development (GDO, article 3), 286
draft development plan. see development plans
duty of care
  planning applications, determination of, 112–13
duty to act fairly
  determination of planning applications, 111–12
dwellinghouses
  development within curtilage of
    addition or alteration to roof, 272
    enlargement, improvement or other alteration, 271–2
    hard surface, 274
    oil or gas storage, 274
    permitted development (GDO, article 3), 271–5
    porch, 273
    satellite antenna, 274
    swimming pools etc., 273
  subdivision of, 74
  use as (class 14), 269, 277
  use within curtilage of, 76

ecclesiastical buildings, 222
  alteration or demolition, 212–13
electricity lines, 103
electricity undertakings, 103
  permitted development (GDO, article 3), 286–8
energy industry
  environmental assessment, 304–5
enforcement notices, 165
  appeals, 178–84
    decision of Commission, 183–4
    deemed application for planning permission, 100
    duty of Planning Appeals Commission, 181–2
    effect of appeal, 183–4
    grounds of appeal, 180–81
    mode of appeal, 179
    powers of Planning Appeals Commission, 182–3
    right of, 178–9
    time for, 179
    who may appeal, 178–9
  cesser of effect, 175–6
  challenges to, 176–8
    article 69(9), 177–8
    nullity or invalidity, whether, 176–7
  compliance with, 184
    entry on land to effect, 184–5
  consequences of notice taking effect, 184–5
  contents, 169
    date on which notice will take effect, 173
    matters alleged to constitute breach, 169–71
    period for taking steps required, 173
    steps for purpose of alleviating injury to amenity, 173
    steps required for compliance with permission, 173
    steps required to remedy breach, 171–3
  defective, 176–7
  effect of appeal, 183–4
  effect of grant of planning permission, 175–6
  'four year rule', 167–9
  invalid, 176–7
  issue of, 173–4

limitation period, 167–9
listed buildings, 219–21
non-compliance, 184–5
  offences, 185–6
offences, 185–6
power to issue, 165–7
  25 August 1974, 166–7
  'breach of planning control', 166
  'may', 167
  'where it appears', 165–6
quashing of, 183
service of, 173–5
  failure to serve copies, 175
  occupier, on, 174–5
  owner, on, 174
  time limits, 175
special notices, 186–7
validity, 176–8
variation of terms, 183
withdrawal, 175
enforcement of development control, 159. *see also* enforcement notices
Attorney-General, by, 160
Department of the Environment, by, 160
discretion to enforce, 160–61
enforcement notices. *see* enforcement notices
entry on land, powers of, 161
information, gathering of, 161–2
injunctions, 191–3
members of the public, by, 159–60
notices requiring planning permission (article 23), 162–4
  appeals, 163–4
  contents of notice, 163
  issue of notice, 163
  offences, 164
  service, 163
  withdrawal of notice, 163
prohibition, 193
special enforcement notices, 186–7
stop notices, 187–91; *see also* stop notices
who can enforce?, 159–60
engineering operations
  meaning, 67
  operational development, as, 63; *see also* operational development
enterprize zone schemes, 35–8, 79
  adoption, 36
  challenge to validity of, 36–7
  grounds of challenge, 38
  persons aggrieved, 37
  substantial prejudice, 38
  effect, 36
  notice of adoption, 36
  planning permission under, 84
  power to make, 35
  procedure for making, 35–6
  publicity, 36
  representations, 36
entry on land, powers of, 161
  enforcement notices, 184–5
environmental protection, 248–51
  applications affecting environment, 100
  assessment of effects, 22
  schedule 1 and schedule 2 applications, 249–50, 303–5
environmental statements, 248, 250–51
  information specified, 250
  time for determination of applications, 251
environmentally sensitive areas, 43
estate in land, 178–9
estoppel, 81–2
European Community, 22
exempted development. *see* permitted development
existing use
  preservation of, 118–19
expiry of limited planning permission, 149
extensions to dwellinghouse. *see* dwellinghouses
exteriors of buildings
  painting of, 276
extractive industry
  environmental assessment, 304
extrinsic evidence
  construction of planning permission, 87–8

false or misleading statements, 104
fees
  planning applications, 105–6
fences, 275
financial, professional and other services (class 2), 267, 276, 277
financial considerations
  determining planning applications, in, 120–21

food and drink
　sale of, 78
food industry
　environmental assessment, 305
forestry buildings and operations
　permitted development (GDO, art. 3), 281
forestry purposes
　use of land for
　　not 'development', 76–7
'four year rule', 68, 167–9
funeral undertakers, 78
funfairs, 77

gas undertakings
　permitted development (GDO, article 3), 288–9
gates, 275
GDO. see General Development Order
General Development Order (GDO), 79, 84–5, 158
　directions from Department, 85
　effect of, 85
　permitted development (article 3)
　　agricultural buildings and operations, 278–81
　　amusement parks, 301
　　aviation development, 293–5
　　caravan sites, 247, 278
　　changes of use, 276–7
　　civil aviation authority, development by, 291–2
　　District Councils, development by, 285
　　dwellinghouse, development within curtilage of, 271–5
　　forestry buildings and operations, 281
　　industrial and warehouse development, 282–4
　　Local or Private Acts or Orders, development under, 284–5
　　mineral exploration, 295–6
　　minor operations, 275–6
　　repairs to services, 284
　　repairs to unadopted street and private ways, 284
　　roads, 302
　　statutory and other undertakers, development by, 285–91

　　telecommunications code system operators, development by, 296–9
　　telecommunications development, 300
　　temporary buildings and uses, 277–8
　time limit for determination of planning applications, 110
general industrial uses (class 5), 267, 276
glass making, 305
grant of planning permission, 124–6; see also planning permission
　conditions, subject to. see conditions
　revocation or modification, 154–6
green belts, 33, 42
guest houses and hostels (class 12), 268, 277

harbour undertakings
　permitted development (GDO, art. 3), 286
hazardous substances, 228
　applications for consent, 228
　contents of consent, 229
　contravention notices, 231–2
　　appeals against, 232
　　service of, 232
　contravention of provisions, 230–31
　determination of applications, 228–9
　district council's entitlement to consultation, 14
　duration of consent, 229–30
　enforcement, 231–2
　modification of consent, 230
　offence, 230–31
　revocation of consent, 230
hearings
　functions of Planning Appeals Commission, 18
　procedure at, 20
Historic Buildings Council, 21, 40, 213, 222
historic interest
　areas of, 3, 14. see also conservation areas; environmentally sensitive areas
　buildings of. see conservation areas; Historic Buildings Council; historic monuments; listed buildings

historic monuments, 207, 212, 222–3
  powers of Department of the Environment, 11
  protection orders, 11
Historic Monuments Council, 223
history of planning control, 3–8
  centralisation of planning administration, 7
  interim development control, 4, 5–6
  planning schemes, 3–6
  reform of planning law (1972), 6
hotels, 78
housing. *see also* dwellinghouses
  Northern Ireland Housing Executive, 22, 50
  redevelopment schemes, 11, 22, 27, 103

illegal decisions, 145
implementation of planning permission, 124–5, 151–2
incidental uses
  not 'development', 76
industrial buildings
  extension or alteration of, 282–3
industrial development
  permitted development (GDO, art. 3), 282–4
industrial uses (classes 4–10), 267–9
infrastructure, adequacy of
  consideration of, in determining applications, 119
infrastructure projects
  environmental assessment, 305
injunctions, 148
  enforcement of planning control, 191–3
  planning agreements, enforcement of, 199
intensification of use, 69–70
interim development control, 3, 4, 5–6
interior of building
  maintenance, improvement or alteration
  not 'development', 75
irrational decisions, 145

judicial review
  application for, 144
  declaratory relief, 148
  development plans, 31
  discretionary nature of remedy, 144
  enforcement notices, 176
  function of court, 144
  grounds for review, 145–6
    illegality, 145
    irrationality, 145–6
    procedural impropriety, 146
  injunctions, 148
  leave to apply, 147
  Planning Appeals Commission, 20, 140, 141
  planning decisions, 144–8
    determination of planning application, 112
    determinations under articles 41, 80
    failure to make a decision, 138
    sufficient interest, 146–7
  private law actions, 148
  simplified planning zone schemes, 35
  standing, 146–7
  time limits, 147

Laganside Corporation, 12, 21–2
  general objects, 22
Lands Tribunal
  blight notices, consideration of objections to, 55–6
  compensation disputes, references of, 143
  purchase notice disputes, reference of, 263
leather industry, 305
leisure uses (class 16), 269
letting of land, 48
licences
  caravan sites. *see* caravan sites
light industrial uses (class 4), 267, 276
lighthouse undertakings
  permitted development (GDO, article 3), 290
limited period, permission for, 86, 149
listed building consent, 211–17
  applications, 213
    fees, 213
    publication of notices, 213
  compensation, 215
  conditional grant, 214–15
  determination of applications, 214
  duration, 216

listed building consent (*contd.*)
  grant or refusal, 214–15
  offences, 216–17
  procedure for obtaining, 213–14
  purchase notices, 214–15, 259
  revocation or modification, 216, 259
  when consent is required, 211–13
listed buildings, 10, 42, 207–9
  acquisition of, 217
    agreement, by, 217
    compulsory acquisition, 218–19
  alterations or extensions, 211–17
  consent. *see* listed building consent
  ecclesiastical buildings, 212
  amendment of list, 207
  categories, 209
  certificates that building will not be listed, 221–2
  consequences of listing, 210–11
  criteria for inclusion, 207, 209–10
  damage to, 217
  demolition, 67, 211–17. *see also* listed building consent
  ecclesiastical buildings, 212–13
  district council, consultation of, 13
  duty to compile list, 207
  ecclesiastical buildings, 212
  endowments, 222
  enforcement notices, 219–21
    appeals, 220–21
  financial assistance towards maintenance, 211
  Historic Buildings Council, 21
  procedure for listing, 210
  what may be protected
    'any object or structure', 208
    fixed to the building or part of the land, 209
    'within the curtilage of the building', 208–9
livestock, keeping of
  domestic purposes, for, 274
local authorities, 3, 5, 12. *see also* district councils
  centralisation of planning administration (1972), 7
  interim development control, 5–6
local enquiries. *see* public enquiries
local government
  reorganisation (1972), 6–7
  Review Body Report (Macrory Report, 1970), 12–13

Local or Private Acts or Orders
  development under, 284–5
Local Plans, 27
locus standi
  application for judicial review, 146–7
  planning appeals, 139–40

Macrory Report (1970), 12–13
maintenance
  building, of, 75
  services, of, 75–6
major planning applications, 100–101
management agreements, 203–4
mandamus. *see* judicial review
map
  development plan, in, 26
markets, 278
material change in use, 63, 69–73
  acts expressly 'development', 74–5
  acts expressly not 'development', 75–7
  use classes, 77–8
  advertisements, display of, 75
  desirability of preserving existing use, 118–19
  determinations under article 41, 79–82
  incidental uses not 'development', 76
  intensification of use, 69–70
  planning unit, 70–73
  primary and ancillary uses, 73
  seasonal use, 73
  subdivision of dwelling house, 74
  use classes, 77–8
  waste, deposit of, 74–5
material considerations in decision-making, 113–23
Matthew, Sir Robert, 6
Matthew Plan (1963), 25
Matthew Report, 7, 25
metals, processing of
  environmental assessment, 305
microwave antennae, 298, 300
mineral exploration
  permitted development (GDO, art. 3), 295–6
minerals extraction, 10
  land used for purposes of agriculture, 280
mining operations, 277
  definition, 67

'four year rule', 68
operational development, as, 63; see also operational development
Ministry of Development, 3, 7, 9
Ministry of Health and Local Government, 3
Ministry of Home Affairs
planning schemes, 3–4
minor operations
permitted development (GDO, art. 3), 275–6
modification of development plan, 29–30
modification of planning permission, 154–6
compensation, 154–5
purchase notice, service of, 155–6, 258
mortgaged land
blight notices, 59
motor car racing, 278
motor vehicles
breaking yards, 78
display or sale of, 78
hire of, 78
sale of fuel for, 78
motorcycle racing, 278
moveable structures
permitted development (GDO, art. 3), 277–8

national nature reserves, 33
national parks, 11
designation, 42
development within, 291, 294, 298, 300
land in, 33
natural justice, rules of
planning decisions, 111, 139, 146
nature conservation
agreements with landowners, 202–3
management agreements, 203–4
areas of outstanding natural beauty, 11, 33, 43
areas of special scientific interest, 11, 33, 43, 204
Council for Nature Conservation and the Countryside, 20–21
environmentally sensitive areas, 43
powers and functions of Department of the Environment, 11, 42–3

nature reserves, 11, 33
management agreements, 204
neighbouring land, occupiers of
meaning of 'neighbouring land', 103
notification of planning applications, 107–8
planning applicant to provide information on, 103, 107
new development, 261
compensation, 141, 142
new towns
designation of, 11, 27
Newbury tests
planning agreements, application to, 195–6
non-residential institutions (class 15), 269
Northern Ireland Housing Executive, 22, 50
redevelopment schemes, 11–12, 51, 103
Northern Ireland Parliament, 7
notices requiring planning permission (art. 23). *see under* enforcement of development control
notifiable occupiers, 107–8
notification of planning applications, 107–8

occupier
blight notice, entitlement to serve. *see* blight notice
enforcement notice served on, 174–5
neighbouring land, of, 107–8
offences
notices requiring planning permission, non-compliance with, 164
open country, access to, 12
operational development, 63
building operations, 64–7
demolition of buildings, 65–7
determinations under article 41, 79–80
engineering operations, 67
mining operations, 67–8
'other operations', 66, 68
'other operations', 63, 68
outline planning permission, 85–6
applications, 92; *see also* applications for planning permission

outline planning permission (contd.)
  approval of reserved matters, 86, 90; see also approval of reserved matters
  duration of, 89
owner of land
  blight notice, service of. see blight notice
  enforcement notice served on, 174

painting of exteriors, 276
paper industry
  environmental assessment, 305
partnership
  blight notice, service of, 60
permitted development
  acts expressly not 'development', 75–8
  General Development Order (art. 3), 84–5, 271–302. see also General Development Order
personal circumstances of planning applicant, 121–2
personal representatives
  blight notices, service of, 59–60
persons aggrieved
  enterprize zone schemes, 37
  vesting orders, by, 46–7
petrol stations, 78
pigeons, keeping of, 274
pipes, lines, cables etc.
  electricity undertakings, development by, 286–8
  gas undertakings, development by, 288–9
planning agreements, 49
  1991 Order, 194–5
  contents, 197
  covenants, 199, 200
  enforcement, 200
  Department cannot bind itself by, 198
  discharge, 200–202
  effect of, 197–9
  enforceability, 197–8
  enforcement, 199–200
  financial contributions, requirement of, 197
  formalities, 199
  modification, 200–202
  Newbury tests, 195–6
  registrable in Registry of Deeds, 199
  relation to planning conditions, 195–6
  seal, made under, 199
planning appeals. see appeals; Planning Appeals Commission
Planning Appeals Commission, 7, 10, 16–20
  assistance in carrying out duties, 18–19
  constitution, 17
  duties, 17–18
    appellate functions, 17
    hearings, 18
    public enquiries, 17–18, 29
  enforcement notices, appeals against, 178–84
    duty in regard to, 181–2
    powers of Commission, 182–3
  hearings, 18, 20, 139–40
  judicial review, 20, 140, 141
  procedure, 19, 139–41
    appeals, 19
    enquiries, 19
    hearings, 20
    regulations, 19
  rules of natural justice, bound by, 139
  remuneration and allowances, 17
planning applications. see applications for planning permission
planning authorities. see also Department of the Environment; Planning Appeals Commission
  estoppel, 81–2
  requests to, for information
    determinations under article 41 and, 80–81
planning blight. see blight
Planning Board, 5
planning conditions. see conditions
planning decisions, 124
  appeals against. see appeals
  challenge to validity of. see judicial review
  conditional permission, 126–36; see also conditions
  failure to make a decision, 138
  grant of permission, 124–6
  grounds for review of, 145–6
  precedent, as, 118
  previous decisions, 117–18
  refusal of permission, 137

Planning Directorate, 10–11
Planning Headquarters, 10
planning permission, 9, 83–90
  advertisements regulations, 84
  applications for. *see* applications for planning permission
  conditions, grant subject to. *see* conditions
  construction of, 87
    buildings, 89
    extrinsic evidence, 87–8
    single or multiple permission, 88–9
  date of notification, 86, 87
  date when permission granted, 86–7
  decisions on applications. *see* planning decisions
  determination of applications. *see* determination of planning applications
  development orders, 84–5
    General Development Order (GDO), 85
  duration of, 89–90, 124
  enterprize zone scheme, designation of, 36, 84
  enures for benefit of land, 89, 124
  environmental assessment, 248–51
  environmental statements, 250–51
  extent of, 89
  failure to make a decision, 138
  full permission, 124–6
  General Development Order, 84–5
  grant of, 124–6
    conditions, subject to. *see* conditions
    enures for benefit of land, 89, 124
    judicial review, 125
    no right of appeal, 125
  implementation, 124–5
    effect of, 151–2
  limited period, for, 86, 149
  means of obtaining permission, 83–5
    adoption of simplified planning zone, 83
    advertisements regulations, 84
    application to Department, 83
    designation of enterprise zone, 84
    development order, 84–5
  modification of, 154–6
  notices requiring (art. 23). *see under* enforcement of development control
  outline. *see* outline planning permission
  'permission spent' principle, 152
  permitted development
    acts expressly not 'development', 75–8
    GDO (art. 3), 84–5, 271–302. *see also* General Development Order
  refusal of, 137
    appeals, 138–41
  renewal of
    applications for, 99–100
  requirement of, 63, 83
  revocation of, 154–6
  simplified planning zone scheme, adoption of, 83–4
  unconditional grant, 124–6
planning policy. *see also* development plans; enterprize zone schemes; simplified planning zone schemes
  Area Plans, 25, 27
  consideration of planning applications, 114–15
  development schemes, 32
  Local Plans, 27
  policy guidance notes, 10
  powers and duties of Department of the Environment, 9, 10
  special controls. *see also* conservation areas; historic monuments; listed buildings; tree preservation
    areas of outstanding natural beauty, 43
    areas of special scientific interest, 43
    environmentally sensitive areas, 43
    green belts, 42
    national parks, 42
  Subject Plans, 27
planning register
  applications for planning permission, information on, 109
planning rights
  termination of. *see* termination of lawful development rights
planning schemes, 3–6, 25
  compensation provisions, 4
Planning Service, 10–11
planning unit, 70–3
  construction of new building, 71, 72–3

planning unit (*contd.*)
  division into separate occupation or ownership, 71–2
  relevant area, 70–71
policy. *see* planning policy
pools
  within curtilage of dwellinghouse, 273
ports, 303
post office
  permitted development (GDO, article 3), 290
poultry-keeping
  domestic purposes, for, 274
power stations, 303
premature development, 137
primary use of land, 73
private interests, 120
private ways
  repairs to, 284
procedural impropriety, 146
professional services (class 2), 267, 276, 277
prohibition, 193. *see also* judicial review
property certificates, 109
public enquiries, 9
  development plans, 29
  functions of Planning Appeals Commission, 17–18
  procedure at, 19
  simplified planning zone schemes, 34
public service vehicles
  permitted development (GDO, art. 3), 289–90
public worship
  use for purposes of, 78
publication of notices
  planning applications, 108–9
purchase notices, 257
  circumstances in which notice may be served, 257–9
  conditions, grant of permission subject to, 133, 257–8
  counternotices, 263
  date for completion of contract, 264
  deemed contract, 263–4
  discontinuance orders, following, 158, 258–9
  effect of valid notice, 263
  'incapable of reasonably beneficial use', 260–62
  new development, 261
  listed building consent
    refusal or conditional grant, 214–15, 259
    revocation or modification of, 259
  owner, service by, 257
  meaning of 'owner', 257
  procedure, 262–3
  reference of disputes to Lands Tribunal, 263
  refusal of permission, following, 137, 257–8
  response from Department, 262–3
  revocation or modification of permission, following, 155–6, 258
  time limits, 262
  withdrawal, 264

railway lines, 303
railway undertakings
  permitted development (GDO, art. 3), 285–6
redevelopment schemes, 11, 22, 27, 51, 103
  functions of Department of the Environment, 11–12
reform of planning law (1972), 6
refusal of planning permission, 137
  appeals, 137, 138–41; *see also* appeals
  compensation, 137
  judicial review of decision, 137
  purchase notices, 137, 257–8
refuse, deposit of, 74–5
regional policies, 10
register, 109
rejection of development plan, 29, 30
religious instruction
  use for purposes of, 78
renewal of planning permission
  applications for, 99–100
reorganisation of local government, 6–7
Report of the Review Body on Local Government in Northern Ireland (Macrory Report, 1970), 12–13
research
  power to make grants for, 9
reserved matters
  approval of. *see* approval of reserved matters
  meaning of, 86

residential institutions (class 13), 268, 277
revocation of planning permission, 154–6
  compensation, 154–5
  purchase notice, service of, 155–6, 258
road passenger transport undertakings
  permitted development (GDO, art. 3), 289–90
roads, 255–6
  extinguishment of right to use, 255
  means of access to, 275
  permitted development (GDO, art. 3), 302
rubber industry, 306

satellite antennae, 274, 300
scientific interest, areas of. *see* areas of special scientific interest
scrapyards, 78
seasonal use, 73
service stations, 78
services
  maintenance of
    not 'development', 75–6
    repairs to, 284
severance of invalid conditions, 131–2
shops (class 1), 267, 276, 277
simplified planning zone schemes, 33–5, 79
  challenge to validity of, 35
  duration of, 34
  effect of adoption, 35, 83–4
  form and content, 34
  land which may not be included in, 33
  modifications, 34
  notice of adoption, 34
  planning permission under, 83–4
  power to make, 33–4
  procedure for making, 34
  public local enquiries, 34
  representations and objections, 34
site licences. *see* caravan sites
special enforcement notices, 186–7
special industrial uses (classes 7–10), 267–8
special roads, designation of, 27
statutory definitions. *see* words and phrases

statutory undertakers
  maintenance of services
    not 'development', 75–6
  permitted development (GDO, art. 3), 285–90
stop notices, 187–91
  activities which may be prohibited, 188–9
  appeals, 190
  cesser of effect, 189
  compensation, 190–91
  contents, 188
  contravention of, 190
  offences, 190
  power to serve, 188
  service of, 189
  withdrawal of, 189
storage or distribution uses (class 11), 268, 276
strategic planning. *see also* acquisition of land; blight; development plans
  areas of outstanding natural beauty, 43
  areas of special scientific interest, 43
  conservation areas, 39–42
  development schemes, 32
  enterprize zone schemes, 35–8
  environmentally sensitive areas, 43
  green belts, 42
  national parks, 42
  simplified planning zone schemes, 33–5
streets
  repairs to unadopted streets, 284
studies, 9
subdivision of dwellinghouse, 74
Subject Plans, 27
surveys, 9
swimming pools
  within curtilage of dwellinghouse, 273

taxi businesses, 78
telecommunications code system operators
  permitted development (GDO, article 3), 296–9
temporary buildings and uses
  GDO (art. 3), 277–8
termination of lawful development rights, 149
  abandonment of use, 150–51
  action/inaction of landowner, 149–53

termination of lawful (*contd.*)
  agreement, by, 152
  automatic termination, 149
  change of use, 151, 152
  completion orders, 153–4
  conditions, by, 158
  Department, by, 153–8
  discontinuance orders, 156
  expiry of planning permission for limited period, 149
  GDO directions, 158
  implementation of planning permission, 151–3
  'permission spent' principle, 152
  revocation or modification of permission, 154–6
textile industry, 306
time limits
  appeals against enforcement notices, 179
  determination of planning applications, 110–11, 251
  enforcement notices, 167–9, 175
  'four year rule', 167–9
  judicial review, 147
  purchase notices, 262
Town and Country Planning—Proposals for Legislation (White Paper, 1972), 7
trading ports, 303
travelling people
  caravan sites, 246–7
tree preservation, 224. *see also* tree preservation orders
  meaning of 'trees', 224
tree preservation orders, 225–7
  compensation, 227
  criterion for making, 225
  Crown land, 227
  enforcement regarding replanting, 226–7
  form, 225
  objections or representations, 225
  offences, 226
  procedure for making, 225–6
  registration of order, 226
trunk roads, designation of, 27

UCO. *see* Use Classes Order
Ulster Countryside Committee, 20
ultra vires
  enterprize zone schemes, 38

unadopted streets
  repairs to, 284
unlawful development. *see* enforcement of development control
unreasonable decisions, 145
use. *see also* material change in use
  abandonment, 150–51
  agricultural purposes, for, 76–7
  change of, 151, 152
  classes of, 77–8; *see also* Use Classes Order
  discontinuance of
    order requiring. *see* discontinuance orders
  forestry purposes, for, 76–7
  incidental uses
    not 'development', 76
  intensification of, 69–70
  meaning, 63, 67
  mining operations, for, 67
  preservation of existing use, 118–19
  primary and ancillary uses, 73
  seasonal, 73
  temporary uses, 277–8
Use Classes Order (UCO), 77–8
  assembly and leisure (class 16), 269
  business (class 3), 267
  changes of use
    permitted development (GDO, art. 3), 276–7
  dwellinghouses (class 14), 269
  excluded uses, 77–8
  financial, professional and other services (class 2), 267
  general industrial (class 5), 267
  guest houses and hostels (class 12), 268
  judicial approach, 78
  light industrial (class 4), 267
  non-residential institutions (class 15), 269
  residential institutions (class 13), 268
  shops (class 1), 267
  special industrial (classes 7–10), 267–8
  storage or distribution (class 11), 268
  uses falling into more than one class, 78

vesting orders, 45–8
  challenges to validity, 46–7

compensation provisions, 47–8
contents, 46
effect, 46
operative date, 46
public inspection, 46
publication of notices, 45, 46
representations, 45–6
suspension, 47

walls, 275
warehouse development
  permitted development (GDO, art. 3), 282–4
waste
  deposit of
    material change in use, constituting, 74–5
    mining operations, in course of, 67
  disposal
    planning applications for, 10
water transport undertakings
  permitted development (GDO, art. 3), 286
wood industry
  environmental assessment, 305
words and phrases
  abandonment, 150
  advertisement, 233
  agricultural land, 280
  agricultural unit, 280
  amusement park, 301
  'any object or structure', 208
  begun, 90
  booths or stalls, 301
  breach of planning control, 166
  building, 64–5, 280
  building operations, 64
  caravan, 237
  caravan site, 237
  consult, 14–16
  destruction, 226
  development, 63–82; see also development
  development in accordance with a licence, 299
  dispose of, 48
  ecclesiastical building, 212
  employee facilities, 283
  engineering operations, 67
  gas undertaker, 289
  hazardous substances, 228
  impediment, 201
  incapable of reasonably beneficial use, 260–2
  industrial building, 284
  industrial land, 283
  knowledge or consent, 236
  land, 258
  land controlled by an operator, 299
  material consideration, 113–14
  may, 167
  mineral exploration, 296
  mining operations, 67
  monument, 222
  neighbouring land, 103
  new development, 141
  occupier, 174
  operations, 63, 64
  other operations, 66, 68
  outline planning permission, 85–6
  owner, 174, 257
  owner-occupier, 52
  painting, 276
  person aggrieved, 37
  planning schemes, 3–4
  planning unit, 70
  public call box, 299
  purpose incidental to the enjoyment of the dwellinghouse, 274
  purposes of agriculture, 280
  reasonable endeavours, 53
  reasonably beneficial use, 260–61
  relevant development, 143
  reserved matters, 86, 92
  resulting building, 275
  structure, 296
  telecommunication system, 299
  telecommunications apparatus, 299
  telecommunications code, 299
  telecommunications code system operator, 299
  trees, 224
  undertaking, 295
  use, 63, 67
  warehouse, 284
  where it appears, 165–6
  'within the curtilage of the building', 208–9
written statement
  development plan, in, 26–7

1. Strategic Planning Guidelines for Dublin.
2. City Development Plan.

Greater Dublin Area.
   2 tier political system.

29 County Councils.
   5 County Boroughs Corporations.
   5 Boroughs Corporations
   49 Urban District Councils.